Western Garden
Book of
Edibles

The Complete A to Z Guide to Growing Your Own Vegetables, Herbs, and Fruits

Sunset

Menlo Park, California

Contents

Introduction

Fragrant basils, juicy tomatoes, sweet strawberries—we want them all, at peak flavor and freshness. That's why kitchen gardens are growing everywhere around the West—even in front yards, on curb strips, and on rooftops. To get started, learn about your climate zone and growing season (see pages 10–15), then find a sunny spot and dig in.

In a sunny corner

You can start small by tucking a tomato plant and a couple of basils into a border, or turn over an entire corner of your yard to food crops. The U-shaped bed above is just 13 feet long and 8 feet wide, yet it's packed with tidy rows of cool-season greens that make it as attractive as it is productive. Large or small, kitchen gardens offer the same rewards come harvesttime—freshness and flavor.

On a driveway

(above) Arugula, beans, strawberries, summer squash, tomatoes, and sunflowers take over this former driveway, whose ribbons of concrete are still visible in the foreground (paving and sod were removed from the back half). Owner Christine Taylor, a garden coach whose mantra is "for the love of nature," forfeited garage access to plant her crops. Here she also grows basil and rosemary in pots alongside edible calendula—for coloring salads. Basalt stones edge the beds.

Along a curb strip

(opposite page, top) Peeling away a strip of grass opened up a sunny patch of soil for this garden along a Portland street. The owner started with just a few plants, then gradually removed more grass to make room for additional crops as the summer progressed. Carrots, chard, green onions, peppers, and squash grow in the foreground; beans ramble around a tall A-frame trellis toward the back. (Check local laws before claiming the curb strip in front of your house.)

On a city rooftop

(right) Where gardening space is hard to find, such as atop this San Francisco high-rise, large containers work well for most crops. These galvanized livestock watering troughs are deep and wide enough for growing broccoli raab (an Italian relative of broccoli that sends up loose spikes of yellow flowers), as well as giant mustard, kale, lettuce, onions, and other cool-season crops. Similar troughs are sold at feed stores; you'll need to add drainage holes in the bottom.

In a side yard

(above) A narrow strip on the south side of the house is where Portland garden designer Darcy Daniels grows her fruits and vegetables. Angular raised beds fit easily into the small yard with room to spare for tending crops. In the beds at left, Daniels grows blueberries, strawberries, garlic, Swiss chard, and columnar apple. 'Autumn Bliss' raspberries grow beneath the window at right.

By an entry

(right) Pots of fruit-laden citrus and fig trees edge this entry path in Northern California, while tomato vines climb the trellis behind. Owner Rosalind Creasy, a cookbook author, landscape designer, and edible landscaping pioneer, grows edibles everywhere—herbs along paths, lettuce in borders, squash up fences.

Along a fence

(opposite page) An espaliered apple tree forms a sculptural backdrop for a quartet of 'Lacinato' kale plants and nasturtiums in this small bed adjacent to a driveway. Steel edging frames the bed.

You're truly "eating local" when you feast on the bounty of your own garden.

BRITISH COLUMBIA

4

1A

1A

4

5

4

Vancouver

2

1A

ALBERTA

SASKATCHEWAN

1B

1B

5

Seattle

1A

5

Tacoma

4

WASHINGTON

Spokane

2

90

2

MONTANA

1B

2

2

Great Falls

15

Portland

2

82

Walla Walla

Columbia River

3

Walla

6

3

84

Eugene

4

OREGON

2

Billings

90

94

4

1A

2

1A

IDAHO

15

2

2

Medford

7

2

Boise

2

3

Idaho Falls

84

2

17

1A

7

3

2

WYOMING

1B

7

15

7

7

Casper

25

4

1A

2

Winnemucca

Great Salt Lake

1A

2

80

2

Ogden

14

4

9

80

Reno

3

Salt Lake City

1A

15

8

Lake Tahoe

2

NEVADA

2

UTAH

Denver

76

Sacramento

17

14

9

1A

70

1A

70

COLORADO

San Francisco

7

1A

2

3

15

14

2

1A

2

Colorado Springs

CALIFORNIA

Fresno

10

10

2

25

8

16

1A

5

13

10

Las Vegas

10

2

1A

NEW MEXICO

17

15

Bakersfield

1A

10

11

Lake Mead

10

3

1A

1A

3

2

16

14

3

2

10

10

40

13

2

Flagstaff

3

Santa Fe

23

21

18

15

10

11

40

1A

3

25

3

Los Angeles

20

19

7

10

11

12

ARIZONA

17

1A

Albuquerque

1A

1A

22

23

18

10

11

2

1A

40

24

21

13

Phoenix

13

1A

10

2

San Diego

24

13

8

10

Pacific Ocean

12

2

2

3

Tucson

10

10

2

2

Climate Zones | 1A | 1B | 2 | 3 | 4 | 5 | 6 | 7 | 8 | 9 | 10 | 11 | 12 | 13 | 14 | 15 | 16 | 17 | 18 | 19 | 20 | 21 | 22 | 23 | 24 | 25

0   100   200   300 miles

The West's Climate Zones

In this book, we assign each of the plants listed numbered climate zones representing regions where it grows best. The maps on these two pages show where the zones are, and on the following pages are descriptions of the individual zones. If you garden near an intersection of zones, pick the one whose description most closely matches the conditions in your garden. (Zone information is also available online at www.sunset.com, under Garden.)

ZONE CONSIDERATIONS
The following factors make each zone unique.

latitude Generally, the farther north an area is, the longer and colder its winters are and the longer its summer days and winter nights.

elevation Gardens high above sea level get longer and colder winters, often with intense sunlight, and lower nighttime temperatures all year.

ocean influence Weather that blows inland off the Pacific Ocean tends to be mild all year and laden with moisture in the cool season.

continental air influence The North American continent generates its own weather. Compared with coastal climates, inland areas are colder in winter, hotter in summer, and more likely to get precipitation and (in open areas) incessant wind anytime of year. The farther inland you live, the stronger this continental influence.

mountains, hills, and valleys These determine whether areas beyond them will be influenced most by marine, continental, or arctic air. The Coast Ranges take some marine influence out of the air that passes eastward over them. The Sierra-Cascades and Southern California's interior mountains further weaken marine influence. East of the Rocky Mountains, continental and arctic air dominate.

microclimates Terrain sharply modifies the climate within any zone and any garden. South-facing slopes get hotter than flat land and north-facing slopes. Slopes also direct airflow, as warm air rises and cold air sinks. Because hillsides are never as cold in winter as the hilltops above them or the ground below them, they're called thermal belts. Lowlands into which cold air flows are called cold-air basins.

Continued on page 12 ▶

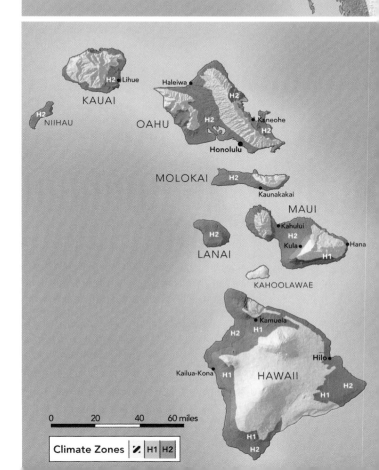

ZONES AND GROWING SEASONS

The following zone descriptions identify local conditions that make each area hospitable to some plants, trouble for others. A zone's growing season also affects which plants will grow there. The main factor determining growing season is the interval between the last frost in spring and the first frost in fall, but other factors include location, temperature, hours of sunlight, and rainfall. The growing season for each zone is shown as a green band in a bar indicating months from January to December. The yellow area at each end of the band represents shoulder seasons, when light frosts are possible but not likely to bother cool-season crops.

Zone A1

J F M A M J J A S O N D

ALASKA'S INTERIOR During summer, plants benefit from long days in the 70s F (low to mid-20s C), with rare spikes to 90°F/32°C. In winter, gardeners can usually depend on snow to insulate plants from winter minimums of –20°F/ –29°C, with occasional dips to –60°F/–51°C. And in permafrost areas, the ground usually thaws to below root level during the warm months.

Zone A2

J F M A M J J A S O N D

ANCHORAGE AND COOK INLET Though mountain ranges protect much of this region, plant success depends largely on each area's microclimate. Winter lows average 6° to 0°F/–14° to –18°C, with drops to –40°F/–40°C every 10 years or so. Summer days are usually cloudy and in the mid-60s F (high teens C), with occasional jumps into the high 70s F (mid-20s C).

Zone A3

J F M A M J J A S O N D

ALASKA'S SOUTHERN MARITIME CLIMATE Cloudy summers stay mostly in the 60s F (16° to 21°C), with occasional jumps to 80°F/27°C, while winter lows are 25° to 16°F/–4° to –9°C, with extreme lows of –20°F/–29°C. Annual precipitation averages 50 to 75 in.—but Homer gets only 25 in. per year, while Pelican gets 150 in. Cool-weather crops thrive here, but warm-season vegetables mature slowly.

Zone 1a

J F M A M J J A S O N D

COLDEST ZONE WEST OF THE ROCKIES A short growing season has mild summer days and cold nights that extend the bloom of summer perennials. Winter snow usually insulates plants against lows from 11° to 0°F/–12° to –18°C (with extremes to –50°F/–46°C). If snow comes late or leaves early, protect plants with a 6-inch layer of organic mulch.

Zone 1b

J F M A M J J A S O N D

COLDEST ZONE EAST OF THE ROCKIES This zone sees January temperatures from 13° to –4°F/–11° to –20°C, with extremes to –50°F/–46°C. Arctic cold fronts sweep through 6 to 12 times a year, sometimes dropping temperatures by 35°F/19°C in 24 hours. The growing season tends to be warm, relentlessly windy, and sometimes subject to hail storms.

Zone 2a

J F M A M J J A S O N D

COLD MOUNTAIN AND INTERMOUNTAIN REGIONS Another snowy winter climate, Zone 2a is considered mild compared with surrounding regions. It is the coldest zone in which sweet cherries and many apples grow. Precipitation averages just 16 in. per year, so irrigation is essential. Winter nights usually hover between 20° and 10°F/–7° and –12°C, with drops to –30°F/–34°C every few years.

Zone 2b

J F M A M J J A S O N D

WARMER-SUMMER INTERMOUNTAIN CLIMATE This zone has a good balance of long, warm summers and chilly winters. That's why commercial orchards locate here. Precipitation averages 16 in. per year, but it's much higher in the west and north ends of the zone. Winter minimums are 22° to 12°F/–6° to –11°C, with extremes in the –10° to –20°F/–23° to –29°C range.

Zone 3a

MILD MOUNTAIN AND INTERMOUNTAIN CLIMATES East of the Sierra and Cascade ranges, this is the premier gardening climate for deciduous fruit trees and such long-season vegetables as melons, gourds, and corn; just keep them watered, since precipitation here averages only 14 in. per year. Winter minimum temperatures run from 25° to 15°F/–4° to –9°C, with extremes down to –18°F/–28°C.

Zone 3b

MILDEST MOUNTAIN AND INTERMOUNTAIN CLIMATES Chilly winters, summers in the 90s F (low 30s C), and a 6- to 7-month growing season make this zone perfect for grapes, watermelons, late apples—anything that needs plenty of time to mature. Winter temperatures range from 29° to 19°F/–2° to –7°C, with extremes as low as –15°F/–26°C. Precipitation averages 11 in. per year.

Zone 4

COOLEST MARITIME AREAS FROM CALIFORNIA TO SOUTHEAST ALASKA As in neighboring Zone 5, wet winters and mild summers prevail here, but Zone 4 is a bit warmer in summer and colder in winter. You can grow most things if you choose early-maturing varieties. Winter lows range from 34° to 28°F/1° to –2°C, with extreme lows reaching 0°F/–18°C.

Zone 5

NORTHWEST COAST AND PUGET SOUND Wet, breezy winters and mild summers favor leaf vegetables, root crops, and berries here. Low heat accumulation slows development of warm-season vegetables and fruits that ripen in fall, but even these prosper if you choose varieties carefully. January minimum temperatures range from 41° to 33°F/5° to 1°C, with 10-year extremes down to 6°F/–14°C.

Zone 6

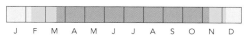

WILLAMETTE AND COLUMBIA RIVER VALLEYS Warm summers, a long growing season, and cool, wet winters make this maritime climate perfect for growing everything from berries and hazelnuts to apples and Pinot Noir grapes. Winter minimums usually hover just above freezing, but chilly interior air occasionally pushes west through the Columbia Gorge, layering trees with ice. Extreme lows may reach 0°F/–18°C.

Zone 7

OREGON'S ROGUE RIVER VALLEY, THE CALIFORNIA GRAY PINE BELT, AND SOUTHERN CALIFORNIA MOUNTAINS Hot summers and mild but pronounced winters give Zone 7 sharply defined seasons without severe winter cold or enervating humidity. Tree fruits thrive here. Typical winter lows range from 35° to 26°F/2° to –3°C, with record lows down to 0°F/–18°C. Rainfall averages 34 in. per year.

Zones 8 and 9

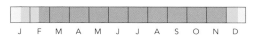

CALIFORNIA CENTRAL VALLEY Zone 9 is the thermal belt that edges California's Central Valley, while Zone 8 is the colder valley floor. The difference is crucial: citrus that flourishes in Zone 9 cannot be grown commercially in Zone 8. Lows in both zones are 38° to 34°F/3° to 1°C, with extremes as low as 16°F/–9°C. Zone 9 gets 20 in. of rain, 5 in. more than Zone 8.

Zone 10

ARIZONA–NEW MEXICO HIGH DESERT This zone lies mostly in the high elevations of the Southwest. Summer highs are in the 90s F (30s C), while average winter temperatures range from 33° to 22°F/1° to –6°C, with drops to around 0°F/–18°C every few years. More rain falls in the east than in the west, and the Pecos River drainage receives more precipitation in summer than in winter.

Zone 11

CALIFORNIA–SOUTHERN NEVADA MEDIUM TO HIGH DESERT In winter, Zone 11 has mild days, nights that hover around freezing, and occasional drops to 10°F/ −12°C; but in summer, many days cross 100°F/38°C, with the highest temperatures recorded at 117°F/ 47°C. Zone 11 has less rain (about 7 in.) and more wind than adjacent parts of Zone 10.

Zone 12

ARIZONA'S INTERMEDIATE DESERT Zone 12 has harder frosts spread over a longer season than Zone 13, with average minimums around freezing and extreme lows to 10°F/−12°C. Still, it doesn't provide enough chill for some deciduous fruits. As in Zone 13, cool-season planting starts in early fall, while warm-season crops go in during late winter. Protect them against strong spring winds.

Zone 13

LOW OR SUBTROPICAL DESERT Whether gardening below sea level in the Imperial Valley or at 1,100 feet in Phoenix, Zone 13 gardeners plant most vegetables in fall and heat-lovers like corn and melons in late winter, all to avoid average summer highs of 107°F/42°C, with spikes to 120°F/49°C. Winter lows average 40°F/4°C, with rare extreme drops to 15°F/−9°C.

Zone 14

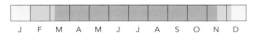

NORTHERN CALIFORNIA AREAS WITH SOME OCEAN INFLUENCE Marine air that moderates Zone 14 pushes clear to Sacramento, Modesto, and even down the Salinas Valley, prospering fruits that need summer heat and winter chill. Winter minimums average 40° to 35°F/4° to 2°C, with extreme lows from 27° to 17°F/−3° to −8°C. Precipitation averages 25 in. over most of the zone.

Zone 15

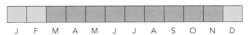

CHILLY-WINTER CALIFORNIA COAST RANGE Zone 15 comprises cold-air basins, hilltops, and areas far enough north to affect plant performance. The region is influenced by marine air 85 percent of the time and by inland air 15 percent, and most of the zone gets a nagging afternoon summer wind. Average January minimum is 39°F/4°C, with record lows to 16°F/−9°C.

Zone 16

CENTRAL AND NORTHERN CALIFORNIA COASTAL THERMAL BELTS This is one of Northern California's finest horticultural climates. Its hillside slopes are dominated by ocean weather 85 percent of the time. Average winter lows are about 40°F/4°C, with extreme lows around 20°F/−7°C. This zone gets more heat in summer than Zone 17 and has warmer winters than Zone 15. That's a happy combination for gardening.

Zone 17

OREGON AND NORTHERN AND CENTRAL CALIFORNIA COASTAL STRIPS Mild, wet, almost frostless winters and cool summers mark this climate. Summer fog comes in high and fast, cooling, shading, and humidifying the land. Winter minimums are in the low 40s F (7° to 4°C), with rare extreme lows in the mid-20s F (about −4°C). Precipitation averages 38 in., but is much higher in the north than the south.

Zone 18

SOUTHERN CALIFORNIA INTERIOR VALLEY COLD ZONES An interior climate, this zone is influenced by ocean air only about 15 percent of the time. Many of Zone 18's chilly valley floors held commercial apricot, peach, apple, and walnut orchards before homes were built there. Average winter lows are 40° to 34°F/4° to 1°C. Over a 20-year period, winter lows bottomed out at 17°F/−8°C.

Zone 19

SOUTHERN CALIFORNIA INTERIOR VALLEY THERMAL BELTS
Interior air dominates the climate of this mostly sloping land 85 percent of the time, keeping it warmer than adjacent Zone 18's valleys and hilltops. Navel oranges, macadamias, and most avocados thrive here. Average January minimums are 43° to 37°F/6° to 3°C, with drops every few years to 25°F/–4°C.

Zone 20

SOUTHERN CALIFORNIA COLD-AIR BASINS, HILLTOPS
As interior and maritime air masses shift across this zone, climate boundaries often move 20 miles in 24 hours. In winter, Zone 20's chilly hilltops and cold-air basins get considerably colder than the thermal belts that connect them. Winter lows are 43° to 37°F/6° to 3°C; 20-year lows average 25° to 22°F/–4° to –6°C.

Zone 21

SOUTHERN CALIFORNIA THERMAL BELTS Gardens here can be bathed in ocean air or sulking under high fog one day and dried out by interior air (perhaps a Santa Ana wind) the next day. This is fine citrus-growing country, with average winter lows around 40°F/4°C and summer highs of 90° to 94°F/32° to 34°C. Ten-year lows have reached 25°F/–4°C.

Zone 22

COLD ZONES ALONG THE SOUTHERN CALIFORNIA COAST
Zone 22 consists of cold-air basins and hilltops influenced by the ocean approximately 85 percent of the time and inland air 15 percent. They get more winter chill than the slopes of neighboring Zone 23. Winter lows average 45° to 40°F/7° to 4°C, with 10-year drops to 25°F/–4°C.

Zone 23

THERMAL BELTS ALONG THE SOUTHERN CALIFORNIA COAST This is the best zone for avocados and is also excellent for cherimoyas, 'Valencia' oranges, guavas, mangoes, and papayas. But mild winters allow only low-chill pears, apples, and peaches. Winter lows average about 45°F/7°C, and summer highs reach 78° to 89°F/ 26° to 32°C. Frosts are rare, but Santa Ana winds dry plants and break branches every fall.

Zone 24

SOUTHERN CALIFORNIA COASTAL STRIP Dominated by marine air, winters here rarely dip below 45°F/7°C, and frosts can be years apart. In late spring, morning overcast is the rule. July highs are in the mid-70s F (about 24°C). Where the beach parallels high cliffs or palisades, Zone 24 extends only to that barrier; but where hills are low or absent, it runs inland several miles.

Zone H1

HAWAII'S MILD VOLCANIC SLOPES Cooler air makes high volcanic slopes good for growing everything from sweet bulbing onions to low-chill varieties of apples, peaches, and plums. Some gardeners in regions high on the dry sides can even succeed with Mediterranean herbs. Warm-season highs range from 65° to 80°F/18° to 27°C; cool-season lows can dip into the 40s F (9° to 4°C), with extreme lows around 35°F/2°C.

Zone H2

HAWAII'S COCONUT PALM BELT Most lowland lees here get heavy rains from November through March, while May through September is relatively dry. On the wind-ward sides, rain comes year-round from passing storms and tradewind showers. The Kona Coast, however, gets most of its rain in the warm season. Highs hover in the mid-80s F (around 30°C); lows can dip to the mid-60s F (around 18°C).

How to Use the Encyclopedia

The encyclopedia entries on pages 17–238 contain all the information you need to grow edibles successfully. Each entry begins with basic identification and growing information (shown in example below). Next, introductory text describes the plant and lists recommended varieties, some in chart form. Finally, the "How to Grow It" section gives detailed instructions on everything from soil and fertilizer requirements to harvest tips and pointers on dealing with common pests and diseases.

[Potato] Common name
[*Solanum tuberosum*] Botanical name
[Nightshade family] Family name
[Perennial Grown as Annual / Cool-season root vegetable] Type of plant and harvest season

climate

✄ Sunset climate zones where the plant grows best (see pages 10–15).

exposure

☼ Plant grows best with unobstructed sunlight all or almost all day.

◑ Plant needs partial shade (some shade for half the day or at least for 3 hours during the hottest part of the day). Some listings contain qualifications, such as "partial shade in hottest climates."

More detailed information about sun exposure may be found in the "How to Grow It" section under "best site."

watering

○ Plant is quite drought-tolerant. Some drought-tolerant plants may need no irrigation once established; others may need a little.

◐ Plant needs less than regular moisture, perhaps a deep soaking every 2 or 3 weeks.

● Plant requires regular moisture, perhaps once a week, or more in hot weather; soil shouldn't be too dry or too wet.

●● Plant needs ample moisture at all times.

A range of moisture needs may be indicated for plants that adapt to more or less water. More information on watering may be found in the "How to Grow It" section.

toxicity

◊ Some part of the plant is known to have toxic or irritant properties.

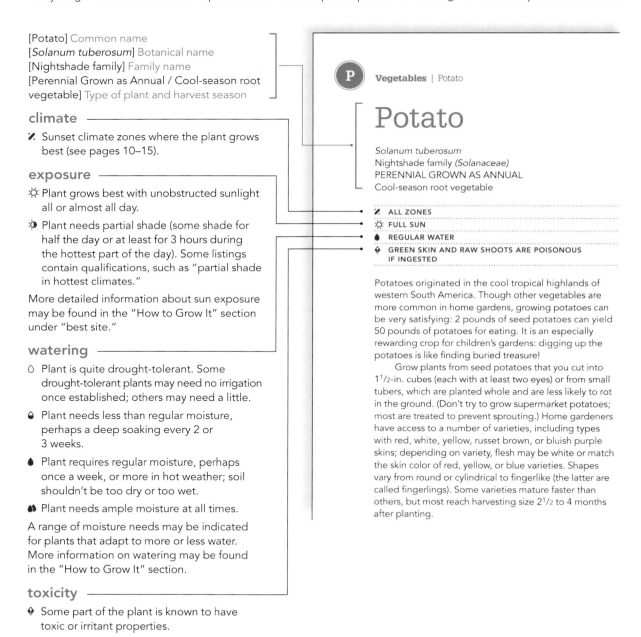

P   **Vegetables** | Potato

Potato

Solanum tuberosum
Nightshade family *(Solanaceae)*
PERENNIAL GROWN AS ANNUAL
Cool-season root vegetable

✄ **ALL ZONES**
☼ **FULL SUN**
● **REGULAR WATER**
◊ **GREEN SKIN AND RAW SHOOTS ARE POISONOUS IF INGESTED**

Potatoes originated in the cool tropical highlands of western South America. Though other vegetables are more common in home gardens, growing potatoes can be very satisfying: 2 pounds of seed potatoes can yield 50 pounds of potatoes for eating. It is an especially rewarding crop for children's gardens: digging up the potatoes is like finding buried treasure!

Grow plants from seed potatoes that you cut into 1½-in. cubes (each with at least two eyes) or from small tubers, which are planted whole and are less likely to rot in the ground. (Don't try to grow supermarket potatoes; most are treated to prevent sprouting.) Home gardeners have access to a number of varieties, including types with red, white, yellow, russet brown, or bluish purple skins; depending on variety, flesh may be white or match the skin color of red, yellow, or blue varieties. Shapes vary from round or cylindrical to fingerlike (the latter are called fingerlings). Some varieties mature faster than others, but most reach harvesting size 2½ to 4 months after planting.

CHAPTER 1

Vegetables

Eat your vegetables, whether warm-season crops (such as beans, corn, melons, peppers, squash, and tomatoes) or cool-season vegetables (like asparagus, beets, cabbage, carrots, lettuce, and onions). Roots, shoots, stems, leaves, buds, blossoms, fruit, and seeds—they all sustain us, and the diversity is a delight.

Artichoke

Cynara cardunculus (Scolymus group)
Sunflower family *(Asteraceae)*
PERENNIAL SOMETIMES GROWN AS ANNUAL
Cool-season vegetable

🌿 ZONES 8, 9, 14–24; AS ANNUAL IN ZONES 3A–7, 10–13
☼ ◑ FULL SUN OR LIGHT SHADE
💧 REGULAR WATER

This attractive Mediterranean native is a big, coarse, ferny-looking plant with an irregular, somewhat fountainlike form to 4 ft. tall, 6–8 ft. wide. Leaves are silvery green. Big flower buds that form at the tops of stalks are the artichokes you cook and eat. If not cut, the buds open into spectacular purple-blue, 6-in., thistlelike flowers that can be cut for arrangements (cut just before blooms are fully open). See *Cardoon* to learn about a close relative of artichoke.

In California Zones 8, 9, and 14–24, artichoke is a dependable perennial crop that grows luxuriantly at least from spring through fall, producing edible buds in early summer only. But in the mildest part of this region—central California coastal Zone 17, where it is grown commercially—artichoke can be both a handsome ornamental plant and a producer of fine, tender artichokes from early fall to late spring.

In Southwest desert Zones 11–13, it is usually treated as an annual and planted in fall for spring harvest, but it may hang on to be a perennial.

In Zones 3a–7 and 10, plant in spring and hope for the best—you will get foliage for sure and a crop if the season is long and mild enough. Plants will likely freeze out in winter, but if a deep layer of organic mulch is applied in fall and if freezes are not deep or long, the plants may make it to another season. You can also dig roots and store them in a frost-free place over winter, replanting them in the garden about a month before the average date of last spring frost.

Favored varieties include standard 'Green Globe' and 'Imperial Star'; among those with violet-tinged buds, try 'Purple Italian Globe' and 'Violetto'. 'Northern Star' has survived at 0°F/–18°C, so it is popular in chilly-winter climates.

HOW TO GROW IT

best site Full sun in mild coastal climates; light afternoon shade where summers are hot.

yield About 12 buds per plant after the first year; fewer when grown as an annual.

Harvest artichokes when plump but still tightly formed.

soil Fertile and well-drained. Prepare garden beds for planting by digging in 4–6 in. of compost along with $^1\!/_2$ pound of complete fertilizer per 100 sq. ft.

planting Start dormant roots or containerized plants in winter or early spring at least a month before the average date of last spring frost. Set root shanks vertically with buds or shoots just above soil level.

Where roots are not available or in cold-winter areas, you can grow artichokes from seed. 'Imperial Star' produces the first season (150 to 180 days from seed to harvest) and can be grown as an annual; 'Green Globe' is ready to harvest the second summer after seeding.

Start seeds indoors 8 to 12 weeks before the average date of last spring frost; set transplants outdoors about a month before that date. Plants need cool temperatures to set flower buds.

Artichokes grown as annuals can be closely spaced.

When cutting buds, include 1½ inches of stem.

spacing Where artichokes are grown as perennials, space them 4–6 ft. apart in rows; where grown as annuals, plant 18 in. apart in rows 2–3 ft. wide.

water After active growth starts, water plants thoroughly once a week, wetting the entire root system. If grown only for ornamental value, artichokes can tolerate much drought, going dormant in summer heat.

fertilizer Artichokes are heavy feeders. Give plants monthly doses of high-nitrogen fertilizer starting 4 weeks after transplanting.

pruning, training To encourage a second crop, cut off the main stalk an inch above soil level after harvesting the last bud of the first crop; new sprouts at the base will grow faster and produce sooner than if the plant were uncut. In all recommended climate zones, cut off old stalks near ground level when leaves begin to yellow. In cold-winter regions, cut tops to 1 ft. in fall, tie them over the root crown, and mulch heavily to protect from frost.

harvest Cut off buds with 1½ in. of stem while they are still tight and plump.

challenges After buds start to form, use strong jets of water to blast off any aphids that appear. Also keep snails, slugs, and earwigs away from plants. For gopher control, plant in raised beds lined with hardware cloth at the bottom or in large containers.

Arugula

Eruca vesicaria sativa
Cabbage family *(Brassicaceae)*
ANNUAL
Cool-season vegetable

ALL ZONES
FULL SUN
REGULAR WATER

This weedy-looking Mediterranean native, sometimes called rocket or roquette, is grown for its 1- to 4-in.-long leaves, which resemble small mustard leaves and lend a nutty zing to green salads. In winter, plants reach about 1 ft. tall; but eventually they shoot up to 3 ft. tall, then bloom. Tender buds and flowers taste like the young leaves. Plants reseed.

HOW TO GROW IT

best site Open, sunny spot.

yield A 10-ft. row will supply a family of four.

soil Well-drained garden soil.

planting Arugula grows best in cool weather. Start from seed about 1 month before the average date of last spring frost. Sow again in late summer or fall for a fall-winter crop. *In containers:* Arugula is an easy container plant. Choose a wide pot at least 6 in. deep.

spacing Thin to 6 in. apart.

water Arugula does best with regular water, but it can grow in dry soil.

fertilizer For fast growth, apply a high-nitrogen fertilizer after true leaves appear.

harvest Cut tender young leaves; older, larger ones usually taste too sharp. Nip off and eat the flower buds or flowers as they appear.

challenges No serious pests in home gardens.

Easy-to-grow arugula has a spicy tang that's somewhere between cress and horseradish.

Asian Greens

Brassica species
Cabbage family *(Brassicaceae)*
ANNUALS AND BIENNIALS
Cool-season vegetables

✿ **ALL ZONES**
☼ **FULL SUN IN COOLER CLIMATES ONLY**
💧 **REGULAR WATER**

The vegetables in this large group are mainstays of stir-fry dishes and excellent in salads. They are primarily quick-maturing cool-season crops planted at the same time as other cool-season vegetables: late winter to early spring for spring-to-summer harvest, late summer to early fall for harvest in fall and winter. In areas with short growing seasons and in mild-summer coastal regions, they can be grown all summer. Many Asian greens, especially the mustards, are attractive foliage plants that make a colorful addition to the vegetable garden and also look good mixed with flowering annuals and spring bulbs.

Specialty seed catalogs carry scores of varieties. Transliteration of names from various Asian languages is inconsistent, so the same variety might show up under multiple spellings—or even called by completely different names—in different catalogs. Read descriptions closely to get exactly what you want.

Bok choy (Chinese white cabbage, pak choi). Annual or biennial. One of the more familiar Asian greens, bok choy is relatively mild, but with a hint of mustard in its flavor. Tender, crisp, sweet, and very mild. Good alone, with meat, and in soups and stir-fries. Many varieties are sold, including the robust 'Joi Choi', smaller-size 'Mei Qing Choi', and the miniature 'Toy Choi'. 'Tatsoi' ('Tah Tsai'), a close relative of bok choy, is similar but more compact. Thin or transplant seedlings to 6–12 in. apart. Harvest approximately 50 days after sowing seed, when plants are loose-headed and 10–12 in. tall.

Broadleaf mustard (dai gai choy). Annual. Large green leaves with a pungent, somewhat bitter, mustardlike flavor that gets stronger as the plant matures. Hot weather or inadequate moisture also increases pungency. Best used in soup to tone down the sharp flavor. Thin or transplant seedlings to 10 in. apart. Harvest plants when they are loose-headed and 10–14 in. tall, about 65 days after sowing. Look for green varieties such as 'Yanagawa Takawa', or ones with colored leaves like 'Osaka Purple' and 'Garnet Giant'.

Chinese broccoli (gai lohn). Annual. Similar in flavor and texture to standard broccoli but with a slight mustardlike

Bok choy is high in nutrition and low in calories.

pungency. Thin or transplant seedlings to 10 in. apart. Harvest central stalk and side shoots when stalk is 8–10 in. tall or when flower buds just begin to form, usually about 70 days after sowing.

Chinese mustard greens (gai choy). Annual. Milder member of the mustard family. Thin or transplant seedlings to 10 in. apart. Harvest the first greens when the plants are 2 in. tall; continue harvesting until leaves turn tough or bitter. It usually takes 45 days after sowing for plants to reach their mature height of 6–8 in.

Flowering cabbage (yao choy, choy sum, ching sow sum). Annual or biennial. Tender, delicate, broccoli-type vegetable favored for its mild, sweet flowering shoots. Leaves are also edible. Thin or transplant seedlings to about 6 in. apart. Harvest about 60 days after sowing, when 8–12 in. tall.

Continued on page 22 ▶

*Cut just a few leaves at a time
to keep mizuna productive.*

RENEE SHEPHERD ON
asian greens

Renee Shepherd knows how to cook up a feast from the garden. Her secret? Asian greens. They grow fast—seemingly overnight—and take only minutes to prepare. "I heat up peanut oil, then throw in some scallions, garlic, and ginger," she explains. "After a few minutes, I add the greens and cook them quickly."

Through her seed company, Renee's Garden, in Felton, CA, Shepherd sells blends of Asian greens, usually including mizuna ("one of the sweetest") and bok choy ("pretty, sturdy, reliable, very juicy, and tender"). She grows these greens cut-and-come-again style. "I plant densely and harvest leaves using kitchen scissors when they are 3–5 inches tall, leaving 1-inch crowns so plants regrow," says Shepherd. "I can harvest these two or three times, depending on time of year and weather."

Mizuna. Annual. Mild-flavored, leafy vegetable with finely cut, frilly, white-stemmed leaves. Great in salads. Thin or transplant seedlings to 8–10 in. apart. Start cutting leaves when plants are a few inches tall or wait until they mature at 8–10 in. tall, about 40 days after sowing.

HOW TO GROW IT

best site Full sun in cool climates, filtered sun where summers heat up quickly.

yield Varies by crop.

soil Fertile, well-drained soil is essential. Dig in compost or composted manure before planting.

planting For planting depth, follow the instructions on the seed packet. *In containers:* You can plant nonheading varieties by sowing seed in wide, 8-in.-deep containers. Eat the thinnings as plants grow.

spacing See individual entries.

water Plants should be kept evenly moist (but never waterlogged).

fertilizer Apply mild fertilizer every 2 weeks during the growing season.

harvest See individual entries.

challenges The goal is to maintain steady, rapid growth, unchecked by dry periods or infertility. Anything that hinders growth tends to force bolting and make the flavors too pungent or strong. Cabbage root maggots and cabbageworms can be defeated with row covers.

Asparagus

Asparagus officinalis
Lily family *(Liliaceae)*
PERENNIAL
Cool-season vegetable

- ☒ **ZONES A1–A3, 1–24**
- ☼ **FULL SUN**
- ⬤ **REGULAR WATER**

Asparagus, native to the Mediterranean, is one of the most dependable of home-garden vegetables. Plants take 2 or 3 years to come into full production but then furnish delicious spears every spring for 10 to 15 years. They take up considerable space but are tall, feathery, and graceful.

Asparagus seeds and roots are sold as "traditional" ('Mary Washington' and others) or "all-male" ('UC 157', 'Jersey Giant', 'Jersey Knight', and 'Jersey Supreme'). The latter produce more and larger spears because they don't have to put energy into seed production. 'Millennium F1' is a cold-hardy all-male variety bred for the Far North.

Among purple-tinged varieties, look for a high-sugar traditional variety sold as 'Purple Passion' or 'Sweet Purple', and the all-male 'Marte'.

HOW TO GROW IT

best site Full sun all day is best.

yield 3 to 4 pounds of asparagus spears per 10-ft. row.

soil Well-drained, deeply dug, and rich. (Where drainage is poor, plant in raised beds.) To prepare the planting site, make trenches 1 ft. wide, 8–10 in. deep, and 4–6 ft. apart. Heap loose, organically amended soil into the bottom of the trenches and soak just before planting.

planting Seeds sown in spring will grow into strong young plants in one season, but roots are more commonly used. Choose roots that are unwilted and no smaller than an adult's hand. Plant in fall or winter in mild-winter climates, in early spring in cold-winter areas, with the crowns 6–8 in. below the surface; spread out roots evenly. Cover with 2 in. of soil and water. As young plants grow, gradually fill in the trench, taking care not to cover growing tips.

spacing Space plants 1 ft. apart.

water Soak deeply whenever the soil begins to dry out.

fertilizer After harvest, feed and irrigate heavily.

Freshly cut asparagus spears

pruning, training Don't harvest the first year; the object at this time is to build a big root mass. When plants turn brown in late fall or early winter, cut stems to the ground. In cold-winter areas, permit dead stalks to stand until spring; they will help protect root crowns.

harvest The following spring, you can cut spears when they are 5–8 in. long; cut only for 4 to 6 weeks or until thin spears appear, indicating that roots are nearing exhaustion. Then permit plants to grow. The third year you should be able to cut spears for 8 to 10 weeks.

challenges Clean up debris from beds in fall to help get rid of overwintering asparagus beetles. Use row covers over beds in spring. If the beetles appear during cutting season, handpick them, knock them off plants using jets of water, or spray them with insecticidal soap. If fusarium or rust is a problem where you garden, grow resistant asparagus varieties.

Bean

Multiple species
Pea family (*Fabaceae*)
ANNUALS AND PERENNIALS
Warm-season vegetables (except cool-season fava bean)

- ▨ **ALL ZONES**
- ☼ **FULL SUN**
- ◗ **REGULAR WATER**

Gardeners can choose from many types of beans, the most common of which are described below. Except for the soybean (from eastern Asia) and the fava bean (from the Mediterranean region), beans are New World plants belonging to the genus *Phaseolus*. Most are frost-sensitive heat lovers and easy to grow from seed, and all are annuals except scarlet runner bean, which is a perennial grown as an annual. The growing instructions that follow apply to all beans except fava, whose contrarian cultural information is listed with its description below.

For more vigorous beans, buy seeds inoculated with *Rhizobium* bacteria, which helps the plants fix nitrogen from the air and store it in their roots. Or buy the inoculant from a nursery or mail-order seed supplier and treat the seeds yourself.

Bean flowers are edible.

Dry bean. 'Pinto', 'Red Kidney', and 'White Marrowfat' belong to this group. Most are grown until pods turn dry or begin to shatter, but some varieties are best when harvested at the green shelling stage ("shelly" beans) and cooked like green limas. These include the flageolet bean (a French favorite) and 'French Horticultural Bean', also known as 'October Bean'. Heirlooms such as 'Aztec Dwarf White', 'Mitla White', and 'New Mexico Appaloosa' were used by Native Americans of the Southwest and are very well adapted to that region.

Fava bean (broad bean, horse bean). This is a cool-season bean (actually a giant vetch, *Vicia faba*), best known and grown in coastal climates. Cook and eat immature pods like edible pod peas; prepare immature and mature seeds the same way as green or dry limas. Note that a few people (mainly of Mediterranean ancestry) have an enzyme deficiency that can cause severe reactions to the beans and even the pollen.

In cold-winter areas, plant as early in spring as soil can be worked; in mild climates, plant in fall for harvest in late winter or early spring. Beans mature in 120 to 150 days. Space rows 1$^1/_2$–2$^1/_2$ ft. apart. Sow seeds 1 in. deep, 4–5 in. apart; thin to 8–10 in. apart. Plants produce bushy growth to 2–4 ft. tall.

Pick snap beans by nipping them off with your thumbnail as seeds begin to swell inside the pods.

Lima bean. Like snap beans (which they resemble), lima beans come in either bush or vine (pole) form. They develop more slowly than snap beans and do not produce as reliably in very hot weather. Before being cooked, they have to be shelled, a tedious chore but worth it if you like fresh limas.

Scarlet runner bean. Perennial twining vine grown as annual pole bean. Showy and ornamental, with slender clusters of vivid scarlet flowers and bright green leaves divided into three roundish, 3- to 5-in.-long leaflets. Use it to cover fences, arbors, or outbuildings; it also provides quick shade on porches. Pink- and white-flowered varieties exist. Flowers are followed by flattened, very dark green pods that are edible and tasty when young but toughen as they reach full size. Beans from older pods can be shelled and cooked like green limas.

Snap bean (string bean, green bean). The most widely planted bean type. Tender, fleshy pods; not stringy. Color may be green, yellow (wax beans), or purple (these turn green when cooked). Plants grow as self-supporting

Continued on page 26 ▶

Fava beans have a slightly nutty flavor.

Purple snap bean bushes also sport purplish flowers.

Look for yellow snap beans under the name "wax beans."

'Yin Yang' dry beans have a distinctive look befitting their name.

A trio of snap beans: yellow 'Ramdor', green 'Emerite', and 'Purple Queen'

bushes (bush beans) or as climbing vines (pole beans). Bush types bear earlier, but vines are more productive. Plants look like scarlet runner bean, but their white or purple flowers are not showy.

Soybean, edamame. Grown in Asia for millennia, *Glycine max* is a relatively recent arrival in American gardens. Plants grow like bush snap beans, producing short, fuzzy pods. The beans themselves are very high in protein. Plants thrive in warm, humid climates but struggle in dry ones. "Edamame" can refer to shelled green soybeans, to a dish made from cooked whole baby soybeans, or to soybeans generally (the Japanese word means "beans on a branch").

HOW TO GROW IT

best site Most beans thrive in heat and sun, though cool-season fava beans prefer mild and sunny conditions.

yield Varies by kind.

soil Soil should be loose and open so that heavy seed leaves (the first leaves that emerge from the bean seed) can push through, but it need not be particularly deep, since beans have shallow roots.

planting Sow seeds as soon as soil is warm. *In containers:* Beans grow well in wide containers at least 6 in. deep. If you grow pole beans, be sure to put a trellis behind or in the container before you plant.

spacing Plant seeds 1 in. deep and 1–3 in. apart. Allow 2–3 ft. between rows of all kinds of bush beans. Pole beans can be managed in a number of ways; see "pruning, training" below.

water Moisten soil thoroughly before planting, then do not water again until seedlings have emerged. Once growth starts, keep soil moist.

fertilizer Fertilize soil after plants are in active growth and again when pods start to form.

pruning, training There are four ways to train pole beans: (1) set three or four 8-ft. poles in the ground and tie them together at the top in tepee fashion and plant four seeds around the base of each, thinning to two plants each; (2) set single poles 3–4 ft. apart and sow six or eight seeds around each, thinning to the three or four strongest seedlings; (3) insert poles 1–2 ft. apart in rows and sow seeds as you would bush beans; or (4) sow seeds along a sunny wall, fence, or trellis and train vines on a web of light string supported by wire or heavy twine.

harvest *Dry beans* take 70 to 80 days to get to the shelly bean stage, then another 2 to 3 weeks to reach true dry bean stage. Let pods remain on the bush until they dry out or begin to shatter; then remove beans from the pods, dry them, and store the beans to soak and cook later. *Lima beans and soybeans* take 65 to 95 days to mature. *Scarlet runner beans and snap beans* are ready in 50 to 80 days, depending on variety. Pick snap beans every 3 to 5 days; if pods mature, plants will stop bearing.

challenges Control aphids, cucumber beetles, spider mites, and whiteflies if any of these pests are problems in your garden. Row covers help with insect control on bush beans; hosing down helps with aphids; and yellow sticky traps help with whiteflies.

Beet

Beta vulgaris
Goosefoot family *(Chenopodiaceae)*
BIENNIAL GROWN AS ANNUAL
Cool-season root vegetable

* **ALL ZONES**
* **FULL SUN**
* **REGULAR WATER**

Though this European native is best known for its edible roots, its tender young leaves are also tasty when chopped fine and added to salads or steamed or sautéed (beets are botanical sisters of Swiss chard). Plants grow best in relatively cool weather.

Types with round, red roots range from old favorite 'Detroit Dark Red' to newer varieties like 'Early Wonder' and 'Red Ace'. 'Bull's Blood' and 'Big Top' have particularly plentiful, tender, tasty greens. Novelties include 'Cylindra' and 'Rodina' (with long cylindrical roots) and 'Chioggia' (rings of red and white); there are also varieties with golden yellow, purple, or white roots.

HOW TO GROW IT

best site Choose a spot where beets won't be shaded by taller plants.

yield 8 to 10 pounds of beets per 10-ft. row.

soil Fertile and well-drained, without lumps or rocks.

planting In hot-summer climates, sow seed in early spring or late summer so that plants will mature in relatively mild weather. In mild-winter areas, you can also plant in late summer for fall and winter harvest. Sow seed 1 in. apart and cover with 1/4 in. of compost, sand, or vermiculite. To harvest beets over a long season, sow seed at monthly intervals. *In containers:* Grow in a container at least 8 in. deep and as wide as you can find, so that you have room for plenty of beets.

spacing Thin plants to 3 in. apart while they are small—the thinnings (both tops and roots) are edible.

water To keep roots tender, keep soil evenly moist. Mulch helps.

fertilizer Beets are light feeders: if you mix in plenty of compost at planting time, then a light dose of complete fertilizer after tops are up is sufficient.

A mix of yellow, red, and purple roots will brighten up a traditional beet salad.

harvest Start by harvesting the tender young leaves when you thin rows. Begin harvesting roots when they are 1 in. wide, and complete harvesting before they exceed 3 in.; they will be woody if allowed to grow bigger. In cold climates, harvest all beets before hard frosts in fall.

challenges Beets may attract flea beetles, leafhoppers, and leaf miners; plant under row covers. Rotate crops to avoid problems with nematodes and wireworms. Temperature or moisture stress causes roots to become woody.

Broccoli

Brassica oleracea (Botrytis group)
Cabbage family *(Brassicaceae)*
ANNUAL
Cool-season vegetable

ALL ZONES

FULL SUN

REGULAR WATER

Among cole crops (cabbage and its other close relatives), broccoli is arguably the best all-around choice for the home gardener: it bears over a long season and is not difficult to grow. Plants reach 2–3 ft. tall, with a branching habit, and send up a central stalk that bears a cluster (to 6 in. wide) of green or purple flower buds. When that central cluster is removed, side branches will lengthen and produce smaller clusters.

Broccoli is thought to be a Mediterranean native. In addition to the traditional heading broccoli, there are other excellent kinds to choose from. Sprouting broccoli forms many small florets that are harvested when the size of buttons. Broccoli raab (broccoli rabe), an Italian relative of broccoli, has slightly stronger flavor. For Chinese broccoli, see *Asian Greens.* For Romanesco, see *Cauliflower.*

All types of broccoli are cool-season plants that tend to bolt into flower at high temperatures, so time your plantings to mature during cool weather.

HOW TO GROW IT

best site Broccoli needs full sun to put on early growth and encourage heads to form.

yield About 4–6 pounds per 10-ft. row. A dozen plants will supply a family.

soil Fertile loam. If soil has too much sand or clay, amend it heavily with compost before planting.

planting In mild climates, plant in late summer, fall, or winter for crops in winter or early spring. In cold-winter areas, set out young plants 2 to 4 weeks before the last frost (young plants resist frost but not hard freezes).

spacing Space plants 1 1/2–2 ft. apart in rows 3 ft. apart.

water Keep plants growing vigorously with regular deep irrigation during dry periods.

fertilizer Feed once or twice with a complete fertilizer before heads or florets start to form.

Heading broccoli is the most familiar form.

harvest Start cutting 50 to 100 days after setting out plants but before clustered buds begin to open. Include 5–6 in. of edible stalk and leaves. Cut the smaller side-branch heads that form after the main head has been harvested; be sure to get them before they flower.

challenges Subject to the same pests as cabbage. To prevent soilborne pest buildup, plant in a different site each year. Row covers will protect plants from pests such as aphids, cabbage loopers, imported cabbage-worms, and cabbage root maggots. Alternatively, prevent root maggots by ringing the base of each plant with a tar-paper collar; or cover each plant with a cone fashioned from window screen. Collars made from paper cups or metal cans (with ends removed) also deter cutworms, which chew off seedlings at the base. *Bacillus thuringiensis (Bt)* can be applied to control young larvae of cabbage-worms and cabbage loopers on plants.

Brussels Sprouts

Brassica oleracea (Gemmifera group)
Cabbage family *(Brassicaceae)*
BIENNIAL GROWN AS ANNUAL
Cool-season vegetable

✔ **ALL ZONES**
☼ **FULL SUN**
💧 **REGULAR WATER**

Brussels sprouts are a close cabbage relative of unusual appearance: the mature plant has an edible crown of fairly large leaves (which can be prepared like cabbage) and a 2- to 3-ft. stem completely covered with golf ball–size, cabbagelike sprouts. These likely Belgian natives are fairly easy to grow where summers are not too hot, long, or dry.

'Jade Cross Hybrid' is the most heat-tolerant. 'Diablo' produces heavy crops of uniform sprouts in most climates. 'Oliver' is the standard early variety for short-season climates. 'Rubine' is an heirloom variety with purple sprouts. Seedlings of brussels sprouts aren't commonly available; you may have to grow your own from seed.

HOW TO GROW IT

best site Full sun promotes quick, sturdy growth and the earliest possible harvest.

yield About 3 to 5 pounds per 10-ft. row. A single plant will yield 50 to 100 sprouts; a dozen plants will easily supply a family over a long season.

soil Best grown in medium to heavy loam; too much organic matter in the soil causes too many leaves and loose sprouts. Add lime to acid soil before planting.

planting In cold-winter climates, set out seedlings you start yourself or nursery transplants in spring for summer-to-fall harvest; in mild-winter areas, plant in late summer and fall for winter-to-spring production.

spacing Space plants 1½–2 ft. apart in rows 3 ft. apart.

water Keep plants growing vigorously by keeping soil evenly moist.

fertilizer Apply complete commercial fertilizer once or twice before sprouts start to form.

harvest Begin picking sprouts when big leaves start to yellow. Snap off sprouts from the bottom first—they're best when slightly smaller than a golf ball. Leave smaller

Brussels sprouts resemble miniature palm trees with spheres growing on their trunks.

sprouts on the upper stem to mature. After picking, remove only the leaves below harvested sprouts. The flavor of sprouts benefits from a frost. Harvest the leafy edible crown a month before first expected fall frost.

challenges To prevent soilborne pest buildup, plant in a different site each year. Row covers will protect plants from pests such as aphids, cabbage loopers, imported cabbageworms, and cabbage root maggots. Alternatively, prevent root maggots by ringing the base of each plant with a tar-paper collar; or cover each plant with a cone fashioned from window screen. Collars made from paper cups or metal cans (with ends removed) also deter cutworms, which chew off seedlings at the base. *Bacillus thuringiensis (Bt)* can be applied to control young larvae of cabbageworms and cabbage loopers on plants.

Cabbage

Brassica oleracea (Capitata group)
Cabbage family *(Brassicaceae)*
BIENNIAL GROWN AS ANNUAL
Cool-season vegetable

☀ **ALL ZONES**
☀ ◑ **LIGHT SHADE IN HOT CLIMATES**
◐ **REGULAR WATER**

Cabbage probably originated along the Mediterranean coast of western Europe. It is grown for its leaves, which come in green, red, and blue- or purple-tinted green. Each plant forms a tight round or pointed head whose size can be barely larger than a softball or big enough to fill a wheelbarrow. Leaves can be smooth or, with savoy types, crinkly.

Early varieties mature 7 to 8 weeks from transplanting; late varieties need 3 to 4 months. Among early varieties, 'Early Jersey Wakefield' and 'Charmont' are recommended. Late varieties that keep well include 'Danish Ballhead' and 'Kaitlin'. Good savoys include 'Samantha' and the red 'Deadon'. 'Gonzalez' is an excellent miniature savoy; and in Alaska, the savoy variety 'O.S. Cross' is the standard for giant cabbage (up to 50 pounds!). Good red cabbages include 'Red Express', 'Ruby Ball', and 'Ruby Perfection'. For a firm round cabbage that develops well in hot weather, try 'Stonehead'.

See also *Chinese Cabbage.*

HOW TO GROW IT

best site Full sun in mild coastal growing conditions; partial shade in hot-summer interiors.

yield Depending on variety, 10 to 25 pounds per 10-ft. row.

soil Fertile, well-drained loam produces the best results.

planting Time plantings so heads will form either before or after hot summer months. In the low or intermediate desert, grow as a winter crop in full sun. Sow seeds 1/2 in. deep in pots or flats about 6 weeks prior to planting-out time. Use a floating row cover for an early start. To avoid overproduction, set out a few plants every week or two, or plant both early and late kinds. Mulch helps maintain uniform moisture.

spacing At transplant, space seedlings 2–2 1/2 ft. apart.

water Plants thrive in moist soil. Water often enough that plants never wilt.

'Danish Ballhead' cabbage keeps well and is good for sauerkraut.

fertilizer Give frequent light applications of nitrogen fertilizer.

harvest Use pruners or loppers to cut off heads when they're firm and well formed, and before they split or crack. Light frost doesn't hurt cabbage, but harvest and store before heavy freezes occur.

challenges To prevent soilborne pest buildup, plant in a different site each year. (Cabbages do well in the ground where peas grew the year before.) Row covers will protect plants from pests such as aphids, cabbage loopers, imported cabbageworms, and cabbage root maggots. Alternatively, prevent root maggots by ringing the base of each plant with a tar-paper collar; or cover each plant with a cone fashioned from window screen. Collars made from paper cups or metal cans (with ends removed) also deter cutworms, which chew off seedlings at the base. *Bacillus thuringiensis (Bt)* can be applied to control young larvae of cabbageworms and cabbage loopers on plants. Handpick snails and slugs, or bait for them.

Heads of savoy cabbage 'Julius' can reach a weight of 5 pounds.

Cardoon

Cynara cardunculus
Sunflower family *(Asteraceae)*
PERENNIAL
Warm-season vegetable

- ✎ ZONES 4–9, 12–24
- ☼ FULL SUN
- ◗ REGULAR WATER

This Mediterranean native is very closely related to artichoke but is grown for its thick, fleshy, edible leafstalks rather than its flower buds. The plant is so striking that it's often grown as an ornamental. It can reach 5 ft. tall and 4 ft. wide (more than twice that size in the Pacific Northwest), with coarse, spiny, gray-green leaves up to 1½ ft. long. In summer, gray stems hold purple, thistle-like blossoms up to 3 in. across. Perennial roots can handle 5°F/–15°C if provided with a thick layer of mulch.

Blanching the stems about a month before harvest makes them more tender and also removes bitterness (see "blanching" below). To cook cardoon, cut heavy leaf midribs into 3- to 4-in. lengths, parboil until tender, then sauté; or serve boiled with butter or a sauce.

HOW TO GROW IT

best site Full sun and protection from wind, which can topple these large plants.

yield 1 to 4 pounds per plant.

soil Light, well-drained soil amended with compost is best, but cardoon will also grow in heavy soil.

planting Start containerized plants in spring after danger of frost is past. If your growing season is at least 6 months long, you can sow seeds directly where you want plants to grow, around the average date of last spring frost.

spacing Plant at 2- to 4-ft. intervals.

water After active growth starts, water plants thoroughly once a week, wetting the entire root system. If grown for ornamental value only, cardoon can tolerate much drought.

fertilizer Cardoon is a heavy feeder. Give plants monthly doses of high-nitrogen fertilizer starting 4 weeks after transplant.

Big, bold cardoon in full bloom

blanching On a dry day in late summer or early fall, 4 to 5 weeks before harvest, blanch leaf stems by gathering them together, tying them up, and wrapping them with paper to shield from sunlight.

harvest In mid-autumn, remove the whole plant by cutting it off just below soil level.

challenges Aphids and slugs like cardoon's tender new growth; control by blasting off aphids with a hose, or by baiting for slugs or killing them as you see them. The plant also naturalizes in mild-winter climates and may become a weed.

Carrot

Daucus carota sativus
Carrot family *(Apiaceae)*
BIENNIAL GROWN AS ANNUAL
Cool-season root vegetable

✎ **ALL ZONES**
☼ **FULL SUN**
💧 **REGULAR WATER**

Carrots were probably first developed in Afghanistan; the familiar orange versions were selected from yellow ones in the Netherlands around 1600.

The best variety to plant depends on your soil: carrots reach smooth perfection only in light-textured soil that is free of stones and clods. Plant long market kinds such as the 12-in. 'Envy' only if you can give them a foot of this ideal, well-prepared soil. If you can provide only a few inches, plant half-long Nantes types such as 'Bolero', 'Mokum', 'Nantes', 'Nelson', or 'Yaya'; all grow 6–8 in. long. Smaller ones are perfect for containers; try miniatures like 'Little Finger' and 'Short 'n Sweet', baby carrots such as 'Baby Sweet' and 'Sweet Baby Jane', and round ones like 'Parmex' and 'Thumbelina'.

Carrots also come in colors other than orange—'Purple Haze', 'Red Samurai', and 'White Satin' are examples—and in high-nutrient versions like 'Sugarsnax 54', a 12-incher with extra-high levels of beta-carotene.

HOW TO GROW IT

best site A sunny location unshaded by taller plants.

yield 7 to 10 pounds per 10-ft. row.

soil Soil should be fine enough for root development and loose enough so crusting won't check sprouting of seeds. (If crust should form, keep soil soft by sprinkling.) Light, deep, stone-free soil is perfect.

planting Sow lightly in rows spaced at least 1 ft. apart. To grow successive plantings, sow seeds when previous planting is up and growing; in cold-winter climates, make last sowing 70 days before anticipated killing frost. For a crop in May or June, plant an overwintering variety like 'Merida' around autumnal equinox. *In containers:* Carrots of all types grow well in containers 8–14 in. deep, depending upon length of carrot variety chosen.

spacing When tops are 1–2 in. tall, thin plants to $1\frac{1}{2}$–2 in. apart; thin again if tops begin to crowd. Spacing is second only to variety in controlling root size: 1-in. spacing

Continued on page 34 ▶

Not all carrots are orange; from left, 'Yellowstone', 'Purple Haze', and 'White Satin'.

Thin carrots at this stage and cover root tops with soil or mulch to prevent bitter green "shoulders."

Freshly harvested 'Bolero' carrots, a particularly sweet Nantes variety

in rows 12 in. apart, for example, results in uniformly smaller carrots than 2-in. spacing in rows 15 in. apart.

water Maintain even soil moisture. Alternating dry and wet conditions causes split roots.

fertilizer After the first thinning, work in a narrow band of commercial fertilizer 2 in. out from the row. Too much nitrogen or manure will result in excessive top growth and cause forking of roots.

harvest Use thinnings steamed in butter or in salads. Begin root harvest when carrots reach finger size, usually 30 to 40 days after sowing. Most types reach maturity in 60 to 70 days. In mild-winter climates, carrots store well in the ground; dig as needed.

challenges Use row covers to exclude carrot rust flies and carrot weevils, which lay their eggs in the soil or in the leafy tops of young carrots. Row covers can be removed when plants are 6–8 in. tall. Wireworms and nematodes can also cause problems; practice crop rotation to minimize pest buildup in soil.

Cauliflower

Brassica oleracea (Botrytis group)
Cabbage family *(Brassicaceae)*
ANNUAL OR BIENNIAL GROWN AS ANNUAL
Cool-season vegetable

⚡ **ALL ZONES**
☼ **FULL SUN**
💧 **REGULAR WATER**

Like broccoli and cabbage, cauliflower is a member of the genus *Brassica* and is thought to have originated in the Mediterranean region. All share similar cultural requirements, but cauliflower is more difficult to grow than the other two plants. Gardeners in cool, humid regions will have the easiest time of it; where summers are hot, select heat-tolerant varieties and time your planting to harvest well before or well after midsummer.

Cauliflower grows 1–3 ft. tall, with large, cabbagey leaves surrounding a white edible head that is sometimes called a curd. Home gardeners usually plant an early variety such as 'Snow Crown' or later-season self-blanching varieties such as 'Amazing' or 'Fremont'. There is also a passel of varieties with colored heads: 'Cheddar' (orange), 'Graffiti' (purple), and 'Panther' (green) are examples.

Romanesco varieties such as 'Orbit' and 'Veronica' are sometimes listed as broccolis. Their flavor is milder and sweeter than broccoli; head color is chartreuse; and shape is rounded, pointy, and spiraled, looking like a cross between a cauliflower and the head of a medieval mace.

HOW TO GROW IT

best site Full sun, but be sure to protect developing heads from sun (see "pruning, training" below) or get a self-blanching variety.

yield 8 to 10 pounds per 10-ft. row.

soil Fertile, well-drained soil.

planting Start with small plants; seed is more difficult.

spacing Space plants 1½–2 ft. apart in rows 3 ft. apart.

water Keep plants growing vigorously by keeping soil moist; supply regular deep irrigation during dry periods.

fertilizer Make one o r two applications of complete commercial fertilizer before heads start to form.

pruning, training When heads first appear, tie up the large leaves around them to keep them white.

'Cassius' has excellent flavor and disease resistance.

(Leaves of self-blanching varieties curl over developing heads without assistance.)

harvest Cut heads as soon as they reach full size. Most varieties are ready to harvest 50 to 100 days after transplanting; overwintering types may take 6 months.

challenges Be sure to keep plants actively growing by watering steadily and fertilizing on schedule; any check in growth is likely to cause premature setting of undersize heads. Cauliflower has the same potential pests as cabbage. To prevent soilborne pest buildup, plant in a different site each year. Row covers will protect plants from aphids, cabbage loopers, imported cabbageworms, and cabbage root maggots. Collars made from paper cups or metal cans (with ends removed) deter cutworms, which chew off seedlings at the base. *Bacillus thuringiensis (Bt)* can be applied to control young larvae of cabbageworms and cabbage loopers on plants.

Celeriac

Apium graveolens rapaceum
Carrot family *(Apiaceae)*
BIENNIAL GROWN AS ANNUAL
Cool-season vegetable

- **ALL ZONES**
- **FULL SUN**
- **REGULAR WATER**

This is the "celery root" sold in markets. Like celery, it is descended from wild plants native to Europe and Asia, but celeriac is grown for its large, rounded, edible roots rather than for leafstalks. The roots are peeled, then cooked or used raw in salads.

Growth requirements are the same as for celery: a long, mild growing season that gets neither very hot nor very cold. If your garden is close to the Pacific, you are in optimal celeriac country.

'Brilliant', 'Giant Prague', and 'Mentor' are among several improved varieties.

HOW TO GROW IT

best site Full sun.

yield One root per plant.

soil Though roots of celeriac don't go as deep as those of celery, soil should still be rich, well amended with compost, and deeply dug. Celeriac does not grow well in clay.

planting Plant seeds in flats or peat pots in late winter or early spring; where winters are virtually frost-free, start in summer for a winter crop. Celeriac is slow to reach planting size; to save time, you can purchase small nursery plants.

spacing Grow plants 6–8 in. apart in rows spaced 1½–2 ft. apart.

water Keep soil evenly moist.

fertilizer Celeriac is a heavy feeder. Apply liquid fertilizer every 2 to 3 weeks.

Try celeriac peeled, cut into matchstick-size strips, parboiled, and tossed with a mustard vinaigrette.

harvest Dig up when roots are 3 in. across or larger—about 100 to 120 days after transplanting.

challenges Generally trouble-free, but aphids, carrot rust fly, and caterpillars may occasionally appear. Screen them out with row covers. Handpick or bait for slugs.

Celery

Apium graveolens dulce
Carrot family (*Apiaceae*)
BIENNIAL GROWN AS ANNUAL
Cool-season vegetable

✎ **ALL ZONES**
☼ **FULL SUN**
💧 **REGULAR WATER**

This salad vegetable is grown for its thick, crunchy stalks. Native to Europe and Asia, it performs best where it has a long, mild growing season. Optimal daytime temperatures should average below 75°F/24°C, and nights should be 50° to 60°F/10° to 16°C. Lower nighttime temperatures cause celery to bolt. In the low and intermediate desert, it's a winter crop. In hot-summer climates, set out transplants about a month before the average date of last spring frost, and mulch plants heavily.

Try 'Conquistador', which is very early and widely adapted; 'Golden Boy', a self-blanching variety whose short stalks are naturally light colored; 'Monterey', an extra-early hybrid; or 'Tall Utah 52-70 Improved', with long, dark green stalks.

HOW TO GROW IT

best site Full sun.

yield Several stalks per plant.

soil Soil should be rich, light, and deep, since roots of direct-sown plants can sink down 4 ft. (roots of transplants don't go as deep). Turn and amend soil at least 20 in. deep before planting, and don't waste effort planting in clay—celery won't grow in it.

planting For a summer crop, plant seeds in flats 10 weeks before the average date of last spring frost; where winters are virtually frost-free, start in summer for a winter crop. Or, you can save time by purchasing small nursery plants. In cold-winter climates, plant seedlings after the average date of last spring frost. In mild-winter climates, plant seedlings in fall, winter, or early spring when nighttime temperatures average above 55°F/13°C.

spacing Set plants 6 in. apart in rows 2 ft. apart.

water Keep soil evenly moist or plants will become tough and stringy.

fertilizer Celery is a heavy feeder. Every 2 to 3 weeks, apply liquid fertilizer with irrigation water.

Celery is stronger tasting and more nutritious when left unblanched.

blanching Market celery is blanched (shielded from sunlight during the growing season to keep stalks light colored and milder flavored). To create the same effect with garden-grown plants, slip a bottomless milk carton, paper sleeve, or section of 6-in. drainpipe over the stalks (leaves must have sunlight). Another technique is to mound up soil around the stalks as they grow—or grow self-blanching varieties.

harvest When plants reach harvestable size (3 to 4 months after transplant), you can cut off the whole bunch below the base, or harvest stalks one at a time with a sharp knife and more will grow.

challenges Though celery is usually trouble-free, aphids, carrot rust fly, caterpillars, and slugs can damage growing plants. You can screen out the first three with row covers. Handpick slugs or bait for them.

Chicory and Radicchio

Cichorium intybus
Sunflower family (*Asteraceae*)
PERENNIALS
Cool-season vegetables

✔ ALL ZONES

☀ FULL SUN

💧 REGULAR WATER

This Mediterranean native grows in much of the West as a roadside weed called blue sailors, recognized by its sky blue flowers. Different forms are grown for different uses.

Chicory. For salad greens, use small-rooted, green-leafed varieties like 'Catalogna', 'Red Rib', or 'Crystal Hat'. For roots to grind as a coffee substitute, look for large-rooted varieties such as 'Magdeburgh' ('Cicoria Siciliana'). For Belgian endive (sometimes called French endive or Witloof chicory), use varieties like 'Witloof Bruxelles' or 'Totem' and blanch to produce tender, pale green, cylindrical heads. (For the standard salad green called endive, see *Endive and Escarole*.)

Radicchio. This is the name given to red-leafed chicories grown for salads. 'Giulio', 'Indigo', 'Palla Rossa', and 'Treviso' are good varieties. Radicchio makes lettucelike heads that color to a deep rosy red as weather grows cold; its slight bitterness lessens as color deepens.

HOW TO GROW IT

best site All kinds need full sun.

yield Varies by type and use.

soil Well-drained and organically amended.

planting *Green-leafed and root-type chicories:* Sow starting in early spring (up to early summer where summers are cool). In areas with mild winters, you can also plant in mid- to late summer for fall and winter harvest (or, in the desert, in fall for winter harvest). *Belgian endive:* Sow in spring or early summer; plants will mature by fall. *Radicchio:* Best sown in mid- to late summer for harvest in autumn, though 'Giulio' can be sown in spring to harvest in summer. *In containers:* Plant any except the root types in pots at least 8 in. deep.

spacing Sow $^1/_4$–$^1/_2$ in. deep and 2–3 in. apart in rows spaced 18 in. apart. Thin seedlings to 6–12 in. apart.

'Alouette' radicchio colors up beautifully in winter.

water Keep soil moist.

fertilizer Apply a complete fertilizer after active growth starts.

blanching Belgian endive is blanched in winter. Just trim the greens to an inch of stem, then dig the roots. Bury them diagonally in moist sand; then set in a dark, cool room until pale, tender new growth has been forced.

harvest *Green-leafed chicories:* Pick tender young leaves as needed. *Root-type chicories:* Dig roots when they're 6 in. long and 1–1$^3/_4$ in. wide at the top. *Belgian endive:* Harvest after new growth has been forced. *Radicchio:* Harvest after heads have formed.

challenges Spray with jets of water to control occasional aphid problems. To keep rot from taking hold, remove any leaves that are wilted or damaged.

Chinese Cabbage

Brassica rapa (Pekinensis group)
Cabbage family *(Brassicaceae)*
BIENNIAL GROWN AS ANNUAL
Cool-season vegetable

🌱 ALL ZONES
☼ FULL SUN
💧 REGULAR WATER

Chinese cabbage, sometimes called celery cabbage, produces heads somewhat looser than ordinary cabbage, a close relative. Raw or cooked, it has a more delicate flavor than cabbage and serves well in sukiyaki, stir-fries, soups, and kimchi. There are three kinds: Michihli types (pe-tsai), with tall, narrow heads; Napa types (wong bok), with short, broad heads; and loose-head varieties.

Favored Michihli varieties are hybrid 'Greenwich' and open-pollinated 'Michihli' itself; among Napa varieties, try 'China Express' and the miniature 'Tenderheart'. To sample a loose-head type, look for 'Tokyo Bekana'.

All types are very prone to bolt in hot weather or in the long days of spring and early summer.

For information on Chinese white cabbage (bok choy), see *Asian Greens*.

HOW TO GROW IT

best site Needs abundant sunlight to grow in the cool weather it favors, but tolerates light shade in hot climates.

yield Varies by type.

soil To make sure soil is fertile and well drained, dig in compost before planting.

planting In Zones 1–6, 10, and 11, plant seeds directly in open ground in midsummer; elsewhere, sow in late summer. *In containers:* Grow one plant in a wide pot at least 8 in. deep.

spacing Sow seeds thinly in rows spaced 2–2½ ft. apart. Thin or transplant to 1–1½ ft. apart.

water Keep soil moist.

fertilizer Apply mild fertilizer every 2 weeks during the growing season.

harvest Pick whole Chinese cabbages when heads are well formed and mature, about 70 to 80 days from planting.

Frilly leaves of 'Greenwich', an excellent Michihli variety

challenges To prevent soilborne pest buildup, plant in a different site each year. Row covers will protect plants from aphids, cabbage loopers, imported cabbageworms, and cabbage root maggots. Collars made from paper cups or metal cans (with ends removed) deter cutworms, which chew off seedlings at the base. *Bacillus thuringiensis (Bt)* can be applied to control young larvae of cabbageworms and cabbage loopers on plants. Handpick snails and slugs, or bait for them.

Corn

Zea mays
Grass family *(Poaceae)*
ANNUAL
Warm-season vegetable

ZONES 1B, 2B–24, H1, H2
FULL SUN
REGULAR WATER

Sweet corn. This is the one cereal crop that home gardeners are likely to grow; the 5- to 10-ft.-tall plants require considerable space but are still well worth planting. Once standard sweet corn is picked, its sugar changes to starch very quickly; by rushing ears from the garden directly to boiling water, you can capture their full sweetness.

Sugar-enhanced (se) varieties like 'Kandy Korn' and supersweet (sh2) varieties like 'Supersweet Jubilee' and the 'Xtra-Tender' series are sweeter than standard sweet kinds such as 'Silver Queen' and 'Golden Bantam'. They also maintain sweetness longer after harvest because of genes that increase the quantity of sugar and slow its conversion to starch. An increasing number of synergistic (sy) varieties are also sold; these blend sugar-enhanced and supersweet genes. 'Honey Select' and the bicolored 'Frisky' and 'Montauk' varieties are examples.

Corn needs heat, but suitable early hybrid varieties will grow even in cool-summer areas. In northern climates and at high altitudes, grow short-season varieties such as 'Earlivee' or 'Fleet', which come to harvest in fewer than 70 days; plant seeds you have pregerminated, and grow with black plastic or infrared transmitting (IRT) mulch and a row cover to hasten growth.

Sugar-enhanced varieties are more widely sold than any others, and have become the new standards. In addition to yellow 'Kandy Korn', other good choices include yellow 'Bodacious' and 'Miracle', white 'Whiteout', and bicolored 'Luscious'.

In Hawaii, try varieties developed especially for Island gardens, such as 'Hawaiian Supersweet #9' and 'Hawaiian Supersweet #10'. For traditional corn, try 'H68'.

Baby corn. Special varieties are harvested very early, when the ears are only a few inches long. The tender ears are eaten whole, often pickled or used in salads or Asian cuisine. Plant seeds 1–2 in. apart; thin seedlings to 4 in. apart. Harvest shortly after the first silks appear, which may be only a few weeks after sowing.

Popcorn. Grow and harvest just like sweet corn, but avoid cross-pollination (see "challenges"). Maturity time tends to be long: 100 days from seed to harvest is typical. White, red, and yellow kinds of popcorn are shaped like other types of corn, while strawberry popcorn has stubby, fat ears packed with red kernels. It is grown for its ornamental value as well as for popping.

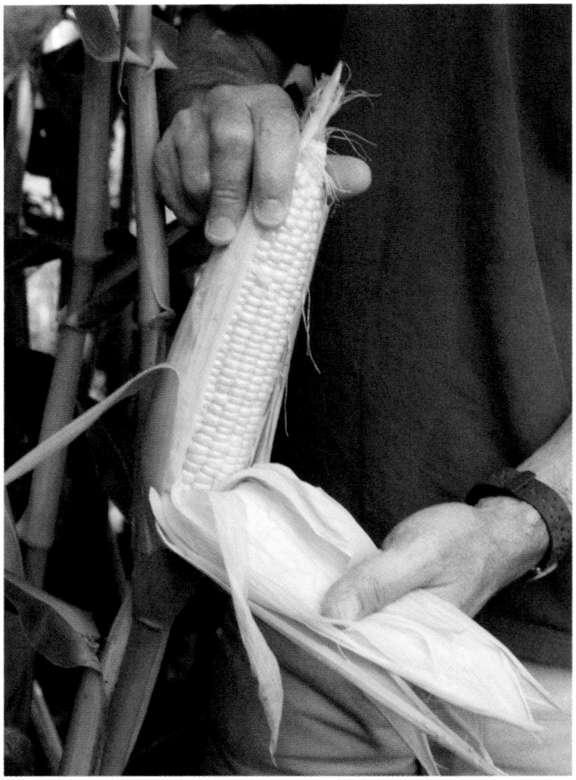

'Honey Select' sweet corn has tender kernels and great corn flavor.

HOW TO GROW IT

best site Maximum sunlight produces the best corn.

yield 1 to 2 ears per plant, 10 to 12 ears per 10-ft. row.

soil Corn grows in various soils but does best in deep, rich ones; good drainage is important.

planting Sow seed 2 weeks after the average last-frost date, then make three or four more plantings at 2-week intervals; or plant early, midseason, and late varieties. In Hawaii, you can plant corn year-round. Plant in blocks of several rows or in hills (clusters) to ensure efficient pollination by wind. Never plant in a single long row or ears will be poorly filled.

Continued on page 42 ▶

Harvest corn when the kernels squirt milky white juice if pinched.

'Sweet Symphony' corn grows well in cool conditions, producing crisp, sweet, yellow-and-white kernels.

Plant like varieties of corn in blocks to ensure good wind pollination.

Expect a yield of 1 to 2 ears per plant.

spacing For block planting, plant seeds 4 in. apart in four or more parallel rows with 3 ft. between them. For hill planting, mound soil 6–8 in. high to form 3-ft.-wide areas spaced 3 ft. apart on all sides. Plant six or seven seeds in each hill and thin to the three strongest plants. (It's easier to weed and harvest hills, and you can fit hills into irregular spaces, but you get more production from blocks.)

water Give plants plenty of water. Just as tassels emerge from stalks, give an especially deep watering that thoroughly wets the entire root zone; repeat when silks form.

fertilizer Feed with high-nitrogen fertilizer when stalks are 12–15 in. tall and again when they are 2–2$^1/_2$ ft. tall.

pruning, training Don't bother removing suckers that appear around the base of the plant. It's extra work for you and doesn't improve the quality or quantity of corn you're growing.

harvest *Sweet corn:* Check your crop when ears are plump and silks have withered; corn is usually ready to eat 3 weeks after silks first appear. To check, pull back husks and try popping a kernel with your thumbnail. It should squirt milky juice. Watery juice means that corn is immature, while toothpaste consistency indicates overmaturity. *Baby corn:* Harvest a few days after first silks appear. *Popcorn:* Allow ears to fully ripen before you harvest: silks will be withered, husks will be the color of straw, and kernels will be firm. After harvested ears are thoroughly dry, rub off kernels and store them in a dry place.

challenges Corn cross-pollinates readily, so if you plant two varieties that release pollen at the same time within 100 ft. of each other, the traits of each type might show up in the other. For example, if popcorn and sweet corn cross-pollinate, many of the kernels in the popcorn ears won't pop, and many of the kernels in the sweet corn ears will be popcorn. If you want to grow unlike varieties, put them on opposite sides of your house, with neither downwind from the other.

Corn earworm is the principal insect pest. There is no simple control. Most gardeners expect some harvested ears to show worm damage at the silk ends, and they just cut off those ends. Prevention is tedious but effective: 3 to 7 days after silks appear, use a medicine dropper to put two drops of mineral oil just inside the tip of each ear.

GARY NABHAN ON
local corn

Gary Nabhan, PhD, author, ecologist, and co-founder of Native Seeds/SEARCH (a nonprofit organization that works to preserve Southwestern native plants) is a strong advocate for growing truly local crops. "Regionally adapted seed is especially important in the desert because our growing conditions are so different," says Dr. Nabhan. "I grow Hopi sweet corn, which is perfectly adapted where I live; it ripens in a short season and outproduces other corn here. The Hopi got their seed at a world's fair in the 1890s, then selected the best plants for replanting year after year."

How do you select the best plants for your garden? Dr. Nabhan says, "You can get seed at Native Seeds/SEARCH, but then you should select your own seed from what you grow. Gradually you'll develop a strain that's best adapted in your own garden. All of us can be plant breeders." Here's how:

Start by buying open-pollinated (non-hybrid) corn seed that does well in your region. Sow it and grow it in isolation from other corn, so it won't be cross-pollinated. When the corn ripens, leave one or two ears on each plant that has the traits you want to perpetuate, such as early harvest, robust plants, especially good flavor, or large ears.

After the silk has dried, put paper (not plastic) bags over the ears to protect them. At season's end, pick the ears, peel back the husks, and hang the ears in a place where the kernels can dry completely. Then break off the seed and store it in a paper bag in a cool, dark place for planting next spring.

By repeating this process over several years, you will end up with corn that is uniquely well adapted to the conditions in your own garden.

Cucumber

Cucumis sativus
Gourd family *(Curcubitaceae)*
ANNUAL VINE
Warm-season vegetable

- **ALL ZONES**
- **FULL SUN**
- **REGULAR WATER**

Most cucumbers are big, trailing vines that need at least 25 sq. ft. to sprawl, but you can run vines up a fence or trellis to conserve space. Seeds require warm soil to sprout, and flowers need heat for pollination. The species is native to south Asia.

There are long, smooth, green slicing cucumbers like 'Marketmore 76'; numerous small pickling cucumbers like 'Alibi'; and roundish, yellow, mild-flavored lemon cucumbers. Novelty varieties include an Asian type called 'Suyo Long' (long, slim, and very mild), Armenian cucumber (actually a long, curving, pale green, ribbed melon that looks like a cucumber and has a mild cucumber flavor), and English greenhouse cucumber. The last type must be grown in a greenhouse to avoid pollination by bees and subsequent loss of form and flavor; when well grown, it's the mildest of all cucumbers.

Bush cucumbers like 'Fanfare' and other varieties with compact vines take up little garden space. Burpless varieties resemble supermarket cucumbers in shape and mild flavor but can be grown outdoors. They're called burpless because the skin can be eaten without causing indigestion.

Catalogs are very specific about cucumber pollination requirements. Most cucumbers bear male and female flowers on the same plant, so bees cross-pollinate them easily. But some produce only female flowers; when you buy these, a few seeds in the packet will be marked to show that they will produce male plants. You must plant at least one of these for every six female plants. Some cucumbers produce seedless fruit without a pollinator, so they're popular both outdoors and in bee-free greenhouses. 'Diva' is a mild-tasting seedless cucumber.

HOW TO GROW IT

best site Give vines room to ramble, with all parts in full sun.

yield 8 to 10 pounds per 10-ft. row.

soil Fertile and well-drained.

'County Fair', a favorite cucumber for pickling

planting Sow seeds in the ground 1 to 2 weeks after the average date of last frost. *In containers:* Grow three bush cucumbers in a wide, 12-in.-deep container with a tomato cage on it.

spacing Plant seeds 1 in. deep and 1–3 ft. apart in rows 3–6 ft. apart, depending upon whether you're growing bush or vining cucumbers (wider spacing for vines). Or plant in hills (clusters) of five or six seeds each, thinning to the two strongest plants. Make hills 6–8 in. high and 3–6 ft. apart.

water Cucumbers need a steady supply of water. Apply it in furrows or by drip irrigation—never overhead, since that encourages downy mildew.

fertilizer Apply complete fertilizer after plants have started vigorous growth, then repeat a month later.

Continued on page 44 ▶

Cucumber choices include Armenian, slicing, and pickling varieties.

Lemon cucumbers, distinguished by their color and shape, bear well on a trellis.

pruning, training To reduce the amount of ground space plants use, you can let cucumber vines grow up a trellis or even to the top of an old stepladder (their tendrils cling). This technique also helps long cucumbers grow straight.

harvest Pickling cucumbers should be harvested as soon as they have reached the proper size: 2 in. long for sweet pickles, 5–6 in. long for dill pickles, 6–8 in. long for slicing (or longer for extra-long varieties). Frequent harvest ensures continued production.

challenges Bait for slugs and snails. Row covers will protect seedlings from various insect pests, including cucumber beetles and flea beetles; remove covers when flowering begins so that pollination can occur. Whiteflies are a potential pest late in season; hose off plants regularly or hang yellow sticky traps. Misshapen fruit is usually due to uneven watering or poor pollination. Bitter fruit is usually a result of uneven irrigation.

Eggplant

Solanum melongena
Nightshade family *(Solanaceae)*
ANNUAL
Warm-season vegetable

✎ **ZONES 1–24, H1, H2**
☼ **FULL SUN**
💧 **REGULAR WATER**

Few vegetable plants are handsomer than eggplant, which hails from Southeast Asia. It resembles a little tree, 2–3 ft. tall and equally wide. Big leaves (usually lobed) are purple tinged; drooping violet flowers are $1^1/2$ in. across. And, of course, the big, usually purple fruits are spectacular. A well-spaced row of eggplant makes a distinguished border between vegetable and flower gardens. Eggplants are also effective in large containers or raised beds.

Large roundish or oval varieties such as 'Black Beauty', 'Burpee Hybrid', 'Dusky', and 'Zebra' are often sold as Italian types.

Long, slender Asian varieties are sold under a number of names, including 'Fairy Tale' and 'Millionaire'.

Specialists in imported vegetable seeds offer numerous colored varieties, including the full-size white 'Casper' and a host of smaller varieties in a range of sizes (down to $1/2$ in.) and colors—for example, white, yellow, red, green, and variegated plum. Some of the smaller ones genuinely resemble eggs. All are edible as well as attractive.

To produce a crop, eggplant needs 2 to 3 months of warm days and nights (nighttime temperatures should be no lower than 65°F/18°C). A second crop for late-summer and fall harvest is even possible in the warmest climates.

HOW TO GROW IT

best site Full sun for good fruit production.

yield Italian (oval) varieties produce about 8 fruits per plant, Asian kinds up to 15.

soil The soil should be well drained and well amended with compost or aged manure.

planting Eggplant can be grown from seed (sow indoors 8 to 10 weeks before the date of the last expected frost), but starting from nursery-grown plants is much easier. Mulch to maintain soil moisture. *In containers:* Plant by themselves or interplant with flowers. Use a container at least 1 ft. deep and 16 in. wide.

Continued on page 46 ▶

'Hansel' eggplants are tender whether picked as "babies" at 2 to 3 inches or when mature.

'Zebra' eggplant bears striking white-streaked fruit.

'Farmer's Long' Japanese eggplant thrives in containers.

spacing Set plants 2–2¹/₂ ft. apart in rows 3 ft. apart.

water Keep soil moist.

fertilizer Feed every week or two with fish fertilizer or half-strength liquid fertilizer.

pruning, training If you enjoy tiny whole eggplants, allow plants to produce freely. If you prefer larger fruits, pinch out some terminal growth and blossoms; three to six large fruits per plant will result. Large-fruited Italian types can be staked or caged like tomatoes to keep fruit from breaking branches.

harvest Pick fruits after they develop some color but don't wait until they lose their glossy shine.

challenges Colorado potato beetles, cutworms, and flea beetles can be a problem on young plants; grow eggplant under row covers until plants are big enough to tolerate leaf damage. Control aphids by blasting them off with a jet of water or spraying with insecticidal soap, and put out yellow sticky traps for whiteflies. Blight and verticillium wilt can also cause problems; as a precaution, don't grow eggplants in the same place 2 years in a row.

Endive and Escarole

Cichorium endivia
Sunflower family *(Asteraceae)*
BIENNIAL OR ANNUAL
Cool-season vegetable

▨ **ALL ZONES**

☼ **FULL SUN**

♦ **REGULAR WATER**

This Mediterranean species includes curly endive (also called frisée) as well as broad-leafed endive (escarole), both of which form rosettes of leaves. Though they tolerate more heat than lettuce does, they grow faster in cold weather, maturing in 90 to 95 days from seed.

'Green Curled', 'Keystone', 'Rhodos', and 'Salad King' are standard curly endives; 'Broad-leaved Batavian', 'Full Heart Batavian', and 'Full Heart NR65' are good full-leafed varieties.

Belgian or French endives are the blanched sprouts of a kind of chicory; see *Chicory*.

HOW TO GROW IT

best site Both kinds take full sun.

yield 3 to 6 pounds per 10-ft. row.

soil Rich soil well amended with compost or rotted manure.

planting In cold-winter areas, sow from spring into summer; in mild-winter climates, sow so that plants mature after summer heat is past. *In containers:* Plant in wide containers at least 6 in. deep.

spacing Seed thinly in rows 15–18 in. apart, then thin plants to 12 in. apart.

water Keep soil moist.

fertilizer Apply complete fertilizer after active growth starts.

pruning, training When plants have reached full size (a foot across), pull outer leaves over the center and tie them up at top (but not when they're wet, as that may cause decay). Covered center leaves will blanch to yellow

Endive, like 'Tres Fine Maraichere' shown here, and escarole add spice to salads and stir-fries.

or white; the process keeps the taste from becoming too bitter. Endive can also be used unblanched by harvesting the outer leaves, as for Swiss chard.

harvest Pick outer leaves from young plants. Pull up the entire plant when it matures, 85 to 100 days after sowing.

challenges Plants can be bothered by aphids, armyworms, flea beetles, leafhoppers, snails and slugs, and downy mildew. Row covers help manage insect problems; bait or handpicking controls snails and slugs; and good air circulation minimizes mildew.

Garlic

Allium species
Lily family *(Liliaceae)*
PERENNIALS
Cool-season bulb vegetables

- **ALL ZONES EXCEPT A1**
- **FULL SUN**
- **REGULAR WATER**

These onion relatives are not known in the wild, but progenitors probably come from Central Asia. Plants grow clumps of 2-ft.-long, 1-in.-wide leaves from bulbs. Both the leaves and the bulbs are edible.

Seed stores and some mail-order seed houses sell disease-free mother bulbs ("sets") for planting—and some gardeners have had good luck planting bulbs from grocery stores.

Softneck garlic (*Allium sativum*). This is what you usually find in grocery stores. Bulbs have an outer layer of medium-size cloves and inner layers of smaller cloves. In this group, you'll find varieties such as 'California Early', 'California Late', 'Silver Rose', and 'Silverskin'.

Hardneck garlic or rocombole garlic (*A. s. ophioscorodon*). Hardneck bulbs have large outside cloves and no inner cloves, and the plants are a little more cold-hardy than softnecks. This type is generally preferred by chefs for its superior flavor. In spring, each plant sends up a scape (leafless flower stalk) that loops around before forming a small bulb on top. These are good in stir-fries and make interesting flower arrangements, but they take energy out of the plants. Cut them off as they form to get larger cloves. This group includes varieties like 'Korean Red', 'Music', 'German Extra Hardy', and 'Spanish Roja'.

Giant or elephant garlic (*A. ampeloprasum*). This type, closely related to leek, has unusually large (fist-size) bulbs and mild garlic flavor. Growth requirements are the same as for regular garlic.

HOW TO GROW IT

best site Full sun for healthy growth and big cloves.

yield 10 to 30 bulbs per 10-ft. row.

soil Rich, well-drained soil.

planting Plant in fall for early summer harvest. Break up bulbs into individual segments ("cloves"), select the largest ones, and plant pointed end up. Mulch to help conserve soil moisture.

To keep your garlic crop going, pull off larger cloves from harvested bulbs and plant in fall.

spacing Plant garlic cloves 3–6 in. apart in rows 15 in. apart. Space elephant garlic 8–12 in. apart.

water Keep soil moist. Stop watering when leaves start to turn brown.

fertilizer Garlic is a light feeder; fertile soil is sufficient.

harvest Snip some young tender leaves to chop into salads in spring. In early summer, when leafy tops fall over, lift garlic with a garden fork (rather than pulling by the tops). Air-dry bulbs, cut off most of the tops and roots, and store in cool, well-ventilated place out of sunlight.

challenges Garlic can survive very cold winters, but bulbs can be displaced when freezing weather causes soil to heave.

Jicama

Pachyrhizus erosus
Pea family *(Fabaceae)*
ANNUAL VINE
Warm-season root vegetable

✎ **ZONES H1, H2; AS ORNAMENTAL IN ZONES 8, 9, 12–14, 18–24**

☼ **FULL SUN**

💧 **AMPLE WATER**

⬦ **SEEDS POISONOUS IF INGESTED**

The edible part of this tropical American plant is actually an enlarged taproot; it develops underground like a beet and tastes something like a sweet water chestnut. Above ground it grows as a very attractive vine, twining to 14 ft. tall or more, with luxuriant deep green foliage and upright spikes of sweet pea–shaped purple or violet flowers in summer. Leaves have three leaflets.

Cultivate jicama for its edible root in Hawaii—it needs a long, warm growing season—or as an ornamental elsewhere. Plants produce poor-quality roots in Southern California, and you'll usually get only foliage and flowers in Northern California.

HOW TO GROW IT

best site Full sun, tropical climate.

yield One 1- to 6-pound tuber per plant.

soil Rich, well-drained sandy loam is perfect.

planting Plant in spring after danger of frost is past.

spacing Sow seeds 2 in. deep and 4 in. apart. Thin seedlings to 8–12 in. apart.

water This is a water lover. Keep soil constantly moist.

fertilizer Apply high-nitrogen fertilizer monthly.

pruning, training Grow on a trellis or on the ground as a trailing mound. Pinch off flowers for maximum root production.

Jicama looks like a potato and tastes like a water chestnut.

harvest Roots enlarge in fall as days begin to grow shorter, but weather must stay warm to produce a good crop; harvest roots before first frost in regions where frosts are likely (if you're fortunate enough to get a crop). In frost-free areas, you can leave them in the ground until they're needed. Peel off the rough brown skin and eat the white flesh raw or cooked.

challenges No serious pests or diseases.

Kale and Collards

Brassica oleracea (Acephala group)
Cabbage family (*Brassicaceae*)
BIENNIAL GROWN AS ANNUAL
Cool-season vegetable

🌿 **ALL ZONES**

☼ ◑ **FULL SUN OR LIGHT SHADE**

💧 **REGULAR WATER**

These cabbage relatives are originally from the north-western Mediterranean coast. They are grown for their leaves, which can be steamed, stir-fried, sautéed, or added to soups. Kale and collards are high in vitamins A and C and in calcium. Both are winter-hardy to as low as 5°F/–15°C.

Kale. This attractive plant grows 14–30 in. tall, depending on variety. Curly-leafed varieties such as 'Redbor' and 'Winterbor' form compact clusters of leaves that are tightly curled. 'Toscano' ('Lacinato') is a noncurly green kale; 'Red Russian' is a noncurly red kale (its leaves are actually gray-green with purple veins). So-called flowering kale is similar to flowering cabbage, with brightly colored, decorative foliage; it, too, is edible and is sometimes sold in markets under the name "salad savoy."

Collards. Often listed as a type of kale, this is a large (2–3 ft.), smooth-leafed plant that does not form a head. Recommended varieties include 'Champion', 'Flash', and 'Vates'.

HOW TO GROW IT

best site Full sun or light shade in mild climates; partial shade where it's hot.

yield 4 to 8 pounds per 10-ft. row.

soil Fertile soil amended with compost or aged manure.

planting *Kale:* Plant in late summer for a fall crop; in cool-summer areas, it can also be planted in early spring for a summer crop (intense sun in hotter climates makes leaves turn bitter). *Collards:* Plant in summer for fall and winter harvest; or plant in early spring for a spring-into-summer crop (collards are heat-tolerant). *In containers:* Plant in wide pots at least 10 in. deep, one plant per pot.

spacing Sow seeds in place and thin to 1¹⁄₂–3 ft. apart, or set out transplants at the same spacing.

Large leaves of 'Toscano' kale, sometimes called "dinosaur kale"

water Keep soil moist during the growing season, but stop watering after the first frost in fall.

fertilizer Top-dress with a high-nitrogen fertilizer in spring.

harvest Eat thinnings as plants fill in. For all types of kale and collards, harvest by removing leaves from the outside of the clusters; or harvest the entire plant by pulling it up and cutting off the base. Light frost sweetens flavor.

challenges Though kale occasionally gets aphids and cabbageworms, plants suffer far fewer pest and disease problems than most other crops in the cabbage family. Crop rotation minimizes problems.

Ornamental kale is more brightly colored—and sweeter tasting—when nipped by frost.

Kohlrabi

Brassica oleracea (Gongylodes group)
Cabbage family *(Brassicaceae)*
BIENNIAL GROWN AS ANNUAL
Cool-season vegetable

ALL ZONES
FULL SUN
REGULAR WATER

Leaves and leafstalks of this 2-ft.-tall plant are edible, but most gardeners grow it for the large, round, bulblike portion of stem formed just above the soil surface. Peel, slice, and serve it raw; or steam or sauté slices or chunks. Young leaves and leafstalks can be steamed.

Kohlrabi probably originated in coastal western Europe. Plants are very fast growing, ready to harvest in 50 to 60 days from seed. Standard varieties are 'Early White Vienna' and 'Early Purple Vienna', which are similar in size and flavor, differing only in skin color. They're harvested when globes are 2–3 in. in diameter. 'Kolibri' is a popular purple-skinned variety that grows 4- to 6-in. globes. 'Superschmelz', 'Kossack', and 'Gigante' all reach 8–10 in. in diameter.

HOW TO GROW IT

best site Full sun, especially for fall planting.

yield 4 to 8 pounds per 10-ft. row.

soil Fertile soil is best. If soil is acid, add lime before planting.

planting Sow seed about 2 weeks after the average date of the last frost. Make successive sowings 2 weeks apart. In areas with warm winters, plant again in late fall and early winter. *In containers:* Plant three seeds or one plant per 12-in.-wide, 8-in.-deep pot.

spacing Sow seed $1/2$ in. deep in rows $1^1/2$ ft. apart. Thin seedlings to 4–6 in. apart in the ground; thin to the strongest seedling in the container.

water Keep soil moist.

fertilizer Feed with complete fertilizer after planting seedlings.

Kohlrabi's distinctive stem looks almost alien, but it's the most delicious part.

harvest Harvest bulbous part of standard varieties when 2–3 in. wide; harvest large-globed varieties when they're just under their advertised diameter. Quality declines if harvest is delayed until after globes are full size (the flavor gets hot and the texture becomes woody).

challenges Plants are not usually bothered by pests or diseases.

Leek

Allium porrum
Lily family *(Liliaceae)*
BIENNIAL GROWN AS ANNUAL
Cool-season vegetable

🗲 **ALL ZONES EXCEPT A1, A2**
☼ ◑ **PARTIAL SHADE IN HOTTEST CLIMATES**
💧 **REGULAR WATER**

Leeks are related to onions but don't form distinct bulbs. They grow 2–3 ft. tall, with an edible, mild-flavored stem that resembles a long, fat green onion. It can be eaten by itself or in soups. Excellent varieties include 'Giant Musselburgh', 'Lancelot', 'Lincoln', and 'Shelton'.

HOW TO GROW IT

best site Full sun in cool-summer climates; also does well in hotter areas if given some shade.

yield 4 to 6 pounds per 10-ft. row.

soil Very rich garden loam. If soil is acid, dig in lime before planting.

planting In cold-winter regions, set out transplants in early spring, or direct-sow seeds in late summer for harvest the following year. In mild-winter areas, set out transplants in fall. Sow seeds indoors $1/2$ in. deep and 1 in. apart 8 weeks prior to planting date. If leeks bloom, small bulbils may appear in flower clusters; plant these for later harvest.

spacing Space seedlings 2–4 in. apart in a 5-in.-deep furrow.

water Keep soil moist.

fertilizer Feed with fish fertilizer every few weeks during the growing season.

pruning, training As plants grow, mound soil around stalks to blanch them; this makes the stem bottoms white and mild. Keep mounded soil just below leaf joints. (If soil gets into leaf joints, it can work its way into the bulb.)

'Giant Musselburgh' leek, a popular heirloom variety

harvest Lift out leeks with a spading fork when stems are $1/2$–2 in. thick, usually about 4 to 7 months after setting out plants. In cold-winter climates, harvest before ground freezes. (Where ground doesn't freeze, you can leave leeks in place and harvest as needed.) Any offsets can be detached and replanted.

challenges Leeks are not bothered by many of the pests and diseases that attack onions.

Lettuce

Lactuca sativa
Sunflower family *(Asteraceae)*
ANNUAL
Cool-season vegetable

✎ **ALL ZONES**
☼ ◐ **PARTIAL SHADE IN HOTTEST CLIMATES**
💧 **REGULAR WATER**

Probably from Asia Minor, leaf lettuce has been popular for at least 2,000 years, and head lettuce for about 500. A short browse through a seed catalog, seed display rack, or selection of nursery seedlings will reveal enough variety to keep your salad bowl crisp and colorful throughout the growing season.

There are four principal types of lettuce: crisphead, butterhead or Boston, loose leaf, and romaine. Most come in both red and green varieties.

Crisphead. The most exasperating type for home gardeners to produce because it often doesn't head up tightly like the Iceberg lettuce you buy in stores. Heads form best when monthly average temperatures are 55° to 60°F/13° to 16°C. In mild climates, this type of lettuce does well over a long season, but in hot-summer areas, timing of planting becomes critical. Start with the Iceberg type 'Summertime', or try one of the easier Batavian varieties (also called Summer Crisp and French Crisp) such as 'Nevada' or 'Loma'. The Batavians have young leaves like leaf lettuce and form small, crisp heads.

Butterhead or Boston. Has a loose head with green, smooth outer leaves and yellow inner leaves. Good varieties include 'Bibb' ('Limestone'), 'Buttercrunch', and 'Tom Thumb'. For red-speckled or red-tinted varieties, try 'Flashy Butter Oak', 'Merveille des Quatre Saisons', and 'Speckles'.

Loose leaf. Makes a rosette rather than a head. Because this type is easy to grow and stands heat well, it is the biggest category of lettuce. Choice selections include 'Black-seeded Simpson', 'Simpson Elite', and 'Oak Leaf' (all with green leaves); 'Salad Bowl' (with deeply cut green leaves); and 'Merlot', 'New Red Fire', 'Red Deer Tongue', and 'Red Sails' (all with red-tinged leaves).

Romaine (also called Cos lettuce, for the Aegean island where it originated). Has an erect, cylindrical head of smooth leaves; outer leaves are green, inner ones whitish. It stands heat moderately well. Try 'Flashy Trout Back', 'Little Gem', 'Remus', or 'Winter Density'; or, for reddish leaves, 'Rouge d'Hiver' and 'Outredgeous'.

'Remus', a classic romaine lettuce

Various loose-leaf and romaine lettuce varieties are typically included in mesclun mixes (see *Salad Blends*).

Many lettuce varieties have been bred to resist bolting when it gets hot. If you live in a hot-summer climate, or one where temperatures jump suddenly, look for these. Besides loose-leaf and romaine, try 'Drunken Woman Frizzy Headed' butterhead and 'Reine des Glaces' crisphead.

HOW TO GROW IT

best site Full sun in cool areas, partial shade where it's hot.

yield 4 to 10 pounds per 10-ft. row.

soil All lettuces need loose, well-drained soil.

planting Sow in open ground; barely cover seeds. Or buy nursery starts, which often have two or three plants to a cell if they haven't been thinned. Cut or tease them apart before planting. *In containers:* Nonheading types are easy in a wide container at least 6 in. deep.

Continued on page 56 ▶

Fresh-cut baby greens are sweet and tender.

'Merveille des Quatre Saisons', a French heirloom butterhead lettuce

'Oak Leaf', an heirloom loose-leaf variety popular since the 1800s

spacing Loose-leaf lettuce can be grown as close as 4 in. apart; thin all other types to 1 ft. apart.

water Spray the seedbed regularly until seeds germinate. Then keep roots of growing lettuce moist; if lack of water checks growth, leaves will become bitter.

fertilizer Lettuce is a relatively light feeder, but it benefits from feeding with a complete fertilizer once or twice during the growing season.

harvest Start with thinnings. *Loose-leaf lettuce and romaine:* Harvest by picking outer leaves as needed or by pulling up whole plants. *Head lettuce:* Harvest by pulling up whole plants when they have matured.

challenges Lettuce goes to seed and the leaves become bitter during warm weather. It is also subject to snails, slugs, aphids, cabbage loopers, cutworms, flea beetles, leafhoppers, leaf miners, downy mildew, and fusarium wilt. Long as this list is, well-raised plants rarely suffer much from any of these problems. Row covers will protect against insects, bait can reduce slug problems, good air circulation helps with mildew, and crop rotation minimizes problems with fusarium.

Mâche

Valerianella locusta
Valerian family *(Valerianaceae)*
ANNUAL
Cool-season vegetable

🌿 **ZONES A1–A3, 1–24, H1**
☀ **FULL SUN**
💧 **REGULAR WATER**

This cool-season European native, sometimes called corn salad or lamb's lettuce, is among the most cold-hardy of traditional salad and cooking greens. Plants form rather loose, 8- to 10-in.-wide rosettes of spoon-shaped leaves to 6 in. long with a mild, nutty flavor. Mâche overwinters in areas where the ground doesn't freeze.

HOW TO GROW IT

best site Open garden with full sun.

yield A 10-ft. row produces enough for a family of four.

soil Grow in well-drained soil.

planting In warmer climates, sow seeds from fall through early spring for harvest in about 90 days. In cooler climates, sow seeds in summer (for fall harvest) or in late winter as soon as soil is workable (for spring harvest). Leave a few plants in the ground to reseed. *In containers:* Mâche is easy to grow in a wide container at least 6 in. deep.

spacing Plant seeds 1/2 in. deep and 1 in. apart in rows 8 in. apart; thin seedlings to 6 in. apart.

water Irrigate when the soil surface starts to dry out.

fertilizer Apply a half-strength dose of complete liquid fertilizer after true leaves appear.

harvest You can harvest the entire rosette anytime after three or four pairs of leaves appear, but before the plant goes to seed.

challenges Mâche quickly bolts in warm weather, so be sure to harvest while temperatures are still cool.

Mâche is prized for its mild flavor and soft texture.

Melon

Cucumis melo
Gourd family *(Cucurbitaceae)*
ANNUAL
Warm-season vegetable

* **ZONES 2–24**
* **FULL SUN**
* **REGULAR WATER**

Melons are thought to have originated in Africa. The principal types cultivated in the West are muskmelons (cantaloupes) and late melons. True cantaloupes are a type of hard-shelled melon rarely grown in North America. Because watermelon *(Citrullus lanatus)* is botanically different, it is listed separately.

Muskmelons *(Cucumis melo reticulatus).* Melons of this type are ribbed, with netted skin and typically salmon-colored flesh. Choice varieties include 'Ambrosia', 'Athena', 'Fastbreak' (very early), and a small, personal-size cantaloupe called 'Lil' Loupe'. Hybrids are superior to others in disease resistance and uniformity of size and quality. (Growing melons resistant to mildew and other diseases is particularly important in humid coastal regions.) Seed packets and catalogs will usually tell you if varieties are hybrids. Other muskmelons include small, tasty, highly perfumed types from the Mediterranean—charentais types such as 'Edonis', for example—and larger galia varieties, such as 'Arava' and 'Passport'.

Late melons *(C. m. inodorus).* This varied group includes canary ('Amy'), honeydew ('Earlidew'), casaba ('Golden Beauty'), and Piel de Sapo ('Lambkin'). Though less widely cultivated than muskmelons, they are gaining in popularity as more garden-friendly varieties are developed. Most dislike high humidity and grow best in areas with hot, relatively dry summers (Zones 8, 9, 12–14, 18, 19).

There are also crosses between muskmelons and late melons—'Crane', 'Crenshaw', and 'Twice as Nice', for example; and wild cards with unknown ancestry, like the heirloom ananas melons (also called pineapple melons)—'Creme de la Creme' and 'San Juan', for examples. As breeding blurs traditional melon categories, many seed sellers are simply lumping together new hybrids as "specialty melons."

HOW TO GROW IT

best site Full sun; to ripen to full sweetness, melons need steady heat for 2$\frac{1}{2}$ to 4 months.

yield Two or three melons per vine.

Cantaloupes are a favorite melon; there are sweet-tasting choices for almost any climate.

soil Melons need well-drained soil with high organic content. Dig in compost before planting.

planting Sow seeds 1 in. deep 2 weeks after the average last-frost date. In regions where summers are cool or relatively short, start plants indoors in pots a few weeks before the last frost date, then plant outdoors in the warmest southern exposure. Plastic mulch can help extend the season: plant through X-shaped slits in clear plastic mulch (in areas where summers are very short) or in black plastic mulch to warm soil, speed harvest, and help keep fruit from rotting. Using row covers to shelter plants at the beginning of the season protects them from cold nights.

In containers: It is possible to grow compact early cantaloupes in containers at least 18 in. wide and deep; a half wine barrel works well. Let vines ramble over the edges, or trellis them.

For the largest harvest, look for melons that bear at least two fruits per running stem.

Flavorful melons, from left: 'Amish', 'Crane', 'Collective Farm Woman', and 'Eden's Gem'

spacing You can plant in hills (clusters) or rows. *Hills:* Make hills about 3 ft. in diameter and space them 3–4 ft. apart; encircle each with a furrow for irrigation. (After you turn and amend the soil where you're planting, the area will naturally be several inches higher than the surrounding garden.) Plant four or five seeds per hill. When plants are well established, thin each hill to the best two plants. *Rows:* Make rows 3 ft. wide and as long as desired, spacing them 3–4 ft. apart; make furrows for irrigation along both sides. Plant two or three seeds per foot of row. Thin to one strong plant per foot.

water Fill furrows with water from time to time (to water plants without wetting foliage), but do not keep soil soaked.

fertilizer Feed in furrows every 6 weeks with a complete fertilizer.

pruning, training Though you can grow melons on sunbathed trellises, the heavy fruit must be supported in individual cloth slings.

harvest *Muskmelons:* Lift the fruit and twist; if ripe, it will easily slip off the stem. A pleasant perfume also indicates ripeness. *Late melons:* These do not slip from stems when ripe. Honeydews are ready to pick when the area of the melon that rests on the ground turns from yellow to white. Harvest 'Crenshaw', casaba, and other late melons when the fruit begins to turn yellow and starts to soften at the blossom end. As 'Crenshaw' melons approach maturity, protect fruits from sunburn.

challenges If aphids, cucumber beetles, mites, or squash vine borers are a problem in your area, use row covers to protect plants. If fusarium wilt or powdery mildew are concerns, select resistant varieties.

Mustard

Brassica species
Cabbage family *(Brassicaceae)*
ANNUALS
Cool-season vegetables

☀ **ALL ZONES**

☼ **FULL SUN**

💧 **REGULAR WATER**

Three kinds of mustard are popular in American gardens, all derived from plants native to the Mediterranean eastward into Asia. All are easy to grow, and grow fast—ready for the table 35 to 60 days after planting.

Curly-leafed mustard (*Brassica juncea*). Looks similar to curly-leafed kale, with leaf margins that are curled and/or frilled, or leaves cut clear to the center vein. It is usually cooked like spinach or cabbage. Young leaves are sometimes eaten raw in salads or used as garnishes. 'Golden Frill', 'Green Wave', 'Ruby Streaks', and 'Southern Giant Curled' are good examples.

Flat-leafed mustard. Less well known but gaining popularity, and probably interchangeable with the broadleaf mustards listed in *Asian Greens*. 'Florida Broadleaf' is a standard. 'Red Giant' ('Chinese Red'), with large, crinkled leaves and strong red shading, is handsome enough for a border.

Tendergreen mustard, or mustard spinach (*B. rapa* Perviridis group). Has smooth, dark green leaves with a spinachy flavor. It matures earlier than curly-leafed mustard and is more tolerant of hot, dry weather. Use young mustard spinach as a salad green; older leaves can be cooked. 'Komatsuna' and 'Tendergreen' are the most common varieties.

To learn about Chinese mustard greens, see *Asian Greens*.

HOW TO GROW IT

best site Full sun; tolerates light shade in hottest climates.

yield 3 to 6 pounds per 10-ft. row.

soil Plants do best in fertile, well-drained soil. Amend with compost or aged manure before planting.

planting Sow in rows in early spring; make successive sowings when young plants from each previous planting are established. Mustard thrives in cool weather but

'Green Wave', one of the tangy hot mustard greens enjoying a new popularity

quickly goes to seed in summer heat, so it's not worth risking in summer. For fall harvest, sow in late summer; in mild-winter areas, plant again in fall and winter. *In containers:* Grow in a wide container at least 8 in. deep.

spacing Thin seedlings to 6 in. apart.

water Keep soil moist.

fertilizer Feed once every 2 to 3 weeks with a complete fertilizer.

harvest Pick outer leaves as needed.

challenges Cabbage loopers, flea beetles, and downy mildew can be pests. Row covers can protect against insects, and good air circulation reduces mildew problems.

Okra

Abelmoschus esculentus
Mallow family *(Malvaceae)*
ANNUAL
Warm-season vegetable

- ☑ **ALL ZONES**
- ☼ **FULL SUN**
- ● **REGULAR WATER**

This heat-loving vegetable hails from tropical Asia. It is a large, erect, bushy plant to 6 ft. tall, with big, bold, deeply lobed leaves. The edible pods, produced in leaf joints, are used to flavor and thicken soups and gumbos; they can also be pickled, sautéed, steamed, or batter-fried.

Okra grows well under the same conditions as sweet corn, and takes 55 to 60 days from planting to harvest. 'Clemson Spineless' and 'Cajun Delight' are early varieties that mature in areas with a short growing season. 'Burgundy' has red stems and pods—an attractive choice for containers.

HOW TO GROW IT

best site Full sun is essential. If you live in a mild climate, choose the hottest spot in your garden, such as against a south-facing wall.

yield 5 to 10 pounds per 10-ft. row.

soil Fertile and well-drained.

planting Plant when danger of frost is past and ground has warmed to 70°F/21°C. To speed germination, soak seeds for 24 hours before planting; use only seeds that are swollen. *In containers:* Grown in a large tub in a warm spot, a single okra plant can yield 1 to 2 pounds of pods.

spacing Set plants 1–1¹/₂ ft. apart in rows that are 2¹/₂–4 ft. apart.

water Keep soil well watered.

fertilizer Apply a complete fertilizer when the first pods set, and again when plants are shoulder high.

harvest Okra is ready to harvest 3 to 4 days after flowering, when pods are 2–4 in. long. Wear gloves, since pods of most varieties are prickly and all will make you itch. Pick every 2 days or so; plants stop producing if pods are not harvested.

The flowers of okra are distinctive, while the edible pods can easily be mistaken for leaves at first glance.

challenges Aphids, mites, nematodes, and corn earworms are possible problems. Row covers help with insects when plants are small enough to cover; rotate crops to minimize nematode problems.

Onion

Allium cepa (Cepa group)
Lily family *(Liliaceae)*
BIENNIAL GROWN AS ANNUAL
Cool-season vegetable

☑ **ALL ZONES**
☼ **FULL SUN**
🌢 **REGULAR WATER**

The bulbing onion has been in cultivation since the time of ancient Egypt; the species is not known in the wild. Scallions, or green onions, are grown from bulbing onions that are harvested young or from bulbless bunching onions. More so than for other vegetables, growing onions successfully requires proper variety selection, appropriate planting methods, and good timing. Consult a local nursery or your Cooperative Extension Office for advice on varieties that grow well in your area.

Bulbing onions. Varieties differ in size, shape, color, flavor, and storage life. More important, many onions require specific amounts of daily sunlight in order to produce bulbs. Day length depends on latitude, and if you choose a type inappropriate for your area, it may bolt, form small premature bulbs, or produce no bulbs at all. Seed suppliers often list optimal latitude ranges for each variety or identify onions as long-, intermediate-, or short-day varieties. (For reference, Maui is at about 20° latitude; San Diego and Tucson 32°; Los Angeles 34°; Albuquerque 35°; San Francisco 37°; Denver 40°; Oregon-California border 42°; Boise, ID, and Eugene, OR, 44°; Portland 46°; Seattle 48°; Vancouver, BC, 49°; Anchorage 61°; and Fairbanks 64°.)

Long-day varieties need 14 to 16 hours of daylight to form bulbs and thus are best adapted to regions in the more northern latitudes, such as Alaska, Canada, and the Pacific Northwest. These varieties tend to be pungent, and many (but not all) store well. Examples include yellows like 'Copra' and 'Walla Walla Sweet'; reds such as 'Mars' and 'Redwing'; and whites like 'White Sweet Spanish'. Generally, long-day onions are planted in early spring and form bulbs as the days get longer in summer.

Intermediate-day onions, requiring 12 to 14 hours of daylight, are best suited to regions such as the San Francisco Bay Area and northern Nevada. They store moderately well. Examples are 'Red Torpedo' and 'Ruby Ring'. They are usually planted in early spring.

Short-day varieties need 10 to 12 hours of daylight and are best adapted to areas in the more southern latitudes, such as Los Angeles, the Southwest, and Hawaii.

Slice red onions to top burgers for a classic barbecue combination.

These onions tend to be sweet and are poor keepers. Examples are yellow onions like 'Granex' and 'Texas Super Sweet'; and reds such as 'Desert Sunrise', 'Red Burgundy' ('Bermuda'), and 'Southern Belle'.

Day-neutrals such as the yellow 'Candy' and the white 'Super Star' are hybrids that bulb up anywhere. Plant these in early spring.

Bunching onions (scallions). Grown for their tops, these have a mixed heritage. Some are perennial, nonbulbing *A. fistulosum* varieties (also unknown in the wild) such as 'Evergreen Hardy White'. There are two races of this species: Welsh onions and (preferred) Japanese bunching onions. Others, such as 'Ishikura Improved' and 'White Lisbon', are bunching forms of *A. cepa*.

Cipollini onions. Very small bulbing onions usually listed as their own class in catalogs. They are flattish, 2- to 3-in.-diameter, sweet, long-day onions that come in red, yellow, and white. These Italian heirlooms are perfect for braiding, storing, cooking, and grilling.

Continued on page 64 ▶

Freshly harvested bunching onions

Sweet spring and summer onions are great in salads and lightly cooked recipes.

A healthy onion crop in a raised bed.

Harvest onions once the tops begin to yellow and fall over.

HOW TO GROW IT

best site Open garden is best, in a sunny spot on the south side of the bed, where these low-mounding plants won't be shaded by taller plants.

yield 7 to 10 pounds of bulbs per 10-ft. row; 1^1/$_2$ pounds of scallions (about 60) per 10-ft. row (but plant the row in 2^1/$_2$-ft. lengths at two-week intervals, or you'll have too many green onions at once).

soil Should be loose, fertile, and well drained. A pH above 6.5 is optimal; add lime if your soil is acid.

planting Onions can be planted from transplants, sets (small bulbs), or seed. Transplants and sets go into the garden 4 to 6 weeks before the average date of last spring frost. Trim back tops of transplants about halfway at planting. If planting sets, push them just under the soil surface so the point of the bulb is visible. Direct-sow scallions starting in spring about 2 weeks before the average date of last frost. Direct-sow seed of short-day onions in fall or early winter; they'll have all winter to put on vegetative growth so they'll be ready to bulb up in spring. Sow all other kinds in flats or pots indoors about 10 weeks before the average date of last spring frost; transplant them into the garden 4 to 6 weeks before the last spring frost. If planting from seed, direct-sow in the garden when the soil temperature has reached at least 45°F/7°C.

In containers: Onion bulbs take up too much room, but scallions are good container plants. Roots are relatively shallow, so the pot needn't be any deeper than 6 in.

spacing Sow seed ^{1}/$_4$ in. deep in rows 15–18 in. apart. Thin seedlings of bulbing onions to 4–5 in. apart; they can be eaten or transplanted to extend planting. Space onion sets or transplants 4–5 in. apart (closer if you want to harvest some as green onions). Thin seedlings of bulbing types used as scallions to 2 in. apart; thin bunching onions to 12-in. intervals.

water Because onions are shallow rooted, they need to be watered often enough that there's always moisture fairly near the soil surface.

fertilizer Feed plants regularly, especially early in the season: the larger and stronger the top growth, the bigger the bulb that will form. Choose a complete fertilizer with relatively low nitrogen for bulbing onions; choose one with normal nitrogen levels for scallions.

harvest Pull up scallions when tops are 12–18 in. long, before bulbs start to form. Harvest bulbs when most of the tops have begun to yellow and fall over. Dig the

Lodging Onions

1. An alternative harvesting method: When half of the tops have withered, push over the remaining tops and let the bulbs cure in place.

2. Three weeks later, lift the bulbs and remove the tops.

bulbs and let them cure and dry on top of the ground for several days. Cover bulbs with tops to prevent sunburn. When the tops and necks are completely dry, pull off the tops and brush dirt from the bulbs; then store the bulbs in a dark, cool, airy place.

challenges Onions are prone to thrips, which you may not notice (or need to act on), wireworms, and mildew. The best defense against wireworms is crop rotation and thorough cultivation before planting. To control mildew, plant in a site that gets good air circulation—a windy spot is fine—and don't space onions too close together.

Parsnip

Pastinaca sativa
Carrot family (*Apiaceae*)
BIENNIAL GROWN AS ANNUAL
Cool-season vegetable

☀ **ALL ZONES**

☼ **FULL SUN**

💧 **REGULAR WATER**

◊ **LEAVES MAY CAUSE RASH**

Parsnip is native to Siberia and Europe and is among the most cold-hardy of vegetables. It is grown for its delicately sweet, creamy white to yellowish roots, most often used in stews. It's also good roasted. Roots can reach 15 in. deep, with tops to 3 ft. tall. Harvest before it flowers; if parsnip goes to seed, it can become a noxious weed. Recommended varieties include 'Andover', 'Gladiator', and 'Javelin'.

Some people develop a sunburnlike rash, and even blistering, after handling parsnip leaves in the sunlight (ultraviolet light triggers the reaction). Wear gloves as a precaution.

HOW TO GROW IT

best site Full sun is optimal, but parsnip will tolerate partial shade where summers are hot.

yield 10 pounds per 10-ft. row.

soil For long roots, parsnip needs well-prepared, loose, deep, rock-free soil.

planting Plant from seed only—and use fresh seed, since parsnip seed isn't viable for long. In cold-winter areas, sow in late spring. In mild-winter climates, sow in fall. Soak seeds in water for a day before planting to improve germination. Sow 1/4–1/2 in. deep in rows spaced 2 ft. apart.

spacing Thin seedlings to 3 in. apart.

water Regular water keeps root growing steadily.

fertilizer Apply complete fertilizer a month after seedlings emerge.

Parsnips taste best after a frost.

harvest In cold-winter climates, harvest in fall. Leave surplus in the ground to be dug as needed in winter; cold makes the roots sweeter. In mild-winter climates, harvest all roots in spring; if left in the ground, mature roots will continue to grow, becoming tough and woody as the plant goes to seed.

challenges Armyworms, cabbage root maggots, flea beetles, leafhoppers, and nematodes can be problems. Row covers help prevent all but the nematodes, which can be managed with crop rotation.

Pea

Pisum sativum
Pea family *(Fabaceae)*
ANNUAL
Cool-season vegetable

✔ **ALL ZONES**
☼ **FULL SUN**
💧 **REGULAR WATER**

Peas are native to southern Europe. They come in two general types: shelling peas and edible-pod peas. The latter includes snow peas, which are eaten when pods are young, before the peas inside mature; and snap peas, which are eaten when pods are filled out. Peas have edible flowers, but if you pick them, they won't get the chance to develop into crops. Most gardeners are unwilling to make the trade.

All peas are easy to grow when conditions are right. They need coolness and humidity and must be planted at just the right time. For more vigorous peas, buy seeds inoculated with *Rhizobium* bacteria, which helps the plants fix nitrogen from the air and store it in their roots. Or buy the inoculant from a nursery or mail-order seed supplier and treat the seeds yourself.

If you have space and don't mind the bother, grow tall (vining) peas on trellises, strings, or chicken wire; they climb by tendrils to 6 ft. or more and bear heavily. Bush types are more commonly grown in home gardens; no support is required, though they can be grown on short trellises for easy picking.

Shelling peas. Superior bush varieties include 'Alderman' ('Tall Telephone'), 'Mr. Big', 'Caseload', and 'Maestro'. In France, tiny peas called petits pois are considered a delicacy because of their tenderness and sweet flavor. These aren't just immature versions of shelling peas; they are genetically smaller (2–3 in. long at maturity), with six to nine small peas per pod. Try 'Waverex'.

Edible-pod peas. An unusually good vegetable (and one popular in Asian cooking), usually called snow or sugar peas. The heirloom 'Mammoth Melting Sugar' is a 4-ft.-tall variety; 'Manoa Sugar' is a another tall type, developed for Hawaiian gardens. 'Oregon Sugar Pod II' and 'Oregon Giant' are bush varieties. 'Atitlan' has few leaves on its upper stems, putting all its energy into producing peas.

'Super Sugar Snap' (tall), 'Sugar Ann' (bush), and short-vine 'Sugar Sprint' (26 in.) combine the qualities of shelling peas and edible-pod peas. You can eat the immature pods, eat pods and peas together as you would string beans (the most popular way), or wait for the peas to mature and harvest them for shelling.

'Oregon Giant' snow pea is a bush type with extra-large pods.

HOW TO GROW IT

best site Full sun in an area with good air circulation.

yield 2 to 6 pounds per 10-ft. row.

soil Grow peas in slightly acid to slightly alkaline soil that is water retentive but fast draining. Organic matter is the key: it adds air spaces to soil for drainage, but individual fragments of compost absorb water, which the roots can access.

planting Where winters are cold, sow as early in spring as the ground can be worked; for a fall crop, sow about 12 weeks before the first frost date. Where winters are mild, plant at any time from fall to early spring—but don't sow after midwinter in areas where spring days quickly become too warm for peas. Successive plantings several days apart will lengthen the bearing season; most varieties are ready to pick 60 to 70 days from planting. Soak seeds overnight in water before planting. If planting in winter, sow $1/2$–1 in. deep. At other times of year, sow 2 in. deep in light soil, $1/2$–1 in. deep in heavy soil.

'Super Sugar Mel' peas boast sweet, crunchy pods.

Purple-podded peas grow tall and put on a colorful show.

In containers: Peas do well in containers at least 6–8 in. deep and 16–18 in. wide.

spacing Leave 2 ft. between rows for bush types, 5 ft. for tall vines; thin seedlings to 2–4 in. apart in the ground, 2–3 in. apart in containers.

water Moisten ground thoroughly before planting; then hold off on watering until seedlings are up. If weather turns warm and dry, supply water in furrows; overhead watering encourages mildew.

fertilizer Plants need little fertilizer, but if soil is very light (sandy), give one application of complete fertilizer about 6 weeks after planting.

pruning, training Have supports in place in advance for tendrils to grab (even bush peas benefit from trellising). You can use sticks, string, bamboo poles, or wide-mesh stock fencing—anything tendrils can grab onto and that you can get your hand through when it comes time to harvest.

harvest When peas reach harvesting size, pick all pods that are ready; if seeds are allowed to ripen, the plant will stop producing. Vines are brittle; steady them with one hand while picking with the other. *Shelling peas:* Begin harvesting when the pods have swelled to almost a cylindrical shape but before they lose their bright green color. *Edible-pod peas:* Pick snow peas when they're 2–3 in. long, before the seeds begin to swell; pick snap peas after pods have filled out. Eat all kinds of peas immediately: like corn, they start converting their sugar to starch as soon as they're picked.

challenges Avoid powdery mildew by planting peas where air circulation is good. Blast off aphids with a jet of water when you see them. Row covers protect emerging plants from cucumber beetles (but remove covers once young plants are growing well). Peas are also subject to a number of viruses and wilts; look for resistant varieties.

Pepper

Capsicum species
Nightshade family *(Solanaceae)*
ANNUAL OR SHORT-LIVED PERENNIAL GROWN
AS ANNUAL
Warm-season vegetable

ALL ZONES
☼ **FULL SUN**
💧 **REGULAR WATER**

Peppers are native to tropical South America. All types grow on attractive bushy plants ranging from less than a foot high to 4 ft. tall. Peppers are classified as sweet or hot, but breeders have blurred the distinction by developing hot bell peppers and sweet jalapeños.

Peppers need a long, warm growing season, so in most areas they must be planted outdoors as seedlings in order to produce fruit. In regions with cool or short summers, extend the season by using floating row covers and clear plastic mulches.

Sweet peppers. These remain mild even after they ripen and change color. This group includes the big stuffing and salad peppers commonly called bell peppers. The best known is 'California Wonder', which starts green and ripens red. Others start green or purple, then ripen yellow, orange, or even brown. Hybrids have been bred for early ripening, high yield, miniature size, and/or disease resistance. Other sweet types include sweet cherry peppers, used for pickling; long, slender Italian frying peppers and Hungarian sweet yellow peppers, both used for cooking; and thick-walled, very sweet pimientos (sometimes called pimentos), used in salads, cooking, and canning. (Allspice, also called pimento, is not a pepper but a spicy seasoning made from the fruits of a tree native to Jamaica.)

Hot peppers (chiles). These vary from pea-size types to narrow, 6- to 7-in.-long forms, but all are pungent, ranging from mildly hot 'Italian Pepperoncini' to nearly incandescent habanero strains like 'Caribbean Red'. Among the most popular hot peppers are jalapeños, used fresh, dried, or pickled. Others include various selections of 'Anaheim', a mildly spicy pepper from New Mexico used for making canned green chiles and the attractively strung bunches called *ristras*; 'Cayenne' types, usually dried, powdered, and used as a spice; and 'Hungarian Yellow Wax (Hot)' and 'Fresno Chile Grande', mostly used for pickling and cooking. Mexican cooking calls for a wide variety of hot peppers, among them 'Ancho' ('Poblano'), 'Mulato', and 'Pasilla'.

'Trinidad Perfume', a mildly hot habanero pepper

HOW TO GROW IT

best site Full sun; add heat in mild-summer regions by planting in a protected place against a south-facing wall. (Warmer growing conditions result in hotter peppers.)

yield 5 to 18 pounds per 10-ft. row.

soil Must be fertile, moisture retentive, and well drained.

planting Sow seed indoors 8 to 10 weeks before the average last-frost date. When the soil is thoroughly warm and nighttime temperatures remain consistently above 55°F/13°C, set seedlings outdoors. Or, much easier, set out nursery transplants after nighttime temperatures remain mostly above 55°F/13°C. *In containers:* Both sweet and hot peppers do well in containers at least 8 in. deep and 16 in. wide. Peppers may be earlier and smaller than those grown in the ground, but they're still well worth the effort.

spacing Set plants 1½–2 ft. apart.

Continued on page 71 ▶

Colorful, mildly spicy 'Mariachi' peppers grow well in pots.

Italian sweet peppers are delicious fresh, sautéed, or roasted.

'Tequila' bell peppers change from yellow to purple to red as they mature.

'Mirasol' chile peppers are popular in Mexican dishes.

Mild and hot forms of jalapeño are available.

Banana peppers are prized for their mild, sweet taste.

water Water regularly so that growth is not checked.

fertilizer After plants are established (but before blossoms set), give them one or two applications of a balanced liquid fertilizer.

pruning, training Tall peppers may have to be caged or staked.

harvest Most peppers can be picked green or purple after they have reached good size, but flavor typically becomes fuller and sweeter as fruit ripens into its mature color, which varies by variety. Pick pimientos only when red-ripe. To harvest any kind of pepper, snip the stem with hand pruners or scissors.

challenges Aphids, flea beetles, and whiteflies can be kept off young peppers early in the growing season with row covers (which also protect plants from unseasonable cold). Later, use yellow sticky traps to control whiteflies. To control pepper weevils (both the larvae and adults attack fruit), destroy infested plants after harvest. Bait for slugs. To avoid viruses, buy resistant varieties.

PAUL BOSLAND ON
pepper flavor

Horticulture professor Dr. Paul Bosland, director of the Chile Pepper Institute at New Mexico State University at Las Cruces, is internationally recognized as a chile breeder. On campus, he's fondly referred to as Chile Man, and when he talks about peppers, you know you're in the presence of a connoisseur.

The complex flavor of tabascos, he explains, has 23 components, while bell peppers and jalapeños are dominated by only one taste—but it ranks as the single most potent flavor in the world.

From mild to wild, below are some of Bosland's favorites.

For heat-free sweetness, try a salad laced with 'Red Heart' pimientos.

Sample moderate heat by making salsa with multicolored 'NuMex Piñata' jalapeños. They're beautiful and full flavored.

Test your tongue's fire tolerance by cooking up a batch of buffalo wings with 'Red Savina' habaneros. The world's hottest pepper, they are more than 100 times as hot as 'NuMex Piñata'.

For the curious but cautious, 'NuMex Suave Red' offers full habanero flavor at very low heat levels.

Potato

Solanum tuberosum
Nightshade family *(Solanaceae)*
PERENNIAL GROWN AS ANNUAL
Cool-season root vegetable

◢ **ALL ZONES**
☼ **FULL SUN**
💧 **REGULAR WATER**
◈ **GREEN SKIN AND RAW SHOOTS ARE POISONOUS IF INGESTED**

Potatoes originated in the cool tropical highlands of western South America. Though other vegetables are more common in home gardens, growing potatoes can be very satisfying: 2 pounds of seed potatoes can yield 50 pounds of potatoes for eating. It is an especially rewarding crop for children's gardens: digging up the potatoes is like finding buried treasure!

Grow plants from seed potatoes that you cut into 1¹/₂-in. cubes (each with at least two eyes) or from small tubers, which are planted whole and are less likely to rot in the ground. (Don't try to grow supermarket potatoes; most are treated to prevent sprouting.) Home gardeners have access to a number of varieties, including types with red, white, yellow, russet brown, or bluish purple skins; depending on variety, flesh may be white or match the skin color of red, yellow, or blue varieties. Shapes vary from round or cylindrical to fingerlike (the latter are called fingerlings). Some varieties mature faster than others, but most reach harvesting size 2¹/₂ to 4 months after planting.

Culinary use depends greatly on whether a potato is moist or dry, and whether the starch it contains is branched (holds its shape in salads and stews) or relatively straight (allows the potato to fall apart in cooking). For baking and mashing, most people prefer a light, dry, fluffy potato like 'Butte' or 'Russet Burbank'. For velvety-textured soups, try 'Carola', which falls apart nicely when cooked. For stews, boiling, and potato salads, choose a waxy, moist potato like 'Reddale'. For fun, make colorful fries or mashed potatoes with 'All Blue'; 'Elba' is another good choice for these dishes, but with traditional buff-colored skin and white flesh.

There are also potatoes for special situations. If you garden in a short-season climate, try an early all-purpose variety like 'Yukon Gold'. In wet climates or soil that tends to be damp, grow 'Nooksack'. If diseases are a problem in your area, try 'Island Sunshine' for resistance to late blight or 'Reddale' for resistance to verticillium wilt.

The aboveground potato plant is sprawling and bushy, with much-divided dark green leaves somewhat

'Yukon Gold' potatoes are a good choice for colder climates.

like those of a tomato plant. Clustered inch-wide flowers may be white, pink, light red, or pale blue, depending on variety; blossoms often reflect the color of the tubers but not always.

New potatoes are just immature potatoes harvested when the plant flowers. They're extra sweet because their sugar hasn't yet converted to starch, as it has in mature tubers.

HOW TO GROW IT

best site Full sun in a place that gives tops a little room to ramble.

yield 10 to 20 pounds per 10-ft. row.

soil Loose, fertile, sandy soil is best. Amend with plenty of compost (potatoes often grow in compost piles). Tubers become deformed in heavy, poorly drained soil.

planting In cold-winter climates, plant as soon as the soil is workable in spring. In mild-winter regions, plant in early spring for a summer crop, in early fall for a winter-into-spring crop. Where frosts are not severe, potatoes can be planted in midwinter—as long as the soil isn't too wet from winter rains. Let seed potato pieces dry for a day or two before planting. Then set the potato pieces or minitubers in furrows 4 in. deep and cover with 2 in. of soil. As tops grow, add more soil until you've built a ridge 4 in. above ground level. Developing tubers should always be covered with soil to keep skin from turning green (and toxic).

Another method of growing potatoes is to prepare the soil so the surface is loose, plant potato pieces or minitubers $1/2$–2 in. deep, and water well. Mound loose soil over plants as directed above; then cover the soil with a 1- to $1^1/2$-ft.-thick layer of straw, hay, or dead leaves. Surround the planting with chicken wire to keep loose material from blowing away. Potatoes will form on the soil surface or just beneath it; you can probe through the mulch with your fingers to harvest them.

In containers: You can grow potatoes in a half wine barrel. Put 6 in. of planting mix in the bottom, lay three seed potatoes on top, cover them with 3–4 in. of additional planting mix, and water. After growth appears, continually add more soil, always leaving the growing tips exposed to light, until soil is 1–2 in. below the container's rim. Keep the soil evenly moist, and fertilize lightly every time you add more soil.

spacing Plant tubers or potato pieces 1–$1^1/2$ ft. apart.

water Keep soil uniformly moist during growth. Water for the last time as leaves turn from yellow to brown.

fertilizer At planting time, mix a complete fertilizer into the soil at least 2 in. away from seed potatoes.

harvest Dig new potatoes when the plants begin to bloom; dig mature potatoes when plants die down. Dig carefully to avoid bruising or cutting the tubers. Well-matured potatoes free of defects are the best keepers; store them in a cool (40°F/4°C), dark, dry place. Where the ground doesn't freeze, late potatoes can remain in the ground until needed. Dig before warmer temperatures start them growing again.

challenges The many pests and diseases that beleaguer commercial growers are not likely to plague home gardeners. To avoid disease problems, plant certified disease-free starter potatoes or disease-resistant varieties. Scab can be a problem where soil pH is above 5.5.

'Anna Cheeka's Ozette'   'Yukon Gold'

'Island Sunshine'   'Butte'

'Reddale'   'Russian Banana'

'Irish Cobbler'   'Caribe'

Potatoes vary widely in size, color, and shape.

Growing Potatoes

1. Cut seed potatoes into chunks with at least two eyes each and allow to dry for 2 days.

2. As sprouts emerge, keep soil ridges mounded around the plants.

Pumpkin

Cucurbita species
Gourd family *(Cucurbitaceae)*
ANNUAL
Warm-season vegetable

✎ **ALL ZONES**
☼ **FULL SUN**
💧 **REGULAR WATER**

The first pumpkins are thought to have originated in
South America. Most are varieties of *Cucurbita pepo*,
which includes summer squash, ornamental gourds, and
many pumpkins, though other squash species have varieties called pumpkins as well. Pumpkins are available in
vining and bush types, and fruit varies greatly in size. One
of the best for a jumbo Halloween pumpkin is 'Atlantic
Giant'. 'Orange Smoothie' is smooth skinned, making
it easy to decorate with paint. 'Small Sugar', a smaller
pumpkin with finer-grained, sweeter flesh, is great for
pies. 'Jack Be Little' and 'Wee-B-Little' are miniature
(3- to 4-in.) types used for decoration. Novelties with
white skin and orange flesh include miniature 'Baby Boo'
and 8- to 10-in. 'Lumina'. Seeds of all types are edible,
but the easiest to eat are those of hull-less varieties, like
'Baby Bear'.

Giant pumpkins aren't special varieties; they are
ordinary full-size vining pumpkins grown in a special
way (though gardeners aiming for colossal fruits do have
favorites, such as 'Dill's Atlantic Giant'). For maximum size,
do this: As the plant develops, cut off all but two main
stems. After blossoms fall and pumpkins start growing,
remove all but one fruit on each stem. Along each stem's
length, mound a 4-in.-wide hill of soil every 2 ft.; roots
will form there, supplying nutrients to the pumpkin.

HOW TO GROW IT

best site Pumpkins need sun and plenty of room:
a single vine can cover 500 sq. ft., and even bush sorts
can spread over 20 sq. ft.

yield 10 to 20 pounds per 10-ft. row.

soil Fertile loam is best.

planting Where the growing season is short, start plants
indoors and use floating row covers early in the season.
In other areas, sow seeds outdoors in late spring after
soil has warmed. *In containers:* Grow bush pumpkins in
containers at least 18 in. tall and wide. If you trellis the
vines to save patio space, support ripening pumpkins
with cloth or net slings.

spacing For vining pumpkins, sow clusters of five or
six seeds 1 in. deep in 6- to 8-in.-high, 3-ft.-wide hills
spaced 4–8 ft. apart. Thin seedlings to two per hill. Plant
bush pumpkins in rows spaced 3 ft. apart; plant seeds
1 in. deep in clusters of three or four, spacing clusters
2 ft. apart along each row, then thin seedlings to one
or two plants per cluster.

water Irrigate regularly during rainless periods, but
keep foliage dry to prevent leaf diseases.

fertilizer Give complete fertilizer periodically.

pruning, training In late summer, slide wooden
shingles or other protection under fruit to protect it
from wet soil and rot (not necessary if soil is sandy).

harvest Depending on variety, pumpkins are ready to
harvest 90 to 120 days after sowing, when the shell has
hardened. Pick after first frost kills the plant. Use a sharp
knife or hand pruners to harvest fruit along with 1–2 in.
of stem.

challenges Squash bugs cause leaves to wilt and
may damage fruit. To control them, destroy yellowish
to brown egg clusters on the undersides of leaves; trap
adults with boards or burlap set in the garden at night,
then collect and destroy your catch each morning. Various
insecticides are also labeled for control of squash bugs.
Mildew can be another problem; get a resistant variety
and/or plant where there's good air circulation, and keep
water off the leaves.

Straw bedding protects a 'Cinderella's Carriage' pumpkin from wet soil and rot.

'Green Hokkaido' may be sold as a pumpkin or as a winter squash.

Ghostlike 'Lumina' pumpkins are great for carving and for eating.

A young 'Atlantic Giant' pumpkin

Radish

Raphanus sativus
Cabbage family *(Brassicaceae)*
ANNUAL
Cool-season root vegetable

ALL ZONES

LIGHT SHADE IN HOTTEST CLIMATES

REGULAR WATER

Cultivation of radishes for food dates back 4,000 years in Mediterranean cultures, 2,500 years in China, and more than a millennium in Japan. These days, the colorful, crunchy root vegetables are most often used to give salads zip.

Radishes are among the easiest vegetables to cultivate and are very fast growing. The most familiar types are short, round, red or red-and-white varieties like 'Cherry Belle', 'Cherriette', and 'Scarlet White-tipped'. You can also get round radishes in white or pink; 'Easter Egg II' produces a mixture of white, pink, red, and purple. 'French Dressing' and 'Red Flame' are long, narrow, white-tipped types with a sweet flavor; they're known as breakfast radishes. Other long radishes have a more typical radish flavor; white 'Icicle' is the best known of these, but there are also novelties like 'Misato Rose Flesh', which is green outside and pink inside. Some types of long, white radishes with a mildly nippy to hot flavor can be found in markets under the name "daikon."

HOW TO GROW IT

best site Full sun in mild climates, partial shade where it's hot.

yield 2 to 5 pounds per 10-ft. row.

soil Containers, raised beds, or open garden soil are fine as long as drainage is good. Blend well-aged manure into the soil at least a month before planting. If your soil is fairly rich, just loosen it before planting and fertilize later (see 'fertilizer').

planting Sow seeds as soon as ground can be worked in spring, then at weekly intervals until warm weather approaches (plants go to seed when temperatures rise, with roots becoming bitter in the process). In mild climates, you can sow at intervals in fall and winter for harvest during these seasons. *In containers:* Radishes are easy to grow in a pot that's 16 in. wide and at least 4 in. deep.

'Cherry Belle' radishes, an early variety, are best in cool weather.

spacing Sow seeds $1/2$ in. deep and 1 in. apart; space rows 1–1$1/2$ ft. apart. In containers, sow seeds 6 in. apart in a diamond pattern. When the tops are up, pull out every other plant; you can eat the thinnings if they are large enough.

water Keep soil evenly moist from seed to harvest. That means daily watering during warm spells.

fertilizer Feed about 10 days after planting, applying dry or liquid fertilizer beside rows (as for carrots).

harvest Radishes are best harvested and eaten as soon as they reach full size; they can become woody and overly pungent in flavor if left in the ground too long. You can pull them for the table as early as 3 weeks after sowing seeds (the slowest kinds take 2 months to reach table-ready size).

challenges If cabbageworms or cabbage root maggots cause trouble, cover radishes with a row cover.

A plateful of radishes in various shapes and colors

Rhubarb

Rheum × hybridum
Knotweed family *(Polygonaceae)*
PERENNIAL
Cool-season vegetable

✎ BEST IN ZONES A1–A3, 1–11; MAY SUCCEED IN 14–24
☼ ☽ PARTIAL SHADE IN HOTTEST CLIMATES
💧 REGULAR WATER
⬧ LEAVES ARE POISONOUS IF INGESTED;
   USE LEAF STEMS ONLY

Rhubarb is probably a hybrid between *Rheum rhaponticum* and *R. palmatum*, both from China. Foliage is showy enough to qualify this plant for a display spot in the garden: huge crinkled leaves with an elongated heart shape are held on thick, typically red-tinted stalks. These plants easily grow 3 ft. tall and 6 ft. wide and develop very large roots. Leafstalks have a delicious tart flavor and are typically used like fruit in sauces and pies. Insignificant flowers bloom in spikelike clusters. Preferred rhubarb varieties include 'Crimson Cherry' and 'MacDonald', both with red stalks; and 'Victoria', which produces greenish stalks.

   The plant needs some winter chill for thick stems and good red color (if you grow a red variety). Rhubarb is deciduous, so in all but the mildest areas, plants will die back completely in winter.

HOW TO GROW IT

best site Full sun in mild climates, partial shade where summers are hot.

yield 1 to 5 pounds per plant per season.

soil Fertile, well-drained soil rich in organic matter.

planting Set out plant divisions containing at least one bud in late winter or early spring. In Zones 10 and 11, treat as a cool-season annual and plant in fall for winter-into-spring harvest (plants tend to rot in the heat of late spring and summer). *In containers:* Rhubarb may be grown in a large container for a few years but will eventually outgrow it. Be sure not to let potted plants dry out.

spacing Set out plants at 3- to 6-ft. intervals (most gardeners plant only one or two).

water Like most plants with large leaves, rhubarb needs regular water.

fertilizer After harvest, feed and water freely.

A forcing pot placed over the dormant crown in winter helps rhubarb grow earlier and longer.

harvest Let plants grow for two full seasons before harvesting. In the third season, you can pull off leafstalks for 4 or 5 weeks in spring; older, huskier plants can take up to 8 weeks of pulling. To harvest leafstalks, grasp them near the base and pull sideways and outward (do not cut with a knife, as cutting will leave a stub that decays). Never remove all the leaves from a single plant; stop harvesting when slender leafstalks appear. Cut out any blossom stalks that appear.

challenges Aphids, flea beetles, and leafhoppers are possible but are rarely problematic on healthy plants.

Salad Blends

Various families and species
ANNUALS
Cool-season vegetables

✎ **ALL ZONES**
☀ ◐ **FULL SUN OR PARTIAL SHADE (SEE BELOW)**
💧 **REGULAR WATER**

Most seed catalogs include a category for salad blends or mixed salad greens, which include everything from lettuce blends to mesclun mixes and microgreens. All these tender, fast-growing greens are meant to be sown together, grown together, and harvested young. Most of the plants that make up these blends have their own listings in this book.

Lettuce blends. These include various kinds of non-heading leaf lettuce and romaine, usually in a wide variety of leaf shapes and colors. Mild tasting.

Mesclun. Usually includes two or three kinds of lettuce, plus three to five greens from the following: arugula, various Asian greens, beet, chervil, chicory, chives, endive, escarole, garden cress, kale, mâche, mustard, parsley, radicchio, salad burnet (a perennial herb with a mild cucumber flavor), and spinach. The mix's ingredients determine its flavor and color. These blends are usually sold as mild or spicy, and colors often include several shades of green, red, and purple.

Microgreens. Also sold as baby greens. These may or may not include lettuce, but they usually contain arugula, beet, broccoli, Chinese cabbage, kale, kohlrabi, mustard, radish, and salad burnet. Seed companies select varieties that come up fast and simultaneously, because they'll be harvested when they're just a couple of inches tall.

HOW TO GROW IT

best site Full sun is best in fall, winter, and spring; partial shade is best in summer.

yield Depends on the mix.

soil Rich, well-drained, with plenty of organic matter.

planting Scatter seeds over a prepared seedbed in early spring for harvest in spring and early summer, and in late summer or fall for harvest in autumn and winter. Make succession plantings every week for microgreens, every 2 or 3 weeks for mesclun and lettuce mixes. *In containers:* All are ideal container subjects. Grow them in a pot at least 4–6 in. tall and as wide as you like.

Paris Market Mix, a mild mesclun blend, includes arugula, chervil, chicory, endive, escarole, and red lettuces.

spacing If you plan to harvest very young plants (as with microgreens mixes), you don't need to thin. For bigger leaves, thin to 3–4 in. apart.

water Keep soil moist.

fertilizer Apply half-strength liquid fertilizer once after seedlings develop true leaves.

harvest Pick lettuce at any size, from thinning stage to full maturity. Harvest mesclun mixes by snipping them off 2 in. above ground level; most will respond by producing new leaves for your next harvest. Harvest microgreens whole when they're 1–4 in. high.

challenges Slugs and snails are the main problems. Bait for them or surround plants with a copper barrier.

Shallot

Allium cepa (Aggregatum group)
Lily family *(Liliaceae)*
PERENNIAL OFTEN GROWN AS ANNUAL
Cool-season vegetable

✎ ALL ZONES
☼ FULL SUN
● REGULAR WATER

This close relative of onion is thought to have originated in tropical western or central Asia. The bulb, which grows in cloves (sections) on a common base, is prized in cooking for its distinctive flavor—a combination of mild onion and pungent garlic. Young green shoots are also used as scallions.

Shallots are usually grown from cloves, like garlic. You can purchase them from a seed company or simply buy shallots in the grocery store and separate them into cloves. Some seed companies also sell shallot seeds. Nurseries with stocks of herbs may sell growing plants.

Dutch shallots have golden brown skin and white cloves; red shallots have coppery skin and purple cloves.

HOW TO GROW IT

best site Plant in an open location with plenty of sun.

yield Usually 2 to 12 cloves per plant.

soil Fertile, slightly sandy, well-drained soil is optimal. Shallots don't succeed in clay.

planting For a summer crop, plant cloves 2 to 4 weeks before the last frost date of spring. For a winter crop in mild climates, plant at least 6 weeks before the average date of first fall frost. Plant cloves with their pointed end up; cover with 1/2 in. of soil. If planting from seed, direct-sow at about the last frost date.

spacing Plant cloves or growing plants 4–8 in. apart in rows 2–4 ft. apart. Direct-sow 12 seeds per ft.; thin to 4–8 in. apart.

water Keep soil moist during growth, but withhold water for a couple of weeks before harvest.

fertilizer Feed plants regularly, especially early in the growing season.

harvest If planting from cloves, you will have green shoots in about 60 days, new bulbs in 90 to 120 days. If planting from seed, bulbs will be ready to harvest in

Shallots are flavorful and easy to grow.

about 100 days. When shallots are mature, shoots yellow and die. Pull up clumps and separate the bulbs; before using them, let them dry for about a month in a cool, dry place. If stored properly, shallots will keep for up to 8 months.

challenges Problems are few, though wireworms, thrips, and mildew are possible. The best defense against wireworms is crop rotation and thorough cultivation before planting. Thrips rarely show up on shallots in home gardens; if they do, hose off plants with a strong jet of water or collect thrips with yellow sticky traps. To control mildew, plant in a site that gets good air circulation—a windy spot is fine—and don't space plants closer than recommended.

Sorrel

Rumex species
Knotweed family *(Polygonaceae)*
PERENNIALS OFTEN GROWN AS ANNUALS
Cool-season vegetables

✎ **ZONES VARY BY SPECIES**
☼ **FULL SUN**
💧 **REGULAR WATER**

Two similar species are grown for their edible leaves, which can be used raw in salads or cooked in soups, sauces, and egg dishes. The flavor is like that of a sharp, sprightly spinach, but sorrel is more heat-tolerant than spinach and produces throughout the growing season.

Cut out flowering stems to encourage leaf production, and replace (or dig and divide) plants of either kind every 3 to 4 years.

Common sorrel (*Rumex acetosa*). Zones A1–A3, 1–9, 14–17; annual anywhere. Native to northern temperate and arctic regions. This is the larger plant (to 3 ft. tall), with leaves to 6 in. long, many shaped like elongated arrowheads.

French sorrel (*R. scutatus*). Zones 3–10, 14–24; annual anywhere. Native to Europe, western Asia, and North Africa. This is a somewhat sprawling plant to 1½ ft. tall, with shorter, broader leaves and a milder, more lemony flavor than common sorrel.

HOW TO GROW IT

best site Full sun for both species.

yield A dozen plants will supply a family of four.

soil Grow in reasonably fertile soil with good drainage.

planting Sow seeds in early spring or set out transplants at any time. *In containers:* Both plants grow well in a pot at least 6 in. deep, 12 in. wide.

spacing Thin perennial plants to 8 in. apart. If grown as annuals, thin to 4 in. apart.

water Provide even moisture for both, but French sorrel can get by with less water than common sorrel.

fertilizer Apply complete fertilizer once after thinning.

Striking leaves of red-veined common sorrel

harvest Pick tender leaves as soon as they are big enough to use (about 2 months from sowing). With row covers, harvest can continue through winter in mild-winter climates.

challenges Sorrel is generally pest-free.

Spinach

Various families
ANNUALS AND PERENNIALS
Cool- and warm-season vegetables

ZONES VARY BY SPECIES
FULL SUN, EXCEPT AS NOTED
REGULAR WATER

The first of the three plants described here is true spinach, which needs cool weather to succeed; the other two are warm-season vegetables used as substitutes for the real thing. All are grown for their edible leaves, used raw or cooked.

True spinach (*Spinacia oleracea*). All zones. This cool-season annual from the goosefoot family (*Chenopodiaceae*) is thought to have originated in central Asia. It grows in upright, leafy clumps to about 1 ft. tall, maturing slowly during fall, winter, and spring. The long days of late spring and the heat of summer make it go to seed quickly.

New Zealand spinach (*Tetragonia tetragonioides*). Evergreen perennial in Zones 15–17, 21–24, H1, H2, though heavy frosts send it into dormancy; summer annual where winters are colder. A member of the ice plant family (*Aizoaceae*) from Australia and New Zealand. Mature plants are spreading, 1- to 2- ft.-tall groundcovers with dense, arrow-shaped leaves that curve under at the edges. Excellent salt tolerance.

Malabar spinach (*Basella alba*). Perennial in Zones H1, H2; annual in Zones 3–24. This vine from India is part of the *Basellaceae* family. It grows 4–6 ft. long (even longer in hot climates), and produces leaves that are bigger and thicker than leaves of true spinach, so you will need fewer per serving. There is an especially attractive red-stemmed form.

HOW TO GROW IT

best site *Spinach* takes full sun in cool months; for later sowing, plant between taller vegetables that will provide partial shade. *New Zealand spinach* is a sun lover that won't tolerate shade, but it does take heat and drought or cool, damp conditions. *Malabar spinach* needs full sun and nighttime temperatures above 58°F/ 14°C; frost kills it.

yield 4 to 7 pounds per 10-ft. row.

True spinach grows best in cool weather.

soil Fertile, well-draining soil for all three, but New Zealand spinach can take sandy, salty soil.

planting *Spinach:* Sow in fall or late winter/early spring (optimal germination temperature is about 50°F/10°C, and plants can take 16°F/–9°C); to get successive harvests, make small sowings at weekly intervals in fall or early spring. *New Zealand spinach:* Sow in spring after danger of frost is past. *Malabar spinach:* Sow in early summer.

In containers: Spinach grows well in a wide container at least 8 in. tall. *New Zealand spinach* cascades over pot sides, so you can grow three plants in a 14-in. pot. *Malabar spinach* will grow to fill an 18-in. pot.

New Zealand spinach is a vigorous, low spreader.

Train Malabar spinach to grow on a wire or trellis.

spacing *Spinach:* Sow 1 in. apart, and thin seedlings to 3–4 in. apart. *New Zealand spinach:* Sow 4 in. apart, then thin established seedlings to 1–1¹/₂ ft. apart. *Malabar spinach:* Sow 4 in. apart; thin to 1 ft. apart.

water All types need regular water.

fertilizer *Spinach* needs high-nitrogen fertilizer, especially in spring. *New Zealand and Malabar spinach* need single applications of complete fertilizer after thinning.

pruning, training Trellis Malabar spinach when it reaches 1 ft.; when it reaches 2 ft., pinch out a few inches of stem tip (harvesting any young, tender leaves) to encourage the plant to branch and form more stems.

harvest *Spinach* is ready for harvest in about 7 weeks, when leaves have reached full size (6–12 in. tall); pick individual leaves, or cut the entire clump at ground level. *New Zealand spinach* can be harvested by plucking off the top few inches of tender stems and attached leaves; a month later, new shoots will have grown up for another harvest. *Malabar spinach* is ready when leaves reach full, succulent size; pick them individually.

challenges *Spinach* can be troubled by leaf miners and aphids; row covers help. Bait for slugs and snails to protect seedlings. *New Zealand spinach* can occasionally have a problem with nematodes, but crop rotation minimizes it. *Malabar spinach* has no significant pests.

Squash

Cucurbita species
Gourd family *(Cucurbitaceae)*
ANNUALS
Warm-season vegetables

◪ ALL ZONES

☼ FULL SUN

◖ REGULAR WATER

There are two general forms of squash, all derived from various species native to the Americas. Each individual squash plant has both male and female flowers, which must be pollinated by bees in order for fruit to set. The blossoms and tiny developing fruit at the base of female flowers can be eaten as delicacies.

Summer squash. Types planted for a warm-weather harvest and eaten when immature are called summer squash; this group includes scalloped white squash (pattypan squash); yellow crookneck and straightneck varieties; and cylindrical green or gray zucchini or Italian squash.

Summer squash yields prodigious crops from just a few plants 50 to 65 days after sowing, and it continues to bear for weeks. Vines are large (2^1/$_2$–4 ft. across at maturity) and need plenty of room; if space is limited, look for bush varieties. There are many vine and bush varieties to choose from.

Winter squash. These are grown for harvest in late summer or fall; they store well and are often used for baking and pies. Winter squash varieties come in many sizes, colors, and shapes (turban, acorn, and banana, to name a few). All have hard rinds and firm, close-grained flesh, with the exception of spaghetti squash, whose flesh is made up of long spaghetti-like strands.

Winter squash is planted and grown on vines like pumpkins; it typically needs even more space than summer squash. There are a few compact varieties such as 'Honey Bear', a green acorn type, and 'Bonbon', a buttercup type. Most kinds of winter squash are ready to harvest 60 to 110 days after sowing. For storing, try small kinds such as 'Table Ace' and other acorn types, butternuts, and buttercups; or the large blue Hubbard varieties and banana squash. Winter squash doesn't grow well in high heat and humidity.

HOW TO GROW IT

best site Squash needs an open site with full sun and plenty of room.

yield 10 to 80 pounds per 10-ft. row.

soil Give all kinds of squash rich, well-draining soil.

planting Start seed indoors 2 weeks before the average date of last spring frost, and transplant into the garden about 2 weeks after frost. Or direct-sow in the garden 1 in. deep when soil temperature reaches at least 55°F/13°C. *In containers:* Of the two types of squash, summer squash is the best bet for containers; one plant per 18-in. (or larger) pot.

spacing Bush and compact varieties can be planted 2–4 ft. apart in rows. If planted in hills (circles), they need more room; allow a 4-ft. diameter for each. Vining summer or winter squash varieties need 5-ft. spacing in rows or 8-ft.-diameter hills.

water Roots need regular moisture, but leaves and stems should be kept as dry as possible to prevent leaf and fruit diseases.

fertilizer Apply a balanced fertilizer periodically.

harvest *Summer squash* should be picked when it is small and tender. *Winter squash* should stay on the vines until it is thoroughly hardened; harvest it with an inch of stem and store in a cool place (about 55°F/13°C).

challenges Squash bugs cause leaves to wilt and may damage fruit. To control, destroy yellowish to brown egg clusters on undersides of leaves; trap adults with boards or burlap set in the garden at night, then collect and destroy your catch each morning. Various insecticides are also labeled for control of squash bugs.

Summer squash is best harvested when small and tender.

Both the flowers and fruits of zucchini are edible; keeping the crop picked is the biggest job.

'Hubbard', an especially attractive winter squash

Winter squashes are characterized by their hard skins; save the seeds, dry them, and roast to eat.

Sweet Potato

Ipomoea batatas
Morning glory family *(Convolvulaceae)*
PERENNIAL GROWN AS ANNUAL
Warm-season vegetable

🌿 **ZONES 8–10, 12–15, 18–24, H1, H2**
☼ **FULL SUN**
💧 **REGULAR WATER**

Sweet potato is actually not a potato but the thickened root of an attractive trailing vine closely related to morning glory *(Convolvulus, Ipomoea)*. The plant is native to tropical South America. Most varieties trail several feet, but bush and short-vine varieties are also available, making it possible to grow these vegetables even in modest-size gardens. Sweet potatoes are good baked, mashed, boiled, and in pies and breads.

Sweet potatoes are classified by flesh type. One has soft, sugary, yellow-orange flesh (examples are 'Centennial', 'Jewel', 'Kona-B', and the bush types 'Vardaman' and 'Vineless Puerto Rico'); the other has firm, dry, whitish flesh (examples are 'Hoolehua Red', 'Waimanalo Red', and 'Yellow Jersey'). The sweet yellow-orange type is sold under the incorrect name "yam" in grocery stores.

HOW TO GROW IT

best site Sweet potatoes need full sun and a long, hot, frost-free growing season; they're easiest to grow in Hawaii. Long-vine varieties need room to sprawl.

yield 8 to 12 pounds per 10-ft. row.

soil Requires well-drained soil, preferably sandy loam.

planting Plant in late spring, when soil temperature has warmed to 70°F/ 21°C. (You can plant year-round in Hawaii, but spring-planted crops mature faster.) Use only certified disease-free slips (rooted cuttings) from a garden center or mail-order nursery. Set slips so only stem tips and leaves are exposed. To ensure good drainage, mark off rows and ditch between them to form planting ridges. *In containers:* Sweet potatoes are easy to grow in pots at least 18 in. high and wide; attractive vines will cascade over the edge and ramble several feet.

spacing Space 1 ft. apart in rows 3 ft. apart.

water Keep soil moist until plants are established; then water regularly but allow the soil to dry slightly between waterings.

Sweet potatoes like these have soft, sugary orange flesh.

fertilizer Work in a low-nitrogen fertilizer once before planting. Too much nitrogen produces leafy growth at the expense of roots.

harvest Most varieties are ready to dig 110 to 120 days after planting. Harvest before first frost; if tops are killed by sudden frost, harvest at once. Dig carefully to avoid cutting or bruising roots. Flavor improves in storage (starch is converted to sugar). Let roots dry in the sun until soil can be brushed off; then cure by storing 10 to 14 days in a warm (about 85°F/ 29°C), humid place. Store in a cool, dry environment (not below 55°F/13°C).

challenges Possible pests include aphids, flea beetles, and leafhoppers; row covers will help control all of them. To avoid buildup of nematodes, wireworms, and disease organisms in the soil, don't grow sweet potatoes in the same location 2 years in a row.

Swiss Chard

Beta vulgaris cicla
Goosefoot family (*Chenopodiaceae*)
BIENNIAL GROWN AS ANNUAL
Cool-season vegetable

✔ **ALL ZONES**

☼ **FULL SUN**

● **REGULAR WATER**

Swiss chard is a form of beet grown for its leaves and stalks rather than its roots. It probably originated in the Mediterranean area. Chard is one of the easiest-to-grow vegetables for home gardens, and leaves can be harvested all summer. Plants seldom bolt, and if one does go to seed, you can simply pull it up and add it to the compost pile.

Regular green-and-white chard looks presentable in a flower garden, but 'Bright Lights' is more decorative, with leaves ranging from green to burgundy and stalks in various shades of yellow, orange, pink, purple, red, and green, as well as white. Red stems and red-veined green leaves of 'Rhubarb' ('Ruby Red') are very decorative in the garden and in floral arrangements. 'Fordhook Giant' is a heavy-yielding variety with dark green leaves and white stalks.

For all types, cook leaves and leafstalks separately, since stalks take longer. Use like spinach.

HOW TO GROW IT

best site Full sun.

yield 8 to 12 pounds per 10-ft. row.

soil Fertile, well-drained soil; chard can take sandy or clay loam.

planting Sow big, crinkly, tan seeds in spaded soil anytime from spring to early summer. Where winters are mild, chard can be grown as a fall-into-spring crop. *In containers:* Plant in a 12- to 18-in.-wide, 8-in.-deep container (it looks especially attractive in combination with pansies and nasturtiums).

spacing Sow seeds 1/2 in. deep, 2 in. apart, in rows spaced 18–30 in. apart. Thin seedlings to 1 ft. apart.

water Keep soil moist.

fertilizer Apply complete fertilizer after plants are established and again 6 weeks later.

Colorful varieties of Swiss chard make a lovely addition to any garden.

harvest About 2 months after sowing (plants will generally have reached 1–1 1/2 ft. tall), you can begin to cut outer leaves as needed for the table. New leaves grow up in the center of the plants.

challenges Snails and slugs can be controlled with bait or a copper barrier. Exclude aphids, cabbageworms, flea beetles, and leaf miners with row covers. Crop rotation helps control nematodes.

Tomatillo

Physalis ixocarpa
Nightshade family *(Solanaceae)*
ANNUAL
Warm-season vegetable

ALL ZONES

FULL SUN

REGULAR WATER

This easy-to-grow tomato relative hails from Mexico. It has bushy, sprawling growth to 4 ft. tall and at least as wide. Summertime fruit swells to fill—and eventually split—the loose, papery husk (calyx) that surrounds it. When fully ripe, the fruit is yellow to purple, about 2 in. wide, and very sweet, but it is usually picked when green and tart, and used in sauces and other dishes.

HOW TO GROW IT

best site Full sun, as for tomatoes.

yield 1 to 2 pounds per plant.

soil Fertile, well-drained soil.

planting Direct-sow seeds 4 to 6 weeks after the last frost, when the soil has warmed (in moist, warm soil, seeds will germinate in 5 days). Or start plants indoors 2 weeks before the average date of last spring frost, then set seedlings in the garden; plant deep, as for tomatoes. Use floating row covers in short-summer areas to speed growth and protect tomatillos from frost. *In containers:* Try a plant trellised in a container 18 in. tall and wide.

spacing Sow seeds $1/8$ in. deep, 2 in. apart, in rows spaced 2 ft. apart. Thin seedlings to 10 in. apart.

water Provide regular water until fruiting begins; then cut back but don't let plants dry out completely and wilt.

fertilizer Feed with low-nitrogen fertilizer when fruit starts to develop.

pruning, training Tomatillos grown in the ground are usually left to sprawl.

harvest Pick when fruit is walnut size (or smaller, if it seems fully developed) and deep green. Don't remove the papery husk until you are ready to use the fruit.

Tomatillos are tough and prolific; use raw in salads or cooked in salsa verde.

challenges Possible insect pests include aphids, Colorado potato beetles, cutworms, flea beetles, leaf miners, nematodes, and whiteflies. Row covers can help protect against all of them except nematodes, and yellow sticky traps are useful against whiteflies. Tomatillos can also get blight, fusarium wilt, and verticillium wilt. Crop rotation helps prevent these plus nematodes; you can also avoid blight by keeping water off the leaves.

Tomato

Solanum lycopersicum
Nightshade family *(Solanaceae)*
PERENNIAL GROWN AS ANNUAL
Warm-season vegetable

- ALL ZONES
- FULL SUN
- REGULAR WATER

Easy and prolific, tomatoes are just about the most widely grown of all garden plants, edible or otherwise. Amateur and commercial growers have different ideas about how best to raise these Andean natives. If you've developed a successful method, continue to follow it—but if you are a novice or have been dissatisfied with previous attempts, you may find the following information useful.

Choose varieties suited to your climate that will yield the kind of tomatoes you like on plants you can handle. Some varieties are determinate, others indeterminate. *Determinate* types are bushier, need little or no staking or trellising, and tend to bear all their crop at once. *Indeterminate* ones are more vinelike, need more training, and generally bear over a longer period. (Though the tomato plant is really a sprawling plant incapable of climbing, you'll often see it referred to as a vine.) Plant a few each of early, midseason, and late varieties for longest possible production. Or, where the growing season is long, plant in spring and again in summer.

HOW TO GROW IT

best site Most kinds of tomatoes grow best in sunny open gardens or raised beds, but small-fruited kinds thrive in big pots and hanging baskets.

yield Typically, six plants grown in open ground can supply a family of four with enough fruit to enjoy fresh and to use for canning or sauce. Two or three plants in containers will keep you in salad tomatoes for 2 to 3 months.

soil Tomato plants prefer well-drained, neutral to slightly acid soil; add lime to very acid soil or sulfur to alkaline soil the autumn before setting out plants.

planting Set out tomato plants after danger of frost has passed and the soil has warmed. Plant in February or early March in desert Zones 12 and 13; in April, May, or early June in Zones 7–9 and 14–24; in May or early June in Zones A1–A3, 1–6, 10, and 11. In Hawaii, tomatoes can be planted year-round in most locations.

'Early Girl', a popular all-purpose tomato

When buying tomato plants, look for compact ones with sturdy stems; avoid those that are tall for the pot or that already have flowers or fruit.

To grow tomatoes from seed, sow in pots of light soil mix 5 to 7 weeks before you intend to set out plants. Cover seeds with 1/2 in. of fine soil; firm soil over the seeds and keep the surface damp. Place the seed container in a cold frame or sunny window—a temperature of 65° to 70°F/18° to 21°C is ideal, although a range of 50°F/10°C at night to as warm as 85°F/29°C in the day will produce acceptable results. When seedlings are 2 in. tall, transplant each into a 3- or 4-in. pot; keep seedlings in a sunny area until they reach planting size.

Make planting holes extra deep, then carefully pinch off the lowest two sets of leaves and set in seedlings so that the lowest remaining leaves are just above soil level. Additional roots will form on the buried stems and provide stronger root systems.

Continued on page 90 ▶

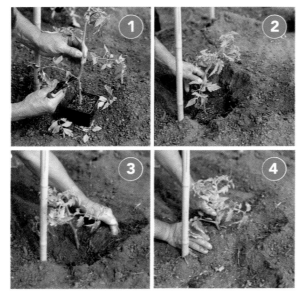

Wire cages are one choice for training tomatoes; you can also use stakes.

Planting Tips

1. Remove the lowest two sets of leaves from seedling.

2. Place seedling next to support stake in a hole that is deeper than the nursery pot.

3. Set seedling so lowest remaining leaves are just above soil level; fill in with soil.

4. Firm the soil in place, then water thoroughly.

Where summers are cool or short, or if you just want to get an early start, take steps to speed growth and protect tomatoes from frost. A combination of plastic mulch and floating row covers is probably most effective. Alternatively, individual plants can be protected with paper or plastic caps known as hot caps (some have water-filled cylinders that trap heat effectively to provide maximum protection).

In containers: Use large containers for large-fruited indeterminate tomatoes; a half-barrel for beefsteak types, for example. Hanging baskets and smaller containers (at least 14 in. wide and 12 in. deep) are usually big enough for determinate varieties of cherry tomatoes.

spacing In the ground, space plants 1¹⁄₂–3 ft. apart if they'll be staked or supported in some way, or 3–4 ft. apart if you plan to let them ramble untrained over the soil. In containers, plant one plant per pot.

water Water regularly and deeply since tomatoes are deep-rooted plants, but avoid overhead irrigation, which can encourage disease. To prevent splitting, reduce watering as fruit ripens.

fertilizer If soil is fairly rich, you won't need to fertilize at all. In ordinary soils, feed lightly every 2 weeks from the time the first blossoms set until the end of harvest; or give a single application of controlled-release fertilizer when planting.

pruning, training Tomato management and harvest will be most satisfying if you keep fruiting vines off the ground. Untrained plants sprawl, and fruits that touch the soil rot, discolor, and suffer pest damage. For training indeterminate varieties, the usual practice is to drive a 6-ft.-long stake (at least 1 by 1 in.) into the ground a foot from each plant. Use soft ties to hold the plant to the stake as it grows.

Slightly easier in the long run—but more work at planting time—is to grow each plant in a wire cylinder made of concrete reinforcing screen (6-in. mesh). The screen is 7 ft. tall, which is just right for cylinder height. Put stakes at opposite sides of the cylinder and tie the cylinder firmly to them. As the vine grows, poke protruding branches back inside the cylinder.

Continued on page 95 ▶

Tomatoes come in an amazing variety of sizes, shapes, and colors.

top picks to grow

Categories and Varieties	Days to Harvest	Fruit	Comments
EARLY TOMATOES: These set fruit at lower temperatures than most other tomatoes.			
'Early Girl'	75	4-ounce red	Indeterminate
'Oregon Spring'	80	7-ounce oval, red	Determinate, compact plant. Sets seedless, unpollinated fruit early, then seeded, pollinated fruit later.
'Prairie Fire'	55	4-ounce smooth, globe-shaped, red	Determinate, small plant. Alaska favorite.
'Quick Pick'	79	4- to 5-in. red in clusters	Indeterminate. Good disease resistance.
'Sub Arctic Maxi'	50	2$^1/_2$-ounce red	Alaska standard
HAWAIIAN TOMATOES: These resist nematodes and diseases common to Hawaii.			
'Anahu'	90	7-ounce round, red-orange	Determinate
'Healani'	90	6-ounce red	Determinate
'Kewalo'	75	7-ounce round, red	Determinate
'Komohana'	70	Grape-size ($^1/_2$-ounce) red	Determinate
'N-5'	85	Green-shouldered red	Semideterminate
'N-63'	85	Green-shouldered red	Indeterminate
'N-65'	85	Green-shouldered red	Indeterminate. Does well in high humidity.
HEIRLOOM TOMATOES: Most are richly flavored vintage favorites that come true from seed.			
'Brandywine'	78	8- to 16-ounce red	Indeterminate. Many versions offered.
'Cherokee Purple'	85	10- to 12-ounce with reddish purple skin, deep red flesh	Indeterminate
'Costoluto Genovese'	78	8-ounce fluted, red	Indeterminate. Produces in much to little heat.
'Mortgage Lifter'	80	16- to 24-ounce pink with few seeds	Indeterminate
'Paul Robeson'	74	8-ounce slicer with deep red flesh, intense flavor	Indeterminate. Sets fruit at colder temperatures than most.
LARGE-FRUITED HYBRIDS: These are grown for slicing and uniformity—perfect for burgers. They don't come true from seed (offspring won't be like parents).			
'Beefmaster'	80	16- to 32-ounce red	Indeterminate. Good disease resistance.
'Beefsteak'	95	16-ounce red	Indeterminate. This is the standard slicer.
'Big Beef'	80	10- to 12-ounce round, red	Indeterminate. Broad disease resistance.
'Burpee's Supersteak Hybrid'	80	Up to 2-pound red	Indeterminate. Good disease resistance.
'Delicious'	90	8-ounce red in clusters	Indeterminate. Resists cracking. Ripens even when nights are cool.
MAIN CROP: These are reliably productive, multipurpose tomatoes.			
'Better Boy'	72	1-pound red	Indeterminate. Good crack and disease resistance.
'Big Boy'	78	1-pound red	Indeterminate. Very large crops.

Categories and Varieties	Days to Harvest	Fruit	Comments
'Celebrity'	70	7- to 10-ounce red	Determinate
'Heatwave II'	70	6-ounce red	Determinate. Yields in very hot weather.
'Pearson'	85	8-ounce round, red	Determinate. Yields well in hot, dry climates.
NOVELTY TOMATOES: These include fruits bred for unusual colors, patterns, keeping quality, uses, and health benefits.			
'Black Prince'	74	3- to 5-ounce with brown and orange-red skin	Indeterminate. Resists cracking.
'Caro Rich'	77	10-ounce orange	Indeterminate. Ten times the beta-carotene of standard varieties.
'Evergreen'	72	16-ounce green	Indeterminate
'Green Zebra'	80	3-ounce green mottled with yellow	Indeterminate
'Health Kick'	75	4-ounce elongated	Determinate with 50 percent more lycopene (an antioxidant) than standard varieties.
'Long Keeper'	78	3-in. orange-red	Determinate. Fruit keeps 3 months if individually wrapped in paper.
'Mountain Gold'	71	8- to 12-ounce round, golden yellow	Determinate
'Yellow Stuffer'	76	Bell pepper–size yellow with hollow insides	Indeterminate
PASTE TOMATOES: Small, oval, thick-meated fruits are bred for canning, sauces, tomato paste, and drying.			
'Roma'	78	3-in. red	Determinate
'San Marzano'	80	$3^1/_2$-in. red	Indeterminate
'Viva Italia'	75	Elongated red	Determinate. Very disease-resistant.
SMALL-FRUITED TOMATOES (often called cherry tomatoes): These are the easiest to grow. Use determinates in containers.			
'Gardener's Delight'	65	1-ounce red in clusters	Indeterminate. Also called 'Sugar Lump'.
'Isis Candy'	67	1-in. marbled red-gold	Indeterminate. Very sweet. Very productive.
'Juliet'	60	1-ounce red	Indeterminate. Very productive.
'Patio'	70	3- to 4-ounce red	Determinate. Good container plant.
'Red Pear'	78	2-in. pear-shaped, bright red	Indeterminate
'Sun Gold'	60	1-in. golden-red in long clusters	Indeterminate. Has unsurpassed sweetness. Can split.
'Supersweet 100'	70	1-in. red in multibranched clusters	Indeterminate
'Sweet 100'	65	$1/_2$-in. red in multibranched clusters	Indeterminate. Sweet. Tends to crack.
'Sweet Million'	70	$1–1^1/_2$ in. red in multibranched clusters	Indeterminate. Resists cracking.
'Tiny Tim'	60	$3/_4$-in. round, red	Determinate. Excellent in pots.
'Yellow Pear'	70	$1^1/_2$-ounce pear-shaped, yellow	Indeterminate

'San Marzano', a meaty variety ideal for tomato paste

'Tigerella', a striped heirloom variety with a tangy flavor

Cherry tomatoes like 'Sweet 100' are popular for salads, or simply eating fresh from the vine.

Heirloom 'Zapotec Pleated', a traditional slicing tomato

GARY IBSEN ON
heirloom tomatoes

Why grow heirloom tomatoes? "Flavor, flavor, and flavor," says Gary Ibsen, tomato expert, author, and impresario of the annual Carmel TomatoFest in Carmel, CA. Below are a few of his favorite heirloom varieties and what he loves about them. All are indeterminate.

....

'Brandywine OTV'. "Big, red fruit with orange undertones has a smooth, creamy texture and a sweet, complex flavor." (72 days to harvest)

....

'Cherokee Chocolate'. "Its flavor isn't intense, but it is rich and has wonderful nuances. The skin of this beefsteak type is a mahogany chocolate color, and each fruit can weigh up to 4 pounds." (80 days)

....

'Dagma's Perfection'. "Delicate, tropical fruit flavor. It's sweet, but has nice acid balance—enough to stand up to the tomato's sugar. The fruit is yellow with red striping, slightly flattish, and weighs about 12 ounces." (73 days)

....

'German Johnson'. "This one is large (1 to 2 pounds), pink, and prolific, and it has excellent flavor." (78 days)

....

'Kellogg's Breakfast'. "Color is deep orange, like orange juice. This is a beefsteak type that produces meaty fruit with few seeds and fantastic, rich flavor." (80 days)

....

'Paul Robeson'. "Its intense flavor has unmatched complexity: it blends rich, almost chocolate, earth tones with fruitiness. And its color is dramatic—black purple outside and deep red inside." (74 days)

harvest Tomatoes are best picked fully ripe, but at the end of the season you'll need to harvest everything before frost. Ripening tomatoes go from dark green to light green, then to their mature color; any tomato you pick that has reached the intermediate light green phase will continue to ripen fully indoors. Put it on a sunny windowsill to speed the process. An alternative harvest method is to pull up the whole plant and hang it upside down in a frost-free garage or porch; much of the fruit will continue to ripen on the dying, drying vine.

challenges Whiteflies are common pests of tomato plants. One good organic control is a yellow sticky trap. Large green caterpillars with diagonal white stripes that feed upside down on leaf undersides are hornworms; handpick them or spray with *Bacillus thuringiensis* (Bt) or spinosad. In Hawaii, wrap developing fruit clusters in paper or cloth bags to protect them from melon flies.

Tomatoes are subject to a long list of diseases, some of which can be addressed with proper watering. For example, you can lessen the chance of late blight (which spots leaves and stems and rots fruit) by avoiding overhead sprinkling. Leaf roll, blossom-end rot, and cracked fruit can be corrected (or prevented) by maintaining uniform soil moisture. Mulching will help conserve moisture in very hot or dry climates.

If plants are growing strongly, then suddenly wilt and die, they may have been sabotaged by gophers. If you can find no evidence of these rodents, plants probably are suffering from verticillium wilt, fusarium wilt, or both; pull them out and discard them. Diseases live over in soil, so plant in a different location every year.

If certain diseases or nematodes cause trouble locally, you may be able to grow varieties that resist one or more problems. Keys to resistance you may see on plant labels or in catalog descriptions include V (verticillium wilt), F (fusarium wilt), FF (Race 1 and Race 2 fusarium wilt), N (nematodes), T (tobacco mosaic virus), A (alternaria leaf spot), and L (septoria leaf spot). For example, a variety labeled VFFNT means that it resists verticillium wilt, two races of fusarium wilt, nematodes, and tobacco mosaic virus. Your Cooperative Extension Office is the best source of information about control measures for most tomato diseases.

Turnip and Rutabaga

Brassica species
Cabbage family *(Brassicaceae)*
BIENNIALS GROWN AS ANNUALS
Cool-season vegetables

🌾 **ALL ZONES**
☼ **FULL SUN, EXCEPT AS NOTED**
💧 **REGULAR WATER**

These European natives are cabbage relatives. Both plants are delicious roasted, mashed (especially with carrots and other root vegetables), and in stews.

Turnip *(Brassica rapa).* Best known for its roots, which come in various colors (white, white with purple on the upper part, and creamy yellow) and shapes (globe and flattened globe). The foliage is also edible, and some varieties, such as 'Seven Top' (summer turnip), are grown for leaves only.

Rutabaga *(B. napus).* Milder and sweeter than turnip, with large yellowish roots; its leaves are palatable only when very young.

HOW TO GROW IT

best site Both turnip and rutabaga grow in full sun. *Turnip*, when sown in summer, does best in partial shade. *Rutabaga* tolerates partial shade in cold-winter, hot-summer climates.

yield *Turnip:* 8 to 12 pounds per 10-ft. row. *Rutabaga:* 8 to 30 pounds per 10-ft. row.

soil Grow in rich, loose, well-drained soil.

planting Where winters are cold, plant in early spring for early-summer harvest, or in summer for fall harvest. Where winters are mild, plant in fall for a winter crop.

spacing *Turnip:* Sow seeds 1 in. apart, then thin to 2–6 in. apart for roots, 1–4 in. apart for greens. *Rutabaga:* Sow seeds 2–4 in. apart, then thin to 5–8 in. apart; each plant needs ample space for the root to reach its full weight of 3–5 pounds.

water Roots are milder if the soil is kept moist; they become more pungent under drier conditions.

'Red Top' turnip, a fine addition to soups or salads

fertilizer *Turnip:* Feed with a liquid fertilizer after seedlings are up, then again monthly. *Rutabaga:* Dig a fertilizer that's high in phosphorus and potassium into the soil at planting time. Apply the same kind of fertilizer a month after active growth starts.

harvest *Turnip* roots grow fast and should be harvested and used as soon as they are big enough to eat, usually about 75 days after sowing. *Rutabaga* roots are ready to harvest 3 to 4 months after planting, when the roots are about 3 in. wide. They store well in the ground, and flavor improves with light frost.

challenges Armyworms, cabbage root maggots, and flea beetles are possible. Row covers help.

Watermelon

Citrullus lanatus
Gourd family *(Cucurbitaceae)*
ANNUAL
Warm-season vegetable

- ZONES 1–24, H1, H2
- FULL SUN
- REGULAR WATER

This native of southern Africa needs a long growing season, more heat than most other melons, and more space than other vine crops—about 8 ft. by 8 ft. for each hill (circle of seed). Most varieties have red flesh, but some have yellow, orange, or pink-and-yellow flesh. And though the fruit is usually large, small watermelons have also become popular in recent years; most of these "personal-size" melons weigh in at 3 to 6 pounds, ripening in less than 3 months.

Watermelons are best grown in hills or mounded rows a few inches tall at the center; you will need to provide considerable space. You can, however, grow small melons on sunbathed trellises to save ground space as long as you support the heavy fruit in individual cloth slings.

Bees pollinate watermelons, with each plant producing both male and female flowers. Seedless varieties need a seeded watermelon nearby to provide pollen or they won't bear fruit.

If your summers are short or cool, choose a fast-maturing early variety (described in catalogs and on seed packets as taking 70 to 75 days from seed to harvest). If your summers are long and warm, choose any variety you like. Among many good choices, try 'Crimson Sweet', a sweet, standard, 20-pound melon with red flesh (88 days to maturity); 'Yellow Doll', which bears oval 4$\frac{1}{2}$- to 7-pound fruits with yellow flesh (68 days); or 'New Queen', with 5- to 6-pound fruits that have bright orange-yellow flesh and few seeds (75 days). For a seedless variety, try 'Orange Sweet', which produces 16- to 25-pound fruit with sweet orange flesh (83 days).

Some of the best varieties for Hawaii gardens are 'Sugar Baby', 'Crimson Sweet', and 'Glory'.

HOW TO GROW IT

best site Watermelons need a spot with plenty of room and full sun.

yield 8 to 40 pounds per 10-ft. row.

Pick watermelons when ripe; thump the end to test.

soil Light, fertile, well-drained soil that's well amended with compost.

planting If your growing season is warm and long enough, sow seeds in light, well-drained soil 2 weeks after the average last-frost date; don't rush it, since melons are truly tropical plants and will perish in even a light frost. In regions where summers are cool or relatively short, start plants indoors in pots a few weeks before the average date of last frost, then plant outdoors in the warmest southern exposure. Indoors or out, seeds need a soil temperature of 70°F/21°C to germinate. Row covers allow for earlier planting outdoors. In areas where summers are very short, place clear or black plastic mulch under melons to warm soil, speed harvest, and help keep fruit from rotting.

Continued on page 98 ▶

Choose a spot that's sunny and hot, with plenty of room for vines to sprawl.

'PureHeart Seedless', a new mini or "personal" watermelon

spacing Plant in hills or rows. *Hills:* Make hills a few inches high and about 4 ft. in diameter; encircle each with a furrow for irrigation. *Rows:* Make rows 4 ft. wide and 8 ft. apart (measuring from center to center), with furrows for irrigation along both sides. Plant seeds 1 in. deep—four or five seeds per hill, one or two seeds every 1 ft. in rows. When plants are well established, thin each hill to the best two plants; thin rows to one strong plant every 4 ft.

water Fill furrows with water from time to time (furrows let you water plants without wetting foliage), but do not keep soil soaked.

fertilizer Feed in furrows with complete fertilizer every 6 weeks.

harvest Watermelon does not become sweeter after harvest—it must be picked ripe. To check for ripeness, thump the melon (it should produce a hollow "thunk"); check to see that the underside has turned from white to pale yellow; and make sure the tendrils where the melon attaches to the stem have darkened and withered. Cut (do not pull) melon from the vine.

challenges Watermelons are subject to aphids, cucumber beetles, squash vine borers, and downy and powdery mildew. Some varieties have been bred for disease and mildew resistance. Row covers offer protection from insects until flowering time, when the covers must be removed so that bees can pollinate flowers.

CHAPTER 2

Herbs

Herbs and other seasonings intensify flavor without increasing fat or calories. Most have aromatic evergreen foliage that wakes up meats, sauces, salads, and soups. Flavors can vary greatly among varieties, even more between species, so taste before you buy. Edible flowers add color to everything from salads to desserts.

Basil

Ocimum basilicum
Mint family *(Lamiaceae)*
ANNUAL OR TENDER PERENNIAL

✔ **ALL ZONES AS ANNUAL;**
   ZONES 13–17, 19, 23, 24 AS PERENNIAL

☼ **FULL SUN**

💧 **REGULAR WATER**

Basil grows about 2 ft. tall and 1 ft. wide, with green, shiny, 1- to 2-in.-long leaves and spikes of white flowers. But there are almost endless variations on this theme, including forms with purple or variegated foliage, dwarf globe or columnar habits, giant or tiny leaves, and purple flowers. Flavors cover a remarkable range, including anise, cinnamon, clove, coriander, lemon, and lime.

As a culinary herb, basil is critical in everything from pesto to Indian and Southeast Asian cuisine. Used fresh or dry, its leaves lend a pleasant, mildly sweet flavor to sauces and cooked dishes of all sorts. The best leaves are from younger stems that have not yet borne flowers. Hailing from tropical and subtropical Asia, basil thrives in sunny, moist locations. There are too many varieties to cover exhaustively, but the following list gives an inkling of what's available. All are annuals unless otherwise noted.

Big leaves. Use leaves of the following as wraps: 'Napolitano', 'Large Green', and 'Mammoth Sweet'.

Compact. Try 'Finissimo Verde a Palla'; 'Greek' ('Spicy Globe'), which makes a fine-leafed, 1-ft. globe; 'Magical Michael' or 'Marseillais Dwarf', which is covered with extremely aromatic leaves.

Flavor. Because basil comes in so many flavors, you should taste before you buy. Most of the varieties that follow have names that describe their flavors: 'Cinnamon', 'Clove', 'Lemon', 'Lettuce Leaf' (licorice), 'Lime', 'Mrs. Burns Lemon Basil', 'Sweet Dani' (intense lemon).

Perennial. Grow these outdoors in virtually frost-free climates or indoors: 'Magic Mountain' (3 ft.) or 'Pesto Perpetua' (to 4 ft., with light green leaves that have cream variegation).

Pesto. Start with a Genovese type such as 'Aroma 1' or 'Aroma 2', 'Genova', 'Genovese', or 'Nufar'; or use a standard variety such as 'Sweet Basil'.

Purple foliage. These *Ocimum basilicum purpurascens* varieties can be a bit touchy to grow, but they're beautiful and much used in Asian cooking: 'Purple Ruffles', 'Red Lettuce Leaved', 'Red Osmin' (an improved 'Dark Opal'), 'Red Rubin', and 'Rubra'.

HOW TO GROW IT

best site Full sun.

soil Basil does best in fertile soil with good drainage.

planting Sow seeds of any basil in early spring or set out nursery plants after all danger of frost is past. In regions with a long growing season, flowering will compromise the flavor of basil before frost knocks plants down. In these regions, make successive sowings about every 2 weeks to ensure a steady supply of leaves throughout the season. *In containers:* Basil grows well in containers; choose 16-in. or larger plastic or glazed pots, which will hold soil moisture longer than wood or unglazed terra-cotta pots.

spacing Space plants 10–12 in. apart or thin to this distance.

water Never let soil dry out completely.

fertilizer Feed once during the growing season with a complete fertilizer.

pruning, training To prolong leaf production—which will cease when plants come into bloom—pinch out flower spikes as they form.

harvest Pick off leaves as you need them.

challenges Susceptible to fusarium wilt, which causes plants to collapse in a day. Defeat it by growing fusarium-tolerant varieties such as one of the 'Aroma' varieties, 'Magical Michael', or 'Nufar', and never plant basil in the same bed more than once every 4 years (plant in containers if you're short on space).

'Genovese' basil, one of the best for making pesto

Pick basil leaves as needed; pinch off flowers as they form.

'Red Osmin' basil, the darkest of the purple-leafed types

'Siam Queen' is one of several flavorful Thai basils.

Chamomile

Matricaria recutita (M. chamomilla)
Sunflower family *(Asteraceae)*
ANNUAL

✄ **ALL ZONES**
☀ **FULL SUN**
💧 **MODERATE WATER**

Though originally from Europe and western Asia, this aromatic plant has naturalized in much of North America. Chamomile, sometimes called German chamomile, grows 1¹/₂–2 ft. tall and 1¹/₂ ft. wide, with finely cut, almost fernlike foliage. White-and-yellow daisy-type flowers to 1 in. wide bloom in summer. Dried flowers are used in making the familiar, fragrant chamomile tea. The scent is sweet with apple overtones.

Plants or seeds sold as *Matricaria* 'White Stars', 'Golden Ball', and 'Snowball' are varieties of the perennial feverfew *(Chrysanthemum parthenium)*. Chamomile sold as a walk-on groundcover is *Chamaemelum nobile (Anthemis nobilis)*. Its dried flowers are also sometimes used for tea, though the plant doesn't produce as many blossoms as *M. recutita* does.

HOW TO GROW IT

best site Full sun.

soil Chamomile grows easily in ordinary soil.

planting Sow seeds in late winter or spring. *In containers:* Grows well in pots at least 12 in. wide and 8 in. deep.

spacing Plant at 14- to 18-in. intervals.

water Moderate water.

fertilizer Little is necessary; mulch with compost and apply complete fertilizer once early in the growing season.

harvest Pick flowers in the morning. They can be used fresh or air-dried on a screen in a place that's protected from direct sun, rain, and dust.

challenges This is a trouble-free herb.

Use chamomile leaves in potpourri; dry the flowers for tea.

Chervil

Anthriscus cerefolium
Carrot family *(Apiaceae)*
ANNUAL

- ✄ **ALL ZONES**
- ◑ **PARTIAL SHADE**
- ◖ **REGULAR WATER**

This native of southeastern Europe and western Asia produces low mounds of fernlike foliage about 1 ft. wide. Flower stems to 1–2 ft. are topped with white blossoms in summer.

The leaves have a parsleylike flavor with overtones of anise; use them like parsley. Flavor is volatile, so fresh leaves are best used right away or added as a cooking ingredient late in preparation. When preserving chervil, freezing retains more flavor than drying.

HOW TO GROW IT

best site Partial shade; too much sun makes plants go to seed.

soil Chervil grows well in average, well-drained garden soils.

planting Sow seeds in place in early spring (in cold-winter areas) or in fall (where winters are mild). Be patient; seeds can take 3 weeks to germinate. Chervil does well interplanted with perennials and other annuals. After the first year, volunteer seedlings will keep you supplied with new plants. *In containers:* Try a single plant in a pot 12 in. wide and 8 in. deep.

spacing Scatter seed, then thin to 9–12 in. apart when seedlings are up.

water Don't let soil dry out completely between watering or plants will tend to bolt.

fertilizer Apply a complete fertilizer once or twice each year.

Chervil leaves taste best when freshly picked.

pruning, training Cut flower clusters to encourage leafy growth.

harvest Snip off leaves as needed.

challenges Chervil goes to seed quickly in hot weather but is fairly winter-hardy; it can survive to 14°F/–10°C.

Chives

Allium species
Lily family *(Liliaceae)*
DECIDUOUS PERENNIALS FROM BULBS

✎ **ALL ZONES**

☼ ◑ **FULL SUN OR PARTIAL SHADE**

🌢 **REGULAR WATER DURING GROWTH AND BLOOM**

These plants are related to onions and garlic but are smaller and prettier. They grow in delicate-looking clumps and make an attractive edging in a flower border or an herb garden. Use leaves and blossoms of both in cooking or as a fresh topping or garnish.

Chives (*Allium schoenoprasum*). European, Asian, and Alaskan natives that form 1 1/2- to 2-ft.-high clumps of round, hollow leaves with a delicate, onionlike flavor. Clusters of rose-purple flowers like clover blossoms are held atop thin stems in spring.

Garlic chives (*A. tuberosum*). Sometimes called Chinese chives, these are native to Southeast Asia. Their 1/4-in.-wide, foot-long leaves are flat, not tubular like regular chives, and have a mild garlic flavor. White flowers appear in summer and smell like violets. There is also a mauve-flowered form.

HOW TO GROW IT

best site Full sun or partial shade.

soil Both prosper in average, well-drained soil.

planting Sow seed 1/8–1/4 in. deep, then thin to 8–12 in. apart. Plants also grow easily from potted seedlings. Leaves die down during winter, but you can extend the season by potting up small divisions in rich soil and growing them on a windowsill. *In containers:* A half-dozen plants will grow well in a 12-in.-wide pot that is at least 6 in. deep.

spacing Plant at 8- to 12-in. intervals.

water Regular water during growth and bloom.

Like its leaves, the flowers of common chives are edible—and pretty as garnishes.

fertilizer Dig in organic compost, rotted manure, or complete fertilizer at planting time.

harvest Use scissors to snip entire leaves from the outside of the clump; this is better for the plant than snipping off the tops of leaves. Chop leaves for garnish. Pick flowers as soon as they open and use them as confetti in salads.

challenges Chives and garlic chives self-sow. Prevent seedlings by removing fading flowers—or just pull and eat unwanted seedlings.

Cilantro, Coriander

Coriandrum sativum
Carrot family (*Apiaceae*)
ANNUAL

✂ **ALL ZONES**
☼ **LIGHT SHADE IN HOTTEST CLIMATES**
💧 **REGULAR WATER**

This western Mediterranean native grows 1–1¹⁄₂ ft. high and 9 in. wide. Delicate fernlike foliage is topped by flat clusters of pinkish white flowers in summer.

Both fresh leaves (cilantro, sometimes called Chinese parsley) and seeds (coriander) are widely used as seasoning, and roots are used in Thai cooking. You can even eat the flowers. Leaves are popular in salads and many cooked dishes. Crush the aromatic seeds for use in sausage, beans, stews, and baked goods.

HOW TO GROW IT

best site Full sun in mild climates; light shade will help prevent bolting in hot-summer climates.

soil Grow in well-drained soil.

planting Cilantro is taprooted and transplants poorly, so start from seed (you can even use the coriander seed sold in grocery stores). In all but low-desert areas, sow in place in early spring after all danger of frost is past. Cilantro grows and flowers extremely quickly. Keep it coming by succession planting every couple of weeks. It does self-sow but is not a problem. In low-desert areas, plant in autumn; cilantro will go to seed and die in late-spring heat. If you're growing cilantro for the seed only, two or three plants is all you need. *In containers:* Try it in a pot at least 12 in. wide and 8 in. deep.

spacing Thin seedlings first to 3–4 in. apart; then, when they touch, to 9 in. apart.

water Regular water encourages steady growth and delays bolting.

fertilizer Plants do best in soils with little nitrogen; if you fertilize at all, use a mild plant food like fish fertilizer or fully composted dairy manure.

Cut cilantro leaves a few at a time to ensure a continuous crop.

pruning, training If you're growing cilantro for the leaves, snip off the flower buds as they appear.

harvest Pull thinnings for the leaves (or snip them off if seedlings are so close that pulling one out would uproot one you want to save), and start harvesting the outer leaves of plants when they reach 8 in. tall. If you have too many leaves, chop them up and freeze them. To collect seeds, pull up whole plants when fruits (which look like seeds) begin to turn gray-brown; then put the plants headfirst into bags and shake them, or hang them over paper and let seeds drop.

challenges Carrot rust flies sometimes attack young plants. Keep them at bay by covering seedlings with a floating row cover until they're 6–8 in. tall. This is an otherwise pest-free plant.

Cress

Lepidium sativum
Cabbage family *(Brassicaceae)*
ANNUAL

🌿 **ALL ZONES**

☼ ◑ **FULL SUN OR PARTIAL SHADE**

🌢 🌢 **REGULAR TO AMPLE WATER**

Garden cress is sometimes called pepper grass because of its peppery taste. It comes in broad- and curly-leafed forms. The broad-leafed form is used most often in soups; both kinds are used in sandwiches and salads. The curly-leafed form can also be used as a garnish.

This Egyptian and western Asian native is easy to grow as long as weather is cool. Sow seed as early in spring as possible. Planted in rich, moist soil, it matures quickly.

HOW TO GROW IT

best site Full sun or partial shade (especially as the warm season advances).

soil Should be rich and moisture retentive.

planting Make successive sowings in the garden every 2 weeks up to the middle of May. Where frosts are mild, sow through fall and winter. *In containers:* Try growing garden cress in shallow pots of planting mix in a sunny kitchen window. It sprouts in a few days and can be harvested with scissors in 2 to 3 weeks. Or grow it by sprinkling seeds on pads of wet cheesecloth; keep damp until harvest in 2 weeks.

spacing Make rows 1 ft. apart; thin plants to 3 in. apart (eat thinnings).

water Garden cress should be kept consistently moist.

fertilizer If your soil isn't rich, mix in a little complete fertilizer at planting time or apply liquid fertilizer once after true leaves appear.

harvest Snip off leaves when plants are 2–5 in. tall. Use them fresh; they don't dry well.

challenges This plant is relatively trouble-free in the garden.

Broad-leafed garden cress has a tangy, peppery taste.

Dill

Anethum graveolens
Carrot family (*Apiaceae*)
ANNUAL

✎ ALL ZONES
☼ FULL SUN
💧 REGULAR WATER

Dill is native to southwestern Asia and has naturalized in the northern U.S. It grows 3–4 ft. tall, with soft, feathery leaves and umbrella-like, 6-in.-wide clusters of small yellow flowers in summer (winter in the desert).

   The pungent aroma of its seeds and leaves make dill a popular culinary herb. Seedlings can be pulled and chopped for use in cooking. Use seeds in pickling and vinegar; fresh or dried leaves flavor cooked dishes, salads, and sauces.

HOW TO GROW IT

best site Full sun, with protection from wind.

soil Well-drained soil is best; rocky soil is fine.

planting Sow seeds where plants are to grow; dill's deep taproot discourages transplanting. For constant supply, sow several times in spring and summer (dill germinates and grows better in spring). In the desert, sow in late summer or fall. *In containers:* Grow a single plant in a container at least 1 ft. deep.

spacing Thin to 1 ft. apart when seedlings are 2–3 in. tall.

water Regular water is best, but dill will grow with only moderate water.

fertilizer For larger plants and later seed setting, dig in fully composted fertilizer before sowing and apply complete fertilizer after plants reach a foot tall.

pruning, training Shear off flower heads before they go to seed if you don't want plants to resow.

Dill flowers attract beneficial insects to your garden.

harvest Snip off leaves as you need them. To collect the seed, tie small bags over seed heads when seeds begin to turn brown. Leave them in place for a week or so. Give each seed head a good shake before removing the bag.

challenges Dry weather makes dill bolt; to delay that, keep the soil moist. Dill will self-sow vigorously if you let it go to seed.

Edible Flowers

ANNUALS AND PERENNIALS

✂ ZONES VARY BY SPECIES

☼ ☽ FULL SUN OR PARTIAL SHADE, EXCEPT AS NOTED

💧 MODERATE WATER UNLESS NOTED

The following are edible flowers you might not normally think of for a food garden; all grow well in either the ground or in containers. Most petals have a short shelf life, so the freshest will be those you raise yourself. Never eat flowers you get from a florist, as there's a risk they've been sprayed with pesticides.

Many food crops also produce blossoms (squash, chives, and pineapple guava are good examples); for edibility, see individual plant listings.

Borage *(Borago officinalis).* Zones A2, A3, 1–24, H1. Annual. Grows 2–3 ft. high, 1$^{1}/_{2}$–2 ft. wide with edible leaves and blue, star-shaped summer flowers. The flowers are beautiful scattered through a salad. Borage doesn't transplant easily, so sow seeds in place in spring after frost danger is past. Tolerates poor soil. Seeds itself but isn't a pest.

Calendula *(Calendula officinalis).* Zones A2, A3, 1–24, H1. Annual. Reaches 1–2 ft. high, 1–1$^{1}/_{2}$ ft. wide; blooms from late fall through spring in mild-winter areas, from spring to midsummer in colder climates. Daisylike 2$^{1}/_{4}$- to 4$^{1}/_{2}$-in. orange or yellow blooms have a tangy flavor. Sow seed in late summer or early fall in mild-winter climates, spring elsewhere. Or buy seedlings at nurseries. Adapts to most soils if drainage is fast. Full sun.

Nasturtium *(Tropaeolum majus).* All zones. Annual. Climbing types grow to 7 ft. and cling with coiling leaf stalks, while mounding kinds grow to 1$^{1}/_{2}$ ft. tall and wide. Leaves are large (to 3-4 in.) and round. Edible flowers have a peppery flavor and come in orange, yellow, red, cream, reddish brown, and maroon. Somewhat drought tolerant.

Pansy and viola *(Viola* species). All zones. Annuals invaluable for winter and spring bloom in mild-winter areas, for spring through summer color in colder climates. Most grow 4–12 in. tall and have brightly colored flowers often blotched or bicolored in white, blue, red-orange, bronze, yellow, or purple. Flowers have a light mellow flavor that recalls the scent of mown hay and heliotrope. Pansies and violas work well in salads, as garnishes on plates and cakes, and candied. Sow seed $^{1}/_{4}$ in. deep; thin to 8 in. apart.

Borage adds a beautiful touch of blue to salads.

Pink *(Dianthus).* Try clove pink *(D. caryophyllus),* Zones A2, A3, 1–24, H1; and cottage pink *(D. plumarius),* Zones A1, 1–24. Both perennials grow to 2 ft. tall and produce clove-flavored flowers in the red, white, and pink range. They thrive in light, rich, fast-draining soil. Organic amendment before planting is helpful. Full sun in all but hottest climates, where light shade is best. Regular water.

Fennel

Foeniculum vulgare
Carrot family *(Apiaceae)*
PERENNIAL SOMETIMES GROWN AS ANNUAL

✎ **ZONES VARY; SEE BELOW**
☼ **FULL SUN**
💧 **MODERATE WATER**

Two forms of this Mediterranean native are commonly grown—one for its flavorful seeds and leaves, the other for its edible leaf bases.

Fennel *(Foeniculum vulgare).* The plain species, which is cultivated for licorice-flavored seeds and young leaves, is a perennial in Zones 2b–11, 14–24, H1, and H2; and a winter annual in desert Zones 12 and 13. It is similar in appearance to dill, growing 3–5 ft. tall and producing flat clusters of yellow flowers in summer, but its yellow-green foliage is somewhat coarser. Fennel often grows as a roadside or garden weed (it is invasive in Hawaii and along the West Coast from California to Washington). The plant is attractive until tops turn brown, and even then birds like the seeds. New stems grow in spring from its perennial root. Bronze fennel ('Purpurascens', 'Smokey') is similar, but has bronzy purple foliage that reaches 6 ft. tall.

Use seeds of either the plain species or bronze fennel to season baked goods. Add young leaves as garnish for salads, fish, and other dishes.

Florence fennel or finocchio *(F. v. azoricum).* This is a summer annual in all areas except desert Zones 12 and 13, where it is a winter annual. Compared with the species, it is lower growing (to 2 ft. tall), with larger, thicker leafstalk bases that are eaten as a cooked or raw vegetable. Its feathery leaves are used as a garnish and seasoning.

HOW TO GROW IT

best site Full sun.

soil Well-drained soil is best.

planting Start from seed where plants are to be grown (a strong taproot prevents easy transplanting). *In containers:* A single plant can go in a container that's at least 1 ft. deep.

spacing Thin seedlings to 1 ft. apart.

Snip off fennel leaves and seeds to use as a summer seasoning.

water Regular water is best, but the plant will grow with little water.

fertilizer Fennel grows larger and delays seed setting if the soil is fertile. Dig in fully composted fertilizer before sowing, or apply complete fertilizer after the plant reaches a foot tall.

harvest Snip off leaves as you need them. To collect the seeds, tie small bags over seed heads when seeds begin to turn brown and leave them on the plant for a few days. Shake the seed heads before removing the bags.

challenges Shear off flower heads before they go to seed if you don't want the plant to self-sow, which it does vigorously.

Horseradish

Armoracia rusticana (Cochlearia armoracia)
Cabbage family *(Brassicaceae)*
PERENNIAL GROWN AS ANNUAL

ALL ZONES

FULL SUN

REGULAR WATER

This large (to about 3 ft.), coarse, weedy-looking plant is cultivated for its large white roots, which are peeled, grated, and mixed with vinegar or cream to make a spicy condiment. It is native to southeastern Europe and temperate parts of Asia, but it grows nearly everywhere, performing best in cool regions. The root, which is at least the size of a large carrot, will put on most of its bulk in late summer and early fall. One plant should provide enough horseradish for a family of four.

Though horseradish is an herbaceous perennial, it's best to treat it like an annual and replant it every spring; perennialized roots become tough and stringy.

HOW TO GROW IT

best site A sunny, out-of-the-way corner.

soil Grows best in deeply cultivated, fertile soil amended with compost and sifted to remove rocks.

planting In late winter or early spring, set pencil-size root horizontally in a trench 3–4 in. deep and cover with 2 in. of soil.

spacing For multiple plants, space them $2\frac{1}{2}$–3 ft. apart.

water Even moisture keeps roots growing steadily.

fertilizer Top-dress with 5-10-10 fertilizer once in early summer. Avoid excess nitrogen, which causes roots to fork.

harvest Through fall, winter, and spring, harvest pieces from the outside of the root clump as you need them—that way, your horseradish will always be fresh and tangy.

Harvest pieces of horseradish root from fall through spring.

challenges Aphids, cabbageworms, flea beetles, and leafhoppers sometimes attack the leaves. But the biggest problem is weediness. If you leave any part of the root in the ground, the plant can spread by underground shoots and become invasive, so dig up every bit when you harvest the last piece that you intend to use.

Lavender

Lavandula species
Mint family *(Lamiaceae)*
EVERGREEN SHRUBS

✂ ZONES VARY BY SPECIES
☼ FULL SUN
◌ ◍ LITTLE TO MODERATE WATER

These natives of the Mediterranean region, Canary Islands, and Madeira are prized for their fragrant lavender or purple flowers, often set off by colorful bracts, and for their aromatic, generally gray-green foliage that grows in perfect mounds.

Blossom spikes of many kinds are used for perfume, aromatic oil, soap, medicine, and sachets. Fresh flowers of English lavender and lavandin varieties can be used in recipes (use only the soft parts of the flowers); other species contain harmful chemicals that should not be ingested. As a flavoring, a little lavender goes a long way. Flowers may be used fresh in teas, lavender lemonade, ice cream, and salads, or as an ingredient in baked goods.

In the landscape, grow lavender as an informal hedge or edging or in borders with plants needing similar cultural conditions. Sunrose *(Helianthemum)*, catmint *(Nepeta)*, rosemary, santolina, and verbena make good companions. Lavender will succeed in cool coastal or mountain climates or inland valleys and deserts but succumbs to root rot in areas where heat is accompanied by humidity. Most types attract bees and butterflies.

English lavender *(Lavandula angustifolia).* Zones 2–24. This is the best culinary variety because it is the sweetest. Common name notwithstanding, it is native to the mountains of southern Europe. English lavender is the hardiest, most widely planted species. In cold-winter Zones 2 and 3, it is short-lived, lasting only 3 to 5 years, but in milder climates it can live 10 years or more. Most varieties are fairly low growing, forming mounds of foliage from 8 in. to 2¹/₂ ft. tall and wide. Leaves are narrow, smooth-edged, gray-green or silvery gray to 2 in. long. Unbranched flower stems rise 4–12 in. above foliage and are topped with 1- to 4-in.-long spikes of flowers in white, pink, lavender-blue, or various shades of purple. It blooms mainly from early to midsummer, but some varieties repeat in late summer or fall.

'Hidcote' was originally selected for its deep violet flowers and medium green foliage on a plant 1¹/₂–2 ft. tall and wide. The plants sold under this name today are frequently grown from seed; they may bear gray foliage and/or vary in size from the original. 'Hidcote Blue' (with

English lavender in full bloom

deep blue flowers) and 'Hidcote Superior' (compact, uniform, 16 in. tall and 18 in. wide) are popular selections. 'Munstead' is another classic; the original is 1¹/₂ ft. tall and 2 ft. wide, with bright lavender-blue flowers and medium green foliage. This long bloomer makes a good low hedge. Like those of 'Hidcote', seed-grown selections of 'Munstead' are quite variable.

Lavandin (*L. × intermedia*). Zones 4–24. This sterile cross between English lavender and spike lavender *(L. latifolia)* has been long used in the perfume and soap industries. Lavandins are vigorous plants that grow 2¹/₂–4 ft. tall and wide, with branching stems topped with interrupted flower spikes that appear from mid- to late summer. They are nearly as hardy as their English lavender parent, and are more tolerant of warm, humid summers.

Continued on page 112 ▶

Pick lavender in midbloom; dry in bundles to preserve.

'Grosso' has the classic lavender scent. It grows 2 1/2 ft. tall and wide, sports violet-blue blossoms that don't fall off in drying, and stays darkest after drying. It often produces a second round of bloom in late summer. 'Provence' has light violet flowers, grows 2 ft. tall and 3 ft. wide, and is the sweetest-smelling lavandin.

HOW TO GROW IT

best site The more sun these plants receive, the more they'll bloom.

soil Soil can be poor, rocky, and a bit alkaline, but it must drain well. If mulching around plants to conserve moisture and keep down weeds, use pea gravel, decomposed granite, or sand rather than organic materials.

planting Though lavender seed is available, start with a cutting-grown plant to make sure it is true to type. *In containers:* Try one of the English lavenders in a big (18-in.-wide, 9-in.-deep) container.

spacing Plant 1–4 ft. apart, depending upon the mature width of the variety you choose.

water Little to moderate water the first year, then little water.

fertilizer Little or none. If soil is acid, apply lime each autumn.

pruning, training To keep plants neat and compact, shear back by one-third to one-half (even by two-thirds) every year immediately after bloom. If plants become woody and open in the center, remove a few of the oldest branches; take out more when new growth comes. If this doesn't work, dig up the plant and replace it.

harvest Pick wands in midbloom.

challenges Lavender is virtually pest-free.

Use lavender flowers sparingly to impart a floral flavor to cakes, custards, teas.

Lemon Grass

Cymbopogon citratus
Grass family *(Poaceae)*
PERENNIAL

🖊 **ZONES 12, 13, 16, 17, 23, 24**

☼ **FULL SUN**

💧 **REGULAR WATER**

All parts of this plant from India are strongly lemon-scented and widely used as an ingredient in Southeast Asian cooking. Clumps of ½- to 1-in.-wide leaves grow 3–4 ft. tall (or more) and 3 ft. wide. The bottom of each clump, composed of overlapping leaf bases, is nearly bulbous in appearance. Lemon grass can live over in the mildest-winter regions, but it's safer to pot up a division and keep it indoors or in a greenhouse over winter.

HOW TO GROW IT

best site Like most true grasses, this one does best in full sun.

soil Grows well in ordinary garden loam.

planting Plant seeds when available or divisions in spring after all danger of frost is past. Lemon grass grows at temperatures above 55°F/13°C. When temperatures drop below that, pot up a division and bring it indoors to extend the season. *In containers:* Grow it in a pot at least 16 in. wide and 6 in. deep.

spacing One plant can cover a 3-ft. circle.

water Regular water during active growth, then less.

fertilizer Requires little fertilizer.

harvest Cut off the thick, bulbous stems just above the crown (ground level). Only the bottom third of each stalk is used; the bigger, the better. Peel off the outer sheath and finely slice or pound the inner stem for salads or cooking. The sharp-edged blades (the upper part of the stems) are too tough to eat.

challenges This is a trouble-free plant.

Lemon grass does double duty as an ornamental.

Marjoram

Origanum species
Mint family *(Lamiaceae)*
PERENNIALS

✎ ZONES VARY BY SPECIES

☼ FULL SUN

◊ ● LITTLE TO MODERATE WATER

The oregano tribe includes several species called marjoram. The two most common culinary marjorams are listed here. Both produce tight clusters of small flowers that are especially attractive to bees and butterflies. They make good groundcovers, trailers that cascade over rocks or retaining walls, and hanging basket plants.

Italian or Sicilian marjoram (*Origanum* × *majoricum*). Zones 4–24. This sterile hybrid is probably a cross between oregano and sweet marjoram. Similar to the latter, but with greater winter-hardiness and wider, greener leaves. Some gourmet cooks consider this the best marjoram for seasoning.

Sweet or knotted marjoram (*O. majorana, Majorana hortensis*). Zones 8–24; summer annual anywhere. Native to the Mediterranean and Turkey. To 1–2 ft. tall and wide. Oval gray-green leaves to ³/₄ in. long. Inconspicuous white flowers emerge from clusters of knotlike heads at the top of the plant. Fresh or dried leaves are used for seasoning meats, scrambled eggs, salads, vinegars, casseroles, and tomato dishes.

HOW TO GROW IT

best site Full sun, but give variegated varieties afternoon shade in hot-summer areas.

soil Marjoram is not fussy about soil type but needs good drainage.

planting Set out nursery plants anytime, or propagate by division or from cuttings taken before flower buds form. Sweet marjoram hybridizes freely, and seedlings may not resemble the parents. *In containers:* Often grown in pots indoors on a sunny windowsill in cold-winter areas.

spacing Plant 9 in. apart.

water Little to moderate water.

Sweet marjoram has a milder, more floral taste than oregano.

fertilizer Needs little fertilizer.

pruning, training Keep blossoms cut off and plant trimmed to encourage fresh growth. In milder climates, marjoram can become woody with age, but wood of previous seasons is seldom as productive as new growth from the base. For best results, cut previous year's stems to the ground in winter or early spring.

harvest Snip off leaves as you need them.

challenges This is a trouble-free plant.

Mint

Mentha species
Mint family *(Lamiaceae)*
PERENNIALS

✎ **ZONES VARY BY SPECIES**
☼ ☽ **FULL SUN OR PARTIAL SHADE**
💧 **REGULAR WATER**

Tough and unfussy, these Mediterranean natives grow almost anywhere but perform best with light, moist, medium-rich soil. Plants spread rapidly by underground stems and can be quite invasive; to keep them in bounds, grow them in pots or boxes. They disappear in winter in the colder part of their range. Replant about every 3 years; propagate from runners.

Apple mint (*Mentha suaveolens, M. rotundifolia*). Zones 3–24. Stiff stems grow 1½–3 ft. tall, bearing rounded, slightly hairy gray-green leaves 1–4 in. long. Purplish white flowers grow in 2- to 3-in. spikes. Foliage has scent combining fragrances of apple and mint. 'Variegata', or pineapple mint, has leaves with white markings and a faint scent of pineapple.

Golden apple mint (*M. × gracilis, M. × gentilis*). Zones 3–24. To 2 ft. tall. Smooth, deep green leaves with yellow variegation have a spicy apple fragrance and flavor. Inconspicuous flowers. Use in flavoring foods. Foliage is also excellent in mixed bouquets.

Orange or bergamot mint (*M. × piperita citrata*). Zones A2, A3, 1–24. To 2 ft. tall, with broad, 2-in.-long leaves that have a slight orange flavor when crushed. It is used in potpourri and for flavoring foods. 'Chocolate' is a popular variety.

Pennyroyal (*M. pulegium*). Zones 4–24. Creeping plant 4–16 in. tall, with inch-wide, bright green, nearly round leaves. Small lavender flowers grow in tight, short whorls. Strong mint fragrance and flavor. Poisonous if consumed in large quantities but safe as a flavoring. Needs a cool, moist site.

Peppermint (*M. × piperita*). Zones A2, A3, 1–24. To 3 ft. tall. Strongly scented, tooth-edged leaves to 3 in. long are dark green often tinged with purple. Small purplish flowers in 1- to 3-in. spikes. Good for flavoring tea.

Chocolate mint tastes like a peppermint patty.

Spearmint (*M. spicata*). Zones A2, A3, 1–24. To 1–3 ft. tall. Dark green, toothed leaves are slightly smaller than those of peppermint. Leafy spikes of pale blue flowers. Use leaves fresh or dried as flavoring for foods, cold drinks, or jelly. Leaves of *M. s. crispa* have curly margins. 'Kentucky Colonel' has large, flavorful leaves.

Continued on page 116 ▶

VJ BILLINGS ON
choice mints

Mint is used to flavor everything from tea to toothpaste. But not every mint will suit every use, says VJ Billings, owner of Mountain Valley Growers in Squaw Valley, CA. Billings, who specializes in growing mint varieties, believes in matching each mint with a specific purpose—"that's the beauty of growing your own."

Peppermint is the traditional "cup-of-tea mint," she says. "It has a very strong flavor, so should be dried first and used sparingly."

Spearmint has a lighter, sweeter flavor and can be used fresh in salads and iced drinks. "The best variety is 'Kentucky Colonel'," says Billings. "It's ideal for the traditional mint julep or the popular Cuban cocktail called mojito."

Curly mint has a nice stiff stem that doubles as a swizzle stick, and its leaves hold up well in a glass of iced tea or lemonade.

The "gray, fuzzy" apple mints are indispensable for adding a sweet, fresh top note to savory dishes. "Use a few leafy stems to scent and flavor roasts, chops, or casseroles as they cook; then just remove them before serving," says Billings.

'Kentucky Colonel' spearmint, a classic ingredient in summer drinks

HOW TO GROW IT

best site Full sun or partial shade.

soil Rich soil amended with organic matter.

planting *In containers:* Mint is best grown in separate containers set on solid surfaces. Plants are just too successful in the open garden, spreading underground by runners and self-sowing wherever seeds drop. Avoid the temptation to plant more than one kind in the same pot or raised bed; they'll become hopelessly intertwined.

If you want mint to appear to be growing with other herbs in an open garden, plant it in a pot and sink the container to its rim in the ground, and weed out mint seedlings as they appear.

spacing In most containers, one plant will do. In large containers or raised beds, plant at 1- to 2-ft. intervals; plants fill in quickly.

water Regular water is optimal.

fertilizer Apply complete fertilizer as growth begins each spring.

harvest Snip off tender new growth as needed. Older growth becomes woody.

challenges Invasiveness.

Oregano

Origanum vulgare
Mint family *(Lamiaceae)*
PERENNIAL

✎ ZONES VARY BY KIND
☼ FULL SUN, EXCEPT AS NOTED
◌ ◖ LITTLE TO MODERATE WATER

These popular "pizza herbs" grow well in rocky soils with good drainage and plenty of sun. Most plants grow 1–2$\frac{1}{2}$ ft. tall with a spread of up to 3 ft., but some dwarf forms are available too. Leaves average 1–1$\frac{1}{2}$ in. long, and tiny summer flowers are usually pink-tinged white or purple. Bees and butterflies love them.

For information on other *Origanum* species used as herbs, see *Marjoram*.

Greek oregano (*Origanum vulgare hirtum, O. heracleoticum*). Zones 8, 9, 12–24. From Greece, Turkey, and the Aegean Islands. Like oregano, but with broader, fuzzy gray-green leaves that have a spicy, pungent flavor.

Oregano, wild marjoram (*O. vulgare*). Zones 1–24. Native to Europe and temperate Asia. Oval, dark green leaves grow to 1$\frac{1}{2}$ in. long and $\frac{3}{4}$ in. wide. Fresh or dried leaves are used in many dishes, especially Spanish and Italian ones.

Most wild forms have scentless leaves; be sure to choose a selected form with a good aroma and a flavor you like. For best flavor, keep plant trimmed to prevent flowering, but let some clumps bloom for bees and butterflies to enjoy. 'Aureum' has bright golden foliage in spring (with morning sun), turning to green by late summer and fall; 'Thumble's Variety' is similar. 'Aureum Crispum' has curly golden leaves. 'Compactum' ('Humile') is a wide-spreading plant just a few inches tall, suitable for a groundcover or between paving stones. 'Country Cream' and 'White Anniversary' are compact growers to 4–6 in. tall and have leaves with a distinct creamy white edge; both are sometimes sold as 'Variegatum'.

HOW TO GROW IT

best site Full sun except for colored-leaf varieties, which can burn in afternoon sun in hot-summer areas.

soil Not fussy about soil type but needs good drainage.

planting Set out nursery plants anytime or propagate by division or from cuttings taken before flower buds form. *In containers:* Can be container-grown in a sunny

Oregano is flavorful fresh or dried.

spot indoors or on a patio. Choose a compact variety for a pot at least 6 in. tall and wide.

spacing Plant 18 in. apart.

water Little to moderate water.

fertilizer Fertilize once at transplanting, and once every spring for established plants.

pruning, training Keep blossoms cut off and the plant trimmed to encourage fresh growth. In milder climates, oregano can become woody with age; for best results, cut previous year's stems to the ground in winter or early spring.

harvest Snip fresh leaves as needed. For freezing or drying, pick leaves just before flower buds open.

challenges This is a trouble-free plant.

Parsley

Petroselinum crispum
Carrot family (*Apiaceae*)
BIENNIAL GROWN AS ANNUAL

✎ ALL ZONES
☼ ◑ AFTERNOON SHADE IN HOTTEST CLIMATES
● REGULAR WATER

Parsley hails from southern Europe. Three kinds are commonly grown: two for their finely cut dark green leaves that are used as a seasoning (both fresh and dried), and one for its roots. Fresh sprigs and minced leaves are classic garnishes. Parsley is also an attractive edging for herb, flower, or vegetable gardens, and good in window boxes and pots.

Curly-leafed French parsley (*Petroselinum crispum crispum*). Grows to 6–18 in. tall and wide. Makes the most attractive garnish. 'Moss Curled' and 'Forest Green' are excellent varieties.

Flat-leafed Italian parsley (*P. c. neapolitanum*). Grows 1½–3 ft. tall and 2 ft. wide. Considered the most flavorful parsley. Standards include 'Dark Green Italian', 'Giant Italian', and 'Single Italian'.

Parsley root (*P. c. tuberosum*). This longer-season parsley (110 days to harvest, about a month longer than leaf parsley) produces a 5- to 8-in.-long white taproot, which is used like carrot in soups and stews. Look for 'Arat' and 'Hamburg'.

HOW TO GROW IT

best site Full sun in mild climates, partial shade where summers are hot.

soil Well-amended, fertile soil is optimal.

planting Parsley is best started fresh each year. Set out small plants or sow seeds in place in spring after average last-frost date in cold-winter climates; in fall or early spring where winters are mild; and in early fall in the low desert. Soak seeds in warm water for 24 hours before planting. (Even after soaking, they may not come up for several weeks.) Three plants of each kind should be sufficient for most gardens. If you use a lot of parsley, sow spring and summer crops.

In containers: All types will grow in containers, and curly-leafed kinds can even grow in a sunny window. Use at least a 6-in.-wide, 8-in.-deep container for curly-leafed parsley; and a 10- to 12-in.-wide, 10-in.-deep container for flat-leafed parsley or parsley root.

Flat-leafed Italian parsley is more flavorful than the curly-leafed kind.

spacing Thin seedlings to 1–1½ ft. apart for flat-leafed parsley or parsley root, 6–8 in. apart for curly-leafed parsley; or space plants at these distances.

water Keep evenly moist.

fertilizer One application of complete fertilizer in spring is enough.

harvest Harvest sprigs from the outside of the plant so that those on the inside will keep coming. Parsley freezes well but doesn't dry well.

challenges If carrot rust flies and aphids are problems in your garden, protect your parsley with a row cover.

Rosemary

Rosmarinus officinalis
Mint family *(Lamiaceae)*
EVERGREEN SHRUB

✿ ZONES 4–24, H1, H2; AS ANNUAL ELSEWHERE
☼ FULL SUN
◊ 🌢 LITTLE TO MODERATE WATER

The genus name, *Rosmarinus*, means "dew of the sea," a reference to the plant's native habitat on seaside cliffs in the Mediterranean region. This tough plant grows most luxuriantly just above the tide line, braving wind and salt spray—but it will also thrive inland, even enduring blistering sun and poor alkaline soil if given moderate water and infrequent light feeding. Leaves are widely used as a seasoning, but flavor and fragrance vary; the best have a mildly pungent flavor and a complex aroma with sweet as well as resinous notes. Rosemary is also used in medicines, cosmetics, potpourri, and moth repellents. Even the flowers are edible; add them to salads or use them as a garnish.

Rosemary varies in growth habit from stiff, erect types through rounded shrubs and squat, dense tufts to rock-hugging creepers. Height ranges from as low as 1 ft. to as tall as 6 ft. or more. Plants are thickly clothed in narrow, typically 1- to 1½-in.-long, resinous, aromatic leaves that are usually glossy dark green above, grayish white beneath. Small clusters of ¼- to ½-in. flowers bloom through winter and spring in various shades of blue (rarely pink or white); bloom occasionally repeats in fall. Flowers attract birds, butterflies, and bees; they produce excellent honey.

Cold-hardiness depends on the selection. In general, upright varieties are hardier, while prostrate ones (originally from Majorca and Corsica) are more tender, suffering damage at 20°F/–7°C or even higher. In cold-winter areas, choose the hardiest types and shelter them from winter winds; in late fall, wrap upright growers in plastic sheeting (leaving tops uncovered) to prevent branches from breaking under the weight of snow. Note that even the hardiest types can succumb to cold if soil remains wet. Beyond its hardiness range, grow rosemary in pots and winter it indoors on a sunny windowsill or treat it as an annual.

Here's a sampling of the many named selections available. (Rosemary plants sold without names are frequently seedlings, which lack the uniformity of cutting-grown, named selections.)

'Arp'. The hardiest rosemary, taking temperatures as low as –10°F/–23°C. Open grower to 4 ft. tall and wide; best with frequent pruning.

Continued on page 120 ▶

An upright rosemary variety in bloom

'Barbecue'. Grows 4–6 ft. tall, half as wide. Stiff, straight stems make perfect skewers for kebabs.

'Blue Boy'. Young plant makes a dense, symmetrical mound 8–12 in. tall, 14–18 in. across. Pleasant fragrance and flavor. Tender.

'Blue Spires'. Strong vertical grower, to 5–6 ft. tall and as wide or wider with age. Superb landscape variety; makes tight sheared hedge. Excellent for seasoning.

'Gorizia'. Vigorous, rigidly upright, to 4–5 ft. tall and wide. Sweet, gingery fragrance.

'Huntington Carpet' ('Huntington Blue'). To 1¹/₂ ft. tall; spreads quickly yet maintains a dense center. Best variety for ground or bank cover.

'Irene'. Vigorous spreader that covers 2–3 ft. or more per year, eventually mounding to 1–1¹/₂ ft. tall and 8 ft. wide. Reputedly one of the most cold-hardy prostrate varieties.

'Prostratus'. To 2 ft. tall, with 4–8-ft. spread. Will trail straight down over a wall or edge of a raised bed to make a green curtain. Effective in hanging containers. Tender.

HOW TO GROW IT

best site Plant in an area that gets plenty of sun and is out of reach of sprinklers. If you garden in a cold-winter area, try a potted dwarf rosemary, like 'Blue Boy', in a window that gets maximum sun. Use taller types as clipped or informal hedges or in dry borders with native and gray-leafed plants. Lower kinds are good groundcovers or bank covers, useful for erosion control.

soil Good drainage is essential; lighten heavy soils with plenty of organic matter.

planting Start from container-grown nursery stock. Plant with the crown slightly above grade. *In containers:* Use a strong, upright rosemary as the focus of a large (at least 18-in.) container, and plant three trailing rosemary plants around the rim to spill over the sides.

spacing Set container-grown plants 2 ft. apart for moderately quick cover.

water Little water is needed after plants are established. Hose down plants occasionally to wash dust off leaves.

fertilizer One application of complete fertilizer in spring is sufficient.

pruning, training Control growth by frequent tip-pinching when plants are small. Prune older plants frequently but lightly; cut to side branch or shear. If plants become woody and bare in center, cut back selected branches by half so plant will fill in with new

Bundled rosemary cuttings ready to dry

growth (be sure to cut into leafy wood; plants will not regrow from bare wood). Or discard plant and start over with a new one. Branches root wherever they touch the ground; creeping types spread indefinitely, forming extensive colonies. To get new plants, root tip cuttings or dig and replant layered branches.

harvest Snip tender tip growth as needed.

challenges Too much water and fertilizer cause rank growth and subsequent woodiness.

Sage

Salvia officinalis
Mint family *(Lamiaceae)*
SHRUBBY PERENNIAL

⬜ **ZONES 2–24, H1, H2**
☀ ◑ **AFTERNOON SHADE IN HOTTEST CLIMATES**
◌ ◍ **LITTLE TO MODERATE WATER**

This Mediterranean native is the traditional culinary and medicinal sage. It grows to 1–3 ft. tall and wide; stems often root where they touch soil. Aromatic, oval to oblong, wrinkled, 2- to 3-in. leaves are gray-green above, white and hairy beneath. Branching, 8- to 12-in. stems bear loose, spikelike clusters of $^1/_2$-in. flowers in late spring and summer. The usual flower color is lavender-blue, but violet, red-violet, pink, and white forms exist. Hummingbirds and bees are attracted to sage. Look for the following named selections.

'Berggarten' ('Mountain Garden'). Compact; just 16 in. tall. Denser growth, rounder leaves, fewer flowers than species; may be longer-lived.

'Compacta' ('Nana', 'Minimus'). A half-size (or even smaller) version of the species, with narrower, closer-set leaves.

'Holt's Mammoth'. Leaves (4–5 in. long) used in making condiments; excellent flavor.

'Icterina'. Variegated gray-green leaves with golden border. Does not bloom.

'Purpurascens' ('Red Sage'). Leaves are flushed with red-violet when new and slowly mature to gray-green.

'Tricolor'. Gray-green leaves with irregular cream border; new foliage is flushed with purplish pink.

HOW TO GROW IT

best site Full sun is fine in cooler areas; provide afternoon shade in hottest climates. Plant sages in an area with good air circulation to help deter mildew and other fungal diseases.

soil Most require good drainage, especially in winter; waterlogged plants rarely make it through hard freezes. If soil is heavy, work in plenty of organic matter and apply a thick mulch of well-rotted compost.

planting Plant from nursery containers with the crown slightly above grade. Replace plants when woody or leggy (every 3 or 4 years). *In containers:* These do well in pots at least 12 in. wide and 8 in. deep—especially small ones like 'Berggarten'.

New leaves of sage are flushed with purplish pink.

spacing Plant at 1- to $2^1/_2$-ft. intervals, depending on variety.

water Moderate water the first year, then little to moderate water.

fertilizer One application of complete fertilizer when growth begins in spring is sufficient.

pruning, training Delay pruning until new leaves begin to unfurl in spring, then cut just above fresh growth; cutting into bare wood usually causes dieback.

harvest Pick leaves as needed; they're good fresh or dried.

challenges Subject to root rot where drainage is less than perfect.

Savory

Satureja species
Mint family *(Lamiaceae)*
ANNUAL AND PERENNIAL

✔ **ZONES VARY BY SPECIES**
☀ **FULL SUN**
💧 **MODERATE WATER**

Summer and winter savory are wonderfully fragrant Mediterranean natives that have been used in cooking since Roman times. Both have notes of mint and thyme, and both are favorites of honeybees.

Summer savory *(Satureja hortensis).* Annual. All zones. From southeastern Europe. Upright to 1½ ft., with loose, open habit. Aromatic, rather narrow leaves to 1½ in. long; use fresh or dried as seasoning for meats, fish, eggs, soups, beans, or vegetables. Whorls of tiny, delicate, pinkish white to rose flowers in summer.

Winter savory *(S. montana).* Shrubby perennial. Zones 3–11, 14–24. From southern Europe. To 15 in. tall, 2 ft. wide. Stiff, narrow to roundish leaves to 1 in. long; not as delicate in flavor as summer savory. Blooms profusely in summer, bearing whorls of small white to lilac flowers.

HOW TO GROW IT

best site A warm spot in full sun. Set out winter savory plants in a rock garden or as a dwarf clipped hedge in an herb garden.

soil Grow either savory in light, well-drained, organically enriched soil.

planting *Summer savory:* Sow seeds in place in spring; fall planting is possible in mild-winter climates. Seeds are very slow to germinate. *Winter savory:* Set out nursery starts in spring. *In containers:* Grow either kind in a pot at least 12 in. wide and 6 in. deep.

spacing Thin summer savory to 1–1½ ft. apart. Plant winter savory plants 1½ ft. apart.

water Moderate water. Both species tolerate occasional missed waterings.

fertilizer *Summer savory:* Amendment with composted manure and dolomitic lime at planting time is sufficient. *Winter savory:* It benefits from one application of complete fertilizer after growth begins in spring.

Winter savory's leaves have pepper and lemon scents.

pruning, training Cut back winter savory as needed to keep compact.

harvest Use leaves of either kind fresh or dried; clip winter savory at the start of the flowering season for drying.

challenges Neither savory tolerates consistently damp soil.

Scented Geranium

Pelargonium species
Geranium family (*Geraniaceae*)
SHRUBBY PERENNIALS

✎ ZONES 8, 9, 12–24; AS ANNUALS ELSEWHERE
☼ ◑ PARTIAL SHADE IN HOTTEST CLIMATES
💧💧 MODERATE TO REGULAR WATER

Though these are commonly called scented geraniums, they're actually pelargoniums. Many aromatic species, hybrids, and selections are available. Most grow 1–3 ft. tall, spreading as wide. Foliage scent is the main draw; clusters of small, typically white or rosy flowers are secondary in appeal. Leaves vary in shape from nearly round to finely cut and almost ferny; they range in size from minute to 4 in. across.

Common names usually refer to leaf fragrance: almond geranium (*Pelargonium quercifolium*), apple geranium (*P. odoratissimum*), lime geranium (*P. nervosum*), nutmeg geranium (*P. × fragrans* 'Nutmeg'), peppermint geranium (*P. tomentosum*). There are several rose geraniums, including *P. capitatum*, *P.* 'Charity', *P. graveolens*, and *P.* 'Lady Plymouth'. Lemon-scented types include *P. crispum* and *P.* 'Prince Rupert'.

Use fresh leaves of all types for flavoring jelly and iced drinks; use dried leaves in potpourri and sachets. All scented geraniums are good for herb gardens, edgings, the front of borders, window boxes, and hanging baskets. Peppermint geranium makes a good groundcover in frost-free gardens.

HOW TO GROW IT

best site Full sun where summers are mild; partial shade in hot-summer climates.

soil Plant in any good, fast-draining soil. Amend poor alkaline soil with plenty of organic matter.

planting Start from transplants (or get cuttings from a friend) and plant after danger of frost is past. *In containers:* These are naturals for pots anywhere; in fact, they bloom best when somewhat pot-bound. Potted plants can be placed where you can see their pretty flowers and brush against their fragrant leaves.

spacing One plant per 6-in. pot, up to 7 plants in an 18-in. container. In the ground, base spacing on the plants' expected mature size.

A variegated form of lemon-scented geranium

water Moderate to regular water.

fertilizer Scented geraniums growing in good garden soil need little fertilizer; those in light sandy soil should receive two or three applications of a balanced fertilizer during active growth.

pruning, training Remove faded flowers regularly to encourage new bloom. Pinch growing tips of young, small plants to force side branches.

harvest Pick leaves as needed.

challenges Though these are usually trouble-free, possible pests include aphids, whiteflies, and spider mites. Geranium (tobacco) budworms may be a problem in some areas; affected flowers look tattered or fail to open at all. Prevent or limit infestation by spraying plants with *Bacillus thuringiensis (Bt)*, available from almost any nursery or garden center.

Sweet Bay

Laurus nobilis
Laurel family *(Lauraceae)*
EVERGREEN TREE OR SHRUB

🖋 **ZONES 5–9, 12–24, H1, H2**

☼ ◑ **FULL SUN OR PARTIAL SHADE**

💧 **MODERATE WATER**

This Mediterranean native grows slowly to 12–40 ft. tall and wide. Its natural habit is compact and multistemmed with a broad base; the plant often resembles a gradually tapering cone. Leathery, 2- to 4-in.-long, dark green aromatic leaves are the traditional bay leaves of cookery. Clusters of small yellow spring flowers are followed by black or dark purple $^1/_2$- to 1-in. fruit.

'Saratoga' has broader leaves and a more treelike habit. Willow-leafed bay, *Laurus nobilis angustifolia,* is a graceful plant well suited to containers. All forms take well to clipping into standards, hedges, or topiary shapes such as globes and cones.

HOW TO GROW IT

best site Full sun or partial shade. Dense habit makes sweet bay a good large background shrub, screen, or small tree (though trees eventually will be large). If you live in a cold-winter climate and grow sweet bay in a container, move it to a greenhouse or cool, well-lighted room when temperatures drop to about 20°F/–7°C.

soil Not fussy about soil but needs good drainage.

planting Plant sweet bay from a nursery pot at any time of year in mild weather. *In containers:* In areas too cold for growing it in the ground, grow sweet bay in an 18-in. box or pot. It will do well for several years, but will eventually need root pruning to remain small.

spacing In the ground, give sweet bay at least a 15-ft.-diameter circle, or space hedge plants 15 ft. apart.

water Regular water for the first summer after planting, then moderate water.

fertilizer An annual springtime application of complete fertilizer is sufficient.

Sweet bay dries well, but fresh-picked leaves have a stronger flavor.

pruning, training If you want a more treelike shape, prune out suckers as they appear, or grow 'Saratoga'. In late winter or early spring, prune for shape.

harvest Pick young leaves as you need them.

challenges Subject to black scale and laurel psyllid ('Saratoga' is resistant to psyllid).

Tarragon

Artemisia dracunculus
Sunflower family *(Asteraceae)*
PERENNIAL

✎ **ZONES A1–A3, 2B–10, 14–24**
☼ **FULL SUN**
💧💧 **MODERATE TO REGULAR WATER**

There are two common forms of this plant, which is native to central and eastern Europe and southern Russia, and the distinction is important for culinary purposes.

Cut sprigs in early summer for seasoning vinegar. Use fresh or dried leaves to season salads or cooked dishes. Plants in all zones die to the ground in winter.

French tarragon (may be labeled 'Sativa') is a sprawling, largely flowerless plant with shiny dark green, aromatic, flavorful leaves. It slowly spreads by creeping rhizomes, the stems becoming slightly woody and the whole plant remaining less than 2 ft. tall. It makes an attractive container subject.

Russian tarragon (may be labeled 'Inodorus') is a less desirable plant, lacking the characteristic flavor and aroma of true tarragon; it has upright, branching growth to about 3 ft. tall and small white flowers. Any seeds you find for sale will be for this culinarily inferior Russian tarragon.

HOW TO GROW IT

best site Full sun; tolerates light shade in hot-summer climates.

soil Rich, well-drained soil.

planting Plant in the open garden from plants only, never from seed. *In containers:* Plant in an 8-in.-deep pot.

spacing Set plants at 2-ft. intervals.

water Moderate to regular water, but be sure to let plants dry out between waterings.

fertilizer Apply complete fertilizer during spring growth and again after major harvests.

pruning, training Divide every 3 or 4 years to keep plants vigorous. Propagate by divisions or cuttings.

harvest Pick leaves as needed.

challenges Snails and slugs find young leaves attractive. Bait or handpick to control them.

French tarragon, the classic for flavoring chicken dishes

Thyme

Thymus species
Mint family *(Lamiaceae)*
SHRUBBY PERENNIALS

☘ **ZONES 1–24**
☼ ☽ **PARTIAL SHADE IN HOTTEST CLIMATES**
◊ ◖ **LITTLE TO MODERATE WATER**

Thymes are diminutive Mediterranean members of the mint family with tiny, usually heavily scented leaves and masses of little flowers in whorls. All forms, but especially compact ones, are well suited to herb or rock gardens. Prostrate, mat-forming types make good small-space groundcovers. Thyme is attractive to bees. Use leaves fresh or dried for seasoning fish, shellfish, poultry stuffing, soups, or vegetables.

Caraway-scented thyme *(Thymus herba-barona).* Fast-growing to 2–4 in. tall, 2 ft. wide or more; stems root as they spread. Forms a dense mat of wiry stems set with widely spaced oval and pointed to lance-shaped, dark green leaves with caraway fragrance. Clusters of rose-pink flowers in midsummer.

Common thyme *(T. vulgaris).* Variable plant to 1 ft. tall, 2 ft. wide, with narrow to oval, gray-green leaves. White to lilac flowers in late spring, early summer. Low edging for flower, vegetable, or herb garden. Good container plant. 'Argenteus', called silver thyme, has leaves variegated with silver. 'Hi-Ho' has even more pronounced silver variegation and is more compact. 'Italian Oregano Thyme' has a strong oregano flavor. 'Orange Balsam' has narrow, orange-scented leaves.

Lemon thyme *(T. × citriodorus).* Variable hybrid with erect or spreading growth to 1 ft. tall, 2 ft. wide. Ovate to lance-shaped, medium green leaves with lemon fragrance. Pale lilac flowers in summer. Leaves of 'Argenteus' are splashed with silver, those of 'Aureus' with gold. 'Lime' has lime green foliage. 'Doone Valley', with yellow-spotted leaves, reaches only 5 in. tall.

HOW TO GROW IT

best site Full sun in mild climates; partial shade where summers are hot.

soil Light, well-drained soil.

planting Start from small nursery plants in spring. *In containers:* Thyme thrives in small pots (6 to 12 in. tall and wide) on patios or windowsills.

Silver thyme makes a fine edging for a path, where sprigs are easily harvested.

spacing Plant at 1-ft. intervals.

water Moderate water to get new plants through the first summer, then little water.

fertilizer You'll never need to fertilize this plant.

pruning, training Shear or cut back established plants to keep them compact. Easy to propagate from cuttings taken in early summer.

harvest Snip off branch tips as needed.

challenges Small patches of thyme may die out after a few years, requiring replanting.

CHAPTER 3

Berries

Berry plants are easy to fit into the garden. Train vining types along a fence and grow blueberries in large half-barrels. Strawberries thrive in pots or baskets or as ground-covers in sunny spots. Berries taste as tangy-sweet when dried as they do when preserved in jams and syrups or baked into breads and muffins.

Blackberry

Rubus species
Rose family *(Rosaceae)*
DECIDUOUS VINES

✎ **ZONES VARY BY VARIETY**
☀ **FULL SUN**
💧 **REGULAR WATER**

Most blackberry varieties are derived from *Rubus* species native to North America. The West has its own varieties, most of which are trailing vines; these include 'Boysen', 'Logan', 'Marion', and 'Olallie', often simply called boysenberry, loganberry, and so on. Midwestern and eastern blackberries are upright and stiff caned; these erect plants are generally hardier and easier to protect in winter (with a thick mulch) than trailing types. Crosses between trailing and erect blackberries are termed semierect.

All kinds of blackberries bear fruit in summer, and a couple of everbearing varieties bear fruit in fall as well. All are self-fruitful.

Some varieties can be grown in the desert, though plants may be short-lived. For best results, amend soil generously with organic matter and provide frequent water, heavy mulch, and protection from wind and intense afternoon sun.

Keep down weeds and pull out suckers; above all, don't let plants get away from you. Some of the varieties available in Western nurseries are listed below. Combine early, midseason, and late varieties to get fresh fruit over the longest possible season.

'Arapaho'. Erect; midseason. Zones 1–24. Thornless, disease-resistant selection. Big crop of medium-size, firm, tasty berries. 'Apache', 'Navaho', and 'Oauchita' are similar thornless varieties; 'Chickasaw', 'Choctaw', 'Kiowa', and 'Shawnee' are also similar but have thorns. All thrive in hot-summer climates and are easy to grow without a trellis.

'Black Satin'. Erect; midseason. Zones 1–24. Thornless hybrid, possibly of *R. laciniatus.* Berries are very large, juicy, and sweet. Heavy producer; nonsuckering. Good disease resistance.

'Boysen' and 'Thornless Boysen'. Trailing; midseason. Zones 2–24; not reliably hardy in Zone 1 but will survive winter if canes are left on the ground and covered with snow or straw mulch. Popular for high yield and flavor. This fruit, propagated from a plant collected at the abandoned farm of Rudolph Boysen in 1923, put Knott's Berry Farm on the map. Its lineage includes 'Logan' berry,

raspberry, and blackberry. Very large berries are reddish (covered with a dusty bloom that slightly dulls color), soft, and sweet-tart, with a delightful aroma. They can be used fresh, cooked, or frozen. 'Nectar' is identical.

'Brazos'. Erect; early. Zones 4–24. Disease-resistant, thorned selection that is well adapted to hot-summer areas. Large, fairly firm, tart fruit.

'Cherokee'. Erect; early. Zones 1–24. Thorned cross between 'Darrow' and 'Brazos' blackberries. Medium-large, firm berries with excellent flavor. Resists anthracnose.

'Chester'. Semierect; late. Zones 2–9, 14–24. Medium-size, firm berries with good flavor. Late ripening, greatly extending season. Thornless; very cold-tolerant.

'Dirkson'. Semierect; midseason. Zones 2–9, 14–24. High yield of large, semitart berries. Thornless; resistant to anthracnose, leaf spot, and powdery mildew.

'Evergreen' and 'Thornless Evergreen' *(R. laciniatus).* Trailing; late. Zones 4–6, 8, 9, 12, 13, 20–24. Probably from Europe. Strong canes bear a heavy crop of large, exceptionally firm, black, sweet berries with large seeds. Leaves are divided into fives, then cut again into ferny subdivisions. Canes can last for years; thus the name "evergreen." Like Himalayan blackberry, 'Evergreen' is often seen along roadsides.

Himalayan blackberry *(R. armeniacus, R. discolor, R. procerus).* Trailing; midseason. Zones 1–6, 8, 9, 12–24. Though native to Armenia, this thorned species grows anywhere moisture is available. An aggressive spreader, it is hard to control and should be kept out of gardens. Nevertheless, its fruit is so tasty that roadside colonies are often picked clean. Because road crews sometimes control encroaching berry patches with toxic herbicides, pick fruit only from healthy canes that are well away from the road.

'Logan' and 'Thornless Logan'. Trailing; early. Zones 2–24. Probably a hybrid of Pacific dewberry *(R. ursinus)* and raspberry *(R. idaeus).* Large berries are light red, not darkening when ripe, with fine hairs that dull the fruit's color. More tart than 'Boysen'; excellent for canning and pies.

'Marion'. Trailing; midseason. Zones 4–9, 14–24. Developed from a cross of 'Chehalem' and 'Olallie' berries. This berry's rich, flavorful fruit sets the standard. Thorny canes can grow 10 ft. in a season but are commonly controlled by pruning and trellising. Similar types include 'Black Diamond', a thornless variety; late-ripening thornless 'Waldo', with berries that maintain their shape when cooked; and 'Black Butte', 'Silvan', and 'Siskiyou', all thorned early ripeners with excellent flavor.

Continued on page 130 ▶

Thornless 'Black Satin' blackberries produce for up to two months.

'Kotata' bears firm, sweet berries in midseason.

'Olallie'. Trailing; early. Zones 4–9, 14–24. A USDA cross of 'Logan' and 'Young' berries that's about one-third raspberry, two-thirds blackberry. Berries are medium to large, shiny black, and firm, with a sweet flavor that has some wild blackberry sprightliness. Thorny canes can grow 10 ft. in a season but are commonly controlled by pruning and trellising.

'Prime Jan'. Erect; everbearing. Zones 4–6, 16, 17. Like everbearing raspberries, this thorned hybrid developed from 'Arapaho' bears on new canes in late summer and second-year canes in spring. Can be cut to the ground each winter, resulting in a single late crop the following season. Very productive. Medium-size, sweet-tart berries. 'Prime Jim' is similar.

'Tay' or 'Tayberry'. Trailing; early. Zones 4–9, 14–24. Hybridized from a blackberry and a raspberry. Heavy bearer of big, mild-flavored, dark red to purple-black fruit. Long, thorny canes. Bears earlier than most other blackberries.

'Triple Crown'. Semierect; late. Zones 1–9, 14–24. This USDA selection is an improved 'Chester' type with large,

very flavorful berries. Vigorous, thornless canes. Hardy. 'Hull' is similar but not as tasty.

'Young' and 'Thornless Young'. Trailing; midseason. Zones 2–24, but does best in Southern California. Hybrid between 'Phenomenal' blackberry and Pacific dewberry *(R. ursinus).* Berries are the same size and color as 'Boysen' but shiny and somewhat sweeter.

HOW TO GROW IT

best site Choose an open, sunny location; a little shade is acceptable but not advised, except in the desert. Don't locate plants where they will be standing in water during dormancy. In cold-winter areas, plant on a slight slope where cold air will drain downhill.

yield *Trailing blackberries:* 10 to 13 pounds per plant. *Erect blackberries:* 4 to 6 pounds per plant. *Semierect blackberries:* 25 to 55 pounds per plant.

soil Deep, well-drained soil.

planting In mild-winter regions, plant bare-root blackberries in winter or early spring. In cold-winter regions, plant after the last hard freeze, when the soil begins to warm. Set bare-root plants an inch deeper than they grew at the nursery, covering their crowns with 1 in. of soil. During the growing season, you can buy blackberries as container plants. Plant in well-amended soil and water them in well.

spacing Rows should be 10 ft. apart for all blackberries. Plant trailing blackberries 5–8 ft. apart, erect blackberries 2–2½ ft. apart, and semierect blackberries 5–6 ft. apart.

water Apply regular moisture throughout the growing season.

fertilizer Fertilize established plantings in the Pacific Northwest at blossom time. In California, split the yearly amount into three applications: before new growth starts, in midspring, and in midsummer. Elsewhere, fertilize just before new growth begins (rapidly swelling buds will tip you off).

pruning, training Blackberry roots are perennial, but the canes of most are biennial; they develop and grow one year, bloom and fruit the next. The distinction between first- and second-year canes is important in the training and pruning instructions that follow.
　　Trailing and semierect types: Allow canes to grow unrestricted their first season, then train year-old canes fanwise onto some kind of trellis the second season. After harvest, cut to the ground all canes that have fruited.

Canes of the current season—those growing beneath the trellis—should now be trained onto it. This can be done in fall or spring.

Prune both trailing and semierect blackberries in midsummer to maximize the following year's crop. Thin trailing varieties to 12 to 16 canes, pruning each to 6–8 ft. long; thin semierect types to 4 to 8 canes, pruning each to 5–6 ft. long. These shortened canes will produce side branches during the remainder of the growing season; cut them back to 1 ft. in early spring. New spring growth will produce small fruiting branches from those side branches.

Erect types: Tie them to wire strictly to help organize the canes—they don't need the support. In midsummer of the first year, cut canes to $2\frac{1}{2}$ ft. to force side growth. Late in the dormant season, cut resulting side branches to 12–15 in. After canes bear fruit in the second year, cut them to the ground. Start the process over again with new canes growing from the ground.

Though 'Prime Jan' and 'Prime Jim' are erect types, they are pruned differently because they are everbearing blackberries, producing two crops per season. The first berries appear in autumn on the top third of each first-year cane, and the second crop appears the following summer on the bottom two-thirds of each second-year cane. Pruning is done in stages. After the fall harvest, cut off the upper (just-harvested) portion of each cane; after the subsequent summer harvest, cut off the remainder of each cane that has fruited. As an easy alternative, you can cut all canes to the ground after fall fruiting has finished (wait until late in the dormant season in cold-winter regions). That sacrifices the first crop the following summer but produces an extended harvest from late summer into fall. Use a power mower to do the job if your berry patch is large.

harvest Pick when berries are full size, fully colored, and come off with a gentle breaking motion (rather than a pulling motion). Put harvested fruit in a shallow container, such as a trug, so bottom fruit won't be crushed.

challenges Blackberries are subject to many pests and diseases, including scale, borers, anthracnose, leaf spot, and powdery mildew, so start with healthy plants from a reputable supplier. Also look for resistant varieties. Because they are susceptible to verticillium wilt, do not plant blackberries where potatoes, tomatoes, eggplant, or peppers have grown in the prior 3 years. To control redberry mites (mostly affecting 'Evergreen' and 'Thornless Evergreen'), spider mites, and whiteflies, apply a dormant spray containing lime sulfur in winter and again as buds are about to break.

'Tayberry' canes wind around a post and down a wire trellis that gives access from both sides.

Blueberry

Vaccinium species
Heath family *(Ericaceae)*
DECIDUOUS SHRUBS

ZONES VARY BY TYPE

☼ **FULL SUN**

♦ **AMPLE WATER**

Blueberries are native to eastern North America. Most types grown for their fruit are also handsome plants suitable for hedges or shrub borders. They thrive under conditions that suit rhododendrons and azaleas, to which they are related. Leaves, to 3 in. long, are bronze when new, maturing to dark green and turning scarlet or yellow in fall. Tiny urn-shaped spring flowers are white or pinkish. Summer fruit is decorative.

All kinds of blueberries have fine roots near the soil surface. A 3- to 4-in.-thick layer of mulch will protect roots, help conserve soil moisture, and keep weeds down. Don't disturb the roots by cultivating around plants.

The following are the major types of blueberries grown. Plants are available bare-root or in containers. Though many blueberries (especially northern highbush) are fully or partially self-fruitful, grow at least two different varieties of each type for better pollination, bigger berries, and superior production, choosing kinds that ripen at different times for a long harvest.

Highbush blueberries. These are the blueberries found in grocery stores. Most varieties grow upright to 6 ft. or more; a few are rather sprawling and under 5 ft. The majority are northern varieties (*Vaccinium corymbosum* selections; Zones 2–9, 14–17); they require definite winter cold and fruit ripens from late spring to late summer. The relatively new southern highbush varieties (hybrids between *V. darrowii* and *V. corymbosum;* Zones 8, 9, 14–24) are better adapted to mild-winter climates and are even finding success in Southern California; in those regions, their fruit ripens in mid- to late spring, even before rabbiteye types. Except as noted, varieties below are northern types.

'Berkeley'. Midseason. Open, spreading, tall. Large, light blue berries.

'Bluecrop'. Midseason. Erect, tall growth. Large berries. Excellent flavor. Attractive shrub.

'Blueray'. Midseason. Vigorous, tall. Large, highly flavored, crisp berries. Attractive shrub. Tolerates more heat than 'Bluecrop'.

'Chandler'. Midseason to late. Tall, upright. Very large, sweet berries produced over a long season.

'Darrow'. Late. Vigorous, upright. Very large fruit, up to the size of a quarter. Heavy producer.

'Bluecrop' blueberries are ready for picking when plump and frosty light blue.

'Earliblue'. Early. Tall, erect. Large, heavy leaves. Large berries of excellent flavor.

'Elliott'. Late. Tall, upright. Medium to large berries of excellent flavor.

'Ivanhoe'. Early to midseason. Grows 6–8 ft. tall and wide. Large, dark berries are firm, crisp, tart.

'Jubilee'. Southern highbush. Early. Tall, upright. Medium to large berries with excellent flavor.

'Legacy'. Late. Upright, arching. Unusual shrub that doesn't lose its leaves in winter. Medium-size berries with fine flavor.

'Misty'. Southern highbush. Very early. Vigorous, upright. Large berries with excellent flavor. Bears heavily.

'Olympia'. Midseason. Vigorous, arching. Medium-size fruit with exceptional, spicy flavor. Large bush has great fall color.

'O'Neal'. Southern highbush. Very early. Upright. Large, flavorful berries.

'Rubel'. Early to late. Erect, tall. Small, firm, tart berries.

'Sharpblue'. Southern highbush. Early to midseason. Fast-growing, spreading habit to 4–6 ft. tall and wide. Large, light blue berries with sweet-tart flavor.

Continued on page 134 ▶

Though yields vary among varieties, most blueberries are prolific producers.

'Bluecrop', a northern highbush variety with large, tasty berries

When ripe, blueberries can be pulled from the bush with just a light touch.

'Southmoon'. Southern highbush. Midseason. Upright, to 4–6 ft. tall. Large, bright blue berries with excellent flavor.

'Spartan'. Early. Vigorous, upright, to 7 ft. tall. Heavy bearer of large, flavorful fruit.

'Sunshine Blue'. Southern highbush. Midseason. Compact, evergreen shrub grows only 3 ft. tall, making an attractive landscape plant. Large, light blue berries with tangy flavor. Self-fertile. Very low chilling requirement. Tolerates a higher soil pH than most other blueberries.

'Top Hat'. Midseason. Dwarf hybrid under 1½ ft. tall. Small fruit with mild flavor. Good for containers.

'Toro'. Midseason. To 6 ft. tall and wide. Large, firm berries with an excellent, sprightly flavor.

Rabbiteye blueberries. Zones 8, 9, 14–24. These selections of *V. virgatum (V. ashei)* are native to the southeastern U.S. and do best in central California, Southern California, and other mild-winter areas if given acid soil conditions. Unlike most blueberries, these tolerate heat. They are also often taller (4½–12 ft.) and rangier than highbush plants, though size can be kept in check with pruning. Large, light blue berries ripen from May to July (late summer and fall in western Oregon). Quality is not as good as that of highbush blueberries.

'Bluebelle'. Midseason. Upright, vigorous. Starts producing when the plant is young and bears its large, light blue, flavorful berries over a long season.

'Southland'. Late midseason. Dense, compact, vigorous. Medium-large, firm, light blue, flavorful fruit.

'Tifblue'. Late midseason. Upright, vigorous. Bears heavy crops of small, very light blue berries. Flavor and fruit quality are only fair; use as a pollinator.

Hardy half-high varieties. Zones A2, A3, 1–3. Highbush blueberries have been hybridized with the northeastern

Birds are a blueberry lover's biggest challenge; use netting to keep them away from the fruit.

U.S. native lowbush blueberry *(V. angustifolium)* to create very hardy types called half-high blueberries. They are bred to be short so they can be protected by snow during harsh winters. Good in containers.

'Chippewa'. Midseason. Upright, to 4 ft. tall and 5 ft. wide. Large, light blue fruit with excellent sweet flavor.

'Northblue'. Midseason to late. Grows 3–4 ft. tall and 5 ft. wide. Large, firm, dark blue berries with trace of wild blueberry flavor.

'Northcountry'. Early midseason. Grows 1^1/$_2$–3 ft. tall and 2^1/$_2$–5 ft. wide. Sweet, very light blue berries.

'Northsky'. Midseason to late. Dense, to 1–1^1/$_2$ ft. tall. Light blue berries with hint of wild blueberry flavor.

'Polaris'. Early. Upright, arching, to 4 ft. tall. Light blue fruit with delightful flavor.

'St. Cloud'. Early. To 3–4 ft. tall and 3^1/$_2$–5 ft. wide. Large, firm, flavorful berries.

HOW TO GROW IT

best site Full sun in a spot that gives access to the plants from all sides for easy harvest.

yield For sufficient fruit throughout the season, allow two plants for each household member. *Hardy half-high:* 2 to 8 pounds per plant. *Highbush and rabbiteye:* 7 to 12 pounds per plant (some old, well-maintained rabbiteyes can produce 20 pounds per plant).

soil Must be cool, moist, well drained, and acidic (pH 4.5 to 5.5). If your soil isn't acid, amend it with peat.

planting Plant in early spring in cold-winter regions, autumn in mild climates. Position the crown no deeper than ^{1}/$_2$ in. below the ground. *In containers:* Grow small kinds in containers at least 18 in. deep and wide, larger ones in half-barrels.

spacing Set plants about 3 ft. apart for an informal hedge; as individual shrubs, space at least 4–5 ft. apart.

water During the first 3 years, give plants a deep soaking—the equivalent of 1 in. of rain—every week during the growing season. In subsequent years, keep plants moist during the growing season but don't subject them to standing water. Avoid overhead irrigation, which can encourage mildew on leaves and gray mold (botrytis) on fruit.

fertilizer Don't fertilize at all the first year, and feed only lightly the second and third years. After that, fertilize once per year in early spring with an acid-forming complete fertilizer. California growers in particular may need to correct chlorosis with iron sulfate or iron chelate.

pruning, training Prune to prevent overbearing. Plants shape themselves but often produce so many fruit buds that berries are undersize and plant growth slows down. Keep first-year plants from bearing by stripping off flowers. On older plants, cut back the ends of twigs to the point where fruit buds are widely spaced. Or simply remove some of the oldest branches each year. Also prune out all weak shoots.

harvest Pick when fruit tastes sweet (some kinds color up before they sweeten up).

challenges Plants seldom have serious problems requiring regular control in home gardens. Netting will keep birds at bay.

Currant and Gooseberry

Ribes species
Currant family *(Grossulariaceae)*
DECIDUOUS SHRUBS

✎ ZONES A1–A3, 1–6, 15–17, EXCEPT AS NOTED
☼ ◑ SOME SHADE IN HOTTEST CLIMATES
💧 REGULAR WATER

These are closely related, many-stemmed shrubs to 3–5 ft. tall and wide, depending on vigor and variety. They have attractively lobed, toothed leaves. The currant plant is thornless, with leaves that drop early in autumn, sometimes turning bright red, orange, or yellow first. Gooseberry is often thorny, and has leaves that usually turn bright colors before they fall. Drooping flower clusters of both bloom in early spring, followed in late spring or summer by fruit. Most currants and gooseberries are self-fruitful.

Gooseberry and currant may host white pine blister rust. Both plants are banned in some areas where white pines grow; check with your Cooperative Extension Office or a local nursery for regulations in your area.

Black currants. Mostly derived from *Ribes nigrum* (from Europe and Asia) or *R. odoratum* (from central North America). These have rich, pungent flavor and are good in jams and preserves. Since they are the most-favored hosts of white pine blister rust, grow rust-immune hybrids such as 'Consort', 'Crandall', 'Minaj Smyriou', and 'Titania'. 'Ben Sarek' has good-quality fruit on a compact, mildew- and rust-resistant plant.

Red and white currants. Derived from *R. sativum,* a western European native. These tart fruits are used mainly for jelly. Red-fruited varieties include 'Cherry', 'Jonkheer Van Tets', 'Red Lake', and 'Wilder'; white types include 'Blanca' and 'Primus'.

Gooseberries. Most are selections of *R. uva-crispa,* a native of Europe and Asia, and the American species *R. hirtellum* and *R. oxycanthoides.* They come in thorny and nearly spineless forms. Fruit is often decorative, marked with longitudinal stripes, and mostly used for pies and canning. 'Black Velvet' is a thorny, disease-resistant variety whose sweet dark red fruit has a hint of blueberry. 'Captivator' has large, teardrop-shaped, sweet pink fruit on an extra-hardy, mildew-resistant, nearly thornless plant. 'Friend' is a thornless Ukranian variety whose large, sweet pink fruit can be eaten fresh or used in pies and jams. 'Invicta' has large green fruit on a thorny bush resistant to mildew. 'Oregon Champion' is a thorny plant that bears a heavy crop of green fruit. Tart, pink-fruited 'Pixwell' is an extremely hardy, nearly thornless variety. 'Poorman' has red fruit that's sweet enough to eat fresh off the bush, though the skin is tart; it is less thorny than most other varieties.

Hybrids between black currants and gooseberries. Zones A3, 1–6, 15–17. These plants are less hardy than currants or gooseberries. The most well known is josta-berry, a disease-resistant, thornless hybrid whose black fruit tastes like a currant but isn't as astringent; it makes great jams and jellies. Another good hybrid is Oregon-bred 'Orus 8'. It resists mildew and aphids; produces medium-size, dark purple fruit; and can be eaten fresh or made into jelly or wine. It has some thorns.

HOW TO GROW IT

best site Full sun or partial shade (part shade is essential in hot-summer climates). Do not grow where water or soil is high in sodium.

yield 6 to 10 pounds per plant.

soil Loam or silt-loam with good drainage.

planting Fall planting is optimal, but winter planting is also good where the ground doesn't freeze. Mulch well. *In containers:* Grow in a container at least 15 in. deep and 18 in. wide.

spacing Allow 3–5 ft. per plant depending on the variety's size at maturity.

water Apply water deeply once a week during the growing season.

fertilizer If plants didn't grow strongly the previous season, feed with ammonium sulfate at the rate of 2 ounces per year of age, to a maximum of 8 ounces.

pruning, training Prune during dormant season. On gooseberries and red and white currants, cut stems older than 3 years to the ground; on black currants and hybrids, remove stems older than 2 years. Older canes are often darker and peeling.

harvest When all the fruit in a cluster has colored up, pick the whole cluster.

challenges Currant worms can defoliate both currant and gooseberry plants; control with *Bacillus thuringiensis (Bt).* The best defense against white pine blister rust and mildew is to plant resistant varieties.

Red currant's delicate fruit is ideal for jellies and preserves.

Grape

Vitis species
Grape family *(Vitaceae)*
DECIDUOUS VINES

✎ **ZONES VARY BY VARIETY**

☼ **FULL SUN**

💧 **MODERATE WATER**

Grapes are grown for fresh fruit, dried fruit (raisins), wine, shade, and fall color. A single grapevine can produce enough new growth every year to arch over a walk, roof an arbor, form a leafy wall, or provide an umbrella of shade over a deck or terrace. Grape is one of the few fruiting vines that looks good all year, offering bold-textured foliage from spring through fall, colorful edible fruit in summer, and a dominant trunk and branch pattern for winter interest. To produce good-quality fruit, you must choose a variety that suits your climate well, train it carefully, and prune it regularly.

European grapes *(Vitis vinifera).* These have tight skin, a generally high heat requirement, and cold tolerance to around 5°F/–15°C. They include the table grapes such as 'Thompson Seedless'. The classic wine grapes, such as 'Cabernet', 'Chardonnay', and 'Pinot Noir', are also European in origin. Production of European wine grapes has greatly increased in the Northwest, but the bulk of the commercial crop is grown in California. For more information about growing wine grapes in your region, consult your local Cooperative Extension Office.

American grapes. These stem from *V. labrusca,* with some influence from other American native species. They include slipskin grapes of the 'Concord' type, which have a moderate summer heat requirement and tolerate temperatures as low as –20° to –35°F/–40° to –31°C. American grapes are used in jelly, in unfermented grape juice, and as a flavoring for soft drinks; some wine, usually sweet, is also made from these grapes.

American hybrid grapes. American varieties crossed with European grapes, with a mix of their parents' characteristics. In general, these vines are almost as disease-resistant and hardy as American species (most will need protection below –15°F/–26°C), but the fruit is more like that of European grapes. Varieties called French hybrids—examples include 'Aurore', 'Baco Noir', 'Foch', and 'Seyval Blanc'—can be used for making wine in cold-winter climates. Consult your Cooperative Extension Office for varieties that will grow best locally.

'Cabernet Sauvignon', a classic European wine grape

Almost all grapes are self-fruitful and do not require pollination from another variety to bear fruit—but since they differ greatly in hardiness and heat requirements, choosing the right type and variety is important. Varieties listed in the accompanying chart are widely available and of high quality where adapted, but they represent only a small portion of what can be grown.

The Pacific Northwest is primarily American grape country, but European grapes grow well in the warmest parts of the Columbia River basin and the lower Willamette Valley. Regions of California and Arizona with a long warm season favor European varieties; California's coastal and inland valleys offer an ideal climate for most types. In short-season, high-elevation areas, choose either American or hardy European varieties, and plant in warm microclimates. If your climate is cooler or your growing season shorter than is desirable for grape growing, look for early-ripening varieties.

The popularity of European grapes, especially wine varieties, has led to their being tried beyond their normal range. In cold-winter climates, the crop may be ruined by spring frosts and summer rains in some years, but vines that are protected or planted in warm microclimates can produce harvestable fruit in other years. Even in Hawaii, European wine grapes are being successfully grown in some high-elevation areas. At lower elevations, where grapes are ravaged by the hard-to-control Chinese rose beetle, crops are rarely successful.

HOW TO GROW IT

best site Open sunny spot with plenty of room.

yield 7 to 30 pounds after the fourth year.

soil Moderately fertile loam with good drainage.

planting Plant year-old bare-root vines during the dormant season (winter in mild-winter regions, about 3 weeks before the last expected frost date in cold-winter areas). Trim roots to 6 in. just before planting in holes spaced 8–10 ft. apart. If planting at an arbor or fence, position each hole about 1½ ft. away from the structure and set the plant at a 45° angle so it leans toward the support. Cut back top growth to two or three buds. Place vines as deep in the soil as they grew in the nursery, spreading roots in all directions. In some areas, planting deeper, with all but the top bud buried, is recommended; check with a local nursery or Cooperative Extension Office. *In containers:* Plant in a wine half-barrel that's near a trellis, fence, or deck rail that the plant can grow on.

spacing Set grapevines 8–10 ft. apart.

water Water regularly. Grapes are prone to fungal diseases, so avoid splashing water on leaves; drip irrigation is ideal.

fertilizer Fertilize each spring with a balanced fertilizer; for newly planted vines, apply one-fourth the amount recommended on the bag, then gradually increase the amount each year until the fourth year, when you can start applying the full recommended dose each spring.

pruning, training Once they are established, grape-vines are rampant. If all you want is a leafy cover for an arbor or a patio with some fruit as a bonus, you need only train a strong vine up and over its support and thin out entangling growth each year. But to prepare grape-vines for good fruit production, provide a sturdy trellis, arbor, chain-link or rail fence, or wall strung with wire to support these big vines and their heavy bunches of grapes. Or to build a custom wire trellis large enough to accommodate two grapevines, set two stout posts in

Continued on page 143 ▶

White seedless 'Himrod' is softer than many other grape varieties but still full of flavor.

'Reliance', a seedless red table grape with great taste

top picks to grow

Variety	Zones	Season	Pruning Methods	Comments
AMERICAN and AMERICAN HYBRID VARIETIES				
'Alden'	6–22	Early midseason	Spur	Large, firm, seeded reddish blue grape with light muscat flavor. Good for fresh eating, juice, wine. Very productive. Good fall leaf color.
'America'	7–22	Midseason	Cane or spur	Seeded blue grape with intense flavor. Good for juice, fresh eating, wine. Resistant to Pierce's disease.
'Black Spanish' ('Lenoir')	7–9, 11–24	Late midseason	Spur	Very old black grape. Small seeded fruit is fine for eating but best for wine and juice. Resistant to Pierce's disease.
'Bluebell'	2–7	Early	Cane or spur	Seeded blue grape with a flavor like that of 'Concord'. Excellent for juice, good for fresh eating. Very hardy (to −35°F/−37°C). Grows in warm-summer areas but may taste flat there.
'Buffalo'	2–7	Early	Cane or spur	Seeded black fruit with spicy flavor. Good for fresh eating or juice. Can produce secondary crop if subjected to early frost.
'Campbell Early'	5–22	Early midseason	Spur	Large, seeded black grape of 'Concord' type. Good for fresh eating, juice. Colors before achieving full flavor.
'Canadice'	2b–9, 11–21	Early	Spur	Seedless red fruit. Excellent for fresh eating or juice. Ripens in very cool areas, such as around Puget Sound. Overcrops easily; must be pruned hard or have crop thinned. Hardy to −20°F/−29°C if well pruned.
'Champanel'	7 (warmer parts), 8, 9, 11–16, 18–24	Midseason	Cane	Seeded black grape. Good for juice, fresh eating. Tolerant of alkaline soil; resistant to Pierce's disease.
'Concord'	2b, 3, 6–9, 14–23	Midseason	Cane or spur	Seeded blue fruit. Standard American slipskin for cooking, juice, jelly.
'Edelweiss'	2–9, 14–21	Early	Cane or spur	Seeded white grape. Good for fresh eating or juice. Milder flavor than 'Niagara', but vine is more manageable. Flavor goes flat in hot-summer areas.
'Golden Muscat' AMERICAN HYBRID	3b, 6–24	Late	Spur	Very large, juicy, seeded green-yellow fruit. Flavor is citruslike, not true muscat; good for fresh eating. Ripens 2 weeks after 'Concord'. Cracks in wet weather.
'Himrod' AMERICAN HYBRID	3–9, 11–21	Very early	Cane	Seedless white fruit with spicy flavor. Good for fresh eating. Very vigorous, suited to arbors. Hardy to −15°F/−26°C.
'Interlaken' AMERICAN HYBRID	2–9, 14–21	Very early	Cane or spur	Firm, seedless green or yellow grape with fruity flavor. Excellent for fresh eating; only one for raisins in cool-summer areas. Ripens a week earlier than 'Himrod'. One of few that matures in the coolest areas of Pacific Northwest.

Variety	Zones	Season	Pruning Methods	Comments
AMERICAN and AMERICAN HYBRID VARIETIES				
'Lakemont'	3, 6–22	Early	Cane or spur	Seedless white fruit with mild flavor; very productive. Fine table grape; keeps well in cold storage.
'Mars'	4–9, 14–21	Early midseason	Cane or spur	Blue fruit; large for a seedless grape. Fine for fresh eating, juice, wine, raisins. Flavor improves after harvest.
'New York Muscat'	2b–9, 14–21	Early	Cane or spur	Seeded blue grape with sweet muscat flavor. Excellent for fresh eating, juice, wine. Less vigorous than other varieties. Can be tried in hotter areas, but quality may suffer.
'Niabell'	7–9, 14–16, 18–22	Early	Cane or spur	Large, seeded black grape similar to 'Concord' at its best. Excellent for arbors. Vigorous and productive in wide range of climates. Succeeds in hot interiors where 'Concord' fails.
'Niagara'	2, 3, 6–10, 14–21	Midseason	Cane	Seedless green to pale yellow fruit. Good for fresh eating, juice, wine.
'Price'	2–9, 14–21	Very early	Spur	Seeded blue grape. Sweet and juicy, with refined 'Concord'-type flavor. Very good for fresh eating and fine for juice. Ripens in coolest areas of range, even around Puget Sound. May even succeed in Zone 1 with cold protection.
'Reliance' AMERICAN HYBRID	2b–9, 14–21	Early midseason	Spur	Seedless red grape with mild, sweet flavor. Good for fresh eating or juice. Dependably productive.
'Swenson Red' AMERICAN HYBRID	2–9, 14–21	Early	Spur	Firm, meaty, seeded red or red-blue grape with unique fruity flavor. Excellent for fresh eating, juice, wine.
'Valiant'	A2, A3, 1–9	Early	Spur	Seeded blue fruit with 'Concord'-like flavor. Makes very good juice and jelly. Hardy to −50°F/−46°C.
'Vanessa'	2–9, 14–21	Early	Cane	Firm, seedless red grape with fruity flavor. Resists cracking. Good replacement for European variety 'Flame' in cool-summer areas. Use for fresh eating or raisins.
'Venus'	3–9, 14–21	Early midseason	Cane or spur	Seedless blue grape. Fruity, muscat-like flavor; fine choice for fresh eating or juice. Excellent fall color.

Continued on page 142 ▶

Variety	Zones	Season	Pruning Methods	Comments
EUROPEAN VARIETIES				
'Autumn Royal'	6–9, 11–16, 18–21	Midseason to late	Cane or spur	Large, seedless purplish black grape. Good for fresh eating or raisins
'Autumn Seedless'	6–9, 11–16, 18–21	Midseason	Cane or spur	Seedless pale green to golden grape. Good for fresh eating or raisins.
'Black Monukka'	3, 6–16, 17 (warmer parts), 18–24	Early midseason	Cane or spur	Seedless purplish black fruit in large, loose clusters. Popular home variety. One of hardiest European grapes.
'Crimson Seedless'	6–9, 12–16, 18–22	Late	Cane	Large, seedless red grape with excellent flavor. Good for fresh eating, raisins.
'Delight'	6–9, 12–16, 17 (warmer parts), 18–24	Early	Spur	Large, seedless, dark greenish yellow fruit. Good for fresh eating, raisins. Succeeds in mild-winter areas.
'Early Muscat'	6–9, 11–16, 18–24	Early midseason	Spur	Seeded green fruit in large clusters. Excellent muscat flavor. Used for muscat wine in Northwest.
'Fantasy'	6–9, 11–14, 18–21	Midseason	Cane	Large, seedless bluish black fruit with sweet, rich flavor. Good fresh or for wine. Vigorous; leave six to eight canes when pruning.
'Flame'	6–9, 11–16, 17 (warmer parts), 18–24	Early midseason	Cane or spur	Seedless red grape. For fresh eating, raisins. Very vigorous. Keep on dry side to reduce vigor, encourage ripening.
'Muscat' ('Muscat of Alexandria')	6–9, 11–16, 18–21	Late midseason	Spur	Large, rounded, seeded green to amber fruit. Renowned for sweet, musky, aged-in-the-vat flavor. Fine for fresh eating, juice, wine, raisins.
'Muscat Hamburg'	6–9, 11–16, 18–21	Late midseason	Spur	Seeded black grape. Intense, almost orangelike muscat flavor. Good fresh or for wine.
'Perlette'	6–9, 11–16, 17 (warmer parts), 18–24	Early	Spur	Seedless pale yellow fruit. Earlier, larger, less sweet than 'Thompson Seedless'. Excellent fresh. Needs less heat than most European varieties.
'Ribier'	7–9, 11–16, 18–21	Early midseason	Spur	Very large, seeded black grape with mild flavor. Good for fresh eating.
'Ruby Seedless' ('King's Ruby')	7–9, 12–16, 18–24	Late midseason	Cane or spur	Large clusters of seedless red to reddish black fruit. Sweet dessert grapes. Very susceptible to powdery mildew.
'Thompson Seedless'	7–14, 18, 19	Midseason	Cane	Big clusters of small, sweet, seedless greenish amber fruit. Good for fresh eating, raisins. Widely planted but does best in hot, dry areas.

Four 'Thompson Seedless' grapevines form a shady canopy over an arbor.

the ground 15–20 ft. apart; posts should rise 5 ft. above the soil. Set two smaller posts (support stakes for the vines) 4–5 ft. from the end posts. String sturdy galvanized wire (10- or 11-gauge) across the tops of the four posts. For a double-wire trellis, string a lower wire at the 2 1/2-ft. level. Space multiple trellises 10–12 ft. apart.

Initial training. The first summer after planting, let each vine grow unchecked from the base of its support structure. During the first winter, select the sturdiest shoot for the trunk and tie it to the support; shorten it to the three or four lowest buds and remove all other shoots at their bases. In the second spring, once the buds have grown out to 6- to 8-in.-long shoots, choose the strongest upright shoot for the continuation of the trunk and tie it to the post. (If you're training plants on a two-wire trellis or against a fence, also select two strong lower shoots for "arms" and tie them to the lower horizontal support.) Cut off all other shoots.

If you're growing your grapevine on a wire trellis, the second summer is the time to stop its vertical ascent. When the trunk reaches the top wire of the trellis, pinch it back to force branching. Train the two strongest resulting shoots along the top wire and remove any others. (For a two-wire trellis, also tie the lower arms' new growth along the lower wire; pinch back any lateral shoots developing from those arms to about 10 in. long.) In the second winter, cut back all growth except the trunk and arms and make sure that both sets of arms are loosely tied to the wire. During the third summer, allow the vine to grow but remove any shoots sprouting on the trunk. At this point, you've established a permanent framework for your trellis-grown vine, and you can choose between cane pruning and spur pruning from the third winter on (see "Yearly pruning," next page).

If you're training your vine onto an arbor, the second summer is the time to direct its growth onto the roof of

Continued on page 144 ▶

the structure. When the vine has grown just beyond the top of the vertical support, gently bend it over and secure it to the roof as it grows. Remove side shoots to encourage the tip to grow. During the second winter, cut back the main stem to a point just beyond where you want the last set of branches. Cut off all the side shoots. During the third spring, thin new shoots to 1 ft. apart. In the third winter, you're ready to create the final framework; its form depends on how you plan to prune your vines in subsequent years. If you plan to do spur pruning, cut back each of the shoots you selected in the spring to two buds. If you'll be cane pruning your vines, cut branches alternately to long canes (12 buds) and spurs (2 buds).

Yearly pruning. Grapes are produced on stems that develop from year-old wood—stems that formed in the previous season. These year-old stems have smooth bark, whereas older stems have rough, shaggy bark. The purpose of yearly pruning is to limit the amount of potential fruiting wood to ensure that the plant doesn't produce too much fruit (resulting in smaller grapes, poorly filled clusters, and exacerbation of the tendency toward alternate bearing) and that the fruit it does bear is of good quality. Pruning should be done in the dormant season—that is, in winter or earliest spring before the buds swell.

The two most widely used methods for pruning grapevines are spur pruning and cane pruning; see the accompanying chart for the recommended method for each variety. Begin using either method in the third winter, and repeat yearly thereafter.

Spur pruning. Start by removing weak side shoots from the arms. Leave the strongest shoots (spurs) spaced 6–10 in. apart; cut each to two buds. Each spur will produce two fruit-bearing shoots during the next growing season. The next winter and every winter thereafter, remove the lower shoot on each spur and cut the upper stem to two buds. Those buds will develop into stems that bear fruit the following summer.

Cane pruning. Select one strong lateral shoot near the trunk on each arm, cut it back to 12 buds, and tie it to the support; these will produce fruiting shoots in the coming summer. Select another strong lateral shoot near the trunk on each arm, and cut it back to two buds; these will be the renewal spurs. Remove all other shoots. Each winter, cut the arms that have fruited back to the renewal spurs, and choose as their replacements the two longest and strongest shoots that grew from the renewal spurs. Cut each to 12 buds and tie the two shoots to the support; select the two next-best shoots as renewal spurs, and cut each to two buds. Remove all other shoots.

LON ROMBOUGH ON
cool table grapes

Many of the nation's table grapes come from hot, sunny California vineyards—but there are varieties that thrive where summers are cool. Just ask Lon Rombough, who has harvested plenty of sweet, fresh fruit from the 200 grape varieties he grows in Aurora, Oregon. "A mature vine of the right variety can produce more than 30 pounds of fruit per year here, usually plenty for a family of four," he says.

For successful production in cool areas, Rombough advises choosing a variety that ripens early, is cold-hardy, and can take fall rains without the fruit cracking. American and American hybrid varieties make his list of tastiest table grapes for the cool Northwest. His favorite seeded grapes are 'New York Muscat', 'Price', and 'Swenson Red'. Among seedless varieties, he recommends 'Canadice', 'Interlaken' (it ripens well in the cool Puget Sound area), 'Reliance', and 'Vanessa' (which has exceptional rain resistance).

harvest Pick grapes when they're sweet to the taste, never sooner, since they stop ripening at the moment of harvest.

challenges Pierce's disease, caused by a bacterium spread by the sharpshooter insect, is a serious threat to grapes in California. It causes afflicted vines to lose productivity, wilt, and die in just a season or two. For more information, contact your Cooperative Extension Office. The grape leafhopper may cause leaf drop on grapevines in California. Get rid of nearby weeds, which may harbor the pest. Spraying with insecticidal soap is somewhat effective; grape leafhopper infestations are rarely serious enough to warrant a stronger pesticide. Grape mealybug may infest vines in the Northwest and parts of California; control with horticultural oil spray in late winter. Powdery mildew is a serious disease of European grapes (most American varieties are immune). To control it, dust vines with sulfur when shoots are 6 in. long, again when they're 12–15 in. long, then every 2 weeks until harvest.

Raspberry

Rubus species
Rose family *(Rosaceae)*
DECIDUOUS SHRUBS

✂ **ZONES A1–A3, 1–24; BEST IN 3–6, 15–17**
☼ **FULL SUN**
💧 **REGULAR WATER**

This luscious fruit is a close relative of the blackberry. Red and yellow raspberries are derived from *Rubus idaeus*, native to North America, Europe, and Asia. Black raspberries are forms of *R. occidentalis*, from eastern and central North America. Purple raspberries are hybrids of red and black kinds.

Raspberries grow from perennial roots that produce thorny biennial stems called canes. Generally, raspberry canes grow to full size in the first year, then bear fruit in their second summer. The red and yellow varieties known as everbearing (or fall bearing) produce two crops on the same canes—the first in fall of the first year, the second in summer of the next year. In all instances, the canes die after fruiting in the second year. New canes grow from the roots every year.

For raspberry fruit to reach perfection, plants need winter chill and a lingering springtime with slowly warming temperatures.

Red and yellow raspberries are produced on erect plants with long, straight canes; they can be grown as freestanding shrubs and staked, but they are tidier and easier to manage if trained on a trellis or confined within a hedgerow (pairs of parallel wires strung at 3 ft. and 5 ft. aboveground along either side of a row of plants).

A caution to gardeners in Hawaii: The very vigorous black-fruited *R. niveus*, called Mysore raspberry, is sometimes grown like a red raspberry in Island gardens; however, it can become a troublesome weed, choking out native vegetation.

Red and yellow varieties. Red varieties are the most common; yellow types are mutations of red raspberries. Plants usually live for about 15 years.

'Anne'. Everbearing. Large, apricot gold berries with excellent, sweet flavor.

'Autumn Bliss'. Everbearing. Very large red berries with fine flavor. Resists root rot.

'Bababerry'. Everbearing. Large, firm red berries. Needs little winter chill; stands heat well. Best in hot-summer climates.

'Boyne'. Summer bearing. Early-ripening, medium-size red fruit. Very hardy variety bred in Manitoba. Subject to anthracnose.

Red raspberries are the most commonly grown.

'Canby'. Summer bearing. Large, bright red berries. Thornless.

'Caroline'. Everbearing. Large red berries with excellent flavor and high levels of nutrients and antioxidants.

'Cascade Delight'. Summer bearing. Long season of large red berries with great flavor. Heavy bearing and resistant to root rot.

'Chilcotin'. Summer bearing. Very large, firm red berries with excellent flavor. Long harvest season.

'Chilliwack'. Summer bearing. Very large red berries with fine flavor. Somewhat resistant to root rot.

'Dinkum'. Everbearing. Medium-size, firm red fruit with good flavor.

'Fallgold'. Everbearing. Large yellow fruit with good flavor.

'Fallred'. Everbearing. Large, firm red fruit with outstanding flavor.

Continued on page 146 ▶

Black raspberries such as 'Allen' have a stronger flavor than their red cousins.

'Heritage'. Everbearing. Small red berries are tasty but a bit dry.

'Indian Summer'. Everbearing. Small crops of large, tasty red berries. Fall crop is often larger.

'Killarney'. Summer bearing. Early harvest of firm, large berries. Very hardy.

'Kiska'. Summer bearing. Small red berries with good flavor. Hardy; developed for Alaska.

'Latham'. Summer bearing. Late-ripening, large red berries that are often crumbly. Older, very hardy variety for coldest regions. Mildews in humid summers.

'Meeker'. Summer bearing. Large, firm bright red berries on long, willowy branches.

'Newburgh'. Summer bearing. Late-ripening, large, light red berries. Takes heavy soil fairly well.

'September'. Everbearing. Small to medium-size red berries of good flavor. Fall crop is heavier.

'Summit'. Everbearing. Large red berries with good flavor. Very productive. Resistant to root rot.

'Tulameen'. Summer bearing. Very large, firm red berries with excellent flavor. Long harvest season. Must have well-drained soil.

'Willamette'. Summer bearing. Large, firm dark red berries that hold color and shape well.

Black and purple varieties. Black raspberries (also called blackcap raspberries) have blue-black fruit that is firmer and seedier than that of red and yellow types, and they have a more pronounced flavor. Expected life is 4 to 8 years. Though purple raspberries grow more like black raspberries, the fruit shares characteristics of both black and red kinds. Purple raspberries are best cooked in pies and jams.

'Brandywine'. Large purple berries. Tart; good for jams, jellies. Ripens late.

'Cumberland'. Large black berries. Old, heavy-bearing variety.

'Jewel'. Large black berries. Vigorous, disease-resistant plant.

'Munger'. Medium-size black berries. Most popular commercial black-fruited variety.

'Royalty'. Large red berries turn purple when ripe. Sweet and fragrant fruit. Vigorous plant.

HOW TO GROW IT

best site Plant in a sunny, open site where you can reach the berries from all sides (not against a fence or wall, where it's too hard to reach ripe berries through the thorns). In warmer zones outside the best raspberry climates, satisfactory production may come from plants grown in light shade and mulched heavily to keep soil cool.

yield *Red and yellow raspberries:* 25 to 35 pounds per 10-ft. row. *Everbearing raspberries:* 15 to 20 pounds per 10-ft. row. *Black and purple raspberries:* 8 to 12 pounds per 10-ft. row.

soil Good drainage is essential; if your garden soil is heavy clay, consider planting in raised beds. Rich, slightly acid soil (pH 6 to 6.5) is ideal.

planting Plant bare-root stock during the dormant season, setting plants so the uppermost roots are buried about 1–2 in. under the soil surface. Cut back the canes to about 6 in. to serve as markers. Some growers have recently been selling tissue-cultured raspberries in small pots in spring and summer. Plant these at the same soil level as they were in the pot, and water carefully and frequently the first summer. Don't accept divisions of raspberry plants from friends: these plants are often tainted with root rot disease organisms and viruses that reduce production. Instead, buy certified disease-free plants from nurseries. Mulch all raspberry plantings to discourage weeds and keep soil moist.

spacing Set red and yellow raspberries 2$\frac{1}{2}$–3 ft. apart in rows spaced 6–10 ft. apart. Set black and purple raspberries 3–4 ft. apart in rows spaced 8–10 ft. apart.

water Provide a deep soaking once a week (avoid overhead watering, which increases disease problems). The need for water is greatest during flowering and fruiting, so don't skip waterings during that season.

fertilizer Apply 5 ounces of 16-16-16 fertilizer per 10-ft. row when new canes start growing in spring. Repeat at the end of May and again at the end of June.

pruning, training Summer-bearing varieties should produce three to five canes in the first year. Tie these to a trellis or confine to a hedgerow. Dig or pull out any canes that grow more than 1 ft. away from the trellis or outside the hedgerow. Late in the dormant season, cut trellised canes to 5–5$\frac{1}{2}$ ft., those in hedgerows to 4 ft. When growth recommences, new canes will appear all around the parent plants and between rows. After the original canes bear fruit, cut them to the ground. Then select the best 5 to 12 new canes and train these (they will bear next summer); cut the remaining new canes to the ground.

Everbearing red and yellow varieties fruit in the first autumn on the top third of the cane, then again in the second summer on the lower two-thirds of the cane. Cut off the upper portion of the cane after the first harvest; cut out the cane entirely after the second harvest. As an alternative, you can cut everbearing canes to the ground yearly in fall after fruiting has finished (wait until late

'Fallgold', a sweet yellow raspberry

dormant season in cold-winter regions). You'll sacrifice one of the annual crops but get an extended harvest from late summer into fall. Use a power mower if your berry patch is large.

harvest Pull off ripe fruit when it separates easily from the plant, and put it in a shallow container so berries on the bottom won't be crushed. Pick every 3 or 4 days.

challenges To lessen the chance of verticillium wilt, avoid planting where you have previously grown tomatoes, potatoes, peppers, or eggplant. To control anthracnose and other fungal diseases on all raspberries, spray with lime sulfur during dormancy and again as leaf buds begin to open; this also helps control many insect pests, including spider mites and cane borers. If borers attack, prune out and destroy damaged canes below the entry points (pinhead-size holes at or near ground level). To keep plants under control, cut off wayward canes as they appear.

Strawberry

Fragaria species
Rose family *(Rosaceae)*
EVERGREEN PERENNIALS

🌿 **ALL ZONES**
☼ ◐ **EXPOSURE VARIES BY TYPE**
💧 **REGULAR WATER**

Standard market strawberries *(Fragaria × ananassa)* are hybrids between *F. chiloense*, which grows along the west coast of North and South America, and *F. virginiana*, from North America and Europe. These hybrids are categorized as June bearing, everbearing, or day neutrals. Alpine and musk strawberries are different species, described at the end of this entry.

Strawberry plants have white flowers and toothed, roundish, medium green leaves. They grow 6–8 in. tall and spread by long runners to about 1 ft. across. Strawberries of one variety or another can be grown in all parts of the West, though it is difficult to succeed with them where soil and water salinity are very high. Varieties tend to be regionally adapted.

June-bearing varieties. June-bearing types produce one crop per year in late spring or early summer; in general, they are the highest-quality strawberries you can grow.

'Benton'. Flavorful, somewhat soft berries. Virus-tolerant, mildew-resistant. Outstanding in the Northwest, especially in mountain and intermountain areas.

'Camarosa'. Huge, conical berries over a long season. Susceptible to mildew. Adapted to California, especially southern areas.

'Chandler'. Large, juicy berries over a long period. Excellent flavor, good texture. Some resistance to leaf spot. Grows well in Southern California; good as an annual elsewhere.

'Earliglow'. Medium-size, deep red, sweet berries come early in the season. Resistant to red stele and verticillium. Does best in cold-winter regions.

'Guardian'. Large, all-purpose fruit with good flavor. Disease-resistant. Recommended for cold-winter regions.

'Honeoye'. Large, symmetrical, bright red fruit with sweet-tart flavor. Recommended for cold-winter regions.

'Hood'. Large, conical to wedge-shaped berries with excellent flavor; good for fresh eating and making into jams and preserves. Early ripening. Resists mildew. Good in the Pacific Northwest.

'Jewel'. Large, firm, bright red berries come at midseason. Best in cold-winter regions.

Straw mulch keeps ripening strawberries clean and dry.

'Puget Reliance'. Large crop of big, tasty berries; excellent flavor for jams and preserves. Vigorous plant. Tolerant of viruses. Adapted to the Pacific Northwest.

'Puget Summer'. A heavy-yielding, late-season variety with excellent, sweet flavor. Holds its fruit off the ground, avoiding fruit rot. Susceptible to powdery mildew; disease-resistant otherwise. Best in the Pacific Northwest.

'Rainier'. Good-size berries that hold size throughout a long season. Fine flavor. Vigorous plant. Fair tolerance to root rot. Best in the Pacific Northwest, west of the Cascades.

'Sequoia'. One of the tastiest strawberries. Bears for many months. Resistant to alkalinity and most leaf diseases. Developed for coastal California but widely adapted, even to cold winters.

'Shuksan'. Soft, mealy berries. Excellent frozen; good fresh. Tolerant of alkalinity. Resistant to botrytis, viruses, red stele. Good away from the coast.

Everbearing and day-neutral varieties. Everbearing strawberries bear one crop in early summer and one in fall, while day neutrals come to peak harvest in early summer and continue to produce fruit (often unevenly) through fall. The exact fruiting pattern for both types depends on variety and heat—plants stop flowering when the temperature rises above 85°F/29°C. Everbearers and day neutrals put out fewer runners than June bearers and generally have smaller fruits. The quality of day-neutral fruit is higher than that of everbearing strawberries.

'Albion'. Day neutral. Long, conical fruit with excellent flavor. Resists verticillium wilt and crown rot. For California.

'Fort Laramie'. Everbearing. Good yield of berries over a long season. Excellent flavor. Tolerates –30°F/–34°C without mulch. Hardy in the Mountain states, High Plains, and milder parts of Alaska. Also good in Southern California.

'Ozark Beauty'. Everbearing. Medium-size red berries; excellent flavor in cold-winter areas, just fair where winters are mild. Vigorous plant.

'Quinault'. Everbearing. Large, attractive berries are tasty, rather soft. Good producer of runners. Resists viruses and red stele. Susceptible to botrytis. Developed for the Pacific Northwest but is widely adapted; grown as an annual in Alaska.

'Seascape'. Day neutral. Good producer of large berries. Very good for eating fresh, making into jam, and freezing. Excellent virus resistance. Very widely adapted, even in Hawaii. Good choice for annual production in colder climates.

'Selva'. Day neutral. First flush of fruit comes as late as July but produces heavily through fall. Large fruit for day-neutral variety; mild flavor develops best in warm areas. Gets red spider mites and leaf spotting in mild climates but has good resistance to red stele. Does best in California.

'Tribute'. Day neutral. Medium to large berries with excellent flavor. Resists red stele and verticillium wilt. Widely adapted but prone to viruses in Pacific Northwest.

'Tristar'. Day neutral. Large berries with excellent flavor. Bears well the first year. Resists red stele and mildew but is moderately susceptible to viruses. Widely adapted.

Alpine strawberry (F. vesca). Zones A3, 2b–9, 14–24, H2. This plant bears a small crop of small but fragrant, delicious berries over a long summer season. It is often grown as a 9-in.-tall edging for flower or herb beds. Alpine strawberries do not produce runners but may be grown from seed, bearing the first year from seed sown

Continued on page 150 ▶

'Tristar', a productive and adaptable variety

Alpine strawberries are tiny but tasty.

Black plastic warms the soil around new plants to encourage early growth.

A wood-framed mesh tent protects fruit from birds, squirrels, and deer.

early. Varieties include red-fruiting 'Alexandria', 'Baron Solemacher', 'Improved Rügen', 'Mignonette', and 'Semperflorens'; yellow-fruiting 'Alpine Yellow'; and white-fruiting 'Alpine White'.

Musk strawberry (*F. moschata*). Zones A3, 2b–9, 14–24, H2. Varieties of this shade-tolerant, June-bearing plant from Italy are renowned for their intense aroma and flavor with hints of musk, raspberry, spice, and pineapple. 'Profumata di Tortona' and 'Capron' are popular, but because they produce mostly female flowers, a male pollinator like 'Male Musk' will increase harvest. Plants take 3 or 4 years to come to full production. They also send out runners, eventually forming an 18-in.-tall groundcover.

HOW TO GROW IT

best site Full sun for standard strawberries, partial shade for alpine strawberries, full sun or partial shade for musk strawberries.

yield *Standard strawberries:* 5 to 10 quarts per 10 ft. of matted row (a row where runners are allowed to root into a groundcover-like swath). *Alpine strawberries:* A 2-ft. clump of a half-dozen plants might yield a small handful of berries at once—small pleasures to be savored. *Musk strawberries:* Between standard and alpine strawberries.

soil Rich, well-draining, acidic soil is best (most varieties do not tolerate alkalinity).

planting Plant on flat ground if soil drains well or is high in salts, on a 5- to 6-in. mound if soil is heavy or drains poorly. (If soil is high in salts and drains poorly, plant in containers.) In mild-winter areas, plant standard strawberries from bare-root stock in late winter or early

Planting a Strawberry Jar

1. Make a watering tube (slightly longer than pot height) from PVC pipe. Cap one end. Drill ⅛-inch-diameter holes 1 inch apart on alternate sides of the pipe.

2. Partially fill with potting soil. Insert watering tube, capped end down, then fill pot to rim with soil.

3. Working from the bottom up, plant each pocket, tamping potting mix firmly around roots. Soak soil well.

4. Using a funnel, water whenever the top inch of soil dries out.

A strawberry jar provides a harvest of sweet fruit in a small space.

spring (they often come bundled in bunches); you can also set out plants of June bearers in late summer or fall for a crop the next spring. In colder climates, set out plants or bare-root stock in early spring; June-bearing kinds will come to harvest the following year; everbearing and day-neutral varieties produce a small crop the year they are planted. Start alpine and musk strawberries anytime from spring through fall from plants in small containers, or start them from seed in spring.

Set out all kinds of strawberry plants with the crown slightly above soil level (a buried crown will rot); topmost roots should be ¼ in. beneath the soil (exposed roots will dry and die). Mulch to deter weeds, conserve moisture, and keep berries clean. Hasten spring growth of standard strawberries by planting through clear or black plastic mulch and covering plants with floating row covers (remove covers as soon as flowers appear). Pinch off the earliest blossoms produced in the first year to increase plants' vigor.

Some home gardeners follow commercial growers' practice of treating strawberries as annuals. Plant in summer or early fall, usually with a plastic mulch; remove runners as they develop. After harvest, tear out plants. Set out new plants in another location the following year (don't replant in the same location until at least 2 years have passed). Benefits are healthier plants, fewer weeds, and bigger fruit. June-bearing 'Chandler' is especially well adapted to this method, but almost any variety can be grown this way if planted at just the right time (you may have to experiment). In the coldest zones, home gardeners are successfully growing some everbearing varieties, particularly 'Quinault', as spring-planted annuals.

Strawberries need winter mulch in cold climates. Cover with a 4- to 6-in. layer of straw or other light, weed-free, organic material in late fall. When temperatures warm in spring, rake mulch between plants.

Continued on page 152 ▶

When harvesting strawberries, pinch the stems to avoid damaging fruit.

In containers: Grow any standard strawberry in a strawberry jar, which has planting holes in the sides and the top, or any kind of strawberry in a container at least 8 in. deep. Strawberries also prosper in large hanging baskets, at least 12 in. deep and wide, since slugs and snails can't reach the fruit as it ripens.

spacing *Standard strawberries:* Space plants 14–18 in. apart in rows 2–2$^1/_2$ ft. apart. *Alpine strawberries:* Set plants 8–12 in. apart. *Musk strawberries:* Space plants 18 in. apart.

water Plants need consistent moisture during the bearing season; don't let them dry out. Drip irrigation is ideal to help reduce disease problems, but overhead irrigation is satisfactory.

fertilizer *June bearers (including musk types):* Feed twice a year—very lightly when growth begins and more heavily after fruiting. *Everbearing and day-neutral types:* These prefer consistent light feedings. *Alpines:* Feed once in early spring and once after fruiting begins.

Use a complete fertilizer for all kinds of strawberries. Don't fertilize heavily in spring or you'll get excessive plant growth, soft fruit, and fruit rot.

pruning, training The majority of varieties reproduce by runners, though some make few or no offsets. Pinch off all runners to get large plants with smaller yields of big berries; let offsets grow 7–10 in. apart for heavy yields of smaller berries. When your plants have made enough offsets, pinch off additional runners.

Most June bearers (not including musk strawberries) benefit greatly from renovation. After harvest, remove foliage with a lawn mower set high so it won't injure the crowns. If diseases were a problem, send leaves out with the trash. Water and fertilize to encourage new growth. This is also a good time to reduce a dense planting by removing the old mother plants and leaving younger, more productive daughter plants. Renovate musk strawberries by dividing them every 3 years.

harvest Pinch through strawberry stems with your thumbnail when fruit has colored up completely. Or, if you plan to use the fruit immediately, hold the stem with one hand and gently pull the fruit away from its calyx (the green part on the stem end) with the other.

challenges Strawberries are subject to many diseases: fruit rots (botrytis, anthracnose, leather rot), leaf diseases (leaf spot, leaf scorch, leaf blight), crown diseases (phytophthora), root diseases (verticillium wilt, red stele, black root rot), and viruses. Root weevils, aphids, mites, slugs, and snails are among potential pests. To reduce problems, use certified disease-free plants; also remove diseased foliage and ripe or rotten fruit. Replace plants with new ones as they begin to decline, usually after 3 years; or, better yet, start a new bed with new plants.

CHAPTER 4

Fruits

Fruits are the superstars of the garden, with some trees and vines yielding up to 300 pounds per year. Anybody with space for a big patio pot, a hedge, or an espalier on a sunny wall can grow them. Best of all, many fruiting plants have flowers and form to match the most eye-catching ornamentals. Now that's tasteful.

Apple

Malus hybrids
Rose family (*Rosaceae*)
DECIDUOUS TREES

✎ ZONES VARY BY VARIETY
☼ FULL SUN
🌢 REGULAR WATER DURING FRUIT DEVELOPMENT

Apples are the world's most widely adapted deciduous fruits. They are probably natural hybrids of *Malus sylvestris* and *M. pumila*, two species whose ranges overlap in southwestern Asia. Most apples ripen from July to early November, depending on variety and climate. Most need hundreds of hours of winter chill to flower and fruit to their full potential, but low-chill varieties can bear apples in mild-winter places such as the low desert and the marine and coastal climates of Southern California.

Although many apples are self-fruitful to varying degrees ('Chehalis', 'Golden Delicious', and 'Mollie's Delicious' are closest to fully self-fruitful), it is generally recommended that, unless there are apples growing nearby, two or more varieties be planted for cross-pollination and good fruit set. If your tree is not bearing, graft a branch of another variety onto it or place fresh bouquets of blossoms from another variety in a can of water at the base of the tree. Certain varieties (triploids) do not produce fertile pollen and thus cannot fertilize their own flowers or those of other apples; they must be pollinated by a fertile apple to bear fruit. Pollen-sterile trees (including 'Gravenstein') are noted in the chart.

Every apple has different storage potential, but the general rule is that the later in the season an apple comes to harvest, the longer its storage life. In practice, early apples must be eaten immediately or made into sauce or cider before they go bad. Late apples can often be stored for months.

If you want nearly perfect fruit, your apple tree will need much care in most regions. But even with less-than-perfect fruit, an apple tree is ornamental: it has more character, better form, and a longer life than most other deciduous fruit trees.

Standard apples. The accompanying chart lists recommended varieties. A standard apple tree grows about 20 ft. tall and wide and takes several years to come to full harvest. If space is at a premium, consider dwarf trees. Multiple-variety trees provide an assortment of different apples, as well as cross-pollination, all on a single tree. Available in standard and dwarf sizes, these trees have three to five varieties grafted onto a single trunk and rootstock; each variety ripens on its own schedule.

'Fuji', a sweet, crisp Japanese variety introduced to the U.S. in the 1980s, is the perfect lunch-bag apple.

In choosing varieties, remember that skin color is not an indicator of quality or taste. And don't let an apple's name or eye appeal or your taste preferences alone influence you to choose a difficult-to-grow variety. If you think 'Golden Delicious' and 'Red Delicious' are equally good-tasting (and you live in an area where either can be grown), consider differences in growing them. 'Golden Delicious' produces fruit without a pollenizer and comes into bearing at a younger age. It keeps well, while 'Red Delicious' becomes mealy if not stored at low temperatures. And 'Golden Delicious' can be used for cooking, while 'Red Delicious' is principally a fresh-eating apple.

In many apple-growing areas, demand for popular varieties seen on fruit stands often causes nurseries to sell unsuitable selections. For example, many nurseries in mild-winter climates offer 'Red Delicious' apple because it is well known—but it won't fruit there. For this reason,

Tart, firm-textured 'Granny Smith' apples are prized for use in pies and sauces.

'Red Delicious', a longtime favorite with deep red skin and sweet, juicy flesh

the accompanying chart indicates where some standard varieties perform best as well as where they are sold. In the coldest climates, rootstock is as important as variety; apples in such areas are best grown on hardy crabapple rootstocks such as *M. baccata, M. antonovka,* or *M. ranetka.* Apple-crabapple hybrids offer another option for coldest-winter areas.

Dwarf apples. Dwarf apple trees (5–8 ft. tall and wide) are made by grafting wood from standard apple varieties onto dwarfing rootstocks such as EMLA 27, M9, and P22. Dwarfs take up little room and bear at a younger age than standard apples, but they have shallow roots and need the support of a post, fence, wall, or sturdy trellis to withstand wind and heavy rain. They are not reliable in the coldest regions. They also need good soil and extra care in fertilizing and watering. Genetic dwarf apples, such

as 'Garden Delicious', are naturally small and stay that way; even grafting them onto a standard (nondwarfing) rootstock would not produce a standard-size tree.

Semidwarf apples. These are larger than dwarfs (and bear bigger crops) but smaller than standard trees. Many commercial orchards get high yields by planting semidwarf trees close together. Semidwarfing rootstocks MARK, M26, and M7 reduce normal tree height by about half; the trees may be espaliered or trellised if planted 12–16 ft. apart and allowed to grow 8–12 ft. tall. Semidwarfing rootstocks MM106 and MM111 reduce height by approximately 15 to 25 percent.

Spur apples. These apple trees bear flowers and fruit on spurs—short branches that grow from wood 2 years old or older. Spurs normally begin to appear only after a tree has grown in place for 3 to 5 years, but on spur apples

Continued on page 160 ▶

top picks to grow

Variety	Zones	Ripening Time	Fruit	Comments
'Adina'	18–24, H1	Early to midseason	Large, round; fragrant, dark red. Firm, sweet, creamy white flesh.	Low-chill variety.
'Akane'	1–7, 14–16	Early to midseason	Small to medium, round to flat; red. Crisp white flesh.	Scab- and mildew-resistant.
'Anna'	7–24, H1	Early; may bear light second and third crops	Large; pale green blushed red. Crisp, sweet with some acid.	Begins producing at a young age. Low-chill variety; useful in warmest-winter areas. Good annual bearer. Good pollenizer for 'Dorsett Golden' and 'Ein Shemer'.
'Arkansas Black'	1–3, 10, 11, 19	Late	Medium size; deep dark red. Hard, crisp, juicy, and aromatic. Flavor is best after storage for 2 months.	'Arkansas Black Spur' is a spurred variation.
'Ashmead's Kernel'	4–9, 14–17	Late	Medium size; red-orange blush over rough-textured yellow-green.	Good disease resistance.
'Beverly Hills'	12–13, 18–24	Early	Small to medium; yellow skin splashed and striped red. Tender flesh is a bit tart. Fair quality. Somewhat resembles 'McIntosh'.	Definitely for cool areas; will not develop good quality in hot interiors. One of the best for Southern California coast.
'Braeburn'	1–4, 6, 14–16, 18, 22, 23	Late	Medium size; orange-red blush over yellow skin. Crisp, sweet-tart flesh. Stores well.	Fruit drops in hot climates. Alternate bearing. Very susceptible to mites.
'Chehalis'	4–6	Early	Large; yellow-green. Similar to 'Golden Delicious'. Mild flavor, melting flesh. Soft but bakes well. Also good in salads. Poor keeper.	Self-fruitful. Resists scab.
'Cox's Orange Pippin'	7, 14–16	Midseason	Medium size; dull orange-red skin. Yellow, firm, juicy flesh. Superb flavor. English dessert favorite.	Susceptible to scab and cracking. Dense growth; thin out branches. Worth trying for its unique flavor.
'Dorsett Golden'	12, 13, 18–24	Early	Medium to large; yellow or greenish yellow. Sweet flavor. Good for eating fresh or cooking. Keeps a few weeks.	Low-chill variety. Good pollenizer for 'Anna' and 'Ein Shemer'.
'Ein Shemer'	12, 13, 18–24	Early	Medium size; yellow to greenish yellow. Juicy, crisp, mildly acidic.	Low-chill variety. Good pollenizer for 'Anna' and 'Dorsett Golden'.
'Empire'	2–7, 14–16	Midseason	Cross between 'McIntosh' and 'Red Delicious'. Small to medium size, roundish; dark red skin. Creamy white flesh is juicy, crisp, mildly tart.	Semispur growth habit. Good tree structure. Susceptible to spring frost damage. Better adapted than 'McIntosh' to hot-summer areas.
'Enterprise'	1–9, 14–16	Late	Medium size; deep red blush over gold. Firm and sweet. Keeps well.	Immune to scab. Subject to preharvest fruit drop.
'Fiesta'	1–9, 14–16	Midseason to late	Medium to large; red-striped yellow skin. Firm fruit is larger and even better flavored than 'Cox's Orange Pippin' and doesn't crack.	Productive. No preharvest fruit drop.
'Fuji'	3b–9, 12–16, 18–22	Late	Medium to large; yellow-green skin with red stripes. Firm flesh with excellent, very sweet flavor. Stores exceptionally well.	Needs a long growing season (160 days) to ripen properly. Fairly low chill requirement. Tends to bear heavy crops in alternate years.

Variety	Zones	Ripening Time	Fruit	Comments
'Gala'	3b–9, 12–16	Early to midseason	Medium size; beautiful red-on-yellow color. Yellow flesh is highly aromatic, firm, crisp, juicy, sweet. Loses flavor in storage.	Vigorous, heavy bearer with long, supple branches that break easily; provide support if necessary. Very susceptible to fireblight.
'Garden Delicious'	1–3, 6–9, 14–20	Midseason	Medium to large; golden green with red blush. Crisp, sweet dessert apple also good for cooking.	Genetic dwarf 5–8 ft. tall and as wide.
'Ginger Gold'	1–9, 14–16	Early midseason	Medium to large; yellow. Firm, crisp, mild flesh. Resembles 'Golden Delicious'. Good keeper. One of the best early yellow apples.	Ripens over 2 to 3 weeks. Susceptible to mildew. Resistant to sunburn.
'Golden Delicious' ('Yellow Delicious')	1–3, 6–11, 14–24	Late midseason	Medium to large; similar in shape to 'Red Delicious' with less prominent knobs. Clear yellow color, though it may develop russeting in some climates. Aromatic, crisp. Excellent for eating fresh and cooking.	Not related to 'Red Delicious'; different taste, habit. Long bloom season, heavy pollen production make it a good pollenizer. Self- fruitful. Spur types include 'Goldspur', 'Yellospur'.
'Golden Russet'	1–3, 6–9, 14–16, 18, 19	Early to midseason	Medium size; greenish yellow to golden brown skin with heavy russeting. Creamy yellow, sweet flesh. Good fresh or cooked.	Vigorous and productive. Partially self-fruitful but better crop with pollenizer.
'Gold Rush'	1–3, 6–9, 14–16	Late	Medium size; yellow, often with some russeting. Crisp, spicy, sweet-tart flesh. Best flavor after storage for 2 to 3 months.	Immune to scab. Good resistance to mildew; some resistance to fireblight.
'Gordon'	12, 13, 18–24, H1	Midseason	Large; greenish yellow blushed red. Sweet-tart flavor.	Vigorous, upright, semidwarf tree. Long blooming, bearing periods. Low-chill variety.
'Granny Smith'	3b, 7–11, 14–16, 19	Midseason (later in cool-summer areas)	Large; bright to yellowish green. Firm, tart flesh. Good quality. Stores well. Makes good pies, sauce.	Australian favorite before it came to U.S. Chancy in cold areas because of late ripening.
'Gravenstein'	Widely sold in 4–11, 14–24; best in 15–17	Early to midseason	Large; deep yellow skin with brilliant red stripes. Crisp, aromatic, juicy. Excellent for fresh eating; makes applesauce with character.	Justly famous variety of California's north coast apple district. Pollen-sterile; won't pollinate other varieties. Susceptible to mildew in Zones 4–6.
'Honeycrisp'	1–7, 14–16	Midseason	Medium size; red. Firm, crisp flesh. Excellent sweet-tart flavor.	Hardy apple from Minnesota. Resistant to fireblight; somewhat resistant to scab.
'Hudson's Golden Gem'	2–6, 7, 14–16	Early to midseason	Large, elongated; gold with light brown russeting. Crisp, nutty flesh. Good for desserts.	Productive. Fruit holds well on the tree. Resistant to scab, mildew, and fireblight.
'Idared'	4–6, 15–17	Late	Medium to large; bright red. Firm white flesh is tart but sweetens in storage.	Begins bearing at a young age. Heavy producer.
'Jonagold'	2–9, 14–17	Late midseason	Large; yellow with heavy red striping. Firm, juicy flesh; fine mildly tart flavor. A frequent taste-test favorite.	Productive medium-size tree. Pollen-sterile; won't pollinate other varieties.

Continued on page 158 ▶

Variety	Zones	Ripening Time	Fruit	Comments
'Jonathan'	Sold everywhere; best in 2, 3, 7	Midseason	Small to medium, roundish oblong; bright red skin. Juicy, moderately tart, crackling crisp, sprightly. All-purpose apple. Good keeper.	Subject to mildew; somewhat resistant to scab.
'Karmijn de Sonnaville'	4–6	Late	Medium size; deep red over yellow with russeting. Excellent sweet-tart flavor. Great fresh or stored.	Pollen-sterile; won't pollinate other varieties. Fertile, midseason bloomers 'Liberty' and 'Melrose' are good choices for pollenizers.
'Liberty'	4–9, 14–16	Late midseason	Medium size; heavy red blush over greenish yellow. Crisp, with fine sweet-tart flavor. Dessert quality.	Productive tree. Immune to scab; can get mildew west of Cascades. Resists rust, fireblight.
'Lodi'	A2, A3, 1–3, 6–11, 14–16	Early	Medium size; greenish yellow. Tart flavor. Good for cooking. Keeps well.	Large, hardy tree. Tends to bear heavily in alternate years.
'McIntosh'	2, 3, 14–16	Midseason	Medium to large, nearly round; bright red. Snowy white, tender flesh. Excellent tart flavor.	Fine choice for cooler climates if given good care. Very susceptible to scab, preharvest fruit drop.
'Melrose'	1–7, 15, 16	Late	Medium to large, roundish; red skin striped deeper red. Flesh is white, mildly tart, aromatic. Stores very well. Good dessert apple.	Cross between 'Jonathan' and 'Red Delicious'. Somewhat mildew-resistant. Considered one of the best in Northwest.
'Mutsu' ('Crispin')	4–9, 15, 16	Late	Very large; greenish yellow blushed red. Cream-colored, very crisp flesh. Excellent dessert and cooking apple with long storage life.	Exceptionally large and vigorous tree. Pollen-sterile; won't pollinate other varieties.
'Newtown Pippin' ('Yellow Newtown')	1–11, 14–22	Late	Large; green. Crisp and tart flesh. Fair for eating, excellent for cooking.	Large, vigorous tree. Excellent for California Central Coast. Gets mildew in Zones 4–6.
'Norland'	A1–A3, 1–3	Early	Medium size, oblong; yellow-green striped with red. Creamy white flesh is sweet-tart; good fresh or cooked. Stores well if picked just before fully ripe.	Hardy variety from Canada. Other Canadian introductions such as 'Noran', 'Norson', 'Parkland', and 'Westland' are also good in coldest-winter areas.
'Northern Spy'	1–3, 6, 7, 14–16	Late	Large; red. Tender, fine-grained flesh with sprightly flavor. Not attractive but excellent dessert and cooking apple. Keeps well.	Slow to reach bearing age.
'Oriole'	A2, A3, 1–3, 7, 14–16	Early	Large; yellow-orange skin striped or spotted with red. Flesh is on the soft side, spicy. Excellent fresh or cooked.	Productive tree with excellent hardiness. Susceptible to mildew.
'Paulared'	2, 3, 6, 7, 14–16	Early	Large, round to flattish; solid red blush. Crisp, mildly tart flesh. One of the best early apples.	Strong, upright tree. Thrives west of Cascades in Northwest. Somewhat resistant to scab.
'Pettingill'	23, 24	Midseason to late	Large, thick-skinned; red-blushed green to red. Firm, tasty, moderately acid white flesh.	Large, upright, productive tree; regular bearer. Very low chill requirement.
'Pink Lady'	6–15, 19	Late	Medium to large; pink blush over yellow skin. Firm, juicy flesh. Sweet-tart flavor; improves with storage. Good fresh or baked.	From Australia; does well in warm-summer areas. Very susceptible to fireblight. Moderately low chill requirement. Self-fruitful.
'Pink Pearl'	1–9, 14–16	Early	Medium size; pale green skin, sometimes blushed red. Sweet-tart pink flesh. Good keeper.	Very attractive in bloom; blossoms deeper pink than on most other varieties.

Variety	Zones	Ripening Time	Fruit	Comments
'Pristine'	3–11, 14–16, 18, 19	Early	Medium size; bright yellow skin. Mildly tart white flesh. Good for eating, baking, applesauce.	Immune to scab; somewhat resistant to mildew, fireblight.
'Red Delicious' ('Delicious')	Sold wherever apples will grow; best in 2, 3, 7	Midseason	Large; color varies with strain, climate (best with sunny, warm days, cool nights). Mildly sweet; good aftertaste. Older, striped kinds often taste better than highly colored commercial types.	Many strains that vary in ripening season, depth and uniformity of coloring. 'Crimson Spur' and 'Bisbee Spur' are popular varieties in home gardens. All types susceptible to scab.
'Redfree'	3b–9, 14–17	Early	Medium size; red. Firm, crisp flesh with good flavor.	Heavy bearer. Immune to scab.
'Rome Beauty' ('Red Rome')	3, 6, 7, 10, 11, 19	Late	Large, round, smooth; red. Greenish white flesh. Outstanding baking apple, only fair for eating fresh.	Bears at an early age.
'Rubinette'	4–6, 19	Midseason	Small to medium; golden with red stripes. Excellent, sweet-tart flavor.	Resists scab and mildew.
'Shizuka'	1–9, 14–16	Late	Large, with full conical shape; gold with light red blush. High-quality fruit with good flavor. Stores well.	Productive tree.
'Sierra Beauty'	2, 3, 6–9, 14–16	Late	Large; exceptionally attractive yellow apple with red stripes. Firm, sweet-tart flesh. Keeps well.	Productive tree.
'Spartan'	3b–7, 15, 16	Midseason	Medium size; dark red with purplish bloom. Crisp flesh. Sweet-tart flavor.	Good tree habit. Heavy producer.
'Spitzenberg' ('Esopus Spitzenberg')	1–7, 14–16; best in 1–3	Late	Medium to large; red-dotted yellow. Crisp, fine-grained, tangy, spicy flesh.	Old favorite that still rates high. Subject to fireblight, mildew.
'Summerred'	A2, A3, 1–7, 15, 16	Early	Medium size; bright red. Tart flavor; good chiefly for cooking until fully ripe, then good dessert quality too.	Hardy. Consistent annual bearer for western Oregon and Washington.
'Sundowner'	6–15	Midseason to late	Medium size; red. Crisp, sweet flesh. Stores well.	From Australia. Tends to bear heavily in alternate years.
'Tropical Beauty'	18–24, H1	Early	Medium to large; bright red. Juicy white flesh with mild, sweet flavor.	Partially self-fruitful; production enhanced if grown near 'Adina'.
'Wealthy' ('Red Wealthy')	1–7, 19	Early midseason	Medium to large; greenish yellow with red overlay. Flesh white with pink veining, firm, tart, juicy. Good cooking variety.	Small, cold-hardy tree that tends to bear in alternate years.
'William's Pride'	1–7, 19	Early	Medium size; dark red. Sweet-spicy flavor. One of the best early reds.	Immune to scab; resistant to fireblight. Susceptible to mildew.
'Winter Banana'	3b, 7–9, 14–24	Late midseason	Large; attractive, pale yellow blushed pink. Tender, tangy, aromatic flesh.	Low-chill variety. There is a 'Spur Winter Banana'.
'Winter Pearmain'	20–24	Midseason	Medium to large; pale greenish yellow skin with pink blush. Tender, fine-grained flesh; excellent flavor.	Low-chill variety. Performs better than standard cold-winter varieties in Southern California.
'Yellow Transparent'	A2, A3, 1–3, 7, 14–16	Early	Medium size; thin yellow skin. Tart white flesh. Good for cooking if harvested when greenish yellow.	Tall, vigorous tree with excellent hardiness.
'Zestar'	A2, A3, 1–7, 15, 16	Early midseason	Medium size; yellow with red stripes. Crisp white, juicy, sweet-tart flesh. Good for eating fresh and baking.	Bred in Minnesota; has excellent winter-hardiness.

Columnar apple trees grow up, not out; they fit nicely into tight spaces.

they form earlier (within 2 years after planting) and grow closer together on shorter branches, producing more apples per foot of branch. Spur apples are natural or genetic semidwarfs about two-thirds the size of standard apple trees. They can be further dwarfed by grafting them onto dwarfing rootstocks; EMLA 27, M9, P22, and MARK produce the smallest trees. Some apples, called semispur varieties, have a fruiting habit intermediate between spur and nonspur kinds.

Columnar apple trees. Zones 2a–9, 14–16. These develop a single spirelike trunk to 8–10 ft. tall, with fruiting spurs directly on the trunk or on very short branchlets. Total width does not exceed 2 ft. Varieties include 'Crimson Spire' (late midseason), which bears red fruit with sweet-tart white flesh; 'Emerald Spire' (midseason), mellow, sweet green fruit with a gold blush; 'Golden Sentinel' (midseason), sweet, juicy yellow fruit;

'Northpole' (early midseason), crisp, juicy 'McIntosh'-type red fruit; 'Scarlet Sentinel' (midseason), large, sweet green-yellow fruit with a red blush; 'Scarlet Spire' (midseason), juicy, red-and-green eating fruit; and 'Ultra Spire' (midseason), tart, tangy red fruit with a yellowish blush. Columnar trees are easy to maintain and attractive as accent, screen, or container plants.

HOW TO GROW IT

best site Full sun is essential for a good crop, as is protection from cold spring winds, which can interfere with pollination.

yield Varies widely according to variety, age, and rootstock.

soil Apples do best in deep, well-drained soil but get by in many imperfect conditions, including heavy soil.

planting Best time to plant bare-root stock is in winter or early spring, but containerized apples can be planted anytime where climates are mild and whenever the soil is workable in cold-winter climates. *In containers:* Any dwarf or columnar apple can be grown in a wine half-barrel. Be sure to plant a variety that doesn't need a pollenizer, a tree that has two different varieties grafted into the same tree, or two different varieties in neighboring containers. Protect containers from sustained temperatures below 15°F/–9°C by bringing them into an unheated garage or porch, or the roots will freeze and the trees will be lost (tops are hardier than roots).

spacing Spacing should equal the mature width of the tree-rootstock combination you're considering. Here are some general examples. *Full-size (standard) apple trees:* 20 ft. apart. *Spur types:* 12–14 ft. apart; on EMLA 27, M9, or P22 rootstocks, 6–8 ft. apart; on MARK rootstock, 8 ft. apart. *Semidwarf trees:* on MM106 or MM111 rootstocks, 15–17 ft. apart; on MARK, M26, or M7 rootstocks, 10 ft. apart. *Dwarf trees:* on EMLA 27, M9, or P22 rootstocks, 5–8 ft. apart. *Columnar types:* $1^{1}/_{2}$ to 2 ft. apart.

water Regular water is especially important in spring and summer as fruit develops. Don't let soil around newly planted trees and shallow-rooted dwarf varieties dry out; mulch helps retain soil moisture and keep weeds down.

fertilizer Give newly planted trees $^{1}/_{4}$ pound of 10-10-10 fertilizer as buds start to open the first year. In every subsequent year, add $^{1}/_{4}$ pound until dwarf trees and columnar types are getting $2^{1}/_{2}$ pounds, semidwarfs 5 pounds, standards 10 pounds. If trees are bearing well and producing 6–8 in. of annual tip growth, you don't need to feed at all.

pruning, training For dwarf or semidwarf trees, the preferred style is a pyramidal or modified leader, in which widely angled branches are encouraged to grow in spiral placement around the trunk. Don't worry about fruit production the first 4 or 5 years—prune to develop strong, evenly spaced scaffold branches late in the dormant season. Keep narrow-angled crotches from developing, and don't let side branches outgrow the leader or let secondary branches outgrow the primary branches.

Prune mature trees late in the dormant season by cutting off weak, dead, or poorly placed branches and twigs, especially those growing toward the center of the tree. Removing such growth will discourage mildew and encourage development of strong new wood with new fruiting spurs. (On apples, spurs may produce for up to 20 years but they tend to weaken after about 3 years.) If you have inherited an old tree, selective thinning of branches will accomplish the same goal.

Dwarf trees can be grown as espaliers tied to wood or wire frames, fences, or other supports. On columnar apples, just remove any wayward growth.

Some apples are alternate bearers, tending to produce heavy crops every other year and light crops in between. To make these trees bear more evenly, thin young fruit aggressively during years when cropping is heavy. Thinning should be done after June drop, when the tree spontaneously thins itself. To thin, remove all but one apple in each cluster, keeping apples about 6 in. apart on the tree.

harvest Pick with fruit nested in your whole palm—not just your fingers—when fruit is fully colored and sweet. Take the stem with the fruit, but be careful not to damage the spur from which the stems grow.

challenges Codling moth is the universal insect pest of apples. Pheromone traps, trichogramma wasps, or horticultural oil may be enough to thwart this pest in home gardens, but proper timing is critical. Spinosad, a relatively new organic control, is also effective. Apple maggot is a problem in some areas (particularly western Washington); it can make fruit soft, rotten, and unusable. Various types of sticky traps may be of some help, as can the application of spinosad. Leaf rollers and aphids are also potentially troublesome.

Apple scab causes hard, corky spots on the fruit, with subsequent defoliation and stunting of immature fruit. It is particularly severe in coastal areas of the Pacific Northwest. Powdery mildew and fireblight can also infect apples in some regions. Planting disease-resistant varieties is the best way to avoid these problems.

For timing of sprays and other control measures for any of the above problems, consult your Cooperative Extension Office or a reliable local nursery.

KEVIN HAUSER ON
low-chill apples

California Rare Fruit Growers is an organization that collects information from a vast network of home gardeners. Longtime member and apple expert Kevin Hauser grows about 100 varieties of apples in Riverside, CA, where winters are mild and warm. Although the majority of apple varieties need cold winters for maximum production and uniformity, Hauser has found that many will bear fruit under considerably warmer conditions—even types not normally known for low chilling requirements. Their bloom period may be later and longer, which can make it hard to time pesticide applications, and trees may have branches with fewer leaves and with fruit clustered at branch ends, but for home gardeners these aren't critical issues. In the end, says Hauser, "What I grow still blows away anything I can get at the store."

His favorite apple is 'Rubinette', which he says is "by far the best." But he's also a big fan of 'Anna'. "It has a nice zing for fresh eating," he says, "and the tree is an overachiever: it explodes with apples." His fondness for 'Dorsett Golden' isn't far behind. Other varieties that get high marks in his garden are 'Arkansas Black', 'Fuji', 'Granny Smith', 'Pink Lady', 'Rome Beauty', 'Wealthy', and 'William's Pride'.

Apricot

Prunus armeniaca
Rose family *(Rosaceae)*
DECIDUOUS TREE

◢ **ZONES VARY BY VARIETY**

☼ **FULL SUN**

💧 **REGULAR WATER DURING FRUIT DEVELOPMENT**

This stone fruit from China can be grown throughout much of the West, with some limitations. Because apricot trees bloom early in the season, they will not fruit in regions with late frosts. In cool, humid coastal areas, tree and fruit are usually subject to brown rot. In mild-winter areas of Southern California, only varieties with low requirements for winter chill do well.

Standard apricot trees reach 15–20 ft. tall and wide and make good, easily maintained, dual-purpose fruit and shade trees; they can also be espaliered. Thin, roundish leaves to 3 in. long are reddish when new, maturing to bright green; flowers are pink or white.

Apricot trees bear most of their fruit on short spurs that form on the previous year's growth and remain fruitful for about 4 years. Most varieties ripen from late spring into summer.

Recommended varieties. The following is a good representation of nursery varieties; many are available on dwarfing and semidwarfing rootstocks. Most varieties are self-fruitful; those that need a pollenizer are noted. For apricot-plum hybrids, see *Plum Hybrids.*

'Autumn Glo'. Zones 8, 9, 12–16, 18–23. Medium-size fruit with exceptional flavor. Late.

'Autumn Royal'. Zones 2, 3, 6–9, 12–16, 18–24. Resembles 'Blenheim' but fruit ripens very late; only fall-ripening apricot tree.

'Blenheim' ('Royal'). Zones 2, 3, 6–23. Standard variety in California's apricot regions. Good for canning or drying. Early to midseason.

'Chinese' ('Mormon'). Zones 1–3, 6. Mild, sweet, and flavorful. Late-blooming, hardy tree; good production in late-frost and cold-winter regions. Mid- to late season.

'Floragold'. Zones 2, 3, 6–23. Full-size fruit grows on natural semidwarf tree (about two-thirds the size of a standard apricot tree). Reliable producer. Early.

'Goldcot'. Zones 1–3. Sweet flavor. Developed for cold climates. Midseason.

'Golden Amber'. Zones 2, 3, 6–9, 12–16, 18–23. Like 'Blenheim' but blooms over a month-long period. Late season.

'Gold Kist'. Zones 8, 9, 12–16, 18–23. Excellent sweet-tart flavor. Heavy bearing, even in mild-winter areas. Early.

Ripe apricots signal the start of the summer fruit season.

'Harcot'. Zones 1–11, 14–16. Medium to large fruit is sweet, rich, and very juicy. Tree is frost-hardy, blooms late. Early.

'Harglow'. Zones 1–11, 14–16. Medium-size orange fruit, sometimes blushed red; firm, sweet, flavorful. Late blooming; disease-resistant. Early.

'Katy'. Zones 2, 3, 6–23. Large yellow fruit with red blush; mild, sweet flavor. Good choice for mild-winter areas. Early.

Manchurian apricot *(Prunus armeniaca mandshurica).* Zones A2, A3, 1–3. Hardy shrub to small tree. Small, mild-flavored orange fruit; good for drying. Early.

'Montrose'. Zones 2–3, 6–12, 14–18. Large yellow fruit with a red blush; sweet and juicy, with excellent flavor. Has edible kernel ("sweet pit"). A hardy, frost-resistant variety from Montrose, Colorado. Late.

'Moongold'. Zones 1–3. Plum-size, golden, sweet, sprightly fruit. Developed for cold-winter climates. Late.

'Moorpark'. Zones 2, 3, 6–11, 14–16. Very large fruit; fine flavor. Color develops unevenly. Good dessert or drying variety; poor canner. Midseason.

'Newcastle'. Zones 10–12, 20–23. Small to medium fruit with soft flesh, red-blushed yellow skin; sweet, juicy, rich flavor. Good Southern California variety; needs little winter chill. Midseason.

'Perfection' ('Goldbeck'). Zones 2–9, 12–16, 18–23. Fruit very large but flavor only mediocre. Low chill requirement; hardy tree. Needs pollenizer. Early.

'Puget Gold'. Zones 4–6. Medium-size fruit with good flavor; low in acid. Consistent bearer in Puget Sound area; fairly resistant to apricot diseases. Late.

'Riland'. Zones 2, 3, 6. Highly colored, roundish fruit. Needs pollenizer. Midseason.

'Rival'. Zones 2–6. Large, oval orange fruit blushed red. Requires an early-flowering pollenizer, such as 'Perfection'. Early.

'Royalty'. Zones 2, 3, 6–9, 12–23. Extra-large fruit on heavy, wind-resistant spurs. Begins bearing at an early age. Early.

'Sun-Glow'. Zones 2–6. Highly colored fruit. Hardy tree with extra-hardy fruit buds. Midseason.

'Sungold'. Zones 1–3. Plum-size, slightly flattened, bright orange, sweet, mild fruit. Developed for cold-winter climates. Early.

'Tilton'. Zones 1–8, 10, 11, 18, 20. Higher chill requirement than 'Blenheim' but less subject to brown rot and sunburn. Midseason.

'Tomcot'. Zones 8, 9, 12–16. Large fruit with sweet orange flesh. Needs a pollenizer. Early.

'Wenatchee' ('Wenatchee Moorpark'). Zones 2, 3, 6. Large fruit with excellent flavor. Difficult to pollinate; 'Perfection' does the best job. Midseason.

HOW TO GROW IT

best site Sunny location with protection from cold spring winds.

yield Varies by variety, age, and size of tree, but 100 pounds is common on a mature, full-size tree.

soil Light loam with good drainage.

planting Set out bare-root stock in late winter or early spring. *In containers:* Choose a variety that comes on a dwarfing rootstock and plant it in a wine half-barrel. Unless you have two containers for two different trees, pick a variety that doesn't need a pollenizer.

spacing Plant 10–20 ft. apart, depending on variety and size.

water Regular water is essential from flowering through harvest, then supply moderate water until all leaves have dropped in autumn. Deep soaking is best.

fertilizer Apply low-nitrogen complete fertilizer once in early spring. Trees growing in containers need an additional application 2 months later, since irrigation washes out much of the fertilizer before it can be used.

pruning, training To get a good crop of large fruit, thin excess fruit from branches in midspring, leaving 2–4 in. between individual fruits. Prune in summer (rather than in the dormant season, as is usually recommended) to avoid Eutypa dieback, a disease characterized by sudden limb dieback and oozing cankers; it is spread by rain and can infect trees through pruning wounds.

harvest Pick fruit when it has colored up and slightly softened.

challenges Apricots are subject to diseases such as brown rot and gummosis. To avert some problems, consult your Cooperative Extension Office for a local timetable and directions for preventive spraying. Essential treatment dates are during dormancy, before and after flowering, and at red-bud stage. You can avoid trouble with verticillium by planting in a location where you have not recently grown tomatoes, peppers, eggplant, potatoes, raspberries, or strawberries.

Asian Pear

Pyrus species
Rose family *(Rosaceae)*
DECIADUOUS TREES

🖊 **ZONES 2–12, 14–21, EXCEPT AS NOTED**
☀ **FULL SUN**
💧 **REGULAR WATER**

These pears are descendants of two Asian species: *Pyrus pyrifolia (P. serotina)* and *P. ussuriensis.* Trees grow to 25–30 ft. tall and about half as wide, but they're easily kept to half that size with pruning. They are quite beautiful trees and would likely be grown as ornamentals even if they didn't bear fruit. They are also available on a range of dwarfing and semidwarfing rootstocks.

Unlike the more familiar European pears, Asian pears are generally round in shape, with a crisp, faintly gritty, firm to hard texture. Asian pears are sometimes called apple pears because of their roundness and crispness, but they are not hybrids of those two fruits. Fresh Asian pears are excellent combined with other fruits and vegetables in salads. Fruit can be stored at room temperature for about 2 weeks or refrigerated for 2 to 3 months.

Asian pears need the same general culture as European pears but have a lower chilling requirement (some need as few as 400 hours) and a greater resistance to fireblight. All benefit from pollination by a second variety that flowers at the same time; consult your local nursery for recommendations. European pears generally bloom too late to be reliable pollenizers for Asian pears.

Recommended varieties. Following are some good choices for the West. In California, harvest runs from mid-July through September; in Washington, it lasts from August through October.

'Chojuro'. Large, russeted brown to orange fruit with crisp, juicy flesh and light spice flavor. Midseason.

'Hosui'. Large fruit with bronzy orange, russeted skin and outstanding flavor. Very susceptible to fireblight. Early midseason.

'Ichiban' ('Ichiban Nashi'). Medium to large, smooth, brown fruit with white flesh that has a slight butterscotch flavor. Handle with care to avoid injuring the fruit's skin. Productive; some tolerance for bacterial infection. Early.

'Kikusui'. Medium-size, flattish, yellow-green fruit with sweet, juicy flesh. Tends to drop fruit early. Fireblight-resistant. Midseason.

'Korean Giant'. Zones 1–12, 14–21. Extra-large, russeted, olive green fruit weighing up to a pound. Keeps in cool (but unrefrigerated) storage for months. Vigorous and cold-hardy. Late.

'Kosui'. Small to medium-size fruit with russeted skin and crisp, sweet, juicy flesh. Vigorous. Susceptible to bacterial infection in western Washington. Early midseason.

'Mishirasu'. Very large fruit with russeted skin and good, crisp flavor; some may weigh over a pound. Very productive. Late midseason.

'Nijisseki' ('Twentieth Century'). Small, round, yellow fruit with white, juicy, sweet, crisp flesh and excellent flavor. Stores well. Self-fruitful. Midseason.

'Seuri'. Small to medium, round fruit with orange-tinted skin and aromatic flesh. Very vigorous and productive; resists fireblight. Late midseason.

'Shinko'. Large round fruit with golden brown, russeted skin and sweet, juicy, crisp flesh. Flavor best in hot climates. Upright growth habit; resists fireblight. Late midseason.

'Shinseiki'. Medium to large fruit with smooth, greenish yellow skin, white crisp flesh, and sweet flavor. Disease-resistant; self-fruitful. Can grow in low desert. Early midseason.

'Tsu Li'. Zones 1–12, 14–21. Elongated, yellow-green fruit; looks like a cross between a European pear and a football. Has aromatic flesh and good flavor that gets even better in storage. Vigorous, upright habit. Low chill requirement; some fireblight tolerance. Late.

'Ya Li'. Zones 1–12, 14–21. Greenish yellow, European pear–shaped fruit with crisp, mild, sweet flesh. Stores well, but fruit is easily marred. Vigorous tree. Late.

'Yoinashi'. Medium to large, brown-speckled pear with sweet, crisp flesh that has a hint of butterscotch flavor. Vigorous; resists bacterial infection. Late midseason.

HOW TO GROW IT

best site Open, sunny spot, preferably on a slope if late frosts are a problem where you garden.

yield More than 100 pounds per mature tree.

soil Asian pears perform best in deep, well-drained loam, but they tolerate heavy soils better than most fruit trees.

planting Plant container-grown stock anytime except in very hot summer weather. Plant bare-root stock when it is available in late winter or spring. Don't plant any deeper than the tree was grown in the nursery or crown rot could kill the tree.

spacing Plant trees 12–15 ft. apart.

water Regular irrigation keeps trees healthy and makes fruit larger.

'Hosui' is one of the most popular Asian pears, thanks to its crunch and its sweet, slightly acidic flavor.

fertilizer Asian pears need little or no fertilizer if tip growth is 12–18 in. per season and fruit crops are abundant. If this isn't the case, give each mature tree 5 pounds of 5-10-10 fertilizer every third or fourth year, before buds open in spring.

pruning, training During winter, cut out dead, injured, crossing, and closely parallel branches. Work to establish strong scaffold branches and open up the center of the tree. Fruit bears most heavily on 2- to 6-year-old spurs. Older fruiting branches should be removed to keep new branches (and spurs) coming. Thin pears to one per fruiting spur.

harvest Pick when fruit is full size and fully colored. Taste tells when it's ready.

challenges Fireblight causes limb dieback; prune into healthy wood below the infection or buy resistant varieties. Bacterial infection from *Pseudomonas syringae* is most common in areas with cool springs when trees are planted during rainy periods; in those places, wait for a dry spell and plant resistant varieties. Codling moth larvae (apple worms) can ruin a crop; treat trees with spinosad or hang pheromone traps to capture them. Check with your Cooperative Extension Office on the best timing. Spinosad can also be used to treat apple maggots. If spider mites take hold (as they are prone to when trees are grown with too little water), treat with neem or sulfur.

Avocado

Persea americana
Laurel family *(Lauraceae)*
EVERGREEN TREE

- ✎ ZONES VARY BY VARIETY
- ☼ FULL SUN
- 💧 REGULAR WATER

In California, two races of avocados are grown: Guatemalan *(Persea americana guatemalensis)* and Mexican *(P. a. drymifolia)*. Widely planted varieties 'Hass' and 'Fuerte' are hybrids. Ideal climates for Guatemalan varieties (generally hardy to 30°F/–1°C) are Zones 21, 23, and 24, but good results can be had in Zones 19, 20, and 22, and some success can be expected in Zones 9 and 15. Mexican varieties, which bear smaller, less attractive fruit, are hardier (down to at least 24°F/–4°C) and grow in Zones 9, 15–24, and some warmer locations in Zones 8 and 14. (See the chart for cold-hardiness of hybrids.) Avocados bloom in late winter to late spring, so even though older trees will survive the seasonal lows, temperatures much below freezing will damage flowers or fruit. In Hawaii, Guatemalan and hybrid varieties are best adapted to (and are grown throughout) Zone H2, but away from exposure to salt spray.

Avocado varieties have flowers categorized as either type A or type B (noted in chart), depending on the time of day they open and when pollen is released. Where avocados are common, isolated trees may produce enough fruit for home consumption; but for best production, plant one of each type or graft a limb of one type onto a bearing tree of the other type. Mexican avocados mature 6 to 8 months after flowering; Guatemalan avocados mature in 12 to 18 months.

Most varieties grow 30–40 ft. tall and spread wider (size can be controlled by pruning). They also produce dense shade and shed leaves throughout the year.

Unless otherwise noted, the avocados listed in the chart have thin, pliable, smooth skin.

HOW TO GROW IT

best site Sloping ground in full sun.

yield 80 to 140 pounds per mature tree.

soil Avocados can grow in a wide range of soils, but perfect drainage year-round is essential.

planting Plant balled-and-burlapped or container plants in early autumn or spring. *In containers:* You can grow small varieties such as 'Holiday' in large containers (no smaller than a wine half-barrel, and preferably larger).

spacing Most types need 15–35 ft., depending on variety and rootstock. Dwarf varieties such as 'Holiday' can be held to 12 ft. with attentive pruning.

water Keep the soil evenly moist by using sprinkler irrigation when the soil near the surface begins to dry. Give plants an occasional deep soaking to wash accumulated salts from the soil around the roots. Let a mulch of fallen leaves build up under the tree to conserve soil moisture.

fertilizer Feed young trees lightly; mature trees need 1 pound of actual nitrogen per year, split into two or more applications in spring and summer.

pruning, training Avocados need to be pruned only for shape and to limit height so you can get to the fruit at harvest time.

harvest Fruit doesn't ripen on the tree, so you'll have to time your harvest to the color of the avocados. For dark-skinned varieties, wait until they have reached full size and color before you pick. For green-skinned types, after fruit has sized up watch for a color shift from shiny bright green to dull, slightly yellowish green, then pick. In mature avocados, the seed coat turns from thick and white to papery thin and dark brown. For all kinds, let the predicted harvest season tell you when to start checking. After you pick a mature fruit, it should soften at room temperature within 10 days without shriveling. If it doesn't, wait a couple of weeks and try again. Mature fruit can hang on the tree for weeks without losing quality, so you have a fair window of time to test for ripeness. Pick high fruit by snipping stems with a pole pruner; catch it in a cloth bag or with a blanket stretched between two people (kids love this).

challenges Avocado trees are very susceptible to *Phytophthora* root rot. Added mulch and gypsum can create soil conditions that suppress this fungus. After an avocado is planted, cover the soil around it with a 6- to 12-in.-deep layer of organic mulch or wood chips, but keep the mulching material at least 6 in. away from the trunk. Scatter a total of 25 pounds of gypsum per year around the tree a little at a time. Control chlorosis with iron and zinc chelates. Persea mite is a problem in Southern California; it causes small yellow and black dead spots on the foliage and excessive leaf drop. It can be partially controlled by releasing one of several species of predatory mites. For more information, contact your Cooperative Extension Office.

Continued on page 168 ▶

The bright green 'Hass' avocado in the foreground is still maturing, but the others are ready to be picked and allowed to ripen fully at room temperature.

top picks to grow

Variety	Zones	Harvest Period	Fruit	Comments
'Bacon'	9, 15–24	Midfall through winter	Medium size; green skin. Good quality.	Mexican. Upright grower. Bears heavier in alternate years. Type A flower. 'Jim Bacon' is a slightly hardier seedling selection.
'Fuerte'	9, 15, 19–24	Late fall through spring	Medium size; green skin. High quality.	Hybrid. Hardy to 27°F/–3°C. Well-known variety. Large tree. Early blooming. Tends to bear in alternate years. Type B flower.
'Gwen'	19–24	Spring into fall	Medium size; green skin. Good quality.	Guatemalan. Medium tree with narrow habit. Bears in alternate years. Type A flower.
'Hass'	16, 17, 19–24	Spring into fall	Medium to large; dark purple, pebbly, thick but pliable skin. Excellent flavor.	Hybrid. Hardy to 30°F/–1°C. Large, spreading tree. Bears heavier in alternate years. Type A flower. 'Lamb Hass' is more productive.
'Holiday'	19–24	Midfall through winter	Large; green skin. Very good flavor.	Guatemalan. Dwarf tree with weeping habit. Bears in alternate years. Often grown in large containers. Type A flower.
'Jim'	9, 15, 19–24	Late fall into winter	Medium size; with green skin and long neck	Mexican. Type B flower.
'Kahaluu'	H2	Fall into winter	Medium to large; green skin. Superb flavor.	Hybrid. Hardy to 30°F/–1°C. Light producer. Type B flower.
'Mexicola'	9, 15–24	Late summer into fall	Small; with tender, dark purple skin. Outstanding, nutty flavor. Large seed.	Mexican. Very cold-hardy, to 20°F/–7°C. Heavy producer. Type A flower. 'Mexicola Grande' is larger and a bit hardier.
'Murashige'	H2	Spring to late summer	Medium to large; with green, pebbly skin. High quality.	Hybrid. Hardy to 30°F/–1°C. Heavy producer. Type B flower.
'Nabal'	19–24	Summer into fall	Medium to large; green skin. Excellent flavor.	Guatemalan. Tends to bear in alternate years. Type B flower.
'Pinkerton'	9, 15, 19–24	Winter through spring	Medium to large; green skin. Very good quality.	Guatemalan. Large tree. Consistent producer. Type A flower.
'Reed'	21–24	Summer into fall	Medium to large; with green, pebbly skin. Fine flavor.	Guatemalan. Slender, upright tree. Tends to bear well alone. Type A flower.
'Sharwil'	H2	Fall into spring	Medium size; with green, pebbly skin. Excellent flavor.	Hybrid. Hardy to 30°F/–1°C. Heavy producer. Type B flower.
'Stewart'	9, 15–24	Fall to winter	Small to medium; with dark purple skin. Excellent flavor.	Mexican. Compact tree. Type B flower.
'Wertz' ('Wurtz')	19–24	Summer	Medium size; with green, pebbly skin. Rich flavor.	Guatemalan. Dwarf tree with weeping branches. Tends to bear in alternate years. Often sold as 'Littlecado' or 'Minicado'. Type A flower.
'Whitsell'	19–24	Midwinter into fall	Medium size; green skin. Very good quality.	Guatemalan. Medium tree. Tends to bear in alternate years. Type B flower.
'Yamagata'	H2	Late spring through summer	Medium to large; with green, pebbly skin. Rich flavor.	Hybrid. Hardy to 30°F/–1°C. Heavy producer. Type B flower.
'Zutano'	9, 16–24	Midfall to midwinter	Medium size; green skin. Average quality.	Hybrid. Hardy to 24°F/–4°C. Upright grower. Used to cross-pollinate 'Hass'. Type B flower.

Cherry

Prunus species
Rose family *(Rosaceae)*
DECIDUOUS TREES

✎ **ZONES VARY BY TYPE**
☼ **FULL SUN**
💧 **REGULAR WATER**

Both sweet and sour cherries are attractive, productive trees in the home garden. Sweet cherry trees are larger and usually require a pollenizer, while sour cherries are smaller, more widely adapted, and self-fruitful (a lone tree will bear). Most people eat sweet cherries fresh and use sour cherries in cooking; both kinds dry well.

Sweet cherry. These are descended from *Prunus avium*, which is native to Europe, northern Africa, and south-western Asia and naturalized in North America. They are the most common market-type cherries and the most widely grown. Trees are 30–35 ft. in height, with some varieties as broad as they are tall. They're at their best in deep, well-drained soil in Zones 2, 6–9, 14, and 15, though at least one variety ('Kristin') has been success-fully grown in Zones A2, A3, and 1. Sweet cherries need many winter hours below 45°F/7°C to flower and fruit, so they are not adapted to mild-winter climates. They also can't take extreme summer heat or intense winter cold; frosts or rain in spring can damage the crop.

In most cases, two trees are needed to produce fruit, and the second tree must be chosen with care as certain varieties won't pollinate each other (these are noted in the list that follows). 'Craig's Crimson', 'Lapins', 'Stella', 'Sweetheart', 'Vandalay', and 'White Gold' are self-fruitful.

Cherry trees are easier to grow and harvest when propagated on a dwarfing rootstock, such as the Giessen 148 (Gisela) series. Such trees can easily be maintained at less than half the size of those growing on standard rootstocks.

Fruiting spurs are long-lived and do not need to be renewed by pruning. Prune trees only to maintain good structure and shape. Fruit appears in late spring to early summer.

The following are among the best varieties:

'Angela'. Small, glossy black fruit with excellent flavor. Resists cracking. Good pollenizer for other cher-ries. Midseason to late.

'Bing'. Top-quality, large, dark red, meaty fruit of fine flavor. Will not pollinate 'Lambert' or 'Royal Ann'. Midseason.

Late-ripening 'Sweetheart' cherries have a mild, sweet flavor and excellent firm texture.

'Black Tartarian'. Purplish black, firm, sweet fruit smaller than that of 'Bing'. Good pollenizer for other cherries. Early.

'Craig's Crimson'. Medium to large, deep red to black fruit with superb flavor. Naturally dwarf tree (about two-thirds normal size). Self-fruitful. Midseason.

'Early Burlat'. Fruit like that of 'Bing' but ripens 2 weeks earlier. Early.

'Early Ruby'. Dark red, purple-fleshed early cherry that performs well in all sweet cherry areas. 'Black Tartarian', 'Royal Ann', and 'Van' are all good pollenizers. Early.

'Emperor Francis'. Medium-size, light red fruit with fine flavor. Favorite in the Northwest. Early.

'Hardy Giant'. Dark red fruit resembles that of 'Bing'. Good pollenizer, especially for 'Lambert'. Midseason.

'Hartland'. Good-flavored black cherry with softer fruit than 'Bing'. Early midseason.

Continued on page 170 ▶

Sour cherries such as 'English Morello' are a perfect choice for jams and pies.

'Kristin'. Large black fruit resists cracking. One of the hardiest sweet cherries; worth a try in Zones A2, A3, and 1. Midseason.

'Lambert'. Very large, very firm black fruit with flavor sprightlier than that of 'Bing'. Late-ripening 'Republican' is the best pollenizer. Will not pollinate 'Bing' or 'Royal Ann'. Late.

'Lapins'. Resembles 'Bing' but is self-fruitful. Early to midseason.

'Mona'. Resembles 'Black Tartarian' but the fruit is larger. Very early.

'Rainier'. Has yellow skin with pink blush. Fruit ripens a few days before 'Bing'. Midseason.

'Republican' ('Black Republican', 'Black Oregon'). Large, spreading tree. Small, round, purplish black fruit with dark juice, tender yet crisp texture, good flavor. Good pollenizer for other cherries. Late.

'Royal Ann' ('Napoleon'). Large, spreading tree; very productive. Light yellow fruit with pink blush, tender and crisp texture, sprightly flavor. Will not pollinate 'Bing' or 'Lambert'. Midseason.

'Sam'. Vigorous tree. Large, firm black fruit with excellent flavor. Good pollenizer for other cherries. Midseason to late.

'Stella'. Dark fruit like 'Lambert', but ripening a few days later. Self-fruitful. Good pollenizer for other cherries (but it will not pollinate 'Bing' in mild-winter climates). Late. 'Compact Stella' is similar, but tree is half the size.

'Sweetheart'. Large, bright red fruit with excellent flavor. Self-fruitful; heavy bearing. Late.

'Utah Giant'. Ripens with 'Bing' but fruit is larger and sweeter, developing sweetness even before fully ripe. Holds color when cooked. Pollinate with 'Van' or 'Stella'. Midseason.

'Van'. Shiny black fruit, firmer and slightly smaller than that of 'Bing', with good flavor. Heavy-bearing tree. Good pollenizer for other cherries. Ripens earlier than 'Bing' in the Northwest but at the same time in California. Early to midseason.

'Vandalay'. Large, black fruit with excellent flavor. Self-fruitful; resists cracking. Midseason.

'White Gold'. Large, red-blushed yellow fruit with fine flavor. This is the only self-fruitful white cherry. Heavy bearing; resists cracking. Midseason.

Sour cherry. *P. cerasus*, also known as pie cherry, may be native from southeastern Europe to northern India. These are spreading trees 15–20 ft. tall. They are self-fruitful but poor pollenizers for sweet cherries. There are far fewer types of sour cherries than sweet cherries; those listed here are the most widely grown. The category name notwithstanding, a few varieties listed here are sweet enough to enjoy fresh.

'Early Richmond'. Small, bright red fruit is soft, juicy, and sweet-tart. Early.

'English Morello'. Darker, tarter fruit than that of 'Early Richmond', with red juice. Late.

'Kansas Sweet' ('Hansen'). Large, semisweet red fruit. Late.

'Meteor'. Fruit similar to that of 'Early Richmond', but tree is smaller (to 12 ft.). Late.

'Montmorency'. Like 'Early Richmond'. Midseason to late.

'North Star'. Red to dark red skin and sour yellow flesh. Small, very hardy tree. Midseason.

'Surefire'. Bright red skin and flesh with very sweet flavor. Late.

HOW TO GROW IT

best site Choose an open site in full sun but not in lawn, which has different water and fertilizer requirements.

yield 20 to 60 pounds per tree, depending on variety and rootstock.

soil Deep garden loam with good drainage is optimal; not sandy or shallow soil.

planting Plant bare-root trees in late winter or early spring, or balled-and-burlapped or container plants any time they're available and the soil is workable. Plant with the bud union (the swollen place where the rootstock meets the scion) about 5 in. above ground level.

spacing *Sweet cherry:* standard trees, 32–40 ft.; on Colt rootstock, 20–26 ft.; on dwarfing rootstock, 15–20 ft. *Sour cherry:* 13–20 ft.

water Regular water throughout the growing season is important. It ensures steady fruit development from flowering to harvest, and proper flower bud development after that. To prevent fruit splitting, cut back on watering as cherries approach harvest.

fertilizer *Standard sweet cherries* need no fertilizer if the trees are putting out 6–12 in. of new growth per year. Otherwise, give full-size, fully bearing trees 5 pounds of 10-10-10 fertilizer in spring and give young trees 1/2 pound per year of age. *For dwarf sweet cherries or sour cherries,* apply 1/2 pound of 10-10-10 fertilizer per inch of trunk diameter.

pruning, training *Sweet cherries* need pruning only to remove injured or diseased branches; do it after harvest in summer to reduce risk of bacterial canker. *Sour cherries* fruit mostly on fairly young wood; prune out old wood in spring to keep new wood coming.

harvest Grasp the top of the cherry stem, where it emerges from the spur, and twist. Be careful not to damage the spur (or the tiny buds growing from it), since it's the source of next year's fruit. Don't pick cherries until they are fully colored and taste ripe (sweet or sweet-tart, depending on type and variety); they don't ripen further after harvest.

Extremely sweet 'Rainier' is prized for its attractive skin and delicately flavored yellow flesh.

challenges Use netting to keep birds from eating the crop, or grow yellow-fruiting varieties as birds tend to leave them alone. For control of brown rot and blossom blight, apply a copper spray just as leaves drop in autumn, then a fungicide when first blooms appear and weekly during bloom. Resume the fungicide program about 2 weeks before harvest or if fruit rot begins to appear. Good sanitation will also help limit disease—remove any mummified fruit, and prune out and discard diseased twigs as soon as you see them. Spray horticultural oil during the dormant period to control many kinds of pests and diseases, including scale insects and mites.

Citrus

Citrus species
Citrus family *(Rutaceae)*
EVERGREEN TREES AND SHRUBS

> ✎ **ZONES 8, 9, 12–24, H1, H2; OR INDOORS**
> ☼ **FULL SUN; BRIGHT LIGHT**
> ● **REGULAR WATER**

Citrus plants offer attractive form and glossy, deep green foliage year-round, as well as flowers with legendary fragrance and decorative, delicious fruit. The flowers also attract bees. Most citrus are self-fruitful, with exceptions noted in the plant descriptions that follow. Citrus of one type or another are grown outdoors all year in regions with warm to hot summers and mild winters. Variety selection depends on climate. You can even buy multiple varieties grafted onto a single tree.

Heat requirements. Generally, sweet-fruited citrus need moderate to high heat to form sugars; sour types require less heat.

Lemons and limes require the least warmth, producing usable fruit in moderately cool-summer areas. Among oranges, 'Valencia' has a low heat requirement and greater frost tolerance; it grows well near the Southern California coast. Navel oranges demand more warmth and grow better inland. Mandarins (tangerines) require high heat for top flavor and are also best adapted inland. Grapefruit develops full flavor only where trees receive prolonged high heat, as in the low desert. (In cooler areas, grapefruit-pummelo hybrids 'Oroblanco' and 'Melogold' are better choices.)

Hardiness. Lemons and limes are the most frost-sensitive. Sweet oranges, 'Improved Meyer' lemon, grapefruit, and most mandarins and their hybrids are intermediate in cold tolerance. Kumquats and satsuma mandarins handle cold best, with kumquats—the hardiest of all—withstanding temperatures below 20°F/–7°C.

Other factors affecting cold tolerance include preconditioning (trees have greater endurance if exposed to cold gradually and when the first freeze comes late), type of rootstock, and garden location. Prolonged exposure to freezing weather is more damaging than a brief plunge in temperature. All citrus fruit is damaged at several degrees below freezing—so choose early-ripening varieties in freeze-prone areas.

Growing citrus in Hawaii. Hawaiians can grow many mainland varieties, plus some types adapted only to the islands (see variety descriptions). However, the fruit often looks and tastes different from the same variety grown in California or Arizona. Hawaiian trees bloom almost year-round, so harvest is nearly continuous. Warm nights result in a thinner, more greenish rind, and warmer nights reduce acid content, making Hawaiian citrus sweeter.

Standard or dwarf. Most citrus are budded or grafted onto an understock that makes them bear fruit in just a few years instead of 10 to 15 years. Standard trees (20–30 ft. tall and wide) are grown on a variety of understocks. Dwarf trees are grafted onto either trifoliate orange *(Poncirus trifoliata),* which usually produces 8- to 10-ft. trees in 10 to 15 years (some varieties reach 15–20 ft.), or 'Flying Dragon' (a contorted, spiny, dwarf form of trifoliate orange), which produces trees 5–7 ft. tall in 13 years.

Harvest periods. Most varieties ripen from late fall into winter, but some, such as 'Valencia' orange, ripen into spring and summer. Many types hold their fruit on the tree for long periods without losing quality. Everbearing citrus, such as lemons and limes, can produce all year, but they fruit most heavily in winter and spring.

Citrus as houseplants. Though there's no guarantee, 'Improved Meyer' and 'Ponderosa' lemons, 'Bearss' lime, and kumquats are the citrus most likely to produce good fruit indoors. Locate them away from heat sources and no farther than 6 ft. from a sunny window. Ideal humidity level is 50 percent. Water sparingly in winter.

Grapefruit (*Citrus* × *paradisi*). Probably hybrids of pummelos and sweet oranges. Trees can reach 25–30 ft. tall (most are shorter), with large, dark green leaves. True grapefruit needs heat for sweet-tart fruit and does best in the desert, where fruit ripens in 9 months (it can take a year or longer where there's less heat). Elsewhere, 'Oroblanco' and 'Melogold' are better bets, ripening in 9 to 12 months, depending on climate.

'Cocktail'. Labeled a grapefruit but actually a mandarin-pummelo hybrid. Large fruit with greenish orange (or mottled orange-and-green) skin and pale orange, very seedy flesh. Sweeter than grapefruit, with distinctive flavor. Best quality in warm-summer areas but worth growing in cooler regions.

'Flame'. Seedless red flesh similar to that of 'Rio Red'; slight rind blush.

'Marsh' ('Marsh Seedless'). Main white-fleshed commercial variety. Large, light yellow fruit.

'Melogold'. Grapefruit-pummelo hybrid developed by the University of California. Needs less heat than true grapefruit, but fruit doesn't hold as well on the tree. Fruit is bigger, heavier, and thinner-skinned than 'Oroblanco', and its seedless white flesh has more of a sweet-tart flavor.

'Oroblanco'. Sister fruit to 'Melogold', with sweeter seedless white flesh. Has the same low heat requirement but is smaller and thicker-skinned.

'Redblush' ('Ruby', 'Ruby Red'). Seedless grapefruit with red-tinted flesh. Red internal color fades to pink then buff by the end of the season.

'Rio Red'. Seedless, with good rind blush and flesh nearly as red as that of 'Star Ruby'. Dependable producer.

Continued on page 174 ▶

'Redblush' is a classic seedless grapefruit with red flesh; the color is more pronounced early in the growing season.

Kumquat's tiny red-orange fruits are sour on the inside, with sweet-tasting skins that are high in vitamin C.

'Star Ruby'. Reddest seedless grapefruit. Tree is prone to cold damage, erratic bearing, and other growing problems. Doesn't withstand desert heat.

Kumquat (*C. kumquat*). From south China. Shrubby plants grow to 6–15 ft. or taller, with yellow to red-orange fruits that look like tiny oranges. They're eaten whole and unpeeled; the rind is sweet and the pulp is tangy. Best in areas with warm to hot summers and chilly nights during fall or winter ripening. Hardy to at least 18°F/–8°C.

'Fukushu'. Large, oval fruit with a prominent neck. Skin and juice are sweet, but not as sweet as 'Meiwa'. Compact, thornless, very attractive tree.

'Marumi'. Slightly thorny plant with round fruit. Sweeter peel than 'Nagami', but the slightly seedy flesh is more acidic.

'Meiwa'. Round fruit is sweeter, juicier, and less seedy than that of other varieties. Performs better than other types in cool-summer areas. Considered the best kumquat for eating fresh. Nearly thornless.

'Nagami'. Main commercial variety. Oval, slightly seedy fruit is more abundant and sweeter in hot-summer climates. Plant is thornless.

Kumquat hybrids. These are the results of early experiments by the citrus industry to produce cold-tolerant kinds of citrus. The fruit has never been a commercial success, but it's good for home gardens. Plants tend to be fairly small even as standards; on dwarfing rootstocks, they reach only 3–6 ft. tall.

Limequat. These hybrids of 'Mexican' lime and kumquat are more cold-tolerant and need less heat than their lime parent. Good lime substitutes; edible rind like kumquat parent. Plants bear some fruit all year, but the main crop comes from fall to spring. 'Eustis' bears fruit shaped like a big olive. 'Tavares' has elongated oval fruit on a more compact, better-looking plant.

Orangequat. The most commonly grown variety is 'Nippon', a cross between 'Meiwa' kumquat and satsuma mandarin. It is cold-tolerant and has a fairly low heat requirement. Small, round, deep orange fruit has a sweet, spongy rind and slightly acidic flesh. Sweeter than kumquat when eaten whole. Ripens winter and spring, but holds on the tree for months.

Lemon (*C. limon*). Origin unknown. May be a hybrid between citron and lime. A low heat requirement makes lemons widely adapted and especially appreciated in regions where sweet oranges and grapefruit won't ripen. Lemons do best year-round near the coast, though some varieties are very successful in the desert.

'Eureka'. Standard market lemon. Bears all year. Not as vigorous as 'Lisbon'. To 20 ft. tall, with somewhat open growth; branches have few thorns. Dwarf is a dense tree with large, dark leaves.

'Improved Meyer' (*C. × meyeri*). It's improved because it's disease-free. The original, virus-carrying 'Meyer' cannot be sold in California or Arizona because officials are afraid the virus will damage both states' citrus industries. This is the best lemon for Hawaii. Fruit of this lemon-orange hybrid is rounder, thinner-skinned, and more orange-yellow than that of standard lemons. It has a tangy aroma but is less acidic than standard lemons; very juicy. Bears fruit year-round and starts bearing at an early age. Reaches 12 ft. tall, 15 ft. wide on its own roots; on a dwarfing rootstock, it's half that size. Excellent container plant.

'Lisbon'. Vigorous, upright, thorny tree to 20–25 ft. tall; denser than 'Eureka'. Can be trimmed up into a highly decorative small tree. Fruit is practically identical to 'Eureka'. Ripens mostly in fall but has some ripe fruit all year. More resistant to cold than 'Eureka' and better adapted to high heat; best lemon for Arizona.

Continued on page 176 ▶

'Eureka' lemon trained on an arching trellis

'Bearss' lime is ready for harvest when skin begins to turn from green to light yellow.

'Ponderosa'. A novelty lemon bearing huge, rough fruit with thick, coarse skin; 2-pound lemons are not unusual. Mild lemon flavor. Bears at an early age, frequently at gallon-can size. Produces its main crop in winter. Open, angular branching; large, widely spaced leaves. To 8–10 ft. tall; dwarf reaches 4–6 ft.

'Sungold'. Attractive semidwarf lemon (to 14 ft. tall, 8 ft. wide) with green-striped yellow fruit and leaves that are mottled with white and cream. Bears main crop in fall and winter.

'Variegated Pink' ('Pink Lemonade'). Sport of 'Eureka' with green-and-white leaves and green stripes on immature fruit; everbearing like 'Eureka'. Light pink flesh doesn't need heat to develop color. Handsome landscape tree.

'Villa Franca'. Generally similar to 'Eureka', but tree is larger and more vigorous, with denser foliage and thornier branches. Fruit is similar to 'Eureka' and comes mainly from fall through winter. Sold in Arizona to grow in Zones 12, 13; not common in California.

Lime (*C. aurantiifolia*). From tropical Asia. Various limes range from moderately to extremely cold-sensitive; they are most reliable in areas where hard frosts are uncommon, but they can succeed in colder areas if grown in pots and protected in winter. Depending on variety, fruit may be intensely sour or nearly devoid of acid.

'Bearss'. Best lime for California and Hawaii gardens. Commonly grown in Florida as a Persian or Tahitian lime. The tree is quite angular and open when young but forms a dense, round crown when mature. Reaches 15–20 ft. tall (half that size on dwarfing rootstock). Thorny and inclined to drop many leaves in winter. Seedless fruit is green when immature, light yellow when ripe, almost the size of a lemon; it is especially juicy when fully ripe. The main crop comes from winter to late spring, though some fruit ripens all year.

'Kieffer'. Leaves are used in Thai and Cambodian cooking, as is the bumpy, sour springtime fruit. Available mainly in California.

'Mexican'. Sometimes called key lime in Hawaii. Small, green to yellow-green fruit; standard bartender's lime. The main harvest is from fall to winter, though you'll get some fruit all year. Very thorny tree to 12–15 ft. tall, with upright, twiggy branches (there is also a thornless form). Very cold-sensitive; best suited to Zones 21–23. Can be grown in Hawaii but is subject to viral diseases there.

'Palestine Sweet' (Indian lime). Shrubby plant with acidless fruit like that of 'Bearss'. Used in Middle Eastern, Indian, and Latin American cooking. Ripens fall or winter.

Mandarin (*C. reticulata*); includes tangerine. Large, diverse group that includes many varieties and hybrids. The original is probably from south China and Vietnam. Varieties with orange-red peel are usually called tangerines. Tend to bear heavily in alternate years. Some are always seedless, while others produce seeds; the latter give seedier fruit if pollinated by another mandarin or mandarin hybrid or by 'Valencia' orange.

'Clementine' (Algerian tangerine). Fruit is a little larger than 'Dancy', with fewer seeds. Ripens late fall into winter; stays juicy and sweet on the tree for months. Develops full flavor in areas too cool for 'Dancy'. Semi-open tree reaches 12 ft. with vertical, spreading, somewhat willowy branches. Usually bears light crops without another variety for pollination.

'Dancy'. Standard tangerine in markets before Christmas. Smaller and seedier than other mandarins. Best flavor in Zones 12 and 13 but also good in Zones 21–23. Ripens late fall into winter; holds well on the tree. Upright dwarf tree with erect branches. Handsome in a container or as espalier.

Continued on page 178 ▶

Mandarin offers sweet-tasting fruit and good looks in the landscape.

Pummelo, the grapefruit's sweeter, milder cousin, turns from dark green to pale green or light yellow when ripe.

'Encore'. Light orange, thin-skinned fruit ripens in summer (latest of all mandarins) and holds until fall. Good quality. Erect tree with slender branches.

'Fairchild'. Hybrid between 'Clementine' mandarin and 'Orlando' tangelo. Medium-size, deep orange fruit peels easily, is seedy but juicy and tasty. Ripens late fall into winter. Small, compact tree bears every year. Needs another variety for pollination. Best in the desert.

'Fremont'. Medium-size, bright orange fruit ripens late fall into winter. Good flavor. Tends to bear in alternate years. Thin fruit when crop is unusually heavy.

'Gold Nugget'. Small to medium size, seedless, with rich, sweet flavor. Light yellow orange, often with rough rind (like 'Pixie'); easy to peel. Ripens late winter to spring; holds well on the tree.

'Honey'. Small, seedy fruit with rich, sweet flavor; matures winter into spring. Typically bears heavily in

alternate years. Vigorous tree. Differs from 'Murcott', a mandarin-orange hybrid often sold as 'Honey'.

'Kara'. Large (2½-in.) fruit with sweet-tart, aromatic flavor when grown in warm interior regions. Ripens winter to spring. Can be very seedy or nearly seedless from one season to the next. Spreading, often drooping branches with large leaves. Grows to a rounded 15–20 ft. tall, half that size as dwarf.

'Kinnow'. Medium-size fruit with rich flavor and fragrance. Ripens winter to early spring; stores well on the tree. Handsome tree shape—columnar, dense, very symmetrical to 20 ft. (dwarf will reach 10 ft.)—with slender leaves. Good in any citrus climate.

'Mediterranean' ('Willow Leaf'). Most important mandarin of the Mediterranean region. Sweet, aromatic fruit ripens in spring. Spreading tree with thin, willowy branches and narrow leaves.

'Page'. Hybrid between 'Clementine' mandarin and 'Minneola' tangelo. Many small, juicy, sweet fruits from fall into winter. Few seeds.

'Pixie'. Easy-peeling, seedless fruit with excellent flavor, usually with a bumpy rind. Ripens late winter into spring. Upright tree.

Satsuma. This group is the source of imported canned "mandarin oranges." Sweet, delicate flavor; nearly seedless, medium-size to large fruit. Loose skin. Earliest mandarin to ripen—early fall to late December. Quickly overripens if left on the tree but keeps well in cool storage. Standard trees are spreading, to 10–15 ft. tall. Dwarf trees can be used as 6-ft. shrubs. Open, angular growth when young, becoming more compact with age. Not suited to the desert. 'Owari' is the main satsuma grown in the West.

'Seedless Kishu'. Very small, loose-skinned, easy to peel; exceptionally rich flavor. Ripens late fall to winter.

'Shasta Gold', 'Tahoe Gold', and 'Yosemite Gold' are three recent introductions from the University of California. All produce large, seedless, deep orange fruit that is easy to peel and has a sweet, rich flavor. They ripen late winter to spring, 'Tahoe Gold' being the earliest of the three.

'W. Murcott' ('Afourer'). Ripens late winter into spring. Medium-size fruit with excellent flavor. Often sold as Delite in supermarkets. Many seeds if cross-pollinated. A seedless form, called 'Tango', has recently been released but may be hard to find in nurseries.

Pummelo (*C. maxima*). Native to Polynesia and a forerunner of the grapefruit. Bears clusters of enormous, round to pear-shaped fruits with thick rind and pith. Once peeled, fruit is just slightly bigger than a grapefruit. Varieties range in flavor from sweet to fairly acidic. Needs a little less heat than grapefruit. Ripening starts in winter in warmest areas. To eat, peel fruit, separate segments, and remove membrane surrounding them. Prune trees to encourage strong branching that will support the heavy fruit.

'Chandler'. Most widely grown variety. Pink fleshed, flavorful, moderately juicy, usually seedless.

'Reinking'. White fleshed, seedy. Not as sweet as 'Chandler'.

'Tahitian' ('Sarawak'). Greenish white flesh has moderately acidic flavor with lime overtones.

Sweet orange (*C. sinensis*). Probably originated in south China and Vietnam. In the following list, 'Washington' and the other navel varieties are described first, then 'Valencia' and its counterparts, and finally the other, lesser-known sweet oranges.

Navel Varieties
'Cara Cara'. First rosy-fleshed navel; bears at the same time as 'Washington'. Rich flavor.

'Lane Late'. Late-ripening navel extends the season into summer. 'Summer Navel' is also late, but flavor and quality are not as good.

'Robertson'. This 'Washington' variant produces identical fruit 2 to 3 weeks earlier, bears prolifically, and tends to carry its fruit in clusters. Smaller tree than 'Washington'; same climate adaptation.

'Skaggs Bonanza'. Another 'Washington' variant whose heavy crops color and ripen earlier. Tree bears young.

'Washington' navel. Widely adapted except in the desert; best in warm interiors. The standard tree is a 20- to 25-ft. globe. On dwarfing stock, it grows 8–12 ft. tall. Bears early to midwinter. 'Tabata' is identical (or nearly so); both it and 'Washington' are grown in Hawaii.

Valencia Types
'Valencia'. The traditional juice orange carried by stores and the most widely planted orange in the world. Though widely adapted in California, it's a poor risk in Arizona; if you try it there, select a warm location or provide some protection for the fruit, which must overwinter on the tree. One of the Arizona Sweets would be a safer bet. 'Valencia' oranges mature in summer and store on the tree for months, improving in sweetness. The tree is vigorous and fuller growing than 'Washington'.

'Campbell', 'Delta', and 'Midknight' are early-ripening, nearly seedless selections of 'Valencia'.

Other Sweet Oranges
Arizona Sweets. Grown in Arizona. They include 'Diller', which bears small to medium-size oranges with few seeds and high-quality juice in late fall (before heavy frost) on a vigorous, large, dense tree with large leaves; 'Hamlin', similar but not as hardy, producing medium-size fruit; 'Marrs', with tasty, low-acid, early-ripening fruit

Sweet oranges, among the most popular citrus choices for home gardens

on a naturally semidwarf tree that bears young; and 'Pineapple', tending to bear rich-flavored, seedy fruit in alternate years.

Blood oranges. Characterized by red pigmentation in flesh, juice, and (to a lesser degree) rind. Color varies with local microclimates and weather. Excellent flavor has raspberry overtones. Thrives wherever sweet oranges produce good fruit. 'Moro' bears fruit with deep red flesh and variable rind color from early winter to early spring (no rind pigmentation on the coast); 'Sanguinelli' bears red-skinned fruit with red-streaked flesh from late winter to midspring; and 'Tarocco' produces fruit with red or red-suffused pulp and pink to red juice from early to midwinter (color varies every year), with good quality in cooler areas. 'Tarocco' is very vigorous and open growing, with long, willowy, vinelike branches; the dwarf version makes an ideal espalier.

Continued on page 180 ▶

'Orlando' tangelo resembles a flattened orange; it is mildly sweet and very juicy.

'Shamouti' ('Palestine Jaffa'). Originated in Israel and considered there to be the finest orange. Large, seedless, no navel. Not a commercial orange in California because it's not sufficiently superior to the 'Washington' navel. Grown on dwarfing rootstock for home gardens because of its beautiful form and foliage. Wider than tall, with larger leaves than those of navel oranges. Heavy crop appears in early spring. 'Pera' is a 'Shamouti' relative grown in Hawaii.

'Trovita'. Originated from seedling of 'Washington' navel. Thin-skinned and about navel size but without navel. Ripens in early spring. Requires less heat than other sweet oranges and develops good-quality fruit near (though not on) the coast, yet produces well enough in heat that it's often sold as an Arizona Sweet. Dwarf tree has 'Washington' navel look, with handsome dark green leaves.

Tangelo (*C. × tangelo*). Early citrus-breeding experiments produced this cross between a mandarin and a grapefruit. It produces the best fruit in warm-summer areas.

'Minneola'. Hybrid of 'Dancy' mandarin and a white-fleshed grapefruit. Large, smooth, bright orange-red fruit tastes much like a mandarin. Few seeds. Ripens mid- to late winter; stores on the tree for 2 months. Tree not as large or dense as grapefruit.

'Orlando'. Same parents as 'Minneola'. Medium-large fruit looks like a flattened orange. Both rind and flesh are orange; rind adheres to flesh. Very juicy, mildly sweet; matures early in season. Similar to 'Minneola' but has distinctly cupped leaves, is less vigorous, and is more resistant to cold.

'Wekiwa' (may be sold as pink tangelo or 'Lavender Gem'). This cross between a tangelo and a grapefruit looks like a small grapefruit but is eaten like a mandarin. Juicy, mild flesh tastes like a mix of sweet orange, grapefruit, and mandarin; flesh color is purplish rose in hot climates. Fruit ripens from late fall into winter.

HOW TO GROW IT

best site Full sun, with protection from frost. In colder areas, plant on a slope, which collects less frost than flat ground.

yield Varies widely by type, variety, and rootstock.

soil Deep, well-draining loam. To improve drainage in average soil, dig a 4- to 6-in. layer of compost or ground bark into the top foot of soil. On poorly drained sites, plant in raised beds or mounds.

planting Plant after danger of spring frost is past, but ahead of summer heat. Remove fruits before planting. Dig a planting hole that's twice as wide as the rootball and mix complete controlled-release fertilizer into the backfill. Plant with the graft union 3 in. above ground level. Mulch with a 2- to 3-in. layer of compost or leaves to support surface roots and maintain soil moisture. In desert or hot-summer areas, whitewash the exposed trunk of the young tree with commercial whitewash or latex paint to protect the bark from sunburn.

In containers: Plant in commercial potting mix in a container at least 18 in. tall and wide. Keep moist; daily watering may be necessary in hot weather. Fertilize monthly from midwinter to midfall with high-nitrogen liquid fertilizer containing chelated zinc, iron, and manganese. Potted citrus can stay outdoors all year in mild-winter climates, but plants should be moved to a protected location if a freeze is predicted and in cold-winter regions. Root-prune and repot in fresh potting soil every 4 or 5 years.

spacing Let mature tree sizes dictate spacing.

water Irrigate established trees every other week during summer, soaking the soil deeply. In clay soils, space watering intervals so the top 4–6 in. of soil dries between irrigations. Never let the tree become dry enough for leaves to wilt. Consistent irrigation prevents fruit splitting (a danger for all citrus—especially navel oranges during autumn). Water newly planted trees twice a week in normal summer weather, more frequently during hot spells. If you build basins to contain and concentrate water, make them wider than the spread of branches; citrus roots extend out twice as far as the distance from the trunk to branch ends. Keep the trunk dry with an inside berm 6–12 in. from the trunk.

fertilizer Nitrogen is the most important nutrient for citrus. (In sandy soil, choose a complete fertilizer containing a full range of nutrients.) Apply 2 ounces of actual nitrogen the first year after a newly planted tree puts on new growth, then increase the amount by 4 ounces each year for the next few years. After the fifth year, apply 1 to 1½ pounds yearly. (Plants growing in raised beds, with restricted root space, or grafted onto 'Flying Dragon' rootstock need only a third to half the recommended amount after the fifth year.)

Divide total fertilizer into several feedings throughout the growing season. In freeze-prone areas, start feeding in late winter and stop in late summer. Make sure trees are well watered before feeding. Spread the fertilizer beneath and a foot or two outside the branch spread of the tree, then water it in deeply.

Citrus trees that receive too much or too little nitrogen show the evidence in leaf color: dark green, lush leaves with burned tips or edges indicate too much nitrogen; yellowish leaves are a sign of nitrogen deficiency.

pruning, training Commercial trees are allowed to carry branches right to the ground. Production is heaviest on lower branches. Growers prune only to remove twiggy growth and weak branches or, in young plants, to nip back wild growth and balance the plant. Espaliering is traditional but reduces the harvest. Lemons can be pruned as hedges. 'Eureka' and 'Lisbon' lemons should be pruned to keep the trees within bounds and the fruit easily reachable. Many citrus are thorny, so wear gloves and a long-sleeved shirt when working with trees. In freeze-prone areas, don't prune in fall or winter; prune frost-damaged trees in spring or summer (new growth reveals which wood is dead). If you have a multiple-variety citrus tree, continually cut back the vigorous growers (lemon, lime, pummelo, grapefruit) so the weaker ones (sweet orange, mandarin) can compete.

Remove all suckers—branches that arise below the graft union—before they overwhelm the desired variety.

(Some tender citrus—limes, for example—are grown from cuttings. Because they're not grafted, they don't have sucker problems; and if they freeze to the ground, they resprout from the roots true to type.)

harvest Citrus fruits ripen only on the tree. Judge ripeness by taste, not rind color (many varieties are fully colored before they are ripe).

challenges Citrus can get aphids, mites, scale insects, and mealybugs. If these pests' natural enemies fail to handle the infestations—and if jets of water fail to keep the pests in check—consult a local garden center for appropriate chemicals. If scale remains troublesome, spray with horticultural oil in early spring.

Control snails and slugs whenever necessary, especially during warm-night spells in winter and spring. Copper bands, available in some areas, will keep snails out of trees. Where it is legal to do so (in Southern California), colonize citrus groves with decollate snails, which prey on the garden snail.

Citrus bud mite causes weirdly deformed fruit (especially lemons). Control with horticultural oil spray in spring and in fall; spray only in fall in hot-summer areas. Keep ants out of trees by using sticky bands on trunks (ants prey on natural predators of the mites).

The few fungal ailments of citrus occur in poorly drained soil. Water molds, causing root rot, show up in yellowing and dropping foliage. The best control is to correct your watering schedule.

Brown rot gummosis usually occurs in older trees at the base of the trunk. Keep the base dry, and trim and clean the oozing wounds, removing decayed bark to a point where discolored wood does not show. Paint areas with Bordeaux paste mixture you make yourself (the formula is available online and from Cooperative Extension Offices), using a sprayer.

Citrus may suffer from chlorosis due to iron, manganese, or zinc deficiency. With iron chlorosis, leaves turn yellow from edges inward; veins remain dark green. (Overwatering presents the same symptoms, so check your irrigation practices.) Manganese deficiency shows up as fine mottling, usually on young leaves, and as pale or yellowish areas between dark green veins. Signs of zinc deficiency are yellowish blotching or mottling between leaf veins. Manganese and zinc deficiencies may occur together and be difficult to distinguish from each other. Commercial products containing chelates of all three nutrients are available as foliar sprays.

Crabapple

Malus species
Rose family *(Rosaceae)*
DECIDUOUS TREES

🌿 **ZONES A1–A3, 1–9, 11–21**
☼ **FULL SUN**
💧 **REGULAR WATER DURING FRUIT DEVELOPMENT**

Crabapple is a small, usually tart apple, typically used for jelly and pickling. Fruit size, not species, distinguishes crabapples from apples (several species are involved). Trees grow 8–25 ft. tall and have beautiful, fragrant spring flowers. The edible varieties listed here are distinct from the many kinds of ornamental crabapples bred strictly for spring flowers. Like apples, crabapples are available as standards, dwarfs, and semidwarfs, and different varieties ripen in different seasons. Use the fruit for apple butter, fresh eating, pickling, or as a tart ingredient in cider.

The following are popular fruiting varieties, all of which grow about as wide as tall: 'Transcendent', with 2-in. red-cheeked yellow crabapples on a 25-ft. tree; 'Evereste', a disease-resistant, white-flowered tree that grows 10 ft. tall and produces 1-in. red, round, tart fruit; or 20-ft. 'Golden Raindrops', whose white flowers are followed by a profusion of small yellow apples. Others include 8-ft. 'Centennial' and 15-ft. 'Dolgo', both with 1¹/₂-in. red fruit; the fruit of 'Centennial' is sweet.

To flower and fruit, crabapple trees need about 600 hours at 45°F/7°C or lower. In coldest areas, crabapples should be grafted onto hardy rootstocks. Trees are self-fruitful, and white-flowered varieties (which attract more bees) are often used as pollinators for standard apples because they have a long flowering season.

HOW TO GROW IT

best site Choose a spot that gets full sun and has protection from cold spring winds, which can interfere with pollination.

yield Varies widely according to variety, age, and rootstock.

soil Crabapples do best in deep, well-drained soil but get by in many imperfect situations, including heavy soil.

planting Plant bare-root stock in winter or early spring. Containerized crabapples can be planted anytime where climates are mild and whenever the soil is workable in cold-winter climates. *In containers:* Grow a dwarf variety or one on a dwarfing rootstock in a wine half-barrel.

Protect a container plant from soil-freezing temperatures by bringing it into an unheated garage or porch.

spacing Let the mature width of your tree determine spacing.

water Regular water is especially important in spring and summer as fruit develops. Don't let soil around newly planted trees and shallow-rooted dwarf varieties dry out. Mulch helps retain soil moisture and keep weeds down.

fertilizer Give newly planted trees ¹/₄ pound of 10-10-10 fertilizer as buds start to open the first year. In every subsequent year, increase the amount by ¹/₄ pound until dwarf trees are getting 2¹/₂ pounds, semidwarfs 5 pounds, standards 10 pounds. If trees are bearing well and producing 6–8 in. of annual tip growth, you don't need to feed at all.

pruning, training For dwarf or semidwarf trees, the preferred growing style is a pyramidal or modified leader, in which widely angled branches are encouraged to grow in spiral placement around the trunk. When the tree is young, prune late in the dormant season to develop strong, evenly spaced scaffold branches. Keep narrow-angled crotches from developing, and don't let side branches outgrow the leader or let secondary branches outgrow the primary branches.

Prune mature trees late in the dormant season by cutting off weak, dead, or poorly placed branches and twigs, especially those growing toward the center of the tree. Removing such growth will discourage mildew and encourage development of strong new wood with new fruiting spurs.

Dwarf trees can be grown as espaliers tied to wood or wire frames, fences, or other supports. The technique requires manipulating the branches to the desired pattern and pruning out excess growth.

harvest Pick when fruit is fully colored and flavorful (remember, some are tart when ripe). Take the stem with the fruit, but be careful not to damage the spur from which the stems grow (it will produce fruit again next year).

challenges The principal pests are coddling moth larvae and, in some regions, apple maggot. Both can be treated organically with spinosad. If mildew and scab are problems where you live, buy resistant trees.

Crabapples offer showy spring flowers and decorative, tasty late-summer fruits.

Fig

Ficus carica
Mulberry family *(Moraceae)*
DECIDUOUS TREE

🌡 **ZONES 4–9, 12–24, H1, H2**
☼ **FULL SUN**
💧💧 **MODERATE TO REGULAR WATER**

Fig is one edible member of a large, mostly ornamental genus native to western Asia and the eastern Mediterranean. It grows fairly fast to 15–30 ft. tall and wide and is generally low branched. Where hard freezes (below 10° to 15°F/–12° to –9°C) are common, fig wood freezes back severely and plants grow more like big shrubs. With pruning, figs can be held to 10 ft. in a large container or espaliered along a fence or wall.

Heavy, smooth, gray trunks are gnarled in really old trees, which are picturesque in silhouette. Rough, bright green leaves with three to five lobes are 4–9 in. long and nearly as wide, casting dense shade. Soft, sweet fruit ripens in shades of purple, yellow-green, brown, or green and are eaten fresh, cooked, or dried. The tree's strong trunk and branch pattern, which looks good by itself in winter and when it's clothed with tropical-looking leaves in summer, also makes fig a top-notch ornamental tree, especially near a patio where it can be illuminated from beneath. Avoid deep cultivation near trees, as this may damage surface roots.

Home-garden figs do not need pollinating, and most varieties bear two crops a year. The first comes in early summer on last year's wood. The second, heavier, main crop comes in late summer or early fall from the current year's growth. In the Northwest, expect only the summer crop; in years when summer and fall are long and warm, you may get a second crop on some varieties.

Varieties differ in climate adaptability. Most require prolonged high temperatures to bear good fruit, but some thrive in cooler conditions. Figs need no frost protection when temperatures remain above 20°F/–7°C. In hot-summer regions, paint trunks of newly planted figs with whitewash or white latex paint to prevent sunburn.

Dried figs from the market are usually 'Calimyrna' or imported Smyrna figs. These require special pollenizers (male trees called caprifigs) and a special pollinating insect, so they aren't recommended for home gardens.

Recommended varieties. The following self-fruitful figs are superior choices.

'Black Jack'. Purple skin with sweet pink flesh. Similar to 'Mission'. Widely adapted to warm climates. Easily kept small by pruning.

'Mission' figs, a legacy of early California's Franciscan missionaries, are fleshy and richly sweet.

'Celeste' ('Blue Celeste', 'Celestial'). Violet-tinged bronzy skin, rosy amber flesh. Good fresh; resists spoilage. Dries well on the tree in warm, dry climates.

'Conadria'. Choice thin-skinned white fig blushed violet, white to red flesh with fine flavor. Best in hot areas.

'Desert King'. Green-skinned, red-fleshed fruit. Adapted to all fig climates but better in cooler areas like the Northwest. Bears one late-summer crop.

'Genoa' ('White Genoa'). Greenish yellow skin, strawberry-colored to yellow flesh. Good quality. Good in coastal valleys and along California coast.

'Improved Brown Turkey'. Brownish purple fruit. Adaptable to most fig-growing climates. Good, small garden tree.

'Italian Everbearing'. Resembles 'Improved Brown Turkey' but has somewhat larger fruit with reddish brown skin. Good fresh or dried.

'Kadota' ('White Kadota'). Tough-skinned, greenish yellow fruit. One of the best figs for Hawaii; on the mainland, it grows best in hot interior valleys.

'Lattarula'. Also known as Italian honey fig. Green skin, amber flesh. In the Northwest, it is more likely than most figs to produce a fall crop in good seasons.

'Mission' ('Black Mission'). Large tree. Purple-black figs with pink flesh. Good fresh or dried. Widely adapted.

'Osborn Prolific' ('Neveralla'). Dark reddish brown skin, amber flesh often tinged pink. Very sweet; best eaten fresh. Best in Northern California coastal areas and the Pacific Northwest. Light bearing in warm climates.

'Panachée' ('Striped Tiger', 'Tiger'). Greenish yellow skin with dark green stripes. Strawberry-colored flesh is sweet but dry. Best eaten fresh. Requires long, warm growing season. Bears one crop late in summer.

'Peter's Honey' ('Rutara'). Greenish yellow skin, amber flesh. Needs extra warmth in mild climates, so plant it in the warmest spot in the garden, such as against a south-facing wall.

'Texas Everbearing'. Mahogany to purple skin, strawberry-colored flesh. Bears at a young age. Produces well in short-season areas of the Southwest.

HOW TO GROW IT

best site Full sun in a place where fallen fruit won't make a mess on a path or patio. In the colder part of its range, trees planted near south walls or trained against them benefit from reflected heat (cut back tops hard at planting time).

yield Expect 40 to 50 pounds per mature tree.

soil Figs are not particular about soil, but good drainage is a plus.

planting Set out nursery plants anytime except during the heat of summer. Plant bare-root trees in late winter or spring. *In containers:* Plant in a half-barrel or other large container. Protect container plants from light frost by covering them at night; protect pots from heavier freezes by bringing them into a cool, frost-free place for winter.

spacing Set trees 15–30 ft. apart. Pruning can easily hold plants at the smaller size.

water Water regularly for the first 2 years, then deeply every 2 weeks during the growing season.

fertilizer Apply a balanced fertilizer once after growth starts in spring. Avoid high-nitrogen fertilizers, which stimulate leafy growth at the expense of fruit.

'Panachée' figs boast distinctively striped skin and strawberry-colored flesh.

pruning, training As the tree grows, prune lightly each winter, cutting out dead wood, crossing branches, and low-hanging branches that interfere with foot traffic. Pinch back runaway shoots in any season.

harvest When figs are ripe, they detach easily when lifted and bent back toward the branch. Keep fruit picked as it ripens. In late fall, pick off any remaining ripe figs and clean up fallen fruit. If the fig's milky white sap irritates your skin, wear gloves.

challenges Few pests or diseases trouble figs, but gophers love the roots; if they or other burrowing animals are a problem in your garden, plant fig trees in ample wire baskets. If necessary, use netting to protect ripe fruit from birds.

Kiwi

Actinidia species
Kiwi family *(Actinidiaceae)*
DECIDUOUS VINES

🌱 **ZONES VARY BY SPECIES**

☀️ ◑ **FULL SUN OR PARTIAL SHADE, EXCEPT AS NOTED**

💧 **REGULAR WATER**

Kiwis are fast-growing, twining vines grown for fruit with flavor that is a combination of melon, strawberry, and banana. Fuzzy-skinned kiwifruit (the type sold in markets) has a delicious piquancy; the hardy kinds, including Arctic beauties, are sweeter. All kiwis hail from eastern Asia.

Unless you have a self-fruitful variety, you will need to grow a male plant nearby to pollinate the fruit-bearing female plant. Supply the vines with sturdy support, such as a trellis, an arbor, or a patio overhead. You can also train kiwi to cover walls or fences; guide and tie vines to the support as necessary.

Fuzzy-skinned kiwi *(Actinidia deliciosa* or *A. chinensis).* This species, sometimes called Chinese gooseberry vine, grows and fruits best in Zones 4–9 and 12–24 (note, however, that a vine can take up to 5 years from planting to flower or set fruit). It twines to 30 ft. if not curbed. Roundish, 5- to 8-in.-long leaves are rich dark green above, velvety white below. New growth often has rich red fuzz. Spring flowers are 1–1¹/₂ in. wide, opening cream colored and fading to buff. Fuzzy, brown-skinned, green-fleshed fruit is the size and roughly the shape of an egg.

'Hayward' is the most common fruiting variety. 'Saanichton', a female type from Vancouver Island, Canada, is a good choice for cooler areas. Use 'Chico Male', 'Tomuri', or plants sold simply as "male" to pollinate 'Hayward' and 'Saanichton'. 'Vincent' is (in spite of its masculine name) a female variety that needs little winter chill and grows well in warmest-winter climates; use 'Chico Male' as a pollenizer. Male hardy kiwi varieties can also supply pollen for female fuzzy-skinned kiwis.

Hardy kiwi *(A. arguta).* Grows and produces well in Zones A1–A3, 1–10, 12, 14–24. It is much like fuzzy-skinned kiwi vine in appearance but has smaller flowers, fruit, and leaves. The 1- to 1¹/₂-in.-long, fuzzless fruits are eaten skin and all.

Green-fruited female varieties 'Ananasnaya', 'Hood River', and 'Jumbo' need a male variety (which may be sold simply as "male") for pollen. 'Issai' is a popular self-fruitful variety. The species *A. purpurea* (formerly classified as *A. a. purpurea* and growing like *A. arguta* in every respect) and its hybrid 'Ken's Red' produce small red fruit with red flesh; each needs a pollenizer.

Fuzzy-skinned 'Hayward' was developed in New Zealand but is popular wherever kiwis are grown.

Arctic beauty kiwi *(A. kolomikta).* Best suited to Zones A2, A3, 1–9, 14–17. Male plants are ornamental vines grown for their splashy, heart-shaped foliage. Female plants typically have somewhat less colorful leaves than males, but they produce green fruit a little smaller than hardy kiwi fruit; a male vine must be growing nearby to supply pollen (but *A. arguta* won't pollinate *A. kolomikta*). Plants typically grow to 15 ft. or more and bear fruit in summer, weeks ahead of most hardy kiwis. These vines prefer partial shade, especially in hotter climates; for good variegation, it is essential. 'September Sun' and 'Sentyabraskaya' have sweet fruit and the best foliage variegation among the female varieties.

HOW TO GROW IT

best site Full sun in a place protected from strong wind.

yield *Fuzzy-skinned kiwi:* To 200 pounds per vine. *Hardy kiwi:* To 100 pounds per vine. *Arctic beauty kiwi:* About 10 pounds per vine.

soil These vines prefer moderately rich, well-drained soil. Plants are sensitive to salt burn in alkaline soils.

planting Bare-root plants can be planted when available in winter and early spring. Plant container plants anytime during mild weather.

spacing Set plants 15 ft. apart.

water Kiwis must be watered regularly; mulch helps retain soil moisture.

fertilizer Dig 1 pound of organic fertilizer into the soil before planting; then, after the first growing season, apply 1 pound of 10-10-10 fertilizer. In the second winter, give dormant plants 1 pound of 10-10-10 in spring and $^3/_4$ pound after bloom. From the third year on, give each vine 2 pounds during the dormant season, 1 pound after bloom. Kiwis are subject to fertilizer burn, so scatter fertilizer widely over the root system.

pruning, training During the dormant season, prune for form and fruit production. Cut back to one or two main trunks and remove closely parallel or crossing branches. Cut out shoots that have fruited for 3 years and shorten younger shoots, leaving three to seven buds beyond the previous summer's fruit. In summer, shorten overlong shoots and unwind any shoots twining around main branches. Newly cut kiwi vines drip sap at an alarming rate, but it doesn't hurt the plant.

harvest *Fuzzy-skinned kiwi:* In fall, start harvesting when the first fruits just start to soften or when the skins turn from greenish brown to fully brown. Let it ripen indoors; egg cartons make perfect ripening/storage containers. Fruit left on the vine too long will spoil or be eaten by birds. *Hardy and Arctic beauty kiwis:* Pick when grape-size fruit starts to soften slightly in late summer and fall; taste is the best test of ripeness.

challenges Kiwis are relatively pest-free.

'Ananasnaya' hardy kiwi bears fuzzless fruits with a sweet-tart flavor.

Luscious emerald green flesh and jet black seeds of fuzzy-skinned kiwi

Olive

Olea europaea
Olive family *(Oleaceae)*
EVERGREEN TREE

🕭 **ZONES 8, 9, 11–24, H1, H2**
☀ **FULL SUN**
◊ ◖ **LITTLE TO MODERATE WATER**

Olives come from the Mediterranean. They thrive in areas with hot, dry summers but also perform adequately in coastal areas. Along with palms, citrus, and eucalyptus, olive trees are now regional trademarks along avenues and in gardens of California and southern Arizona. Their beauty has been appreciated in those areas since they were introduced to mission gardens for the oil their fruit produces. In recent years, growers have experimented with extra-hardy olives that fruit in Oregon.

Willowlike foliage is a soft grayish green that goes well with most colors. Smooth gray trunks and branches become gnarled and picturesque with age. Trees grow slowly, typically to 25–30 ft. tall and as wide; however, young ones put on height (if not substance) fairly fast. Large old trees can (with reasonable care) be boxed and transplanted with near certainty of survival.

Standard olives take temperatures down to 15°F/ −9°C. Most, but not all, are only partially self-fruitful and bear best with pollination from a different variety. Some are completely self-fruitful and some bear no fruit without a pollenizer. A final group, not listed here, consists of essentially fruitless varieties bred for landscape situations where messy fruit drop is unwelcome. Many gardeners grow groundcovers under olive trees so that unused fruit disappears when it drops.

Gardeners who grow olives for fruit or oil have to deal with fruit fly infestation before it spoils the crop, and to cure the olives after harvest. Curing can be done with salt, brine, or lye; for instructions, order a publication called *Olives: Safe Methods for Home Pickling,* from the University of California.

Recommended varieties. 'Arbequina'. Spanish variety grown for fruit, oil, and home gardens. Widely sold in the Pacific Northwest, where it is said to be hardy to 10°F/−12°C, but needs warm summers to bear fruit. Worth growing in the Willamette Valley.

'Ascolana'. A variety grown commercially for fruit; available as a specimen tree from landscaping firms. Large fruit, small pit.

'Leccino'. Needs pollination by 'Maurino' to bear fruit. Hardy to 10°F/−12°C.

Olives can be picked green or left to ripen to a dark purple color.

'Manzanillo'. Commercial-grove kind most often sold as a specimen tree by landscaping firms. Grows to 15–30 ft. tall with a more spreading habit than most. Apple-shaped fruit.

'Maurino'. Cold-hardy to 10°F/−12°C.

'Mission' Commercial-grove kind sold as a specimen tree by landscaping firms. Grows to 36–45 ft. tall.

'Sevillano'. Another commercial-grove kind offered as a specimen tree by landscaping firms. Grows to 24–34 ft. tall with an oaklike form.

'Skylark Dwarf'. Typically a large, compact, multi-trunked shrub to 16 ft. tall and wide. Sets a very small fruit crop in some years.

HOW TO GROW IT

best site Plant olives in an open, sunny part of the garden, but not over a patio or walkway that would be stained by fallen fruit.

yield 50 to 150 pounds per tree.

soil Olive trees look best when grown in deep, rich soil, but they will also grow in shallow, alkaline, or stony soil.

planting Trees are most often sold in plastic nursery containers, but you can buy quite large ones in wooden boxes for transplanting. Plant them anytime in mild parts of California and Arizona; late spring is best in the Pacific Northwest.

In containers: Trees can grow for several years in a container 18 in. deep and wide. Root-prune or transplant when roots start to wind around the inside of the pot or come out the bottom.

spacing Plant trees 25–30 ft. apart.

water Olive trees need two deep soakings per month for optimal production. They'll survive at a small fraction of this but at the expense of their crops.

fertilizer Olives are light feeders; it's sufficient to mulch trees with compost or well-rotted manure each spring.

pruning, training Begin training early. For a single trunk, prune out or shorten side branches below the point where you want branching to begin; cut off basal suckers. For multiple trunks, stake lower branches or basal suckers to continue growth at desired angles. Mature olives withstand heavy pruning. Thinning each year shows off the branch pattern and eliminates some flowering/fruiting wood, reducing the fruit crop (which can be a nuisance in ornamental plantings).

harvest Olives ripen and drop late in the year. Green olives are picked in early fall, blond olives in midautumn, and black olives in late autumn. To pick them, put a tarp on the ground, hand-strip the fruit, and let it fall to the tarp. Separate fruit and leaves.

challenges The larvae (maggots) of olive fruit fly eat virtually all the fruit on affected trees; chemical sprays are available to fight them. Verticillium wilt is a soilborne disease that causes branch dieback and sometimes the death of the tree. Cut off wilted branches and hope for the best, as there is no cure.

A bountiful harvest of olives ready for curing

Peach and Nectarine

Prunus persica
Rose family *(Rosaceae)*
DECIDUOUS TREES

✎ **ZONES VARY BY VARIETY**
☼ **FULL SUN**
◗ **REGULAR WATER**

Peach *(Prunus persica)* and nectarine *(P. p. nucipersica)* trees are both native to China, look alike, and have the same cultural needs. Where fruit is concerned, both may be clingstone (flesh adheres to the pit), freestone (flesh easily separates from the pit), or semifreestone (in between the two). But nectarines differ from peaches in several other respects: they have smooth rather than fuzzy skin; in some varieties, flavor is slightly different; and many are more susceptible to brown rot of stone fruit.

In most regions, crops ripen between June and September, depending on variety; early varieties grown in mild-winter climates may mature as early as April. Most peaches and nectarines need 600 to 900 hours of winter temperatures at or below 45°F/7°C. Insufficient chilling results in delayed leaf-out, a scanty crop, and eventual death of the tree. In extremely mild-winter areas, only low-chill varieties do well (and very few of those are satisfactory in the low desert). A few low-chill peach varieties have been tried successfully at higher elevations in Hawaii, but nectarines tend to split in Hawaii and so are not commonly grown there. In areas subject to late frosts, early-blooming varieties are risky. Where spring is particularly cold and rainy, plants set few flowers, pollinate poorly, and get peach leaf curl. They need clear, hot weather during the growing season.

A standard-size peach or nectarine tree grows rapidly to 25 ft. tall and wide, but properly pruned trees are usually kept to 10–12 ft. tall and a little wider. They start bearing large crops when 3 or 4 years old and reach peak production at 8 to 12 years. Genetic or natural dwarf trees, most of which grow to 5–6 ft. tall and produce medium-size fruit, are useful in containers and small planting areas. You can also save space by planting three or four full-size varieties in one hole; prune the new bare-root trees so that each retains just one primary branch, and point those branches outward as you plant the trees in the hole. With a few exceptions, peaches and nectarines are self-fruitful, so you don't need a pollenizer; it's fine to grow just one tree by itself.

'Frost' peach, a heavy-bearing freestone variety, is cold-hardy and disease-resistant.

HOW TO GROW IT

best site Choose a spot with full sun and protection from cold spring winds.

yield Varies by type and tree size, but a full-size tree generally yields about 50 pounds of fruit.

soil Deep loam or sandy loam. If you have clay soil, plant in containers, raised beds, or mounds.

planting Plant bare-root stock in late winter or spring, or container stock anytime except in the hottest days of summer. *In containers:* Dwarf peaches and nectarines are good subjects for growing in wine half-barrels.

spacing Set trees 5–25 ft. apart depending on the anticipated ultimate size.

water Give regular deep soakings. Water full-size trees when the top 3–4 in. of soil dries out, and genetic or natural dwarf trees when the top 2 in. of soil dries out.

fertilizer Use a 10-10-10 complete fertilizer applied at bud-break in late March. Give young trees $1/2$ pound per year of age and give mature trees up to 5 pounds (for full-size, full-grown trees). Spread fertilizer evenly over the entire root zone.

pruning, training These trees need heavier pruning than other fruit trees because they produce fruit on year-old branches. Severe annual pruning not only renews fruiting wood, but also encourages production of fruit throughout the tree rather than at ends of sagging branches that can easily break. Even with good pruning, peaches and nectarines form too much fruit. When fruits are 1 in. wide, thin out (remove) enough fruit so those that remain are 8–10 in. apart. Genetic dwarf trees need less pruning than standard ones. When planting a bare-root tree that is an unbranched "whip," cut it back to 2–3$1/2$ ft. above ground (the thicker the trunk, the less severe the cutting back). New branches will form below the cut. After the first year's growth, select three well-placed branches for scaffold limbs. On mature trees, in each dormant season cut off two-thirds of the previous year's growth by removing two of every three branches formed that year, or head back each branch to one-third its length, or head back some and cut out others. Peaches and nectarines can be trained as espaliers.

harvest When peaches and nectarines are ripe, they will be fully colored and will pull easily off the tree with a gentle twist.

challenges Among the most serious diseases of peaches and nectarines are peach leaf curl and brown rot of stone fruit. The fungus responsible for peach leaf curl causes emerging new leaves to thicken and pucker. Infected foliage may be tinged red, pink, yellow, or white; it usually occurs in midsummer. Severely infected trees are weakened and may stop producing. Brown rot fungus causes flowers to wilt and decay and twigs to crack and ooze sap. To control both diseases, practice good sanitation—get rid of diseased plant parts to keep fungus from reinfecting the tree the next year. Also apply fixed copper or lime sulfur dormant sprays once after autumn leaf drop and again just as buds begin to swell but before they open. In places where winter and spring are almost always rainy, spray three times, starting in late December and repeating at 2- to 4-week intervals. Some gardeners reduce peach leaf curl by planting the trees under eaves and training them in a fan shape against a south-facing wall (dry leaves aren't susceptible to infection). Move potted genetic dwarf peaches and nectarines

Nectarines produce beautiful spring blossoms followed by sweet, juicy fruit.

to a covered location in rainy weather. To control the diseases as well as scale insects, use sprays combining horticultural oil with either lime sulfur or fixed copper.

Peach tree borer, which tends to attack trees stressed by poor growing conditions or wounds, causes defoliation, branch dieback, and possibly death. Jellylike matter exuding from the base of the tree is the first indication of the pest's presence. The insect holes will be evident at or just below ground level. Prevention through good growing conditions is the best control; if a tree is attacked, consult your Cooperative Extension Office for the best treatment.

Continued on page 193 ▶

A mature, well-tended peach tree can yield 50 pounds of fruit per year.

top picks to grow

Name	Zones	Fruit	Comments
PEACHES			
'Arctic Supreme'	7–9, 14, 15, 18	Large. Clingstone. Red-over-cream skin; white flesh. Superb flavor. Midseason.	Among the finest flavored of all peaches.
'August Pride'	7–9, 14, 15, 18–24	Large. Freestone. Yellow skin with red blush; yellow flesh. Aromatic fruit with rich flavor. Midseason.	Low chill requirement.
'Babcock'	12, 13, 15, 16, 19–24, H1	Small to medium. Freestone. Light pink skin with red blush; little fuzz. White flesh reddens near pit. Sweet flavor with some tang. Early.	Low chill requirement. Old-time favorite.
'Baby Crawford'	7–9, 14, 15, 18	Small. Freestone. Golden orange, very fuzzy skin with slight blush; yellow flesh. Intense flavor. Midseason.	An exceptionally flavorful variety.
'Bonanza II'	2, 3, 7–12, 14–16, 18–23	Large. Freestone. Attractive red-and-yellow skin; deep yellow to orange flesh. Good flavor. Midseason.	Genetic dwarf. Showy flowers. Fruit more flavorful than that of 'Bonanza', the original dwarf variety for home gardens.
'Bonita'	15–24	Large. Freestone. Yellow skin with medium red blush; firm yellow flesh. Fine flavor. Midseason.	Low chill requirement.
'Champagne'	6–11, 14, 15, 18	Medium to large. Freestone. Yellow skin with light red blush; white flesh with red near the pit. Fine, sweet flavor. Midseason.	Vigorous and productive.
'Desertgold'	8, 9, 12, 13, 18–24	Medium size. Semifreestone. Yellow skin and flesh. Good quality. Very early.	Very early bloom rules it out wherever spring frosts are likely.
'Donut' ('Stark Saturn')	7–9, 13–15, 18–23	Medium size. Freestone. Shaped like a doughnut, with a sunken middle. White skin with red blush; white flesh. Mildly sweet flavor with a hint of almond. Early.	Low chill requirement. Almost evergreen in mild-winter areas.
'Double Jewel'	2, 3, 7–12, 14, 15, 18	Large. Freestone. Peach pink skin; yellow-orange flesh. Good flavor. Early.	Bears a profusion of double pink flowers late in spring.
'Earligrande'	8–24	Medium to large. Semifreestone. Yellow with red blush; yellow flesh. Excellent flavor. Early.	Fine quality. Low-chill variety for mild-winter climates.
'Elberta'	1–3, 6–11, 14	Medium to large. Freestone. Yellow skin with red blush; yellow flesh. High quality. Midseason.	Needs good amount of winter chill and high summer heat to ripen to full flavor.
'El Dorado'	2, 3, 7–12, 14, 15, 18	Medium size. Freestone. Yellow skin with red blush; yellow flesh. Rich flavor. Early.	Genetic dwarf.
'Eva's Pride'	12, 13, 18–24	Medium to large. Freestone. Yellow skin and flesh. Fine flavor. Early to midseason.	Low chill requirement.
'Fay Elberta' ('Gold Medal')	2, 3, 6–11, 14, 15, 18, 19	Medium to large. Freestone. Has more red blush on skin than 'Elberta'; yellow flesh. Midseason (ripens with 'Elberta' but keeps better).	Bears large, handsome single flowers. 'Fantastic Elberta' is a double-flowered sport; its fruit has excellent flavor.
'Flordaprince'	12, 13, 18–24, H1	Medium to large. Semifreestone, becoming freestone when fully ripe. Red-blushed yellow skin; yellow flesh. Very good quality. Very early.	Low chill requirement.
'Fortyniner'	5–9, 14–16, 18	Large. Freestone. Yellow skin with bright red blush; yellow flesh. Fine flavor. Early midseason.	Looks like its parent, 'J.H. Hale'; blooms about 1 week earlier.

Continued on page 194 ▶

Name	Zones	Fruit	Comments
'Frost'	3–9, 14, 15, 18	Medium size. Freestone. Yellow skin with slight red blush; yellow flesh. Tangy flavor. Midseason to late.	Resistant to peach leaf curl.
'Gleason's Early Elberta' ('Lemon Elberta', 'Improved Elberta')	2–11, 14, 15	Like 'Elberta' but has better color and even better flavor; ripens about 10 days later.	Late blooming and cold-hardy. Needs somewhat less heat than 'Elberta'.
'Halehaven'	1–3, 6–11, 14–16	Medium to large. Freestone. Red skin; firm yellow flesh. Juicy and flavorful. Midseason.	Flower and leaf buds are very winter-hardy. Good fresh or canned.
'Harken'	1–7	Large. Freestone. Yellow skin with red blush; yellow flesh. Very sweet. Midseason.	Good performer in cold climates and coastal Northwest.
'Honey Babe'	3–12, 14–16, 18–20	Small to medium. Freestone. Yellow skin with red blush; yellow flesh. Fine flavor. Midseason.	Genetic dwarf. Needs another genetic dwarf peach or nectarine for pollination in the Northwest.
'Indian Blood Cling' ('Indian Cling')	1–3, 6–11, 14–16	Medium size. Clingstone. Red skin; firm yellow flesh streaked with red. Rich flavor. Late.	Old-fashioned variety with small but devoted band of enthusiasts. Good for preserves.
'Indian Free'	7–11, 14–16	Large. Freestone. Greenish white skin with red blush; red-tinged yellow flesh, deep red at the pit. Rich and aromatic when fully ripe. Late midseason.	An old favorite with a unique flavor. Needs pollinating by any other peach except 'J.H. Hale'.
'J.H. Hale'	1–3, 7–11, 14–16	Very large. Freestone. Yellow skin overlaid with deep red; little fuzz. Yellow flesh. High quality; fine keeper. Midseason.	Needs pollinating by any other peach except 'Indian Blood Cling' or 'Indian Free'.
'July Elberta' ('Kim Elberta')	2, 3, 6–12, 14–16, 18, 19	Medium to large. Freestone. Yellow skin blushed red; yellow flesh. High quality. Early, 3 weeks before 'Elberta'.	Prolific bearer.
'Loring'	7–9, 14, 15, 18	Large. Freestone. Attractive yellow skin blushed red; little fuzz. Moderately juicy yellow flesh. Good quality. Midseason.	Vigorous. Showy flowers.
'Midpride'	7–9, 12–16, 18–24	Medium size. Freestone. Red-blushed yellow skin; yellow flesh. Exceptional flavor. Midseason.	Excellent variety with low chill requirement.
'Nectar'	7–11, 14–16	Medium to large. Freestone. Creamy white skin with red blush; white flesh. Excellent flavor. Early midseason.	Produces among the best white peaches.
'O'Henry'	7–10, 14–16, 18	Large. Freestone. Yellow skin with red blush; yellow flesh streaked red. Fine flavor. Midseason.	Good commercial and home-garden variety.
'Pix Zee'	2, 3, 7–9, 14, 15, 18	Large. Freestone. Yellow skin with red blush; yellow flesh. Good flavor. Early to midseason.	Genetic dwarf.
'Polly'	1–3, 10	Medium size. Freestone. White skin blushed red; juicy white flesh. Excellent flavor. Late midseason.	Tree and buds are very hardy to cold.
'Q 1-8'	3–9, 14, 15, 18	Medium size. Semifreestone. Yellow skin with red blush; white flesh. Sweet, flavorful. Early.	Resistant to peach leaf curl.
'Ranger'	2, 3, 6–12, 14, 15	Large. Freestone. Red-blushed skin; firm, yellow flesh. Good flavor. Early.	Vigorous, productive tree. Good for areas with late spring frosts. Fruit is good fresh, canned, or frozen.

Name	Zones	Fruit	Comments
'Red Baron'	7–9, 14–16, 18–23	Large. Freestone. Yellow skin and flesh. Sweet, rich flavor. Midseason to late.	Ornamental tree with double red blossoms.
'Redhaven'	3, 5, 12, 14–16	Medium size. Freestone. Yellow skin with bright red blush; firm yellow flesh. Good flavor. Long ripening season permits numerous harvests. Early.	Colors up early, so test for ripeness. One of the best varieties. Fruit is good fresh or frozen. 'Early Redhaven' ripens 2 weeks earlier.
'Redskin'	1–3, 6–12, 14–16	Medium to large. Freestone. Yellow skin heavily blushed red; yellow flesh. Excellent quality. Midseason.	Productive tree. Fruit is good fresh, canned, or frozen.
'Reliance'	1–11	Medium to large. Freestone. Yellow skin blushed dull red; soft yellow flesh. Good flavor. Early.	Outstanding cold-hardiness.
'Rio Grande'	8–10, 15, 18–20	Medium to large. Freestone. Yellow skin with red blush; firm yellow flesh. Good flavor. Early.	Productive tree with showy flowers.
'Rio Oso Gem'	3, 7–11, 14, 15	Medium to large. Freestone. Yellow skin with red blush; firm yellow flesh. Excellent flavor. Late midseason.	Small tree; not vigorous. Fruit is excellent fresh or frozen.
'Santa Barbara'	18–24, H1	Large. Freestone. Red-blushed yellow skin; yellow flesh. Excellent flavor; best used fresh. Midseason.	Low chill requirement. Sport of 'Ventura'.
'Snow Beauty'	7–9, 14, 15, 18	Large. Freestone. Red skin; white flesh. Sweet; exceptionally good flavor. Midseason.	Among the best flavored of white peaches.
'Strawberry Free'	7–9, 14–16, 18–20	Medium size. Freestone. Medium red blush on yellow skin; firm white flesh. Excellent flavor. Early midseason.	An old favorite among white peaches.
'Suncrest'	7–9, 14, 15, 18	Large. Freestone. Yellow skin with bright red blush; yellow flesh. Excellent flavor. Midseason.	Variety made famous in *Epitaph for a Peach: Four Seasons on My Family Farm*, by David Mas Masumoto.
'Tra-Zee'	6–9, 14, 15, 18	Medium size. Freestone. Dark red skin; firm yellow flesh. Excellent flavor. Late.	Vigorous and productive.
'Tropi-berta'	8, 9, 14–16, 18–22, H1	Large. Freestone. Yellow skin blushed red; juicy yellow flesh. Good flavor. Late midseason.	Moderately low chill requirement.
'Tropic Snow'	12, 13, 18–23, H1	Medium size. Freestone. Red skin; white flesh. Superb flavor. Early.	Best low-chill white peach.
'Ventura'	18–23, H1	Medium size. Freestone. Very smooth yellow skin; yellow flesh. Attractive fruit with fair flavor. Midseason.	Low chill requirement. Developed especially for Southern California.
'White Lady'	2b–9, 12, 14–16	Medium to large. Freestone. Red skin; white flesh. Low-acid, high-sugar content. Midseason.	Fairly high chill requirement, but widely adapted where it gets enough cold.
NECTARINES			
'Arctic Jay'	7–9, 14–16, 18	Large. Freestone. Deep red skin; white flesh. Excellent, rich flavor. Early to midseason.	'Arctic' series nectarines are named for white flesh, not frost tolerance.
'Arctic Rose'	7–9, 14–16, 18	Medium size. Freestone. White to pale yellow skin with red blush; white flesh. Delicious sweet flavor. Midseason.	One of the best-tasting nectarines.
'Arctic Star'	7–9, 14, 15, 18–24	Large. Semifreestone. Bright red skin; white flesh. Very sweet, rich flavor. Early.	Low chill requirement. One of the best white nectarines for mild-winter areas.

Continued on page 196 ▶

Name	Zones	Fruit	Comments
'Double Delight'	7–9, 14–16, 18–20	Medium size. Freestone. Dark red skin; yellow flesh. Rich flavor. Midseason.	Ornamental double pink flowers. Low chill requirement.
'Fantasia'	3, 7–9, 14–16, 18–22	Large. Freestone. Bright yellow-and-red skin; firm yellow flesh. Sweet, rich flavor. Midseason.	Vigorous. Relatively low chill requirement. Good in colder areas.
'Flavortop'	2, 3, 6–12, 14, 15, 18	Large. Freestone. Yellow skin, heavily blushed red; yellow flesh. Good flavor. Midseason.	Vigorous, productive. Showy flowers.
'Goldmine'	7–12, 14–16, 18–22	Large. Freestone. Creamy yellow, tough skin with red blush; firm white flesh. Excellent, distinctive flavor. Late midseason.	Low chill requirement. Fruit is excellent fresh or frozen. 'Arctic Fantasy' is an improved form with even better flavor.
'Heavenly White'	7–9, 14–16, 18	Very large. Freestone. Creamy white skin heavily blushed with red; white flesh. Especially fine flavor. Midseason.	Has been called a connoisseur's delight.
'Independence'	7–9, 14–16, 18, 19	Large. Freestone. Red skin; yellow flesh. Good flavor. Early.	Moderately vigorous, moderately productive tree.
'Juneglo'	3–9, 14–16, 18	Medium size. Freestone. Red skin; yellow flesh. Fine flavor. Early.	One of the most reliable varieties in the coastal Northwest.
'Le Grand'	7–9, 14–16, 18	Large. Clingstone. Bright yellow-and-red skin; yellow flesh. Delicate, sweet-tart flavor. Late.	Fruit holds well on the tree.
'Liz's Late'	7–9, 14–16, 18	Medium size. Freestone. Red-over-yellow skin; yellow flesh. Sprightly, sweet-spicy flavor. Good keeper. Late.	Unusual flavor makes this nectarine a favorite.
'Mericrest'	1–3, 10, 11, 14–16, 18	Medium size. Freestone. Bright red skin; yellow flesh. Flavorful. Midseason.	May be as cold-hardy as 'Reliance' peach. Good resistance to brown rot.
'Nectar Babe'	2–12, 14–16, 18–20	Small to medium. Freestone. Dark red skin; yellow flesh. Good flavor. Midseason.	Genetic dwarf. Good pollinator for 'Honey Babe' peach.
'Necta Zee'	2–12, 14–16, 18–20	Medium size. Freestone. Red skin; yellow flesh. Sweet and flavorful. Early to midseason.	Genetic dwarf.
'Panamint'	7–9, 14–16, 18–24	Medium to large. Freestone. Bright red skin; yellow flesh. Very good flavor. Midseason.	Low chill requirement.
'Ruby Grand'	2, 3, 6–12, 14, 15, 18	Large. Freestone. Red skin; firm yellow flesh. Exceptional flavor and quality. Early to midseason.	Good all-purpose nectarine.
'Silver Lode'	7–9, 14–16, 18–20	Medium size. Freestone. Scarlet-and-white skin; white flesh. Good flavor. Early.	Low chill requirement.
'Snow Queen'	7–9, 14–16, 18–23	Medium size. Freestone. Red skin; white flesh. Sweet and juicy. Early.	Low chill requirement.
'Southern Belle'	7–12, 14–16, 18–23	Large. Freestone. Yellow skin with red blush; yellow flesh. Good flavor. Early.	Genetic dwarf. Low chill requirement.
'Sunred'	18–23	Medium size. Semifreestone. Bright red skin; yellow flesh. Good flavor. Very early.	Low chill requirement.

Pear

Pyrus communis
Rose family *(Rosaceae)*
DECIDUOUS TREE

- ✎ **ZONES VARY BY VARIETY**
- ☀ **FULL SUN**
- 💧 **REGULAR WATER**

Pears are mostly descended from a European species. They are among the longest-lived fruit trees. Pyramidal in form, with strongly vertical branching, they grow 30–40 ft. tall and 15–25 ft. wide. Pears on dwarfing understocks make good small-garden trees; they range from one-half to three-fourths the size of standard-size trees. Pears also make excellent espaliers. All types have leathery, glossy bright green leaves and bear handsome clusters of white flowers in early spring.

To produce good crops, pears need winter chill. In cold climates, their early bloom makes them prone to damage from spring frosts; in such areas, they are often planted in protected locations, such as on slopes.

Pears are not self-fruitful: you'll need to plant two varieties to ensure pollination. Fruit is produced on knobby spurs that remain productive for up to 5 years.

Pear trees are resistant to oak root fungus.

HOW TO GROW IT

best site Plant in a sunny spot, on a protected slope if there's potential for late spring frosts in your garden.

yield To 75 pounds per tree.

soil Pears grow best in well-drained loam, but they tolerate damp, heavy soil better than other fruit trees.

planting Nursery-grown trees can be planted anytime except during extreme summer heat. Plant bare-root stock in late winter or early spring, as available. *In containers:* Dwarf pears grow well in wine half-barrels.

spacing Set trees 8–25 ft. apart, depending on variety.

water Provide regular water.

fertilizer Apply 1 pound of 10-10-10 fertilizer per inch of trunk diameter every spring. Keep 1 ft. from the trunk.

pruning, training During winter, cut out dead, injured, crossing, and closely parallel branches.

'Bosc' pears are crisp, with a soft grainy texture.

harvest Harvest season is July to late October, depending on variety. Fruit does not ripen properly on the tree; pick it when it is full size but not yet ripe. Mature fruit should snap easily from the branch when you lift it to the horizontal. Put fruits of 'Anjou', 'Bosc', and 'Comice' in cold storage (32° to 40°F/0° to 4°C) for about a month after picking, then bring them into a warm room for 2 or 3 days to ripen. Store all other varieties in a cool, dark place, such as a shed, cellar, or garage. Bring them indoors to ripen 2 or 3 days before you plan to eat them.

challenges In fireblight-prone areas, plant resistant varieties. To prevent profuse new growth, which brings on risk of fireblight, fertilize sparingly and do not prune heavily in any one dormant season. Dormant oil sprays will control pear psylla and various other pests. To control codling moth, pheromone traps may be effective in a home garden; or treat with spinosad, an organic control.

Continued on page 198 ▶

top picks to grow

Name	Zones	Fruit	Comments
'Anjou' ('d'Anjou', 'Beurre d'Anjou')	2, 3, 6–9	Medium to large fruit; may be round or have a short neck. Yellow to russeted yellow. Fine flavor. Ripens after cold storage. Late.	Upright, vigorous tree. Tie down limbs for more consistent bearing. Moderately susceptible to fireblight. 'Red d'Anjou' is a red-skinned form.
'Bartlett'	2–11, 14–18	Medium to large, with short but definite neck. Thin-skinned; yellow or slightly blushed. Very sweet and tender. Midseason.	Standard summer pear of fruit markets. Good home variety, though tree does not have the best form and is susceptible to fireblight. Generally self-fruitful but may need a pollenizer in cool California coastal areas and the Northwest; use any variety except 'Seckel'.
'Blake's Pride'	2–9, 14–18	Medium-size, bell-shaped fruit. Yellow to gold skin with light russeting. Fine, melting flavor. Midseason.	Recent introduction with excellent resistance to fireblight.
'Bosc' ('Beurre Bosc', 'Golden Russet')	2–9, 14–18; best in the Northwest and higher elevations farther south	Medium to large; quite long neck, interesting and attractive in form. Heavy russeting on green or yellow skin. Fine flavor; firm, juicy flesh. Holds shape when cooked. Ripens after cold storage. Late.	Large, upright, vigorous tree. Needs pruning in youth. Highly susceptible to fireblight.
'Clapp's Favorite'	2–9, 14–18; best in the Northwest and intermountain areas	Resembles 'Bartlett' but is more heavily blushed and matures 2 weeks earlier. Soft, sweet flesh. Early.	Productive, shapely tree; attractive foliage. Highly prone to fireblight. 'Bennett', popular in the Northwest, is a red-blushed strain, as is 'Red Clapp's Favorite'.
'Comice' ('Doyenne du Comice', 'Royal Riviera')	2–9, 14–18	Large to very large; roundish to pear-shaped. Thick, greenish yellow skin is russeted, sometimes blushed. Superb flavor and texture. Ripens after cold storage. Late.	Big, vigorous tree; slow to reach bearing age. Bears good crops when soil, climate, and exposure are right. Moderately susceptible to fireblight. Generally self-fruitful but does better in the Northwest with a pollenizer. 'Red Comice' is a red-skinned sport.
'Conference'	2–9, 14–18	Large, elongated fruit borne in clusters. Yellow skin. Very juicy, sweet flesh with buttery texture. Late.	Very productive. Good resistance to fireblight.
'Fan Stil'	2, 3, 7–12, 14–23	Medium-size, bell-shaped fruit. Yellow with slight red blush. Crisp, juicy; good fresh and cooked. Midseason.	Asian pear hybrid. Vigorous, upright growth. Consistently large crops. Needs little winter chill; tolerates heat. Highly resistant to fireblight.
'Flordahome'	2, 3, 7–23	Small to medium, with short pear shape. Light green fruit. Juicy flesh. Early.	Needs little winter chill. Resistant to fireblight. Pollinate with 'Hood'.
'Harrow Delight'	1b, 2–7	Resembles 'Bartlett' but is smaller. Smooth texture, very good flavor. Early.	Cold-hardy variety developed in Canada. Excellent resistance to fireblight.
'Hood'	2, 3, 7–24, H1	Large fruit with typical pear shape. Yellow-green skin. Ripens a little later than 'Flordahome'.	Vigorous tree. Needs very little winter chill. Resistant to fireblight. Pollinate with 'Flordahome'.
'Kieffer'	2, 3, 7–23	Medium to large, oval-shaped fruit. Greenish yellow skin blushed red. Gritty texture; fair flavor. Good for canning, baking. Late.	Asian pear hybrid. Low-chill variety. Good for hot or cold climates. Quite resistant to fireblight.

Name	Zones	Fruit	Comments
'Max-Red Bartlett'	2–11, 14–18	Resembles 'Bartlett' but has bright red skin and a somewhat sweeter flavor. Midseason.	Red color extends to twigs and tints leaves. Susceptible to fireblight. Bears better in the Northwest with a pollenizer; use any except 'Seckel'.
'Monterrey'	2, 3, 7–12, 14–23	Large, apple-shaped fruit. Yellow skin. Good flavor; texture not too gritty. Midseason.	Probably an Asian pear hybrid. Needs little winter chill. Very resistant to fireblight.
'Moonglow'	2, 3, 7–12, 14–23	Somewhat like 'Bartlett' in looks. Juicy, soft fruit with good flavor. Early.	Upright, vigorous tree; very heavy bearer. Highly resistant to fireblight.
'Orcas'	2–7, 14–17	Large, pear-shaped fruit with a pointier stem end than a typical pear. Yellow skin with red blush. Flavorful, melt-in-the-mouth flesh. Midseason.	Vigorous, spreading tree.
'Orient'	2–21	Large, bell-shaped fruit. Yellow skin with russeting. Firm, juicy, and somewhat sweet flesh; good for canning, baking. Late.	Asian pear hybrid. Heavy producer. Highly resistant to fireblight.
'Potomac'	2-4, 14-21	Medium-size, pear-shaped fruit. Light green skin with red blush. Flesh is buttery with fine, 'Anjou'-like flavor. Fruit keeps 8 to 10 weeks in the refrigerator. Midseason.	Tree is very productive, fireblight-resistant.
'Rescue'	2–7, 14–17	Large fruit with traditional pear shape. Yellow skin blushed red-orange. Sweet, juicy, and smooth-textured flesh. Good keeper. Midseason.	Vigorous, productive, upright tree. Northwest favorite.
'Seckel' ('Sugar')	2–11, 14–21	Very small; roundish to pear-shaped. Yellow-brown skin. Granular, very sweet, aromatic flesh. A favorite for home gardens, preserving. Early midseason.	Highly productive. Fairly resistant to fireblight. Self-fruitful but bears more heavily with pollenizer (any except 'Bartlett' and its strains will do).
'Sensation Red Bartlett'	2–9, 14–18	Looks much like 'Bartlett' but skin is bright red over most of fruit. Midseason.	Medium-size tree, less vigorous than 'Bartlett'. Susceptible to fireblight.
'Summer Crisp'	A2, A3, 1–3	Small, roundish fruit. Red-blushed green skin. Crisp, mildly sweet flesh. Late.	Cold-hardy variety from Minnesota. Quite resistant to fireblight.
'Sure Crop'	2–9, 14–18	Resembles 'Bartlett' in looks and flavor. Late midseason.	Consistent annual bearer. Prolonged bloom makes it safe to grow where spring frosts come late. Fairly resistant to fireblight.
'Ure'	A2, A3, 1–3	Small, roundish fruit. Greenish yellow skin. Sweet and juicy. Good fresh or canned. Midseason.	Cold-hardy hybrid developed in Canada. Small tree, to 20 ft. tall, 12 ft. wide. Resistant to fireblight.
'Warren'	1b–9, 14–18	Medium to large fruit with teardrop shape. Pale green skin, often with a red blush. Buttery, juicy flesh with excellent flavor. Good keeper. Late.	Cold-hardy tree. Extremely resistant to fireblight.
'Winter Nelis'	2, 3, 7–9, 14–18	Small to medium, roundish fruit. Rough, dull green or yellowish skin. Not attractive but has a very fine flavor. Very good keeper; fine for baking. Late.	Moderately susceptible to fireblight.

Persimmon

Diospyros species and hybrids
Ebony family *(Ebenaceae)*
DECIDUOUS TREES

✎ ZONES VARY BY SPECIES
☼ FULL SUN
◑ ● MODERATE TO REGULAR WATER

Three kinds of persimmons are grown in the West. The native American species is a bigger, more cold-tolerant tree than the Japanese species, but the latter bears larger fruit—the kind sold in markets. The third type is a hybrid between the two. All three have inconspicuous flowers, and all are resistant to oak root fungus.

Fruit of American, hybrid, and some Japanese persimmon varieties is astringent until soft-ripe: eat it before then and tannins in the flesh make you pucker; eat it when the flesh is mushy and puddinglike, and flavor is very sweet. Nonastringent Japanese varieties are hard (like apples) when ripe, with a mildly sweet flavor. They can be eaten hard, but their flavor improves when they're allowed to soften slightly off the tree. All types can be used in cooking and baking.

Japanese or Oriental persimmon *(Diospyros kaki)*.
Zones 6–9, 14–16, 18–24, H1 (fruiting may be inconsistent in Hawaii—does best in dry highlands). This species grows at least 30 ft. tall and wide. It has a handsome branch pattern and is one of the best fruit trees for ornamental use; it also makes a good small shade tree or espalier. Leaves are light green when new, maturing to dark green, leathery ovals 6–7 in. long. Foliage turns vivid yellow, orange, or red in fall, even in mild climates. After leaves drop, brilliant orange-scarlet, 3- to 4-in. fruits brighten the tree for weeks and persist until winter unless harvested. The tree sets fruit without pollination, though trees pollinated by another Japanese persimmon often produce tastier, more abundant crops.

The following are superior varieties for home gardens.

'Chocolate'. Medium-size, acorn-shaped fruit. Nonastringent when unpollinated, with seedless yellow-orange flesh. Astringent until soft-ripe when pollinated, with seeded flesh that has dark streaks. Fruit from pollinated trees has best flavor.

'Fuyu'. Firm fleshed; about the size of a baseball but flattened like a tomato. Nonastringent. Favorite variety in Hawaii. 'Jiro' is very similiar and often mislabeled as 'Fuyu'.

'Gosho' ('Giant Fuyu'). Very large, round fruit. Nonastringent. Sweet and flavorful. Widely adapted.

'Hachiya'. Big, slightly pointed fruit. Astringent. Very shapely tree for ornamental use.

Japanese persimmons like 'Saijo' have elongated fruits that turn a brilliant orange-scarlet as they ripen.

'Izu'. Medium-size, round fruit borne on a tree about half the standard size. Nonastringent. Ripens early (end of summer, beginning of fall).

'Maru'. Medium-size, round fruit with shiny orange skin and dark cinnamon–colored flesh. Nonastringent and seeded when pollinated by another variety; astringent if unpollinated. Has best flavor when pollinated.

'Nishimura Wase' ('Coffee Cake'). Large, round fruit. Nonastringent when pollinated by another variety, with spicy-sweet, chocolate-colored flesh; astringent, with lighter-colored flesh, if unpollinated. Ripens early. Good choice in climates that are too cool to ripen 'Fuyu'. Use 'Chocolate' as a pollenizer.

'Saijo'. Elongated, dull yellow fruit. Astringent. Hardy, productive, early-ripening variety. One of the most reliable for the Pacific Northwest.

'Tamopan'. Large, acorn-shaped fruit. Astringent.

American persimmon (*D. virginiana*). Zones 3–9, 14–16, 18–23. Native to the eastern U.S. This species can grow 15–30 ft. tall and about as wide, with attractive gray-brown bark that is fissured in a checkered pattern. Glossy green, broadly oval leaves to 6 in. long turn yellow, pink, or reddish purple in fall. Round, 1½- to 2-in.-wide fruit is yellow to orange (often blushed red) and very astringent until soft-ripe, then very sweet. Fruit ripens in early fall after frost; some varieties do not require winter chill. Both male and female trees are usually needed to get fruit.

'Meader' is self-fruitful; its fruit is seedless if not pollinated. 'Early Golden' has more flavorful fruit; it needs cross-pollination by another American persimmon for the best crop.

Hybrid persimmons. Zones 3–9, 14–16, 18–23. These are hybrids between American and Japanese persimmons. Two of the best are 'Russian Beauty' and 'Nikita's Gift', both developed in Russia. They are as hardy as American persimmon, with larger fruit (2–2½ in. across) that is sweet and flavorful when allowed to fully soften. Hybrids are self-fruitful.

HOW TO GROW IT

best site *Japanese persimmon:* Full sun. *American and hybrid persimmons:* Young trees can take partial shade.

yield *Japanese persimmon:* More than 300 pounds of fruit per year. *American persimmon:* 35 to 75 pounds. *Hybrids:* 150 pounds.

soil All persimmons tolerate many soil types if drainage is good.

planting Plant bare-root trees in winter or early spring, as available, or container stock anytime except in extreme heat. Loosen soil deeply to make it easier for the persimmon's taproot to grow. Plant at the same depth as the plant grew at nursery, keeping the graft union 2–4 in. above ground level.

spacing Set trees 20–30 ft. apart.

water *Japanese persimmon:* Let soil dry out between waterings, but not completely. Too much or too little watering causes fruit drop; consistent watering prevents it. *American and hybrid persimmons:* Do best with regular moisture but will also perform well with moderate water.

fertilizer If tip growth is at least 12 in. long in a season, and if leaves are healthy and green, there is no need to fertilize. When fertilizer is needed, apply 1 pound of 10-10-10 fertilizer per inch of trunk diameter in late winter or early spring.

'Fuyu' bears firm, flat-bottomed persimmons and brings lovely colors to the autumn garden.

pruning, training *Japanese persimmon:* Prune trees when they are young to establish a good framework; thereafter, prune only to remove dead wood, shape the tree, or open up a dense interior. Remove any suckers that shoot up from below the graft line. *American and hybrid persimmons:* Trees usually need pruning only to remove broken or dead branches.

harvest To save the crop from birds, you can pick persimmons when they're fully colored (deep orange) and firm, then take them inside to ripen. Cut the fruit free with stem and calyx (the leathery collar at the base of the fruit) intact.

challenges Insects and diseases are generally not problems.

Plum and Prune

Prunus species
Rose family *(Rosaceae)*
DECIDUOUS TREES

✎ ZONES VARY BY VARIETY
☼ FULL SUN
💧 MODERATE WATER

Like their cherry, peach, and apricot relatives, these are stone fruits of the genus *Prunus*. (To learn about crosses involving plums, apricots, and peaches, see the next entry, *Plum Hybrids*.) Plums come in many colors—both inside and out. Skin may be yellow, red, purple, green, blue, or almost black; flesh may be yellow, red, or green.

Three categories of edible plums and prunes are grown in the West: European, Japanese, and hardy hybrids. All bloom in late winter or early spring; fruit ripens at some point from May into September, depending on variety and climate. Prunes are European plum varieties with a high sugar content that makes it possible to sun-dry the fruit without it fermenting.

European and Japanese plums. The two most widely grown groups are European plums *(P. × domestica)* and Japanese plums *(P. salicina)*. 'Damson' plum, which is sometimes considered a separate species *(P. insititia)*, is probably a type of European plum *(P. × domestica insititia)*. 'Damson' interbreeds freely with other European plums.

European plums and prunes bloom later than Japanese plums and are better adapted to areas with late frosts or cool, rainy spring weather. Most European varieties have a moderately high chill need that excludes them from extremely mild-winter areas. Many European and Japanese varieties are self-fruitful, but others need cross-pollination to produce good crops. The accompanying chart lists proven pollenizers, but other choices also exist; consult a knowledgeable local nursery for more information.

As orchard trees, both Japanese and European plums reach 15–20 ft. tall with a somewhat wider spread, but with pruning they are easily kept to 10–15 ft. tall and wide. Differences in growth habit are discussed in the chart. There are no truly dwarfing rootstocks for plums, and semidwarf trees are only slightly smaller than standards.

European plums have flesh that is firmer and can be cooked or eaten fresh; prune varieties are largely used for drying or canning, but they can also be eaten fresh if you like their very sweet flavor. Japanese plums are the largest and juiciest of all, with a pleasant blend of acid and sugar; they are mainly eaten fresh.

Japanese plums bear large, juicy fruits that are just right for fresh eating.

Hardy hybrids. Where winters are severe, a third plum category dominates. This is a complex group of hybrids involving Japanese plum, several species of native American wild plums, and the native Western sand cherry *(P. besseyi)*. The hardy hybrids originated in Canada, the Dakotas, and Minnesota, and are exceptionally tolerant of cold and wind. Pollination of hardy hybrids is difficult; ask local nurseries about effective pollenizers.

Some of these hardy hybrids are trees; others grow as bushes to about 6 ft. tall and at least as broad. Those with fruit near the size and quality of Japanese plums are sometimes called Japanese-American hybrids; those with smaller fruit closer in flavor to wild species are often called cherry-plum hybrids. Many hardy plums are tasty fresh, while others are better cooked or used in preserves.

HOW TO GROW IT

best site Choose a spot with full sun where fallen fruit won't be a problem.

yield 50 to 150 pounds per tree, depending on species and variety.

soil Fertile soil is best, but these trees can grow in a wide range of soils when drainage is good.

planting Plant bare-root plum trees when available in late winter or early spring; container-grown nursery plants can go in whenever they're available, except during extreme summer heat. *In containers:* Try a small variety like 'Weeping Santa Rosa' in a container 18 in. or larger in diameter.

spacing Set trees 10–20 ft. apart.

water Irrigate moderately but consistently for best fruit.

fertilizer Before leaf-out in spring, apply ¹/₂ pound of 10-10-10 fertilizer for each year of the tree's age, up to 6 pounds.

pruning, training *Japanese plums:* Trees should be trained to a vase shape, with five or six main scaffold branches; fruiting laterals grow from these scaffolds. Where space is limited, trees can be trained in a more linear fashion (against a wall or fence, for example). Regardless of training method, Japanese varieties of all ages need rather severe pruning to control vigorous shoot growth. Remove new, nonfruiting growth in June. Many varieties produce excessive vertical growth; shorten these shoots to outside-facing branchlets. Thin plums to 4–6 in. apart as soon as fruit forms, or fruit load may break branches. *European plums:* These do not branch as freely as Japanese types, so selection of frame-work branches is limited; these plums are usually trained to a central leader. Mature European plums require pruning mainly to thin out annual shoot growth; other-wise, little is needed. *Hardy hybrids:* Prune them to renew unfruitful branches (on shrubby types, remove older shoots to the ground every few years) and to keep the plant's center open.

harvest Pick plums when they've colored and started to soften.

'Stanley', a European plum with deep purple skin, is popular for drying into prunes.

challenges In the dry-summer West, plums are subject to far fewer problems than peaches or apples. Dormant-season sprays combining horticultural oil with lime sulfur or fixed copper will control the fungal disease brown rot and various insect pests, including scale. Peach tree borer, which tends to attack trees stressed by poor growing conditions or wounds, causes defoliation, branch dieback, and possibly death. Jellylike matter exuding from the base of the tree is the first indication of the pest's pres-ence. The insect holes will be evident at or just below ground level. If a tree is attacked, consult your Cooperative Extension Office for best treatment.

Continued on page 204 ▶

top picks to grow

Name	Zones	Pollination	Fruit	Comments
EUROPEAN VARIETIES				
'Brooks'	2–12, 14–22	Self-fruitful	Large. Yellowish red to blue skin; yellow flesh. Sweet with a little tartness. Midseason.	Good canning variety or dried prune. Produces reliably in Pacific Northwest.
'Coe's Golden Drop'	2–12, 14–22	Any other European plum	Medium to large; oblong. Straw yellow skin, often blushed red; golden flesh. Sweet, juicy, apricot-like flavor. Late.	Intense flavor. Highly regarded in Europe.
'Damson' ('Blue Damson')	2–23	Self-fruitful	Small. Purple or blue-black skin; green flesh. Very tart. Late.	Low chill requirement. Makes fine jam and jelly. Strains of this variety are sold as 'French Damson', 'Shropshire'.
'Early Laxton'	2–12, 14–20	Any other European plum	Medium size. Pinkish orange skin; yellow flesh. Deliciously sweet flavor. Early.	Excellent for cooking. Upright, very productive tree.
'French Prune' ('Agen', 'Petite')	2, 3, 7–12, 14–22	Self-fruitful	Small. Red to purplish black skin; greenish yellow flesh. Very sweet and mild. Late.	Standard drying prune of California. Also suitable for canning.
'Green Gage' ('Reine Claude')	2–22, H1	Self-fruitful	Small to medium. Greenish yellow skin; amber flesh. Very rich, sweet flavor. Midseason.	Very old variety; still a favorite for eating fresh, cooking, canning, jam. Selected strains are sold as 'Jefferson'.
'Imperial' ('Imperial Epineuse')	3–12, 14–18	Any other European plum	Large. Red-purple to black-purple skin; greenish yellow flesh. Fine-quality fruit with sweet, intense flavor. Late midseason.	Excellent fresh. Makes a premium dried prune or canned product.
'Italian Prune' ('Fellenburg')	2–12, 14–18	Self-fruitful	Medium size. Purplish black skin; yellow-green flesh. Sweet flavor. Late midseason.	Standard variety for prunes in the Pacific Northwest. Excellent fresh as well as for canning; dries well. 'Early Italian' ripens 2 weeks earlier.
'Mirabelle'	2–12, 14–22	Any midseason non-'Mirabelle' European plum	Small. Yellow fruit with orange to red dots on the skin; yellow flesh. Mild, sweet flavor. Ripening time varies.	A type favored in Europe for making brandy. Also good in preserves. Look for 'Geneva Mirabelle' and 'Reine de Mirabelle'.
'Reine Claude de Bavay' ('Bavay Green Gage')	2–12, 14–20	Self-fruitful	Large. Yellow skin with white dots; yellow flesh. Juicy and sweet; flavor similar to 'Green Gage' but better. Late.	Form of 'Green Gage' on a compact tree; good choice for smaller gardens.
'Seneca'	2–12, 14–20	Any other European plum	Very large. Red skin; yellow flesh. Deliciously sweet. Late.	Productive. One of the best for the Pacific Northwest.
'Stanley'	2–12, 14–22	Self-fruitful	Large. Purplish black skin; yellow flesh. Sweet and juicy. Midseason.	Good canning or dried prune variety. Fruit resembles a larger 'Italian Prune'.
'Sugar'	2–12, 14–22	Self-fruitful	Medium size. Dark blue skin; yellow flesh. Intensely flavored; very sweet. Early midseason.	Good fresh as well as canned; good home-drying prune. Tends to bear heavily in alternate years.

Name	Zones	Pollination	Fruit	Comments
JAPANESE VARIETIES				
'Autumn Rosa'	7–12, 14–23	Self-fruitful	Medium to large. Purplish red skin; yellow flesh with red streaks. Good, sweet flavor. Very late.	Low chill requirement. Ripens over a long period; holds well on tree.
'Beauty'	2–24	Self-fruitful; yield improved with 'Santa Rosa'	Medium size. Bright red skin; amber flesh with scarlet streaks. Good, sweet flavor. Very early.	Low chill requirement. Consistent, heavy bearer. Fruit softens quickly and must be harvested promptly.
'Burbank'	2–12, 14–20	'Beauty', 'Santa Rosa'	Large. Red skin; amber flesh. Excellent, sweet flavor. Midseason.	Hardier to cold than most Japanese plums.
'Burgundy'	7–12, 14–24	Self-fruitful	Small. Dark red skin and flesh. Excellent, rich flavor. Early to midseason.	Low chill requirement. Great fresh or canned. Fruit holds well on tree.
'Casselman'	2, 3, 7–12, 14–22	Self-fruitful	Small to medium. Purplish red skin; amber flesh (red near skin). Sweet flavor. Late.	Sport of 'Late Santa Rosa'. Ripens a few days later.
'Catalina'	7–12, 14–24	Self-fruitful	Large. Deep purple skin and flesh. Juicy and sweet. Late.	Low chill requirement. Very productive.
'Elephant Heart'	2, 3, 7–12, 14–22	'Santa Rosa'	Very large. Dark red skin; rich red flesh. Fine flavor. Midseason to late.	Skin is tart until fruit is fully ripe. Long harvest season.
'Emerald Beaut'	7–12, 14–20	'Beauty', 'Burgundy', 'Late Santa Rosa'	Medium size. Light green skin; greenish yellow to orange flesh. Exceptional, sweet, rich flavor. Midseason to late.	Fruit holds well on the tree without losing quality.
'Friar'	2, 3, 7–12, 14–20	'Santa Rosa', 'Late Santa Rosa'	Large. Purplish black skin; amber flesh. Good, sweet flavor. Late midseason.	Fruit resists cracking; softens slowly after picking. Very vigorous, productive tree.
'Golden Nectar'	2, 3, 7–12, 14–20	Self-fruitful	Very large. Yellow skin and flesh. Excellent, sweet flavor. Small pit. Midseason.	Fruit keeps well after harvest.
'Hollywood'	2–9, 14–20	Self-fruitful	Medium size; oblong. Dark red skin; red flesh. Flavorful. Late.	Not very productive. Pink flowers and purple foliage make this double as a good ornamental.
'Howard Miracle'	7–10, 14–20	'Santa Rosa', 'Wickson'	Medium size. Yellow skin with red blush; yellow flesh. Spicy flavor reminiscent of pineapple. Midseason.	Very vigorous. Fruit more acid than that of most Japanese plums but truly distinctive in flavor.
'Kelsey'	2, 3, 7–12, 14–18, H1	Self-fruitful	Large. Green to greenish yellow skin splashed red; firm yellow flesh. Sweet but not juicy. Late midseason.	Fruit keeps well after harvest.
'Laroda'	7–12, 14–22	'Burgundy', 'Santa Rosa', 'Late Santa Rosa'	Large. Red skin; amber flesh (red near skin). Rich and juicy. Midseason.	Fruit holds well on the tree.
'Late Santa Rosa'	7–12, 14–22	Self-fruitful	Medium to large. Purplish crimson skin; amber flesh (red near skin). Sweet-tart, sprightly flavor. Late.	Ripens a month after 'Santa Rosa'.

Continued on page 206 ▶

Name	Zones	Pollination	Fruit	Comments
'Mariposa' ('Improved Satsuma')	2, 3, 7–12, 14–22, H1	'Autumn Rosa', 'Beauty', 'Late Santa Rosa', 'Santa Rosa', 'Wickson'	Large. Purple-red skin; deep red flesh. Sweet. Midseason.	Good for cooking and fresh eating.
'Methley'	2–9, 12–24, H1	Self-fruitful	Medium size. Reddish purple skin; dark red flesh. Sweet and mild. Early.	Low chill requirement. Good bloom-hardiness.
'Nubiana'	2, 3, 7–12, 14–20	Self-fruitful	Large. Deep purple-black skin; amber flesh. Sweet and firm. Midseason.	Good for fresh eating and for cooking (flesh turns red when cooked). Good keeper.
'Santa Rosa'	2, 3, 7–23	Self-fruitful	Medium to large. Purplish red skin with heavy blue bloom; yellow flesh (dark red near skin). Rich, pleasing, tart flavor. Early.	Low chill requirement. Important commercial variety for fresh eating. Good canned if skin is removed. 'Weeping Santa Rosa' has unique drooping habit, grows only 6–8 ft. tall.
'Satsuma'	2–22	'Beauty', 'Santa Rosa', 'Wickson'	Small to medium. Dull deep red skin; dark red, solid, meaty flesh. Mild, sweet flavor. Small pit. Early midseason.	Preferred for jams and jellies. Sometimes called blood plum because of red juice.
'Shiro'	2–4, 7–12, 14–22	Self-fruitful	Medium to large. Yellow skin and flesh. Mild but good flavor. Early midseason.	Heavy producer. Fruit good for fresh eating and for cooking. Pretty in flower and fruit.
'Wickson'	2–12, 14–22	'Beauty', 'Santa Rosa'	Large. Greenish yellow to yellow skin, blushed with red when fruit is ripe; firm yellow flesh. Mild but fine flavor. Early midseason.	Showy fruit. Keeps well after harvest. Good for jams and jellies.
HARDY HYBRIDS				
'Opata'	A2, A3, 1–3	Check locally	Small. Purple skin; green flesh. Sweet. Late.	Cherry-plum hybrid from South Dakota. Bush form. Upper branches often freeze in coldest areas, but lower branches usually fruit well. Fruit is good fresh and for preserves.
'Pipestone'	A2, A3, 1–3	Check locally	Large. Tough red skin; yellow flesh. A little stringy but juicy and sweet. Midseason.	Vigorous Japanese-American hybrid developed in Minnesota. Tree form. Needs little heat to ripen. Very good for fresh eating and jam; good for jelly.
'Sapalta'	A2, A3, 1–3	Check locally	Small. Red-purple skin; almost black flesh. Mildly sweet. Late.	Cherry-plum hybrid developed in Canada. Bush form. Good for fresh eating, juice, canning, preserves.
'Superior'	A2, A3, 1–3	Check locally	Very large. Golden with red-blushed, lightly russeted skin; firm yellow flesh. Flavor is slightly tart near skin, dessert quality. Late midseason.	Japanese-American hybrid developed in Minnesota. Tree form. Bears at an early age and heavily. Good fresh or for jam, jelly.
'Underwood'	A2, A3, 1–3	Check locally	Medium to large. Dark red skin; amber flesh. Tender, juicy, sweet. Early.	Vigorous Japanese-American hybrid developed in Minnesota. Tree form. Good for fresh eating and jam; fair for jelly.

Plum Hybrids

Prunus hybrids
Rose family *(Rosaceae)*
DECIDUOUS TREES

✒ ZONES VARY BY TYPE

☼ FULL SUN

💧 MODERATE WATER

These hybrids between plum and apricot, plum and peach, and plum and nectarine combine characteristics of their parent fruits in varying degrees. Most grow 10–20 ft. tall and wide but can be held to half that width with consistent pruning. Like their parents, they need winter chill for good fruit production. Plants are not yet widely tested, so the following climate-zone numbers are best guesses for each category. Individual hybrids have such complex ancestry that their climate needs may vary, even within categories.

Aprium. Zones 3–16, 18–22. This plum-apricot hybrid will grow where apricots succeed. 'Cot-N-Candy', a self-fertile aprium, has extra-sweet, apricot-like fruit whose light-colored flesh has a plum aftertaste. 'Flavor Delight' is similar-looking but a little juicier. It is partially self-fruitful, but for the best crop pollinate it with an apricot that blooms at the same time or with 'Flavor Supreme' pluot. 'Cot-N-Candy' ripens just after 'Flavor Delight' in late spring or early summer.

Nectarine-plum hybrid (Nectaplum). Zones 7–9, 14–16, 18–20. 'Spice Zee', the first nectarine-plum cross, has red skin and yellow spicy-sweet flesh redolent of both parents. Red spring leaves mature to a green-red. It is self-fruitful, late ripening, and productive.

Peach-plum hybrid. Zones 3, 7–9, 14–16, 18. 'Tri-Lite' has red skin with white flesh and a mild, classic peach flavor with a plum aftertaste. It is self-fertile and an early ripener.

Plumcot. Zones 3, 7–12, 14–16, 18–23. This was the original plum-apricot cross made by Luther Burbank. 'Flavorella' is the most promising variety, producing medium-size golden fruit with a red blush and firm, juicy, sweet-tart flesh. It has a low chill requirement and needs pollination with 'Flavorosa' plumcot or 'Floragold' or 'Gold Kist' apricot to bear fruit. 'Plum Parfait' is an older plumcot variety with pinkish orange skin, flesh marbled in crimson and amber, and a sweet-tart, plumlike flavor. Both 'Flavorella' and 'Plum Parfait' ripen in late spring or early summer.

Apriums like 'Flavor Delight' taste much like their apricot parent, with just a touch of plum flavor.

Pluot. Zones 3, 7–12, 14–16, 18–23. The fruit of pluot, another plum-apricot hybrid, is very sweet, closer in flavor to a plum. It is most likely to succeed where 'Santa Rosa' plum does. Early ripeners (late spring or early summer) include 'Flavor Supreme', with mottled green-and-maroon skin and deep red flesh; medium- to large-fruited 'Emerald Drop', with green skin and apricot-colored flesh; and 'Splash', an ornamental edible with yellow-, orange-, or red-skinned fruit and extra-sweet yellow-orange flesh. Mid- to late-summer ripeners include 'Dapple Dandy' (often sold in markets under the name "dinosaur egg"), with mottled maroon-and-yellow skin and creamy white flesh streaked with red; 'Flavor King', with purplish red skin and flesh; and 'Flavor Queen', with greenish yellow skin and golden flesh. 'Flavor Grenade' bears elongated green fruit flushed

Continued on page 208 ▶

Ripening 'Splash' pluots take on a red blush.

with red at the end of the season; it has amber flesh. In California, it can hang on the tree until Thanksgiving. Both 'Dapple Dandy' and 'Flavor Supreme' will pollinate any other pluot; you can also use a Japanese plum that blooms at the same time.

HOW TO GROW IT

best site Sunny, open location.

yield Varies by type; 50 to 100 pounds per tree is possible, depending on tree size and extent of fruit thinning.

soil Fertile, with good drainage.

planting Plant bare-root trees when available in late winter or early spring; plant container-grown nursery plants anytime except during extreme summer heat.

spacing Set trees 5–15 ft. apart.

water Moderate water through the growing season. Mulch to maintain soil moisture between waterings.

fertilizer Before leaf-out in spring, sprinkle organic 5-5-5 fertilizer over the tree's root zone.

pruning, training In years when the crop is heavy, thin fruit to 8 or 9 in. apart. This keeps the heavy crop from being followed by a light crop. In winter, prune out injured, diseased, crossing, and closely parallel branches. Prune in summer to control the tree's size.

harvest Pick fruit when it is fully colored, gives slightly when you gently squeeze it, and tastes ripe.

challenges All of these plum hybrids are subject to brown rot, gummosis, and peach tree borers; crosses from peaches and nectarines can also get peach leaf curl. Trees that have good sanitation (injured and diseased branches pruned out), regular watering, periodic feeding, good soil, and plenty of sun are less likely to have problems. If diseases and insects become issues, consult your local Cooperative Extension Office for a treatment plan.

'Flavor Rich', a large pluot with medium-sweet orange flesh

Pomegranate

Punica granatum
Pomegranate family *(Punicaceae)*
DECIDUOUS TREE

🌡 **ZONES 7–16, 18–24, H1, H2; MARGINAL IN 5, 6, 17**
☼ **FULL SUN**
💧 **REGULAR WATER**

This small, showy tree from Iran and northern India has naturalized throughout the Mediterranean. It grows 15–20 ft. tall and broad, though it is often kept pruned to half that size. Showy red flowers appear in spring and develop into roundish, 5-in.-wide fruits that ripen in fall. Each fruit contains hundreds of sacs of seedy, sweet-tart, juicy pulp. Trees are self-fruitful, so you need plant only one to get fruit. Plants are resistant to oak root fungus.

To use pomegranates fresh, cut them into quarters or eighths and pull the rind back (starting from the ends) to expose the juicy sacs; eat them seeds and all. To remove juice, cut the fruit in half and ream with a juicer; or roll fruit firmly on a hard surface, then cut a hole in the stem end and squeeze juice into a container.

'Wonderful', with orangish red flowers, burnished red fruit, and red pulp, is the best-known variety. Other available varieties include the following. (Unless noted, all have red or orangish red flowers and yellow skin overlaid with pink or red.) 'Ambrosia' bears huge fruits (up to three times larger than those of 'Wonderful'), with pale pink skin and purple pulp. 'Eversweet' ripens very early and bears virtually seedless fruit with transparent red pulp and clear, nonstaining juice. 'Granada' has pink flowers and pink pulp. 'Kashmir' has pinkish red fruit and deep red seeds with intense flavor that's great for juice. 'Pink Satin' has pinkish red fruit with light pink, soft seeds whose juice is nonstaining. 'Red Silk' bears medium to large red fruit with excellent sweet-tart red pulp on a 6- to 8-ft. tree, ideal for containers. 'Sweet' has yellow flowers and pink pulp. 'White' bears pink fruit with sweet, transparent pulp.

HOW TO GROW IT

best site Full sun. In Zones 5, 6, and 17, locate it against a south or west wall for maximum heat.

yield 60 pounds per tree.

soil Not particular about soil.

planting Plant bare-root stock when available in spring, and container-grown trees anytime except during the

Pomegranates can be juiced, eaten fresh, or cooked.

hottest days of summer. *In containers:* Small varieties do well in containers at least 18 in. wide and deep.

spacing Set plants 6–18 ft. apart, depending on variety.

water For best fruit, provide regular irrigation.

fertilizer Scatter 10-10-10 fertilizer lightly over the root zone every spring.

pruning, training Remove suckers from plant base.

harvest Pick when fruit reaches full color; any left on the tree is likely to split and rot, especially in rainy weather. Fruit can be stored for up to 7 months in the refrigerator.

challenges Treat aphids by blasting them off with a jet of water when they appear in spring. Apply a sulfur-based miticide to take care of flat mites in late spring and early summer. For leaf rollers, apply *Bacillus thuringiensis (Bt)*.

Quince

Cydonia oblonga
Rose family *(Rosaceae)*
DECIDUOUS OR SEMIEVERGREEN SHRUB OR TREE

✎ **ZONES 2–24**
☼ **FULL SUN**
◖◗ **MODERATE TO REGULAR WATER**

Quince is a relative of the pear and native to western Asia. It reaches 10–25 ft. tall and wide at a growth rate of about a foot a year, with gnarled, twisted branches that are attractive when leafless in winter. Like pear, it is long-lived. Oval, 2- to 4-in. leaves are dark green above, whitish beneath, turning yellow in autumn. White or pale pink, 2-in. flowers are followed by 3- to 4-in., round to pear-shaped, fragrant yellow fruit. It is typically tart and used for jams and jellies, made into candy, or combined with other fruits in pies.

Quince bears fruit 2 or 3 years after planting, is self-pollinating, and needs little winter chill to be productive. Avoid deep cultivation near the trunk; this damages its shallow roots and encourages growth of suckers.

Recommended varieties include the following. 'Apple' ('Orange') is an old favorite with round fruit and tender orange-yellow flesh. 'Aromatnaya' has round fruit with yellow flesh that tastes like pineapple; it can be sliced and eaten fresh. 'Cooke's Jumbo' has very large pear-shaped fruit with sweet white flesh. 'Havran' produces large pear-shaped fruit with very sweet white flesh. 'Pineapple' bears nearly round fruit with tender white flesh that tastes like pineapple. 'Smyrna' has round to oblong fruit with white flesh; strongly aromatic. 'Van Deman' bears large, oblong fruit with spicy yellow flesh.

HOW TO GROW IT

best site Full sun.

yield 50 pounds per tree.

soil Grows in most soils but needs good drainage.

planting Plant bare-root stock when available in late winter or spring, or plant container-grown stock anytime except in the hottest days of summer. Plant no deeper than the soil line on the trunk. *In containers:* Quince can be grown in half-barrels.

spacing Set plants 10–25 ft. apart.

water Water deeply every 2 to 3 weeks during the growing season.

The tender white flesh of 'Pineapple' quince has the aroma and taste of its namesake fruit.

fertilizer Lightly scatter 5-10-10 fertilizer over the root zone in late winter and early summer.

pruning, training Little pruning is required beyond initial shaping and periodic thinning to keep the plant's center open to sunlight. Remove any suckers that sprout around the base of the tree.

harvest Pick when fruit has fully colored up (all yellow, no green) and is fragrant. Fruit is susceptible to bruising, so handle it carefully. It can be stored in a refrigerator for up to 2 months.

challenges Fireblight is the only serious problem. Prune off affected branches in healthy wood well below the wilted part; disinfect pruners between cuts.

CHAPTER 5

Nuts

Crunchy, tasty, and easy to grow, nuts are also good sources of protein, carbohydrates, and dietary fiber. Although their oil contains fat, it's primarily the unsaturated kind. Most nuts are also high in vitamin E. In this chapter, we include tree nuts as well as sunflower seeds and peanuts, which have many of the same health benefits.

Almond

Prunus dulcis
Rose family *(Rosaceae)*
DECIDUOUS TREE

✎   **ZONES 2B, 3B, 8–10, 12–16, 19–21**
☀   **FULL SUN**
💧   **MODERATE WATER**

The almond, native to Asia Minor and North Africa, is nearly as hardy as the peach (its close relative) but is more exacting in climate adaptation. Trees bear best where summers are long, hot, and dry; nuts will not develop properly in areas with cool summers or high humidity. They need some winter chill yet must be spared from frosts at the wrong time. Trees bloom early (in winter or early spring), and frost then will cut the crop; late frosts will destroy small nuts that are forming. To experiment in areas where frost is a hazard, choose late-blooming varieties.

Unless you choose a self-fruitful type, two varieties that bloom at the same time are needed for pollination (they can be planted in the same hole if space is tight). Nuts are borne on spurs that are productive for about 5 years.

Trees reach 20–30 ft. tall and are erect when young, spreading and dome shaped in age. Leaves are 3–5 in. long, pale green with a gray tinge. Flowers are palest pink or white. The fruit looks like a leathery, flattened, undersize green peach. In late summer or fall, the hull splits to reveal the shell; the kernel inside is the edible part of the almond.

Recommended varieties. The following are the main varieties sold for nuts.

'All-in-One'. Semidwarf tree with medium to large, sweet, soft-shelled nuts. Self-fruitful. Highly recommended for home gardens.

'Butte'. Very productive tree with semihard-shelled nuts, slightly smaller than 'Mission'. Late bloomer, flowering just before 'Mission'. Pollinate with 'All-in-One', 'Mission', or 'Nonpareil'.

'Garden Prince'. Genetic dwarf with showy pink blooms and medium-size, soft-shelled nuts. Self-fruitful.

'Hall' ('Hall's Hardy'). Tree may actually be a peach-almond hybrid. Bears hard-shelled, bitter, small nuts of low quality. Pink bloom comes late, an advantage in late-frost regions. Partially self-fruitful but better with 'Mission' as pollenizer.

'Mission' ('Texas'). Regular, heavy producer of small, semihard-shelled nuts. Late bloomer, one of the safest for cold-winter, late-frost areas. Pollinate with 'Hall'.

'Ne Plus Ultra'. Bears large kernels in attractive soft shells. Pollinate with 'Nonpareil'.

'Nonpareil'. Excellent all-around variety with paper-thin soft shells that are easily removed by hand. Midseason bloomer; some bud failure where summers are very hot. Pollinate with 'All-in-One', 'Mission', or 'Ne Plus Ultra'.

HOW TO GROW IT

best site Full sun. In areas where hard frosts are still possible in March and April, plant on a slope, where good air drainage reduces the risk of frost.

yield 5 to 20 pounds per tree.

soil Almonds adapt to all soils except heavy, slow-draining ones. They also need deep soil (at least 6 ft.).

planting Plant bare-root stock when available in late winter or spring. Plant container-grown trees anytime of year except during the hottest days of summer. *In containers:* 'Garden Prince' is worth trying in an 18-in. (or larger) container.

spacing Set trees 20–30 ft. apart.

water Whenever the top 2 or 3 in. of soil dries out, soak the root zone.

fertilizer As long as the tree puts on at least 8 in. of new growth every year, it needs no fertilizer. When growth is less than that, apply 7 pounds of 10-10-10 fertilizer per mature tree before buds emerge; repeat after harvest.

pruning, training Each dormant season, remove about a fifth of the oldest fruiting wood to encourage development of new spurs.

harvest Harvest nuts after hulls have cracked open and are partially dry. Knock or shake them from the tree; waiting for nuts to drop takes too long and carries risk of rotting. Peel off hulls and spread the nuts in the sun for a day or two to dry. To test for adequate dryness, shake the nuts—the kernels should rattle inside their shells. Freeze almonds for 48 hours to kill any insects hiding inside the shells, then seal the nuts in an airtight container. In-shell almonds can be stored 6 months in a cool, dry place.

challenges Trees are subject to attack by brown rot (which causes fruit rot, twig dieback, and cankers on the trunk and branches) and mites (which cause premature yellowing and falling of leaves).

The distinctively shriveled hulls of almonds begin to split by late summer, revealing the shell inside.

Chestnut

Castanea species
Beech family *(Fagaceae)*
DECIDUOUS TREES

🌿 **ZONES 2–9, 14–17, EXCEPT AS NOTED**
☼ **FULL SUN**
💧 **MODERATE WATER**

The American chestnut *(Castanea dentata)* has become nearly extinct in its native range in eastern North America as a result of chestnut blight, but other species and hybrids are available. They make wonderful, dense shade trees where there is space to accommodate them and where their litter and rank-smelling pollen won't be too obtrusive. All have handsome dark to bright green foliage. Small, creamy white flowers in long (8- to 10-in.), slim catkins make quite a display in summer. The large edible nuts are enclosed in prickly burs.

Plant two or more trees to ensure cross-pollination and a substantial crop; single trees bear lightly or not at all.

Chinese chestnut *(C. mollissima).* Native to China, Korea, Taiwan. To 35–40 ft. tall with a rounded crown that may spread to 20–25 ft. Leaves are 3–7 in. long with coarsely toothed edges. Most nursery trees are grown from seed, not cuttings, so nuts are variable but generally of good quality. Resistant to chestnut blight. Intolerant of alkaline soil.

European chestnut *(C. sativa).* Native to southern Europe, North Africa, western Asia. Can reach 100 ft. tall with greater spread, but typically grows 40–60 ft. tall and wide in gardens. Leaves are 4–9 in. long with sharply toothed edges. Large, excellent-quality nuts are the type usually sold in markets. Resistant to oak root fungus. Susceptible to chestnut blight.

Hybrid chestnuts. Zones 2–9, 14–24. Mostly offspring of Japanese *(C. crenata)* or Chinese chestnuts crossed with American or European chestnuts. Trees usually grow 40–60 ft. tall and wide. Intolerant of alkaline soils. Some resist chestnut blight. Varieties include 'Colossal', which sets the standard for nuts; 'Dunstan', an American cross with high-quality, medium-size nuts and blight resistance; 'Nevada', a small-nutted variety and proven pollenizer for 'Colossal'; 'Skioka', a heavy producer of small nuts that won't pollinate other trees; and 'Sleeping Giant', which produces sweet, large nuts and is blight-resistant.

HOW TO GROW IT

best site These need full sun and plenty of room.

yield *Chinese chestnut:* 40 to 70 pounds per tree. *European chestnut:* To 300 pounds per tree. *Hybrids:* 30 to 80 pounds per tree.

soil Best in deep, well-drained, slightly acid soil.

planting Plant bare-root trees when available in late winter or spring; plant container-grown stock anytime of year except during the hottest days of summer. Set trees at the same soil depth as they grew at the nursery.

spacing Set trees 35–60 ft. apart, depending on the variety's mature size.

water Flood the root zone every 3 or 4 weeks from May through September. Create a small berm to keep water 1 or 2 ft. from tree trunk.

fertilizer As leaves open in spring, apply 5 pounds of 10-10-10 fertilizer per tree.

pruning, training Remove dead, injured, diseased, or weak branches every winter.

harvest Burs with full-size ripe nuts inside start to split open on the tree a couple of weeks after unpollinated burs (containing shriveled nuts) fall to the ground. Wearing gloves, harvest all the burs from the tree. Let them dry in the sun (shade in hot climates), picking the nuts out as the burs continue to dry and open. Not all will open; remove those nuts with a knife. Wash nuts for a few minutes in a mixture of 6 ounces bleach to 1 gallon of water, picking out and discarding floating nuts. Drain and dry nuts, then refrigerate in freezer bags, each containing a dry paper towel to absorb moisture, for up to 3 months.

challenges Chestnut blight is the biggest threat to susceptible trees. To minimize its potential for damage, irrigate only by flooding the soil—never with sprinklers that get the leaves wet. *Phytophthora* root rot and crown rot can be controlled by letting trees dry out between waterings and by keeping water away from the trunk. Protect young trees from deer (dogs and fencing are the two most common methods), and set traps if gophers are a problem in your area.

When chestnuts are ripe (typically in October in the West), their prickly burs split open to reveal large edible nuts.

Hazelnut

Corylus avellana
Birch family *(Betulaceae)*
DECIDUOUS TREE

☀ **ZONES 2–7, EXCEPT AS NOTED**
☼ ◑ **AFTERNOON SHADE IN HOTTEST CLIMATES**
◊ ◖ **LITTLE TO MODERATE WATER**

Hazelnuts, sometimes called filberts, are selections of the European species *Corylus avellana;* their nuts are the commercial ones sold in stores. The trees are handsome and nicely structured, growing 10–18 ft. tall and wide—a good choice for a garden or terrace. From spring to fall, the roundish, ruffle-edged leaves cast a pleasant spot of shade. Showy catkins (male flowers) hang long and full on bare branches in winter.

Hazelnuts ripen in late summer and drop in early fall; the roundish or oblong nuts form inside frilled husks. Since cross-pollination is necessary, plant at least two varieties. Cold-winter areas get the best crops.

Recommended varieties. Eastern filbert blight, a destructive bark disease, has devastated old standby varieties 'Butler', 'Daviana', 'Du Chilly', and 'Ennis'; they are no longer recommended in the prime hazelnut-growing areas of Oregon. The following varieties have partial to excellent blight resistance.

'Barcelona'. Fine flavor. Some resistance to blight. Good pollenizer for 'Santiam'.

'Delta'. Richly flavored nuts on a compact plant. High blight resistance. Pollinates 'Gamma', 'Jefferson', and 'Lewis', but not 'Barcelona' or 'Ennis.'

'Eta'. Large harvests of thin-shelled, small nuts with good flavor on a compact tree. Very high blight resistance. Pollinates nearly all varieties except 'Ennis'.

'Gamma'. Sweet, good-quality nuts on a vigorous tree. High blight resistance. Good pollenizer for 'Barcelona', 'Delta', 'Hall's Giant', 'Lewis', 'Sacajawea', 'Santiam', 'Tonda di Giffoni', and 'Yamhill'.

'Hall's Giant'. Flavorful. Good resistance to blight. Pollinates 'Gamma', 'Jefferson', 'Lewis', and 'Sacajawea'.

'Jefferson'. Big yields of attractive, tasty nuts. High blight resistance. Pollinates 'Yamhill'.

'Lewis'. Good-quality nuts. High blight resistance. Pollinates 'Gamma', 'Hall's Giant', and 'Sacajawea', but not 'Yamhill'.

'Sacajawea'. Attractive nuts with excellent flavor. High resistance to blight. Pollinates 'Gamma', 'Hall's Giant', and 'Lewis'.

'Santiam'. New blight-resistant variety that produces abundant, high-quality nuts on a smallish tree. Good pollenizer for 'Yamhill'.

Hazelnut grows throughout the Pacific Northwest and is the official state nut of Oregon.

'Theta'. Large harvests of thin-shelled, small nuts with good flavor on a vigorous, upright tree. Very high blight resistance. Pollinates nearly all hazelnuts except 'Delta' and 'Hall's Giant'.

'Tonda di Giffoni'. Excellent flavor. Highly resistant to blight. Pollinates all varieties except 'Barcelona'.

'Yamhill'. Good-quality nuts on a small tree. Highly resistant to blight. Good pollenizer for 'Delta', 'Gamma', 'Hall's Giant', and 'Santiam'.

Two types of hybrids, called filazels and trazels, can be grown into Zone 1a. Filazels—hardy, 10- to 15-ft.-tall producers of good-quality nuts—are hybrids between *C. avellana* and the North American beaked hazelnut *(C. cornuta)*. Trazels—upright, 20- to 30-ft.-tall trees that produce sweet, fine-flavored nuts—are crosses between *C. avellana* and Turkish hazel *(C. colurna)*. Plant two of the same type for cross-pollination.

HOW TO GROW IT

best site Full sun west of the Cascades but partial afternoon shade in hot areas east of the Sierra Nevada–Cascade ranges.

yield A 10-year-old tree may yield up to 20 pounds of nuts per year.

soil Deep, well-drained soil is optimal.

planting Plant bare-root stock as available in late winter or early spring, or plant container stock at any time of year except during the hottest days of summer.

spacing Set individual nut trees 10–18 ft. apart. For a boundary hedgerow, plant mixed varieties 4 ft. apart and let suckers grow.

water There's little need for supplemental irrigation in mild parts of the Pacific Northwest. Elsewhere, soak trees monthly in drought and hot summer months.

fertilizer If the tree is growing and producing well, don't fertilize. If the tree struggles or yield declines, apply 1 1/2 pounds of 10-10-10 fertilizer in February where winters are mild, in March where winters are cold.

pruning, training Trees tend to sucker, so clear out suckers three or four times a year if you wish to maintain a clean trunk.

harvest Pick up nuts from the ground, then dry them in the sun for a few days. Stored in a dry place below 50°F/10°C, in-shell unroasted hazelnuts can last up to 2 years. In the same conditions, shelled, roasted hazelnuts last up to 6 months.

challenges Eastern filbert blight (*Anisogramma anomala*) shows as raised, oval black bumps in vertical lines on infected branches and twigs. Individual branches die out, and the entire plant can succumb. Protect existing plants by spraying with copper and horticultural oil together at bud break (usually in late March), again in mid-April, and a third time in early May. Remove dead branches, cutting 2 ft. back into healthy growth. Burn or bury prunings. Severely infected trees should be removed entirely. Squirrels and jays are a nuisance, often picking the nuts before they fall. Handpicking when the nuts are tree-ripe (when they separate easily from the hulls) will thwart animal thieves.

Toast hazelnuts to intensify their flavor and make the skins easier to remove.

Macadamia

Macadamia species
Protea family *(Proteaceae)*
EVERGREEN TREES

⚟ **ZONES 9, 16, 17, 19–24, H1, H2**
☼ **FULL SUN**
◐ **REGULAR WATER**

Macadamias are clean, handsome ornamental trees. They produce clusters of delicious hard-shelled nuts, usually within 3 to 5 years after planting, and reach full production in 12 to 15 years. Though these Australia natives are best adapted in subtropical Zones 23 and 24 and tropical Zones H1 and H2, they are also known to grow successfully in Zones 9, 16, 17, and 19–22 when frosts are light.

Trees grow 30–40 ft. tall and almost as wide, with whorls of glossy, leathery, 5- to 12-in.-long leaves. New growth that emerges during winter is usually yellow (caused by cold); later growth is green. Mature foliage is durable and attractive in arrangements. Trees bloom in winter and spring, bearing small, sometimes fragrant, white to pink flowers in dense, pendent, foot-long clusters. The fruit that follows is a roundish leathery husk to 1$^1\!/_2$ in. wide that contains a hard-shelled nut.

Though most macadamias are sold under the name *Macadamia ternifolia*, any tree you buy will likely be one of the two species described below or a hybrid between them. Look for grafted, named varieties of proven nut-bearing ability rather than unnamed seedlings. Seedlings take longer to bear nuts, and their quality is unpredictable. Macadamias are self-fruitful, but planting two different varieties often produces bigger harvests. Macadamias are resistant to oak root fungus.

Roughshell macadamia *(M. tetraphylla).* More widely grown than smoothshell macadamia in California, where it performs best slightly inland. Differs from smoothshell macadamia in having a more open growth habit, spiny leaves, and thinner-shelled nuts that ripen from fall to midwinter. Varieties include 'Burdick', 'Cate', and 'Fenton'.

Smoothshell macadamia *(M. integrifolia).* Commercial species best adapted to Hawaii. Can be grown near the coast in Southern California. Leaves are smooth-edged, and nuts ripen from late fall to late spring. Popular varieties include 'Kakea', 'Kau', 'Keaau', 'Mauka', and 'Purvis'.

Hybrid macadamias. Crosses between *M. integrifolia* and *M. tetraphylla.* 'Beaumont', which bears over a very long period, is one of the best varieties for Southern

Creamy white macadamias grow in hard shells.

California and the most widely available there. It produces medium to large nuts with moderately thick shells; new leaves are reddish. 'Cooper' has small nuts, also with moderately thick shells. 'Vista' produces small to medium-size, very thin-shelled nuts.

HOW TO GROW IT

best site A sunny spot protected from wind.

yield 150 pounds per tree.

soil Macadamias perform best in deep, rich loam.

planting Set out plants from nursery containers at any time of year, but they'll suffer less stress from moisture loss and heat if planted in fall.

When macadamias mature, the green husks split to reveal the shell-covered nut inside each one.

spacing Set trees 30 ft. apart.

water Resists drought, but bears better with moderate watering.

fertilizer Apply light applications of 10-10-10 fertilizer at least twice a year.

pruning, training Trees are weak-wooded, so prune young plants to encourage a strong main trunk with near-horizontal scaffold branches.

harvest Pick up nuts as they fall from tree (husks of ripe nuts split, making the nuts easy to remove). If nuts don't fall naturally, strip the tree when birds and squirrels start to take them. Store the nuts in an airtight container in the refrigerator for up to 6 months or in the freezer for up to a year. To get frozen nuts ready for eating, put them into a food dehydrator for 10 minutes to restore crunchiness and fresh flavor.

challenges Though mites, scale, and thrips sometimes appear, macadamias rarely have serious pest problems in California. In Hawaii, tropical nut borer pierces the shell and lays eggs in the nut; it is a serious and widespread pest. The best controls are to harvest frequently and pick up fallen nuts as soon as possible. Don't let sticktights—mature nuts that remain on the tree—go unharvested. Southern green stinkbug is most serious in Hawaii during drought. Combat it by keeping trees well watered during stretches of dry weather.

Peanut

Arachis hypogaea
Pea family *(Fabaceae)*
ANNUAL

✀ **ZONES 2–24**
☼ **FULL SUN**
💧 **REGULAR WATER**

The peanut originated in South America and produces most heavily where summers are long and warm. It is tender to frost but worth growing even in cool regions. Peanuts are actually legumes rather than true nuts, and in bloom plants look like 10- to 20-in.-tall bush sweet peas *(Lathyrus)* with bright yellow flowers. After the flowers fade, a "peg" (shootlike structure) develops at each flower's base and grows down into the soil, where the peanuts develop.

The four basic classes of peanuts are Virginia and Runner types, with two large seeds per pod; Spanish, with two or three small seeds per pod; and Valencia, with three to six small seeds per pod.

Buy seeds (unroasted peanuts) from mail-order suppliers. In cool-summer areas, grow the plants under floating row covers to hasten growth.

HOW TO GROW IT

best site An open, sunny location. If you live in a cool-summer area, grow peanuts against a south-facing wall for maximum heat (plants do best when soil temperature is 70° to 80°F/21° to 27°C).

yield 40 peanut pods per plant.

soil Peanuts grow best in fertile, well-drained soil; sandy or other light-textured soil is ideal for penetration by pegs.

planting Plant as soon as soil has warmed in spring, setting seeds (with shells removed but skins intact) 1½– 2 in. deep. *In containers:* Possible in a container at least 16 in. wide and 8 in. deep.

spacing Sow seeds of Virginia and Runner peanuts 6–8 in. apart; sow Spanish and Valencia peanuts 4–6 in. apart.

water Water deeply at planting time and whenever the top inch of soil dries out.

fertilizer Apply complete fertilizer at planting time. Sprinkle the soil around the plants with gypsum when flowering starts.

Ripe peanuts cluster among the plants' roots.

harvest Plants are ready to dig 110 to 120 days after planting, when foliage yellows; loosen soil with a spading fork, then pull up plants. Let peanuts dry on vines in a warm, airy, shaded place for 2 to 3 weeks; then strip them from the plants. In a sealed container, refrigerated peanuts keep for up to 3 months, frozen nuts up to 6 months.

challenges Any of a number of leaf-eating caterpillars are possible. Treat with *Bacillus thuringiensis (Bt)*.

Pecan

Carya illinoinensis
Walnut family *(Juglandaceae)*
DECIDUOUS TREE

- **ZONES 2–3 (WARMER PARTS), 6–10, 12–14, 18–20**
- **FULL SUN**
- **REGULAR WATER**

This native of the south-central U.S. is a graceful, shapely tree to 70 ft. tall and wide; it is too large for small gardens but attractive where space is available. The foliage casts light shade. Leaves have 11 to 17 narrow leaflets, each 4–7 in. long. Inconspicuous flowers are followed by nuts enclosed in husks. The best nut production is in areas with long, hot summers; crops in other recommended zones are less certain but possible.

Most pecans set light crops without cross-pollination. For a good-size crop, plant a type 1 variety (produces pollen early, is receptive to pollen late) near a type 2 variety (receptive early, but makes pollen late). The best selections include 'Burkett' (type 2), 'Mohawk' (type 2), 'Western Schley' (type 1), and 'Wichita' (type 2). Early-ripening 'Pawnee' (type 1) is the best choice for areas that normally don't have warm summer temperatures over a long enough time for pecans to ripen (Zones 6 and 7, and the warmer parts of Zones 2 and 3). Other early-ripening varieties that may succeed in these short-season areas include 'Kanza' and 'Shoshoni' (both type 2). Note that pecans tend to be alternate bearers, with a heavy crop one year followed by a light crop the next.

Pecan trees resist oak root fungus.

Bright green husks dry and darken as pecans ripen.

HOW TO GROW IT

best site An open location with full sun and lots of space. Don't plant a pecan tree near a walkway, driveway, or patio, since honeydew from aphids can make things sticky below.

yield 50 to 100 pounds per tree.

soil Pecan trees need well-drained soil loosened to a depth of 6–10 ft. to accommodate their long taproots; they won't grow well in salt-laden soil.

planting Set out bare-root trees in winter, positioning the bud unions above soil level. Firm soil around the roots, then water thoroughly.

spacing Set trees 70 ft. apart.

water If you're counting on a quality nut crop, don't let the soil dry out.

fertilizer Trees need a lot of zinc. Spray it on three to five times each spring (more in drier climates). Younger trees should be sprayed every 2 weeks from mid-April through July. If tree growth is healthy, there's no need to do more. If not, apply a complete high-nitrogen fertilizer just before leaf-out and again in May.

pruning, training Pruning is needed only to remove suckers from below the bud union and to clear out dead, broken, or poorly placed limbs.

Continued on page 222 ▶

Once their husks begin to split and fall, pecans are ready for harvest.

harvest Gather pecans in fall anytime after the husks are open and partly dried. You can do it by picking nuts off the trees, shaking or beating the branches, or just waiting for pecans to fall; however you do it, remove the husks right away. Leave the nuts in a dry, moderately warm place for several days until pecans are crisp. Crack open to check. Store them in sealed containers or freezer bags so they won't pick up odors. In-shell pecans keep in a pantry for about 4 months, in a refrigerator for about 9 months, and in a freezer for several years. For shelled pecans, storage times will be about a third less.

challenges Prevent pecan rosette (abnormal clumps of twigs caused by zinc deficiency) by spraying zinc sulfate on expanding leaves in spring. Pecan trees are prone to aphid infestations and resulting sticky honey-dew droppings. Though there is a treatment, pecan trees are so big that you would need professional arborist spray gear to reach infested areas, so the most practical option for home gardeners is to plant in a place (like over a lawn) where the honeydew droppings won't be a problem.

Pistachio

Pistacia vera
Cashew family (*Anacardiaceae*)
DECIDUOUS TREE

✎ BEST IN ZONES 8–11; ALSO GROWS IN 7, 12, 14, 15, 18–21

☀ FULL SUN

💧 MODERATE WATER

This native of southwestern and central Asia produces the pistachio nuts sold in markets. The tree grows to 25–30 ft. tall and as wide, with one or several trunks. Its gray-green leaves are divided into three to five roundish, 2- to 4-in.-long leaflets.

Plants are either male or female; to get nuts, be sure to include at least one of each in your planting. 'Peters' is the most commonly grown male; 'Kerman' is the principal female (fruiting) variety. On female trees, small brownish green spring flowers are followed by heavy clusters of soft, wrinkled, reddish husks that contain the hard-shelled pistachio nuts.

Nut production is best in Zones 8–11, where trees get just the right amount of summer heat and winter chill. Trees grow well in Zones 7, 12, 14, 15, and 18–21, but crops are unpredictable—and when they do appear, nut meats often do not properly fill shells. Pistachios take 5 to 8 years to begin bearing and many years to reach full yield. Trees tend to bear more heavily in alternate years.

HOW TO GROW IT

best site Full sun in a spot with plenty of room.

yield Up to 80 pounds per mature tree.

soil Deep, well-drained soils are optimal, but pistachios can also grow in rocky, shallow, saline, or high-lime soils.

planting Plant from containers anytime of year except during the hottest days of summer. When planting, avoid rough handling; budded tops are easily broken.

spacing Set trees 25 ft. apart.

water Established trees will survive with little water, but nut quality is best if trees receive periodic deep soakings.

fertilizer Lightly scatter 10-10-10 fertilizer over the root zone every spring; pistachios don't need much.

pruning, training Pistachios are inclined to spread and droop, so stake the trees and train them to a good

Pistachio nuts grow in attractive clusters.

framework of four or five limbs beginning 4 ft. or so aboveground. Prune to develop a central leader and strong horizontal scaffold branches.

harvest In early autumn, when pistachio hulls start to slip easily from the shells, spread a tarp beneath the tree, shake the tree until nuts fall, then strip off and discard the hulls. Put the nuts in water, skimming off and discarding those that float (these are empty "blanks"), and dry them in the sun for 3 or 4 days until the shells split (the water helps the shells split). Some people like to add flavor by boiling the husked nuts in salted water for a few minutes before drying them. Dried pistachios can be stored for a year at room temperature, 18 months at 50°F/10°C, and 2 years in a freezer.

challenges Pistachios are susceptible to verticillium wilt and oak root fungus; to lessen disease risk, grow them in well-drained soil and water deeply and infrequently.

Sunflower

Helianthus annuus
Aster family *(Asteraceae)*
ANNUAL

✎ **ALL ZONES**

☼ **FULL SUN**

💧 💧 **REGULAR TO AMPLE WATER**

The wild ancestor of today's various sunflower varieties is a coarse, hairy plant with 2- to 3-in.-wide flowers native to much of the central U.S. and southward to Central America. Compact, smaller-flowered varieties are bred for use as garden ornaments and cut flowers, while tall, large-headed (10 in.–2 ft. wide) kinds are the ones to use for seed. (Note: Pollenless varieties do not produce seed; be sure to check catalog or seed-packet descriptions.) Birds are especially fond of black-seeded varieties (called black-oil or oilseed sunflowers), while people favor those with bigger, white-striped seeds (called confectionery sunflowers).

Best known among the giant forms are 'Mammoth Russian' and 'Russian Giant'. They grow 10 ft. (sometimes even 15 ft.) tall and 2 ft. wide, typically producing a single huge head (sometimes more than a foot across) consisting of a circle of short yellow rays with a brown central cushion of seeds. The newer variety 'Kong' is just as large. 'Sunspot' carries flower heads 10 in. wide on 2-ft.-tall plants, and 'Sunseed' has foot-wide heads on plants to 5 ft. tall.

HOW TO GROW IT

best site Full sun in a spot that's not too windy.

yield 1/2 pound per 10-ft. row.

soil Rich, moist soil.

planting Sow seeds in spring where plants are to grow. *In containers:* Shorter varieties like 'Sunspot' and 'Sunseed' grow well in 16-in. containers.

spacing Thin to 2–3 ft. apart.

water Water regularly to produce big plants with large heads and lots of seeds.

fertilizer Though sunflowers grow best with fertilizer, seedlings can be burned by fertilizer salts. You can avoid that by digging in complete fertilizer 2 in. beside and below the seed at planting time.

These sunny giants brighten the garden before they set their bounty of edible seeds.

pruning, training You may need to stake tall, top-heavy sunflower plants to keep them from falling over.

harvest After the petals have dropped, cut off the head with about a foot of stalk attached and hang it upside down in a dry place with good air circulation. When seeds are dry, rub them out of the flower head. They are good raw or lightly roasted. Store in sealed containers.

challenges To protect seeds from birds, you can cover fading flower heads with paper bags or with fabric cut from floating row covers.

Walnut

Juglans regia
Walnut family (*Juglandaceae*)
DECIDUOUS TREE

- ZONES 1–9, 14–23
- FULL SUN
- MODERATE TO REGULAR WATER

The tree described here, often called English walnut, is a widely grown orchard plant native to southeast Europe and southwest Asia; its nuts are the familiar ones sold commercially.

The species is hardy to –5°F/–21°C, but certain varieties are injured by early and late frosts. The tree grows fast, especially when young, and reaches a mature size of 40–80 ft. tall and wide. Smooth gray bark covers its trunk and heavy horizontal or upward-angled branches. The aromatic leaves are an attractive purple when young and have five to seven (rarely more) 3- to 6-in.-long leaflets.

Plant English walnut as a landscape tree only on large lots. Its branches are bare for a long season, and it is messy in leaf (because of honeydew drip and sooty mold due to aphid infestations) and in fruit (husks can stain). Many people are allergic to the wind-borne pollen. Keep other plants beyond its dripline, where feeder roots grow.

Most English walnuts are partially self-fruitful but bear better with a pollenizer.

Recommended varieties. The following walnut varieties do best in indicated zones.

In Zones 1–3, grow walnuts described as Carpathian or Hardy Persian. Varieties include 'Ambassador', 'Cascade', 'Chopaka', 'Hansen', 'Mesa', 'Russian', and 'Somers'; these range in hardiness from –25°F/–32°C to –35°F/–37°C.

In Zones 4–7, 'Chambers', 'Cooke's Giant Sweet', 'Franquette', and 'Spurgeon' bloom late enough to escape spring frosts and yield high-quality nuts.

In Zones 8 and 9, grow 'Carmelo', 'Chandler', 'Cooke's Giant Sweet', 'Hartley', 'Idaho', 'Payne', 'Pedro', or 'Serr'.

In Zones 14–16 and warm parts of 17, try 'Carmelo', 'Chandler', 'Cooke's Giant Sweet', 'Franquette', 'Hartley', 'Payne', 'Pedro', or 'Serr'.

In Zones 18–20, grow 'Payne', 'Pedro', or 'Placentia'.

In Zones 21–23, the best choices are 'Pedro' and 'Placentia'.

English walnuts are big landscape trees with velvety green husks concealing ripening nuts.

HOW TO GROW IT

best site An open, sunny spot with full sun. In cold-winter areas, grow on a slope to minimize frost damage.

yield 100 to 150 pounds per tree.

soil Grow in deep, fertile soil.

planting Plant bare-root walnuts as soon as they are available in winter or early spring.

spacing Set trees 30–60 ft. apart.

Continued on page 226 ▶

Fall is harvest season for walnuts. Be prepared: nut drop is messy and husks can stain hands and clothing.

Paul Vossen is a fruit and nut expert with the University of California Cooperative Extension, Sonoma County, and he knows his walnuts. "In home gardens, 'Hartley' is the best variety," says Vossen. "It's not going to produce as many nuts, but you don't need to prune it heavily to get it to grow, and it will give you a great shade tree with good nuts, like what you buy in a store. The same is true with 'Franquette'."

Here's why. Most commercial walnut varieties are bred to bear on both branch tip buds and lateral buds. But without vigorous, expert pruning, the trees grow slowly and yield small nuts. 'Hartley' and 'Franquette' are fast-growing tip-bearers, yielding fewer (but still plentiful), high-quality nuts with little pruning.

water Established plants survive with little supplemental moisture but need occasional deep watering to produce top-quality nuts.

fertilizer Don't fertilize until the tree has been in the ground at least one year; even then, there's no need to fertilize unless your tree is putting out less than 18 in. of new growth per year. If growth is less, follow this regimen each late winter or early spring: for trees 2 to 5 years old, scatter 3 to 5 pounds of 10-10-10 fertilizer around the outer half of the root zone; for trees 6 to 7 years old, apply 5 to 7$\frac{1}{2}$ pounds; for older trees, 7$\frac{1}{2}$ pounds.

pruning, training Train young trees to a central leader with near-horizontal scaffold branches (cut out branches with narrow crotch angles); mature trees need pruning only to remove dead wood or correct shape.

harvest Walnut husks open in the fall, dropping nuts to the ground. To hasten drop, knock nuts from the tree. Gather fallen nuts immediately, remove any adhering husks, and dry in a single layer in airy shade until kernels are brittle (crack a nut open to test). Store unshelled nuts at room temperature for up to a month, in a sealed container in the refrigerator for up to 6 months, or in the freezer up to a year.

challenges In addition to aphids, potential pests include scale, codling moths, and spider mites. Aphids have many natural enemies; to let these predators work effectively, keep ants (which protect aphids) out of trees by encircling the base of the trunk with a sticky barrier sold at nurseries. An application of horticultural oil applied as buds start swelling in spring will reduce scale and aphid problems. Walnut husk fly attacks husks, causing them to turn black and adhere to the shell; this stains the shells and makes the husks difficult to remove, but the nut meats are not damaged.

CHAPTER 6

Tropicals

Nothing says "tropics" like the fruits that grow on sunny South Pacific islands—banana, mango, and papaya, among others. Fortunately, most of these tasty crops thrive in mild parts of California as well as in Hawaii. Trees, perennials, and an exotic vine make our list; there's something delicious for every garden.

Banana

Musa species
Banana family (*Musaceae*)
PERENNIALS

✎ **ZONES 15, 16, 19–24, H2**
☼ **FULL SUN**
💧 **AMPLE WATER**

This attractive, fast-growing plant from Southeast Asia spreads by suckers and underground roots to form clumps 6–10 ft. wide or wider. Its trunklike stem is soft and thick. Striking orange-yellow flowers appear on long, drooping stalks in spring. Spectacular broad leaves (5–9 ft. long) are easily tattered by wind. Banana sap will permanently stain fabric, so wear old clothes when harvesting or pruning.

Fruiting varieties are often grouped botanically under *Musa acuminata*, though some are *M.* × *paradisiaca* hybrids. They are best adapted to Zone H2 in Hawaii and to Zones 21–24 in California, where planting near a warm, south-facing wall encourages development of sweet fruit. But even in warm microclimates of Zones 15, 16, 19, and 20, gardeners sometimes harvest edible bananas. Bananas bear fruit without pollination.

Recommended varieties. Dwarf varieties are the best bet for home gardens. The following ripen fruit 70 to 100 days after blooming.

'Apple' ('Manzano'). Grows 10–12 ft. tall, with small (3- to 6-in.), apple-flavored fruit.

'Dwarf Brazilian'. Grows 6–8 ft. tall and bears high-quality fruit.

'Dwarf Cavendish' ('Chinese'). Grows 4–8 ft. tall; produces bunches of 5-in. bananas within 2 to 3 years.

'Enano Gigante' ('Dwarf Mexican'). Grows 6–8 ft. tall; produces rich yellow bananas. "Gigante" refers to its broad leaves.

'Goldfinger'. Vigorous plant grows 9 ft. tall; produces fruit very similar to supermarket bananas.

'High Color Mini'. Grows about 4 ft. tall, with wide, maroon-striped leaves and small bunches of yellow bananas.

'Ice Cream' ('Blue Java'). To 15 ft. tall, with medium-size fruit that has a silvery blue cast when young.

'Rajapuri'. Grows 6–10 ft. tall and 15 ft. wide, bearing fine-flavored, small to medium-size bananas.

'Williams'. Grows 16 ft. tall; bears standard-size bananas.

HOW TO GROW IT

best site Choose a spot that gets full sun, with protection from wind.

yield Varies by type, but a 'Dwarf Cavendish' plant can yield 150 to 200 bananas.

soil Bananas need rich soil.

planting Plant container-grown bananas in spring in soil dug at least 15 in. deep and 18 in. wide. *In containers:* Small varieties can grow in a wine half-barrel with ample fertilizer and water.

spacing Grow 6–8 ft. apart in rows spaced 12 ft. apart.

water Bananas thrive on water; supply it abundantly.

fertilizer Bananas are heavy feeders. Apply 1½ pounds of 10-10-10 fertilizer in spring before new growth emerges, then feed again 2 and 4 months later, keeping fertilizer at least 1 ft. from the base of the plants.

pruning, training To get good-quality fruit, let only one or two stalks per clump grow; prune out all others as they emerge. Allow replacement stalks (for next year's fruit) to develop after the fruiting stalks have bloomed. Remove stalks that have fruited.

harvest Crops usually ripen in late summer into fall, or whenever the fruit at the top of the cluster starts to turn yellow. Cut the whole cluster and let it ripen at room temperature. If left on the plant, fruit will split and rot.

challenges Control ants on banana trees to help prevent scale, aphids, and sooty mold.

Banana clusters grow on drooping stalks; pick when top fruits begin to turn yellow.

Breadfruit

Artocarpus altilis
Mulberry family *(Moraceae)*
EVERGREEN TREE

- ☑ **ZONE H2**
- ☼ **FULL SUN**
- ● **REGULAR WATER**

Breadfruit is a distinctly beautiful tropical fruit tree native to the South Pacific region and Malaysia; its Hawaiian name is *'ulu*. This impressive evergreen eventually reaches 40–60 ft. tall and just as wide, with huge (to 3-ft.-long), deeply lobed, leathery, shiny deep green leaves. Plants are self-fruitful: yellow male catkins and prickly-looking female flowers appear on the same tree but are borne in different clusters.

Round to oblong green fruit is 8–12 in. long, bumpy, and thin-skinned. Each fruit weighs 2 to 9 pounds and usually contains large seeds (seeded types are called breadnuts). Fruits in all stages of development are present on the tree throughout the year, as fruiting occurs more or less continually; peak fruiting period in Hawaii is summer to midwinter. Peel the fruit to reveal its sweet, soft, white flesh, which can be boiled, roasted, fried, baked as a vegetable, or used in soups and stews. It can also be steamed as a dessert.

'Ma'afala' and 'Maopo' are good seedless varieties.

HOW TO GROW IT

best site Breadfruit needs a warm, humid, sunny location with high nighttime temperatures—preferably over 60°F/16°C. Plants need lots of room.

yield 25 to 100 fruits per tree.

soil Accepts a wide range of soil types—even sand and saline soil—but must have good drainage.

planting Plant nursery-grown stock anytime.

spacing Set trees 25–40 ft. apart.

water Does best where rainfall averages 50 to 100 in. per year. Soak root zone whenever the top inch or two of soil dries out.

fertilizer Lightly scatter 10-10-10 fertilizer over the root zone every spring.

pruning, training Prune off branches that have borne fruit.

Breadfruit bears its distinctive lime green fruits throughout the year.

harvest Fruit is ripe when the rind turns brownish green and is dotted with whitish spots of latex. Consume breadfruit within 2 weeks of picking; refrigeration damages the fruit.

challenges Insect and disease problems vary by location. Consult your Cooperative Extension Office or nursery for good local advice.

Cherimoya

Annona cherimola
Annona family *(Annonaceae)*
BRIEFLY DECIDUOUS SHRUB OR TREE

- 🖊 ZONES 21–24, H1, H2
- ☼ FULL SUN
- 💧 REGULAR WATER

Cherimoya is native to the high Andean valleys of Bolivia, Colombia, and Ecuador. It is hardy to about 25°F/–4°C. In Hawaii, it grows best above 1,000 ft. Cherimoya grows at least 15 ft. tall and 15–20 ft. wide. Leaves are 4–10 in. long, dull green above, velvety-hairy beneath; they drop in late spring, but tree remains leafless for only a brief time. Thick, fleshy, inch-wide, hairy brownish or yellow blossoms with a fruity fragrance begin opening about the time of leaf drop; over the next 3 to 4 months, they develop large fruits weighing ½ to 1½ pounds. The skin of most varieties resembles short overlapping leaves; skin is thin and tender, so handle carefully. The creamy white flesh contains large black seeds and is almost custardlike, with a flavor something like pineapple crossed with banana. Eat it with a spoon; it tastes best cold.

Cherimoyas host few pollinating insects, and the male and female parts of their flowers don't mature at the same rate, so self-pollination is usually poor. To ensure fruit set, gather just-opening flowers and place them in a small jar. Keep jar in a cool place for 24 hours, by which time the pollen will have shed. Use a small paintbrush to dab pollen grains onto the sticky white central stigma of freshly opened flowers on the same or different trees. Repeat every few days.

Specialty nurseries offer several improved varieties, including exceptionally flavorful 'El Bumpo', 'Honeyhart', 'Pierce', and 'Sabor' in California. 'Spain' does well in Hawaii. 'McPherson' is popular everywhere because it does a better job of self-pollinating than most.

HOW TO GROW IT

best site Full sun, with protection from strong winds. Locate tree where you can enjoy its fragrance.

yield Expect 25 to 100 fruits per tree.

soil Cherimoya thrives in average garden loam with good drainage, but will tolerate a fairly wide range of soils.

planting Plant nursery-grown stock at any time of year except during the hottest days of summer.

spacing Set trees 25–30 ft. apart.

Cherimoya's unusual skin covers creamy-textured flesh with a mild, exotic flavor.

water Irrigate young trees deeply every 2 to 3 weeks.

fertilizer After a tree has been growing for 6 months, apply ½ pound of complete fertilizer in a wide band starting 5 ft. from the trunk. Every 6 months, feed again, adding ½ pound to the fertilizer total. After the fifth year, give the tree 5 pounds of fertilizer every year.

pruning, training Leave young trees unpruned. After 4 or 5 years, begin pruning yearly during the dormant season, cutting the previous year's growth back to 6–8 in.

harvest Pick fruit in late fall or winter, when it turns yellowish green. Let ripen at room temperature; when ripe, it turns a dull brownish green and yields to gentle pressure. Fruit can be refrigerated for a week or so.

challenges If mealybugs cluster at the base of the fruit, blast them off with a jet of water.

Guava

Psidium species
Myrtle family *(Myrtaceae)*
EVERGREEN SHRUBS OR TREES

🖋 ZONES VARY BY SPECIES; MAY BE INVASIVE IN H1, H2
☼ ◑ FULL SUN OR PARTIAL SHADE
💧 MODERATE WATER

These natives of the tropical Americas bear white brush-like flowers that develop into round to pear-shaped fruits. Guavas mature from late summer into fall, though some may be produced year-round. They are good eaten fresh or used in jellies, purées, or juice drinks. Though self-fruitful, guava trees may yield a heavier crop when grown near another variety of the same species for pollination.

Common or tropical guava (Psidium guajava). Zones 23, 24, H1, H2 (a weed in Hawaii, where it chokes out native species). It grows to 25 ft. tall and nearly as wide, with strongly veined leaves to 6 in. long. Yellow-skinned, 1- to 3-in.-wide fruit has white, pink, or yellow flesh and a musky, mildly acidic flavor. 'Holmberg', 'Indonesian Seedless', and 'Ruby X Supreme' are sweet dessert varieties. 'Beaumont', 'Ka Hua Kula', and 'Waiakea' are somewhat tart and used mainly for juice.

Strawberry guava (P. cattleianum). Zones 9 and 14 (sheltered locations), 15–24, H1, H2 (has naturalized throughout Hawaii, where it threatens endemic habitats). In Hawaii, it is usually grown as single-trunked tree to 20 ft. tall and wide; in California, it is more often seen as a shrub to 8–10 ft. tall and wide. The plant has especially beautiful reddish to golden brown bark. Leaves to 3 in. long are bronze when new, maturing to glossy green. Fruit is dark red (nearly black when fully ripe) and 1½ in. wide, with white flesh and a sweet-tart, slightly resinous flavor.

HOW TO GROW IT

best site Full sun in mild coastal climates, partial shade in interior valleys.

yield 25 pounds per plant.

soil Grows best in rich soil but tolerates poor soil.

planting Plant container-grown stock anytime of year except during the hottest days of summer. *In containers:* Strawberry guava can be grown in an 18-in. pot.

spacing *Common guava:* Space 25–30 ft. apart (16 ft. apart if grown as a hedge). *Strawberry guava:* Plant 10 ft. apart.

Guavas are rich in vitamins A and C and are a good source of antioxidants.

water Provide regular moisture for best fruit quality. Soak deeply every 2 to 3 weeks during the growing season and monthly in winter.

fertilizer Apply a light sprinkling of complete fertilizer every other month during spring, summer, and fall.

pruning, training Plants take pruning well. (They can even be sheared into a hedge, but at the expense of fruit.) When production starts to decline on older plants, hard pruning can reinvigorate them and increase crop sizes.

harvest Fruit is best picked when skin is fully colored, though it can be harvested when still greenish, then ripened for a few days at room temperature. Fresh guavas don't store well; use them right away.

challenges Guava is fairly pest-free.

Mango

Mangifera indica
Cashew family *(Anacardiaceae)*
EVERGREEN TREE

🗲 **ZONES 23, 24, H1, H2**

☼ **FULL SUN**

💧 **REGULAR WATER**

⬧ **SAP AND JUICE FROM FRUIT CAUSE SKIN RASH
ON SOME PEOPLE**

Mangoes are native to tropical Asia. In Hawaii, the trees can reach 50 ft. tall and spread to 30 ft. or more; they are very long-lived and produce heavy crops of fruit. In the mildest parts of Southern California, plants often remain shrubby (growing 8–10 ft. tall and nearly as wide) and are likely to fruit only in the most favorable frost-free locations. Large handsome leaves, 8–16 in. long, are often coppery red or purple when new and turn dark green as they mature.

Long clusters of yellow to reddish flowers appear at branch ends from spring into summer; these are followed by oval fruits up to 9 in. long and weighing up to 2 pounds in good growing conditions. Fruit has green to reddish or yellowish skin, a large seed, and very juicy pale yellow to deep orange flesh that tastes somewhat like a peach with flowery overtones. Poorer-quality fruit may be stringy and/or have a flavor reminiscent of varnish or turpentine. In Southern California, skin may not color well, but fruit quality can still be excellent. Trees are self-fruitful, and they tend to bear more heavily in alternate years.

Many reliable varieties are sold. Among them are standard-size 'Ah Ping' and 'Pope', and compact 'Carrie', 'Fairchild', 'Keitt', and 'Rapoza'. 'Manila' is a compact grower widely sold in California.

HOW TO GROW IT

best site Full sun. In areas where frost is possible, plant on a slope.

yield 200 to 300 fruits per tree.

soil Trees tolerate fairly poor, shallow soil as long as it has excellent drainage.

planting Plant nursery-grown stock anytime. *In containers:* Smaller varieties can be held in large containers for many years.

spacing Set trees 10–30 ft. apart.

When ready for harvest, these pink-blushed mangoes will soften slightly.

water Mangoes need regular, deep irrigation from June through September and very little water beyond rainfall for the rest of the year.

fertilizer Every month from March through October, feed trees a 50/50 blend of chicken manure and cotton-seed meal. Give young trees one cup per month, scattered evenly over the root zone. In the trees' fourth year, increase the dose to 1½ cups per month. In the fifth and following years, apply 2 cups per month (or 4 cups per application in March, June, and September). Starting the March, June, or September after planting, supplement with 1 cup powdered gypsum or iron sulfate per label directions at alternate feedings (never at the same time).

pruning, training After harvest, prune for shape and to remove diseased or injured branches. Wear gloves when pruning, and try not to let the sap touch your skin.

Continued on page 234 ▶

Mangoes make handsome landscape accents; they reach treelike proportions only in Hawaii.

ALEX SILBER ON
mangoes for southern california

As owner of Papaya Tree Nursery in Granada Hills, CA, Alex Silber sells 10 tested mango varieties. He says that in Southern California, "'Manila' is the most common variety sold, and you have a decent chance of getting fruit with it if you live within 10 miles of the coast." But he acknowledges that it's on the tender side. "You're better off with more cold-tolerant, grafted varieties like 'Carrie' (a true dwarf), 'Edward', 'Thompson', 'Kensington Pride', 'Valencia Pride', or 'Reliable'," he says.

Silber adds that even the right variety needs years to mature before it's strong enough to bear fruit. "Early fruiting weakens the tree," says Silber, "then winter shows up, disease comes in, and the tree dies." His advice for best results: Pick off all fruit when it is pea size for the first three years after planting. For the next three years, allow a healthy tree to bear a few fruits, and by the seventh year, let it go into full production.

harvest Mangoes are most flavorful if allowed to ripen on the tree; they are usually ready to harvest 4 to 5 months after bloom. When fruits are ready, they snap free with a light tug; if you have to pull hard, wait a few days and try again. Rinse mangoes after harvest or sap will burn the fruit's skin. Refrigerated fruit will keep for a month. Harvest with gloves and don't touch the sap: it can cause a severe allergic reaction and blistering.

challenges For anthracnose control, homemade Bordeaux mix is helpful while trees are small enough to spray (the formula is available online and from Cooperative Extension Offices), or buy a resistant variety like 'Fairchild'. Powdery mildew can be controlled with a fungicide such as neem oil. Horticultural oil may be needed for scale control.

Papaya

Carica species
Papaya family *(Caricaceae)*
PERENNIALS

⚡ **ZONES VARY BY SPECIES**

☼ **FULL SUN, EXCEPT AS NOTED**

💧 **REGULAR WATER**

They may look like trees or large shrubs, but papayas are actually perennials with hollow stems. All are tall, upright, narrow plants, 3–6 ft. wide at the top. Cream-colored flowers are inconspicuous. Fruit forms directly on the main stem and takes 6 to 10 months to ripen, depending on climate; in Hawaii, it is borne throughout the year. Plants produce crops only when young. To get the most fruit, don't grow papayas as permanent plants; keep a few plants coming along each year and remove old ones.

Papaya *(Carica papaya).* Zones 21–24 and H2. Native to tropical America. This is the most frequently grown species and the papaya found in markets. It thrives in Hawaii, where it gets the year-round warmth it needs. In California, the key to success is choosing the right location; root rot in cold, wet soil is the principal cause of failure, so locate plants on a south slope or the south side of the house, where winter sun can heat the soil. Plants will also benefit from reflected heat in winter.

This species grows 20–25 ft. tall in Hawaii, perhaps half that in California, with a straight stem topped by a crown of broad, fanlike, deeply lobed leaves on 2-ft.-long stalks. Grow three to five "trees" in a group; you ordinarily need both male and female plants for fruit production, though some types are self-fruitful, producing either bisexual flowers or both male and female flowers on the same plant.

Varieties with yellow-orange flesh grown primarily in Hawaii include 'Kapoho', 'Solo', and dwarf 'Waimanalo'. Types with pinkish flesh grown in Hawaii and California include 'Sunrise', 'Sunset', and 'Thai Dwarf'. Varieties grown in Hawaii have pear-shaped fruit 6–9 in. long and weighing 1 to 2 pounds. Mexican varieties bear much bigger fruit (to more than 1 ft. long and up to 10 pounds), with yellow, orange, or pink flesh and a less intense flavor. Harvest papayas of both types when skin begins to turn yellow; let them ripen fully at room temperature. Papaya seeds are edible, with a somewhat peppery flavor.

Mountain papaya *(C. pubescens).* Zones 21–24, H1, H2. From the Andean highlands of South America. This species reaches 10–12 ft. tall, with foliage borne in dense clusters at the tops of its multiple trunks. Elaborately

Papaya flesh is as smooth as its skin, with a subtle floral taste and a musky aroma.

lobed, foot-wide leaves are fan shaped, deeply veined, and sandpapery in texture; they are dark green above, lighter beneath. The small fruit is edible when cooked (it's unpalatable raw). Male and female plants must be grown near each other in order for fruit to set.

Babaco *(C. × heilbornii pentagona).* Zones 17, 19–24, H1. Ecuadoran native. This self-fruitful plant is a naturally occurring hybrid between *C. pubescens* and another Andean species. It looks like a 5- to 8-ft.-tall *C. papaya*. Foot-long, seedless fruit has juicy flesh similar to that of 'Crenshaw' melon in color and texture; the unique sweet-tart flavor combines papaya, pineapple, and strawberry. Babaco can take more cold than the other papayas but needs partial shade in hottest climates. It can be grown as a houseplant in a sunny window.

Continued on page 236 ▶

Papaya grows from 5 to 25 feet tall, depending on the species, and bears all fruit on the main stem.

HOW TO GROW IT

best site *Papaya* and *mountain papaya* do best in full sun. *Babaco* needs partial shade in hottest climates.

yield All three types of papayas bear up to 75 pounds per plant per year.

soil Grows in a wide range of soils but needs excellent drainage.

planting *Papaya and mountain papaya:* Grow from seeds saved from fruit or start with purchased plants. *Babaco* is seedless and must be started from transplants; handle carefully, disturbing the root ball as little as possible. *In containers:* All types can grow in a container 18 in. wide or larger.

spacing Set plants 6–8 ft. apart.

water Provide regular water, especially in warm weather.

fertilizer Apply a sprinkling of complete fertilizer every 2 months.

pruning, training Train papaya and babaco to a single trunk.

harvest Pick when fruit is 80 percent colored, then eat right away. You can also pick it when the color first shows and then ripen the fruit indoors. Most papaya varieties don't store well, though babaco can be refrigerated for a month or more.

challenges In Hawaii, papaya is subject to mosaic virus carried by aphids. Keep ants (which protect aphids) out of trees and spray for aphids as they appear. Anthracnose and *Phytophthora* can be controlled with fungicides, and powdery mildew on all kinds of papaya is treatable with sulfur. Predatory mites can control mite infestations on babaco. Bait for slugs and snails, and fence young trees where deer are prevalent.

Passion Fruit

Passiflora edulis
Passion flower family *(Passifloraceae)*
EVERGREEN OR SEMIEVERGREEN VINE

🗶 ZONES 15–17, 21–24, H1, H2; MAY BE INVASIVE IN H1, H2
☀ FULL SUN
💧 REGULAR WATER

This vigorous South American native climbs by tendrils to 20–30 ft. Light yellow-green leaves are divided into three lobes. The vine blooms during warm weather, bearing white, 2- to 3-in.-wide flowers with a white-and-purple crown. Fragrant, roundish fruit $1\frac{1}{2}$–3 in. wide ripens mainly in summer and fall; the vine doesn't need cross-pollination to bear fruit. The orange pulp has an exotic, citrusy flavor. Drink the juice or cut the fruit in half and eat the pulp, seeds and all, with a spoon. There is a form with larger, more acidic, yellow-skinned fruit.

Sweet-fruited varieties that have good-size fruit include red-skinned 'Red Rover' and 'Frederick', and purple-skinned 'Edgehill' (particularly good in Southern California) and 'Kahuna'.

Passion fruit is semievergreen in colder zones, and it is often short-lived wherever it is grown. This plant has naturalized in Hawaii and is a serious pest there.

HOW TO GROW IT

best site Grow on a trellis, arbor, or fence in a sunny spot out of the wind.

yield 15 pounds per plant.

soil Must be well drained, and should be amended with organic matter before planting.

planting Plant in mild weather or on an overcast day. *In containers:* Good plant for a large container when there's support nearby for its twining stems.

spacing Set vines 10 ft. apart.

water Water regularly during the growing season, increasing irrigation as fruits mature. Withhold water during cold months.

fertilizer Apply 3 pounds of 10-5-20 fertilizer every 3 months.

Freeze the juice of ripe passion fruit in ice-cube trays, then use cubes to add a citrusy flavor to drinks.

pruning, training Train on a trellis or wall to show off flowers. Every year after harvest, thin out excess stems by cutting them to the ground and cut back vigorous growth by a third.

harvest When fruit matures, the waxy rind turns from green to deep purple and the fruit falls from the vine. Either pick the fruit when it turns color or gather it from the ground every few days. Even with refrigeration, passion fruit lasts only a week or so off the vine.

challenges Don't mow or use a string trimmer around the base of the plant, since injury invites diseases.

Pineapple

Ananas comosus
Pineapple family (*Bromeliaceae*)
PERENNIAL

- **ZONES 24, H1, H2**
- **FULL SUN**
- **REGULAR WATER**

This South American native is well adapted to Hawaii, where it is a commercial crop. It also grows well in Southern California in warm, protected sites; black plastic mulch over the soil increases chances of success. Plants grow 2½–5 ft. tall, 3–4 ft. wide, with a short, thick stem surrounded by a rosette of long (1½- to 6-ft.), narrow, dark green leaves with saw-toothed edges. At bloom time, the stem lengthens and produces a head composed of small red or purple flowers. The blossoms form individual fruits that fuse together and develop into the pineapple, which in ideal outdoor growing conditions can reach the size and heft of ones sold in markets.

Pineapples take up to 2 years to begin bearing. After the fruit is harvested, the plant will continue to produce for several more years.

Without pollination, pineapples bear seedless fruit, but if their principal pollinator, the hummingbird, gets to the flowers, the resulting fruit may have seeds.

Recommended varieties include 'Del Monte Gold', 'Queen', 'Smooth Cayenne', and 'Sugarloaf'. Several ornamental pineapple varieties are sold as houseplants; they can take reduced light, and some produce small, colorful fruit, but the fruit is inedible.

Pineapple plants bear one bristly fruit per stem.

HOW TO GROW IT

best site Choose a spot with full sun and plenty of warmth. Pineapples are excellent container subjects for a greenhouse or sunroom kept above 68°F/20°C.

yield 1 pineapple per stem.

soil Slightly acid sandy loam amended 2 ft. deep with organic matter, or (for container plants) potting mix. Good drainage is essential.

planting Plant divisions sold in nurseries 3–4 in. deep. Alternatively, slice off the leafy top of a market pineapple (cut about an inch below the leaf rosette), work the leaf cluster free from the top of the fruit, and let it dry for a couple of days; then plant it with the base of the leaf rosette 2 in. deep. *In containers:* Grow in pots at least 12 in. wide and deep.

spacing Set plants at 1-ft. intervals in rows 2 ft. apart.

water Provide regular water.

fertilizer Apply high-nitrogen fertilizer per label directions every 2 to 3 months.

pruning, training As the pineapple ripens, the mother plant may produce suckers. Leave one or two to produce more fruit.

harvest Fruit is ready to harvest when it reaches a good size and starts to take on a yellow cast, with the bottom half turning golden. After cutting the fruit off the mother plant, let ripen fully at room temperature.

challenges Mealybugs, mites, and scale insects can colonize plants. If they appear, wash these pests off with warm, soapy water, then rinse plants with clear water.

CHAPTER 7

Garden Design

Growing edibles to produce crops doesn't mean your garden has to look like a farm. By paying attention to the shape of your kitchen garden, the materials you use, and the placement of containers, arbors, and raised beds, you can create a living pantry that's as pleasing to the eye as it is to the palate.

Color, Texture, and Form

When choosing and planting edibles, take note of their leaf and fruit colors. Many shades of green and gray make a soothing picture, but a few bright colors add accents. Contrasting textures, such as a row of lacy carrot tops planted next to wide-leafed lettuces, enhance one another. Also, varying your plant shapes and heights—an upright grower surrounded by low mounds, for instance—keeps your kitchen garden interesting.

1 **Hints of pink** add visual punch to your edible plots. Here, mustard greens with broad purple leaves grow among frilly green ones, and a bright pink flowering cabbage provides a colorful accent.

2 **Brilliant bands** of lime green arugula, red-leafed lettuce, and curly-leafed kale form a lush, low carpet; placing the red between the two greens makes all three colors pop. In the background, the tall, striking leaves of 'Toscano' kale form an upright fountain of deep green.

3 **A classic combination** of herbs includes chives, with rose-purple flowers and slender, grassy foliage; common sage, with broad, soft leaves of fresh green; and thyme, with tiny leaves that resemble light green foam. Plant these three along a path for an edible edging that needs little maintenance besides harvesting.

4 **The burst of burgundy** is a cluster of 'Rhubarb' Swiss chard plants, whose dark leaves demand attention among multicolored chards and lettuces. Backed by a lacy curtain of pole beans, this pretty U-shaped garden packs a lot of variety into an area of only 12 feet by 11 feet.

5 **Towering tepees** and soaring sunflowers give height to this little patch. There's plenty of variation in foliage, with glossy basil leaves on the left, oversize squash in the center, and fine-leafed tomatoes on the right. A golden sage and white cosmos provide bright contrast to the sunflowers' rich mahogany.

Balance and Repetition

With so many choices available, you may be tempted to plant one of this and one of that, but doing so can give your garden a jumbled look. An easily recognizable pattern is more pleasing to the eye. When you plant, consider balancing a large plant at one end of a bed with one of equal size at the other. Or plant the same varieties in groupings that you repeat throughout the garden.

1 Mirror images show up in the two sides of this U-shaped bed in *Sunset's* test garden. Blocks of leafy winter greens and cool-season vegetables echo one another on opposite sides of the central path. A methodical planting scheme like this one—which is just 13 feet long and 8 feet wide—takes maximum advantage of the space.

2 Pots on either side of the path bring a sense of order to this casual kitchen garden, as do alternating clumps of large purple foliage. Matching chairs face each other at path's end.

3 Diamond-shaped beds surround a diamond-shaped patio of flagstones edged with thyme. A twig trellis on the left balances the wooden fence of about the same height on the right.

4 Matching mounds of basil and lavender in the foreground give way to repeated plantings of squash on the left and tomatoes on the right, backed by vining crops on poles. In the distance, vines on a trellis next to the house repeat the vertical lines.

Focal Points

Large urns, sundials, sculptures, and benches are the garden's attention-getters. But even a single fruit tree or a dramatic vegetable can double as a focal point. To make a small garden seem larger, orient the view along the longest possible line, often a diagonal, and place your focal point at one end.

1 **The center point** where these V-shaped beds meet is the middle of a Washington garden. The tip of the V is a natural spot for a colorful accent such as the golden Swiss chard shown here. This living focal point changes with the seasons.

2 **A blue chair** draws attention to the Puget Sound view and a spray of sunflowers nearby. By placing this focal point squarely at the end of the path, you give the visitor a visual—and an actual—destination.

3 **This stone birdbath** appears to organize two half-moon-shaped beds around it. Chosen to match the gravel paths, it also echoes the earthy hues of the bed's Sonoma fieldstone edging.

Relating to Architecture

A sprawling mass of vegetables next to a formal house can look out of place. To add order, contain them inside trimmed hedges or sleek steel containers, and line up their edges with a patio or house doors. To match a brick house, consider a brick-edged path or raised beds made from brick. Even if you're planting a small orchard at the back of the property, you may want to align it with the house.

1 **Three raised beds** fill this sunny front yard and complement the contemporary style of a California house. Each bed measures 4 feet wide by 12 feet long, providing nearly 150 square feet for growing crops such as cauliflower, corn, and zucchini. Wide caps double as benches; pea gravel adds to the garden's clean look.

2 **A cobble-edged bed** fits neatly against an 8- by 10-foot Craftsman-style garden shed built from recycled windows and doors. The smooth stones match the building's charcoal-colored roof and light gray siding.

Arbors and Trellises

To save space and bring your crops up to eye level, grow plants on arbors and trellises whenever possible. Beans, cane berries, cucumbers, grapes, peas, and squash, among other edibles, can be grown above-ground to beautiful effect. You can devise your own fanciful structures or invest in a piece of permanent architecture that will serve the garden year-round.

1 **A tall tuteur** topped with a colorful birdhouse supports scarlet runner beans and nasturtiums. Even after the vines finish their annual show, the structure will continue to bring height—and the birdhouse a touch of red—to the garden.

2 **The lemon arbor** makes harvesting easy; it's made of a series of simple metal arches with trees trained over them. Apples, figs, and peaches would work just as well on such a framework, but lemons have a particular sunny appeal.

3 **An all-stake trellis** provides sturdy support for pole beans. The stakes are casually placed and lashed together with sturdy string.

4 **Multipurpose trellises** made from wood and bamboo keep raspberries (left) and tomatoes (right) tidy. They also provide air circulation, and keep fruit off the ground in this Portland garden. These structures could easily be draped with netting to keep birds away.

5 **A trio of A-frames** provides structure in this kitchen garden. On the left behind an established asparagus bed, an old ladder is called back into service. A large custom-built structure in the center holds vigorous hops, while a small green trellis on the right is strung to support twining vines.

Paths

A path creates a journey through the garden. It should be wide enough (2 to 3 feet) to work on and pleasing to walk along. Firm, flat surfaces such as brick or cut stone are best where you need to roll wheelbarrows or garden carts easily. Add a simple seat and a pot of strawberries or scented geraniums at the end of the path to create a destination.

1 **A straight stone path** leads between edible beds to a gate beneath an arch, which in turn frames a specimen fruit tree. Stone paths are easy to keep clean with a broom or hose.

2 **A bark-mulched path** has an edging of recycled bricks to keep the bits in bounds and to serve as a retainer for slightly raised beds. Edgings accentuate the lines of a path and give the garden a well-cared-for, permanent look. You can also make them from wooden boards, metal strips, stones cleared from the garden, or objects such as pots.

3 **Curving gracefully** through the garden, a gravel path invites a leisurely stroll. Gravel suits both casual and formal gardens. Installed on a layer of larger-diameter gravel, it allows water to percolate through it.

4 **This decomposed-granite path** is edged with brick and softened by woolly thyme. Rusted metal edgers echo the shape of the arched trellis and help keep the garden's bounty contained within the beds.

Raised Beds

Where soil is poor or space is limited, raised beds offer the perfect growing ground. Fill them with organically amended, well-draining soil, and your crops will thrive. Soil in raised beds warms quickly in spring, so planting can be done earlier. And because the soil remains loose, it's easier for roots to penetrate. Enclose raised beds with lumber, dry-stacked rocks, flagstones, bricks, or interlocking concrete blocks.

1 **Recycled concrete** was used to make these raised beds. They are about 4 feet across, so the middle can be reached easily from either side. Make your beds at least 12 inches deep to allow for good root growth.

2 **Wooden beds** in a Santa Monica front yard raise lettuce, basil, and sage to a height convenient for harvest. Covered storage bins on the ends serve as benches; they keep a hose, tools, and soil amendments hidden yet close at hand.

3 **Wattles,** fabric sacks filled with rice straw, can be used to create beds of any shape. Here they surround vibrant Swiss chards and leaf lettuces in circular beds of different diameters.

4 **Recycled scrap metal sheets** inspired these edgy veggie beds of various sizes. Four pieces, secured on the inside corners with galvanized L-brackets, make up each bottomless "box"; each piece was cut to size at a scrap metal yard. The deep beds hold plenty of soil for a variety of crops; rebar stakes support climbers.

Continued on page 253 ▶

Building an 8- by 4-Foot Raised Bed

MATERIALS

One 6-ft.-long 4-by-4 board (cedar or redwood)

Six 8-ft.-long 2-by-6 boards (cedar or redwood)

One 10-ft.-long 1-in. schedule 40 PVC pipe

Two 10-ft.-long $1/2$-in. schedule 120 PVC pipes

$1/2$ gallon semitransparent exterior oil stain

32 $3^1/2$-in. #14 wood screws and 16 $1/2$-in. #8 wood screws

One 4- by 10-ft. roll of $1/4$-in.-mesh hardware cloth

Eight 1-in. galvanized tube straps (semicircular brackets)

32 cubic ft. planting mix

PREP: With a table or power saw, cut the 4-by-4 into four 16-in.-tall corner posts. Cut two of the 2-by-6s in half. Cut the 1-in. PVC pipe into four 12-in.-long pieces and the $1/2$-in. PVC pipes into two 6-ft.-long pieces. Stain lumber; let dry overnight.

1. Build the bed upside down on a hard, flat surface. Set a 4-ft.-long 2-by-6 on edge, and place a 16-in. post at one end. Secure post with two $3^1/2$-in. screws. Repeat at other end of board and with other short board. Join short sides with 8-ft. boards and secure with two screws at each end. Add second pair of long and short boards.

2. Flip the bed right side up. Move it into position in the yard, marking each corner post's location. Move the bed aside; dig a 5- to 6-in.-deep hole for each post. Put the bed back into place, with posts in holes; fill around posts with soil.

3. Rake the existing soil at the bottom of the bed to level it, then tamp it smooth. Line the bed with hardware cloth to keep out gophers or other burrowing pests.

4. To hold hoops for bird netting or row covers, attach the four 12-in. pieces of 1-in. PVC pipe inside the bed. On the long sides, space pipes 4 ft. apart, 2 ft. from each end; screw on two tube straps to secure each pipe.

5. Fill the bed with planting mix, and moisten it with a gentle spray from the hose. Plant crops.

6. To cover newly planted seedlings with bird netting or row covers, bend the two 6-ft. pieces of $1/2$-inch PVC pipe to form semicircles, and slip their ends into the 1-in. pipes inside the bed. Then drape the bird netting or row covers over them.

6

5 **Four square beds** make a stylish home for vegetables in this Jackson, Wyoming, garden. Sunken posts secure the corners of each bed. A strip of wire fencing stretching around the perimeter between posts is lined inside with dry-stacked stone to match the paths. Above the stones, cedar boards, painted red, give the beds a finished look.

6 **A bed of basils** is the perfect addition to a garden with lots of tomatoes. This diminutive bed, just 3¹/₂ feet square, is edged with 2-by-6 boards. The soil was dug to a depth of 10 inches and enriched with compost before six varieties of basil were planted.

Containers

Most edibles grow beautifully in containers. Even if you garden on a balcony or a tiny patio, you probably have space for a couple of pots or a hanging basket. Just about any large vessel with a drain hole can be filled with planting mix. Herbs grow especially well in pots, and many smaller vegetables, berries, and dwarf fruit trees thrive in deep containers.

1 **A galvanized trough** filled with broccoli rabe and cabbage is one of several portable veggie gardens on a San Francisco rooftop. Any spot that gets at least 6 hours of sun per day is fine for a contained edible garden. Try pots on steps, in a bare spot in a flower bed, or along a garden path.

2 **Big glazed pots** play host to squash, tomato, and cucumber plants. Large containers such as these have a distinct presence; they also provide extra room for roots and don't dry out as quickly as smaller pots. Water as often as needed to keep soil in containers as moist as a wrung-out sponge.

3 **Recycled oil drums** painted vibrant colors contain edible and ornamental plants that, together, create a fast-growing screen. If plants in containers need supports, such as stakes or trellises, install them at planting time to avoid damaging the roots later.

4 **Salad-to-go** near a kitchen door echoes the reddish-bronze color of the ceramic pot it calls home. For any container, choose a top-quality potting mix and cover drain holes with fine wire screen to keep soil from washing out.

5 **Garage-sale finds,** like these lovely vintage pieces filled with lettuces and edible flowers, are great for creating a container garden. Frequent watering leaches nutrients from any pot, so mix a controlled-release fertilizer into the potting soil before planting. Or feed your plants with fish emulsion or a liquid fertilizer every 2 to 4 weeks, depending on the crop.

6 **An eye-level herb garden,** such as this one in a flat-backed terra-cotta pot, makes harvesting easy. Gardening in wall-mounted planters opens up space below and keeps crops out of reach of dogs, rabbits, slugs, and snails.

Space-Saving Garden Plans

For many gardeners, space is at a premium. But with careful planning, you can have a bountiful harvest from a small space. Just choose compact but prolific varieties such as 'Patio', a small-fruited determinate tomato, or 'Bush Baby' summer squash, and avoid space-gobbling, low-yield crops like sweet corn. Also, try succession planting: whenever one crop is harvested, be ready to set out new plants in its place.

Garden plan scale: 1 square = 1 foot

Herb Garden

This modest collection of herbs is just right for planting a few steps from the kitchen door. A two-part raised bed holds shrubby perennials and annuals, and spearmint is confined to a circular container set on a liner in the larger bed. A single bay tree grows in a pot of its own.

PLANT LIST
A. Basil (5)
B. Chives (8)
C. French Tarragon (2)
D. Oregano (2)
E. Parsley (2)
F. Rosemary (1)
G. Sage (2)
H. Spearmint (2)
I. Sweet Bay (1)
J. Sweet Marjoram (1)
K. Thyme, Common (2)
L. Thyme, Lemon (2)
M. Winter Savory (2)

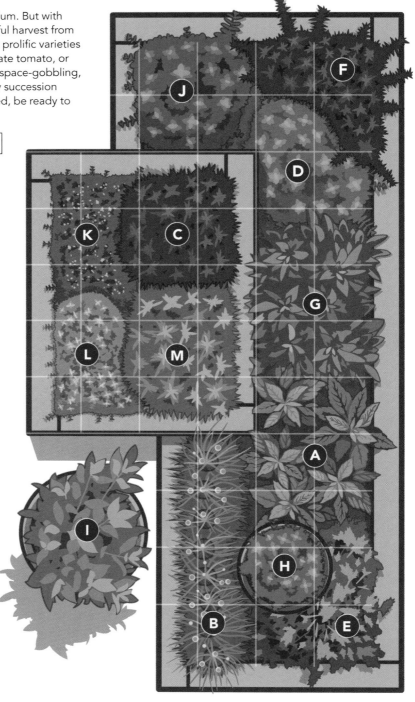

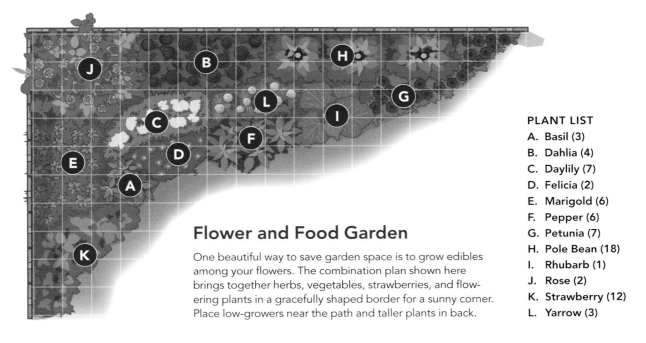

PLANT LIST
A. Basil (3)
B. Dahlia (4)
C. Daylily (7)
D. Felicia (2)
E. Marigold (6)
F. Pepper (6)
G. Petunia (7)
H. Pole Bean (18)
I. Rhubarb (1)
J. Rose (2)
K. Strawberry (12)
L. Yarrow (3)

Flower and Food Garden

One beautiful way to save garden space is to grow edibles among your flowers. The combination plan shown here brings together herbs, vegetables, strawberries, and flowering plants in a gracefully shaped border for a sunny corner. Place low-growers near the path and taller plants in back.

French-Intensive Garden

This bed is closely planted in a narrow rectangle designed for tending from the perimeter. To encourage deep roots, prepare the soil by double-digging: using a shovel, dig out the top 10 to 11 inches of soil, mix it with rich compost, loosen and turn the soil in the bottom of the bed, and return the top layer of soil and compost to the planting bed.

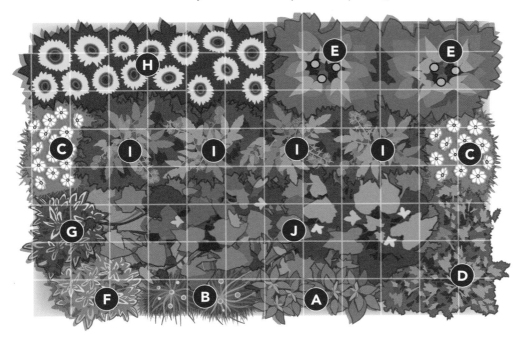

PLANT LIST
A. Basil (2)
B. Chives (2)
C. Cosmos (12)
D. Parsley (10)
E. Pole Bean (24)
F. Sage, Golden (1)
G. Sage, Tricolor (1)
H. Sunflower (6)
I. Tomato (4)
J. Zucchini (2)

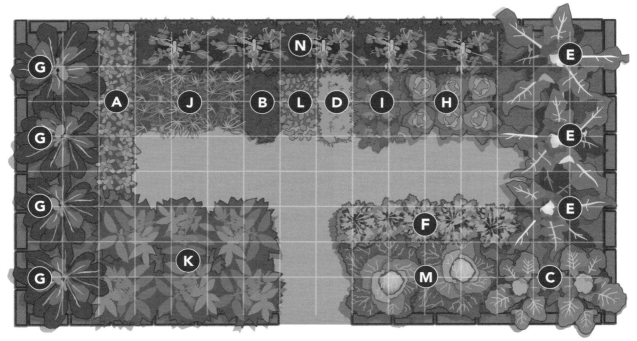

Keyhole Garden

This collection of cool-season vegetables is arranged around a T-shaped path just wide enough for comfortable tending and harvesting. Snap peas grow on tepee trellises opposite the entry to the keyhole, and compact growers like beets, onions, and radishes are planted in neat rows.

PLANT LIST

A. Arugula (20)
B. Beet (18)
C. Broccoli (2)
D. Carrot (12)
E. Cauliflower (3)
F. Celery (5)
G. Kale (4)

H. Lettuce (6)
I. Mustard (8)
J. Onion (24)
K. Potato (6)
L. Radish (24)
M. Savoy Cabbage (2)
N. Snap Pea (30)

U-Shaped Garden

Warm-season vegetables are tightly packed into this nearly square plot, but all have plenty of room to grow and produce a delicious harvest. The central path is mulched to discourage weeds and make the ground easy to walk on, even in wet weather.

PLANT LIST

A. Basil (2)
B. Bush Bean (4)
C. Carrot (24)
D. Chives (6)
E. Eggplant (4)
F. Green Onion (9)

G. Lettuce (6)
H. Pepper (5)
I. Summer Squash (3)
J. Swiss Chard (6)
K. Tomato (4)
L. Zucchini (3)

CHAPTER 8

Practical Guide

The most satisfying kitchen gardens start with the basics: the right location, good soil preparation, consistent watering and feeding, and protection against pests and diseases. Follow the guidelines in this chapter, and you'll soon have a garden full of healthy, vigorous plants—and an abundance of crops come harvesttime.

Getting Started

WHERE TO PLANT

Deciding where to plant your edible crops is the first step in producing healthy, tasty vegetables, herbs, fruits, berries, and nuts. Whether you plan to grow edibles among your ornamental plants, in containers, or in a special plot set aside for food gardening—or all three—it's important to select sites that meet certain requirements if you want your crops to thrive. When looking around your garden for suitable places, keep the following factors in mind.

sunlight The majority of edibles need 6 to 8 hours of full sun daily for top production and flavor. Select a site that is not shaded by buildings, trees, or shrubs. Remember that shadows lengthen in fall and winter to the north of tall structures, so use a compass to determine the direction of north and make sure any tall plants or structures to the south won't cast shadows on your site in those seasons. In addition to blocking sunlight, trees and shrubs send roots far and wide, competing with your edibles for water and nutrients.

air circulation While most edibles do not thrive in heavy winds, airflow from gentle breezes helps keep foliage dry, reducing the possibility of diseases. If your garden is exposed to constant winds, consider planting a sheltering windbreak or hedge.

level ground Planting, watering, and general care are easier in a level garden. If you must plant crops on a slope, run planting beds or rows across the slope, not up and down, to keep the soil from washing away. Exceptions include certain fruit and nut trees that do best with the improved drainage provided by sloping ground.

frost pockets Cold air settles in low-lying spots. Plants in such areas may suffer damage from frost in late spring and early fall.

soil Most crops prefer rich, well-drained soil; see pages 262–266 for information on soils and how to improve them. In very poor soil, consider planting in raised beds.

irrigation Locate your garden where you can easily reach it with a garden hose, or plan to install an automated watering system; see pages 280–281 for choices among watering methods.

Choose a sunny, wind-sheltered spot on level ground for vegetable beds.

convenience If possible, locate edibles fairly close to the kitchen door. That way, it's easy to dash out before dinner for a few vegetables or a handful of herbs.

WHAT TO PLANT

Deciding which edibles to grow can be both exciting and a bit daunting. Keep the following points in mind as you make your selections and decide how much of each crop to plant.

family preferences What crops do you and your family really enjoy eating? Will you use the harvest right away, or do you plan to store some food for winter? Beyond the tried-and-true favorites, it's fun to sample a few new varieties each season.

efficient planting

To make the most of your garden, especially if space is tight or your growing season is short, use one or more of the following planting methods.

Succession planting: Many herbs and some vegetables grow so fast that you can plant another crop as soon as the first one is finished. Planting at roughly two-week intervals for a continuous supply rather than one big harvest is another kind of succession planting.

Interplanting: This is the practice of growing two different crops in the same spot. Some vegetables, such as cabbages and tomatoes, grow fairly slowly. Around or alongside them, you can plant a fast-growing crop that will be ready for harvest before the slower crop needs the entire space. For another sort of interplanting, try growing small, compact crops (such as beets, parsley, and basil) close to tall crops (such as corn, pole beans, or tomatoes trained on a trellis) or around fruit trees.

Planting "cut and come again" crops: If you have only a small space for growing edibles, consider planting leaf lettuces, arugula, mustard greens, kale, and spinach. You can cut leaves as you need them, and the plants will grow more leaves for future harvests.

Plant compact, productive crops like peppers for a big harvest from a small space.

climate See pages 10–15 to find your zone and learn about the length of your growing season and average frost dates. Then check the requirements for the crops you want to plant.

available space How much space can you devote to edibles? In a small garden, for example, sprawling winter squash takes up too much territory for the payback of only a few squashes. In general, it is a good idea to start with a fairly small plot, especially if you are new to growing edibles. That way you won't be overwhelmed with too much work and perhaps far too much produce. Smaller gardens are also easier to keep tidy.

Where summers are hot, grow lettuce where it will receive some shade.

Soil

Most edible crops require rich, fertile, well-drained soil to produce healthy, flavorful harvests. Knowing what type of soil naturally occurs in your garden and how to improve it (if necessary) are basic steps to success in growing edibles. Where soil is poor, plan to plant in raised beds or containers. You may also wish to have your soil tested to determine its pH (acidity or alkalinity), any nutrient deficiencies, and the percentage of organic matter your soil contains. Simple tests are sold at garden centers; for a more precise reading, have the test done at a laboratory. In some states, the Cooperative Extension Office will test your soil.

SOIL TEXTURE

All soils consist of mineral particles formed by the natural breakdown of rock. They also contain varying amounts of organic matter, air, and water, as well as numerous living creatures—earthworms, nematodes, bacteria, fungi, and many others. The size and shape of a soil's mineral particles determine its basic characteristics, or texture.

clay (heavy) soils These are made up of very small particles that pack together tightly, producing a compact mass with microscopic pore spaces (the areas between soil particles). Drainage is usually slow, since water and nutrients percolate slowly through the tiny pores. It's not easy for roots to penetrate clay soil, and during prolonged rainy spells (or if overwatered) the soil remains saturated, even to the point of causing root rot. Working clay soil is a miserable job: it's sticky when wet and rock-hard when dry. On the plus side, its slower drainage does allow you to water and fertilize less often. To loosen clay soil and improve drainage, add organic matter such as compost or manure (see following pages).

sandy (light) soils At the other end of the spectrum are soils with large, irregularly rounded particles and large pore spaces that allow water and nutrients to drain away freely. Plants growing in sand are unlikely to suffer root rot, but you need to water them more often to keep their roots moist. The frequent watering leaches nutrients away, so you'll have to fertilize more often too. Adding organic matter enhances moisture retention in sandy soil by wedging into the large pore spaces between the particles of soil.

Rich, crumbly loam

loam Fortunately, most garden soils fall somewhere between the extremes of clay and sand. The best type for plant growth, referred to as loam, has mineral particles in a mixture of sizes. Loam also contains a generous proportion of organic matter. It drains well but doesn't dry out too fast, loses nutrients at a moderate rate, and contains enough air for healthy root growth.

To determine soil texture, thoroughly wet a patch of soil and then let it dry out for a day. Now pick up a handful of soil and squeeze it firmly in your fist. If it forms a tight ball and has a slippery feel, it's predominantly clay. If it feels gritty, doesn't hold its shape, and crumbles when you open your hand, it's sandy. If it is slightly crumbly but still holds a loose ball, it is closer to loam.

PREPARING THE SOIL

Getting ready to plant edibles in a new area, such as a former lawn, or in an area that has not been cultivated recently takes some time and effort. But the payoff is soil that is fertile and easy to work, so that sowing seeds and setting out transplants become a pleasure. If possible, prepare the soil a few weeks before planting to let the soil settle. You can also get a head start on spring planting by preparing your soil in fall, but wait until spring to spread and rake in fertilizer so it isn't leached away during the winter.

The following steps will help you prepare a new area for planting.

1. If you're removing a lawn, use a sharp spade to cut the sod into sections; then push the spade under each section to sever the roots. Lift the sections away with your hands. If you have weeds rather than sod, remove them by pulling or digging.

2. Dampen the soil slightly before you start to dig and loosen it; don't try to work soil that's too wet or completely dry. In small areas, use a spading fork; for larger beds, you may wish to use a rotary tiller. Dig to a depth of about 10 inches, breaking up clods of earth and removing any stones and debris as you go.

3. Spread 3 to 4 inches of organic material over the area (see following pages). Add fertilizer now as well (see pages 282–283). Phosphorus and potassium (two of the major plant nutrients) should be placed near plant roots to have the greatest benefit, so work a fertilizer high in these nutrients, such as 5-10-10, into the soil before planting. Spread the fertilizer over the soil, using the amount indicated on the label. Also add any amendments needed to alter your soil pH.

4. With a spading fork or tiller, incorporate all the amendments evenly into the soil. Then level the bed with a rake, breaking up any remaining clods of earth. Water well, and let the improved soil settle for at least a few days before planting.

Each time you replant a bed with new crops, you'll first need to rejuvenate the soil by repeating steps 3 and 4 above, adding only 1 to 2 inches of organic matter instead of 3 to 4 inches. Preparation will take less time and effort each year as your soil improves.

tools for working with soil

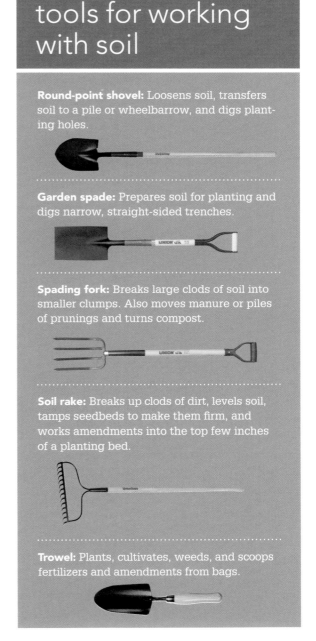

Round-point shovel: Loosens soil, transfers soil to a pile or wheelbarrow, and digs planting holes.

Garden spade: Prepares soil for planting and digs narrow, straight-sided trenches.

Spading fork: Breaks large clods of soil into smaller clumps. Also moves manure or piles of prunings and turns compost.

Soil rake: Breaks up clods of dirt, levels soil, tamps seedbeds to make them firm, and works amendments into the top few inches of a planting bed.

Trowel: Plants, cultivates, weeds, and scoops fertilizers and amendments from bags.

Organic Amendments

Adding organic matter such as compost, manure, or wood products improves and enriches all soil types. Organic matter helps loosen the soil, allowing air and water to penetrate and making the soil more hospitable to plant roots. Use generous amounts of it when you prepare soil for edible crops. Each year your soil will become easier to work and will reward you with larger harvests. As a rule of thumb, a cubic yard of organic material will cover 100 square feet of planting bed to a depth of nearly 4 inches. Cover crops are also excellent sources of organic matter.

MANURE

Aged or composted manure (such as dry poultry or steer manure) contains more plant nutrients than other soil amendments. However, these manures may have high concentrations of soluble salts, which can harm plant roots, so you need to apply them sparingly. Add about 1 pound of dry steer manure per square foot of soil surface; 1 pound of dry poultry manure is plenty for 4 to 5 square feet. Working manure into the soil a month or so before planting allows some of the excess salts to leach below root level.

WOOD PRODUCTS

Sawdust, wood shavings, ground bark, and other wood products are especially useful in clay soils, where they help separate the fine clay particles. However, most wood products take up nitrogen from the soil as they decompose, so you need to add nitrogen along with them to have sufficient nitrogen for plant growth. Some wood products, such as redwood soil conditioner, can be purchased already fortified with nitrogen; check the label to be sure.

MYCORRHIZAL FUNGI

These are naturally occurring soil organisms that colonize the roots of plants, helping them use water and nutrients more efficiently and suppressing diseases. Adding them to your garden soil or potting mixes can improve plant growth and production. You can find them in tablet form or as additives in organic fertilizers.

COMPOST

Compost is one of the best soil amendments and easy to make. A pile of leaves, branches, or other garden trimmings tossed in a corner of the garden will eventually decompose with no intervention on your part. However, it can take as long as a year to produce results. With a little effort, you can hasten the process considerably. If you create optimum conditions for the organisms responsible for decay by giving them the mixture of air, water, and materials rich in carbon and nitrogen that they need, your compost pile will heat up quickly and decompose in a few months. This process also destroys many (though not all) weeds and disease pathogens. Gardeners often need more compost than they can produce; fortunately, good-quality compost is also widely available from commercial sources.

composting systems You can make compost in a freestanding pile or in a homemade structure; various plastic compost bins and barrels are also sold at garden centers. An unenclosed pile should be 3 to 5 feet tall and wide; any larger and it may not receive enough air at its center. For a wire-enclosed system, form a cylinder with welded wire, chicken wire, or snow fencing, supported with stakes, if necessary. The cylinder or hoop should be about 4 feet in diameter and 3 to 4 feet tall. To turn the pile, lift the cylinder and move it to one side, then fork the materials back into it. A more complex composting system can be made by using three compost bins in a row. The left bin holds new green and brown material; the center one contains partly decomposed material; the right bin holds nearly finished or finished compost.

compost tea This nutrient-rich brew is easy to make and use. Half-fill a burlap bag (or, for smaller batches, an old nylon stocking) with finished compost. Place the bag in a barrel, large bucket, or watering can and fill the container with water. Let the brew steep for several days. Another option is to mix loose compost and water in a bucket, then strain it. Sprinkle the resulting brownish liquid around your plants. Do this several times during the growing season to give plants a quick boost. Some mail-order suppliers offer compost tea machines that aerate and stir the brew, increasing the number of beneficial microbes it contains.

Preparing Compost

1. Gather and prepare the ingredients. You'll need approximately twice as much (by volume) brown matter as green matter. Brown matter is high in carbon and includes dry leaves, hay, sawdust, wood chips, and woody prunings. Green matter is high in nitrogen and includes grass, kitchen scraps (do not use bones or dairy products), and animal manure (do not include dog or cat manure). Avoid badly diseased or insect-infested plants, weeds with seeds, and pernicious perennial weeds that might survive composting. Shredding or chopping large, rough materials into smaller pieces allows decay-producing organisms to reach more surfaces, speeding the composting process.

2. Build the pile. Constructing the pile like a layer cake makes it easy to judge the ratio of brown to green materials. Start with a 4- to 8-inch layer of brown material, then add a layer of green material about 2 to 4 inches deep. (Layers of grass clippings should be only 2 inches deep; less-dense green materials can be layered more thickly.) Add another layer of brown material and sprinkle the pile with water. Mix these first three layers with a spading fork. Continue adding layers, watering, and mixing.

3. Turn the pile. In just a few days, the pile should heat up dramatically. In time, it will decompose on its own, but you can hurry things along by turning the contents to introduce more oxygen. Using a spading fork or pitchfork, restack the pile, redistributing it so that the materials originally on the outside are moved to the pile's center, where they'll be exposed to higher heat. If necessary, add water; the pile should be as moist as a wrung-out sponge. Adding an occasional shovelful of aged manure or finished compost gives the pile a dose of extra nutrients and speeds decomposition. Turn the pile weekly, if possible, until it is no longer generating internal heat and most of the materials have decomposed.

4. Use the compost. Finished compost is dark and crumbly and has a pleasant, earthy aroma. Mix it into your planting beds or use it as mulch. If some of the material is coarser than you like, incorporate it into your next compost pile. To obtain a fine-textured compost to use as potting soil, sift the finished compost through a screen with $1/2$-inch mesh.

Distinctive flowers precede fava beans.

COVER CROPS

Cover crops are legumes (pea-family plants) or grasses planted to improve garden soil. Most are planted in fall and dug into the soil in spring. As they decay, cover crops add valuable organic matter, making the soil easier to work and helping it retain moisture. They also reduce erosion, choke out weeds, and provide early spring flowers to supply nectar and pollen for beneficial insects. Seeds for cover crops, and information on how much of each kind you need to cover specific areas, are available from mail-order suppliers and some nurseries.

how they work Legumes such as fava beans, Austrian peas, clovers, and vetch add nitrogen to the soil, due to their association with *Rhizobium* bacteria that live symbiotically on their roots. These organisms draw nitrogen from the air and "fix" (concentrate) it in root nodules. When the legumes decompose, the nitrogen is released into the soil. Grasses such as barley, rye, and oats don't contribute extra nitrogen to the soil, but they do produce plenty of organic matter. Gardeners often combine legumes and grasses to reap the benefits of both.

how to use them Plant cover crops in fall, after the rains begin in mild-winter climates or 6 to 8 weeks before the first expected frost in cold regions. Before planting, treat the seeds of legumes (those grown for cover crops as well as garden peas and beans) with an inoculant powder to be certain that *Rhizobium* bacteria are present. To produce the maximum amount of nitrogen from fava beans and other legumes, let them grow until after they start blooming in spring. Let grasses grow until several weeks before you want to plant other crops. Cut or mow your cover crops, by hand or with a heavy-duty mower. Either till or dig the entire mass of stems, foliage, and roots into the soil, or, if that is too difficult, add the cut stems and leaves to your compost pile and dig just the roots into the soil. Wait two to four weeks for the cover crop to decompose before planting spring or summer vegetables.

Seeds and Transplants

Once you've decided which crops to grow, you'll need to decide whether to buy seeds and start your own plants or to buy transplants from the nursery. With seeds, you can order exactly what you want from a mail-order company if your local nursery doesn't carry the plant you're looking for. Nursery plants are more expensive, but they have the advantage of being ready to plant at once.

BUYING AND STORING SEEDS

Be sure the seeds you buy are fresh; they should be dated for the current year. A packet often contains far more seeds than you can use in one year, especially in a small garden. You can save many kinds of seeds for future use. Some, such as beans, beets, cabbage, cucumbers, lettuce, melons, and squash, remain viable for several years if stored in an airtight container in a cool, dry place. Onions, parsley, and parsnips have a shorter shelf life, so it's best to buy new seeds each year.

STARTING SEEDS

Warm-season vegetables need a long, warm growing season to produce a harvest. If you plan to grow your own seedlings, start such crops indoors in early spring in order to have plants ready to set out in the garden when the weather has warmed up. Starting seeds in containers is also a useful way to have plants of cool-season crops ready to transplant into the garden in early spring or fall.

You can use any of a variety of containers, including flats or trays, small individual pots, or cell-packs. If you're reusing old containers, scrub them out, then soak them for a half-hour in a solution of 1 part household bleach to 9 parts hot water to destroy any disease organisms. Follow these steps for sure success.

1. Fill your containers to just below the rim with a light, porous seed-starting or potting mix. Moisten the mix, and let it drain.

2. Scatter seeds thinly over the surface. Check the seed packet for the recommended planting depth and cover the seeds with the proper amount of mix. (As a rule of thumb, cover seeds to a depth equal to twice their diameter.)

3. Moisten the soil lightly.

4. Label each container with the plant's name and the date.

Continued on page 269 ▶

Mist newly planted seeds.

Label pots with stickers or stakes.

Transplant seedlings when they've developed two sets of true leaves.

Harden off seedlings by gradually moving them into full sun.

5. If you are starting heat-loving plants (tomatoes, cucumbers, eggplant, okra, peppers, squash, or melons), set the containers on a water heater or use a heating mat (see sidebar) to keep the soil warm. Most cool-season vegetables will germinate at room temperature.

6. When the seeds germinate, move the pots into an area with bright light and temperatures between 60° and 75°F/16° and 24°C.

TRANSPLANTING SEEDLINGS

When seedlings develop their second set of true leaves, it's time to transplant them to individual pots, such as 3- or 4-inch plastic pots.

1. Fill the new containers with potting mix, moisten the mix, and let it drain.

2. Gently remove the seedlings from their original pots. Squeeze each pot's sides with one hand and turn the pot upside down so your other hand cradles the soil ball as it slides out. With both hands, carefully pull the soil ball apart, and set it down on a flat surface.

3. Separate the fragile root balls of the seedlings from one another with a toothpick or skewer, or tease them apart with your fingers.

4. Poke a hole in each new container's potting mix. Carefully lift each seedling and its root ball, keeping your fingers under it for support. Place the seedling in its new container and firm the mix around it.

5. Water immediately, then set the pots in bright light (but keep them out of direct sunlight for a few days).

6. Feed seedlings weekly with a fertilizer sold for starting seeds or with a liquid type diluted to half-strength.

HARDENING OFF SEEDLINGS

Plants started indoors and most vegetable starts from the nursery have been raised in warm conditions. To prevent undue stress to these tender seedlings, gradually accustom them to the bright sun and cooler temperatures outdoors. Start the acclimation process, called hardening off, about 10 days before planting the seedlings in the garden. Stop fertilizing, and set the containers outside for a few hours each day in a spot with filtered light and shelter from the wind. Over the next week, gradually increase exposure until the plants are in full sun all day. Bring them back indoors whenever cold or freezing temperatures are predicted. After several nights outdoors in their containers, seedlings are ready to transplant. Alternatively, harden them off by placing seedlings in a cold frame (see page 274) and opening its cover a bit more each day.

starting seeds indoors

Seedlings of edible crops need bright light to develop properly; when grown in conditions that are too dark, the seedlings are spindly and weak.

If you don't have a suitable place for your seedlings, try growing them under fluorescent lights. As soon as the seeds sprout, give them 12 to 14 hours of light each day, setting the light fixture 6 to 8 inches above the tops of the plants.

Seeds of heat-loving summer crops also need warm soil to germinate quickly and strongly. Thin waterproof heating mats placed under the containers keep the soil 15° to 20°F/8° to 11°C above room temperature.

Nurseries and mail-order catalogs sell both fluorescent light kits and heating mats to keep the soil of germinating plants warm.

Planting

SOWING SEEDS DIRECTLY IN THE GARDEN

Many vegetables grow best if you plant the seeds where they are to grow in the garden rather than starting them indoors and transplanting them later. These include root crops (carrots, beets, radishes, turnips, and parsnips) and corn, peas, and beans.

Plan to sow seeds after the soil has warmed in spring; if sown in cold soil, most will germinate poorly or not at all. Check the seed packet (or the plant entries in this book) for sowing time for each crop. Soil should be loose and crumbly; rake it smooth, so seedlings can push through. Refer to the plant listings here or to the seed packet for the proper planting depth; seeds planted too deep will not sprout. In general, seeds should be covered to a depth equal to twice the diameter of the seed.

The right amount of water after sowing keeps the soil moist but not soggy and prevents crusts from forming on the soil surface. Water with a fine mist, so that seeds aren't washed away. In hot weather, covering the soil with damp burlap helps retain moisture. Be sure to remove the burlap as soon as seeds begin to sprout. If you plan to water with basins or furrows, make them before sowing seeds (see page 281).

Some seeds will not germinate, no matter how careful you are. For this reason, gardeners usually sow seeds close together and then thin any overcrowded seedlings to their proper spacing (noted in the plant listings in this book and on seed packets) when they are 1 to 2 inches tall. Following are three methods of sowing.

Make shallow furrows to sow seeds in rows. Use a trowel or the corner of a hoe to make a furrow the correct depth for the seeds you are planting. Sow seeds evenly, and pat soil gently over them. To make straight rows, stretch a string between two stakes, and plant beneath it. Or lay a board on the surface of the soil, then plant along its edge.

Use hills—groups of plants growing in a cluster, often in a low mound of soil—rather than rows for sprawling plants, if you wish. This is a traditional way to grow squash and melons. Sow 5 or 6 seeds in a circle, and pat soil over them.

Broadcast seeds to sow wide bands of vegetables across a bed. This is more space efficient than row-planting for smaller crops such as lettuce, carrots, radishes, or mesclun. Scatter the seeds evenly over the soil. Cover by scattering soil over the seeds or by raking gently, first in one direction and then again at right angles. Pat the soil to firm it.

SETTING OUT SEEDLINGS

Seedlings of annual vegetables that you've grown yourself or purchased from a nursery are usually set out from small containers such as 4-inch pots. Transplant seedlings of warm-season crops after all danger of frost is past, when the soil is fairly dry and has warmed up. Water the seedlings before transplanting them. Dig a hole for each plant, making it the same depth as the seedling container and an inch or two wider.

1. **With your fingers,** lightly separate the roots so they can grow out into the soil. If there is a pad of coiled roots at the bottom of the root ball, pull it off.

2. **Place each plant** in its hole so that the top of the root ball is even with the soil surface. (Tomatoes are an exception; they are planted more deeply.) Firm the soil around the roots.

3. **Water each plant** with a gentle flow that won't disturb soil or roots. After planting, water frequently to keep the soil moist but not soggy.

PLANTING FROM NURSERY CONTAINERS

During the growing season, larger plants such as fruit trees and cane berries are sold in 1-gallon or larger containers. They can be planted throughout the growing season, except during the heat of summer. Be sure to select healthy plants with strong shoots. Avoid root-bound plants—those with roots above the soil level or growing through the pot's drainage holes.

1. **Dig a planting hole** at least twice as wide as the root ball and just as deep, leaving a central plateau of firm soil 1 to 2 inches tall at the bottom of the hole on which to set the root system. This prevents the plant from settling too much. Roughen the sides of the hole with a spading fork to help the roots penetrate the soil.

2. **Set the plant in the hole**, spreading its roots over the plateau of soil. The top of the root ball should be 1 to 2 inches above the surrounding soil. Backfill with the soil you dug from the hole, working in stages and firming the soil around the roots with your hands.

3. **Make a berm of soil** to form a watering basin. Irrigate gently.

4. **Spread mulch** around the plant, keeping it several inches away from the stem or trunk.

PLANTING BARE-ROOT

During the winter dormant season, you can plant bare-root trees (and cane berries and grapes as well). Bare-root stock is available in late winter and very early spring from retail nurseries and mail-order companies. If you're planting fruit trees grown on dwarfing rootstock, you may need to stake them as soon as they are planted; check with the supplier to find out whether your trees are shallow-rooting and should be staked. Grapes and cane berries are also cut back at planting time; see individual plant listings for information on each type.

Before planting, soak the roots in a bucket of water for a minimum of 4 hours (preferably overnight). Just before planting, cut any broken or damaged roots back to healthy tissue; also prune roots that are much longer than all the others.

1. **Dig a planting hole** that is about the same depth as the plant's roots and twice as wide as it is deep. Shape a firm cone of soil on which to set the roots so the plant's crown will be above the soil line. Roughen the sides of the hole with a spading fork.

2. **Hold the plant in place** while you backfill the hole and water the plant to settle the soil.

Mulch

Mulching is the practice of applying organic or inorganic materials to the surface of the soil around plants or on pathways. Mulch reduces evaporation, so the soil stays moist longer after you irrigate your crops. Mulch also helps prevent the growth of weeds and gives the garden a tidy look.

ORGANIC MULCHES

Organic mulches are derived from once-living matter and improve the soil and add nutrients as they slowly decompose. Mulches that work well around plants in garden beds include compost, leaf mold, straw, and grass clippings (be sure to apply clippings in thin layers, letting each layer dry before applying another). For permanent garden paths, choose materials that break down more slowly, such as shredded or ground bark or wood chips.

Nurseries and garden supply centers sell a selection of organic mulches by the bag or in bulk. Farm supply stores offer straw; wood chips are often available from tree maintenance firms.

Because organic mulches keep the soil beneath them cool—a bonus in hot weather—you should delay applying them to planting beds until warm weather arrives; soil has to be warm to get most plants off to a good start. Apply organic mulches in a 2- to 4-inch layer, but take care not to cover the plants' crowns (where the stem meets the soil); too much moisture near the crown can cause rot.

PLASTIC MULCHES

Various sorts of plastic sheeting are useful aids in edible gardening for warming the soil, controlling weed growth, conserving moisture, and keeping developing fruits clean. After preparing the soil for planting, cover it with sheeting; hold down the edges with soil, pieces of lumber, or U-shaped irrigation pins. Cut small holes or Xs when you are ready to set out plants or sow seeds.

The most familiar sheeting, black plastic, absorbs heat to warm the soil in spring, allowing you to plant heat-loving crops earlier. It also blocks light, so weeds can't grow, and conserves water by reducing evaporation.

Infrared-transmitting (IRT) mulch sheeting is green plastic sheeting that allows infrared light to penetrate. It is more effective than black plastic in warming the soil, increasing early yields of warm-weather crops such as melons, cucumbers, squash, pumpkins, and peppers. It also suppresses weed growth and holds moisture in the soil.

SRM-Red mulch

how much mulch?

A half-ton pickup truck holds about 1 cubic yard of mulch (five wheelbarrow loads). Landscape supply companies will deliver bulk orders; nurseries sell bagged mulch. Here's how much you need to add a 2-, 3-, or 4-inch layer of mulch to four different-size garden beds.

Bed size	2" deep	3" deep	4" deep
100 sq. ft.	$2/3$ cubic yd.	1 cubic yd.	$1^1/4$ cubic yds.
250 sq. ft.	$1^1/2$ cubic yds.	$2^1/3$ cubic yds.	3 cubic yds.
500 sq. ft.	3 cubic yds.	$4^2/3$ cubic yds.	$6^1/4$ cubic yds.
1,000 sq. ft.	$6^1/4$ cubic yds.	$9^1/4$ cubic yds.	$12^1/3$ cubic yds.

Red plastic selective reflecting mulch (SRM-Red), developed especially for tomatoes and related plants (such as eggplant), reflects light waves in the red spectrum up into the foliage. Compared with plants grown with black plastic mulch, plants grown with SRM-Red are larger and produce more heavily. SRM-Red also helps retain moisture and warm the soil but is not as effective at blocking weeds. Strawberries benefit from this mulch too.

STRAW. Light, loose option. Good for vegetable and strawberry beds. Avoid hay, which contains weed seeds.

HAZELNUT HULLS. Good for general use and ideal for paths because hulls let water through easily and don't stick to shoes.

GROUND BARK. Made from different types of local wood. Good all-purpose choice, available in various sizes.

DECOMPOSED GRANITE (DG). Compacts quickly and doesn't tend to blow away. Good for paths and herb gardens.

SHREDDED BARK. Irregular bits and shredded pieces knit together, so it stays in place. Useful on slopes and in windy places.

TUMBLED GLASS. Used mainly to add color and punch to small areas. Excellent for containers.

Crop Protection

PROTECTING YOUNG PLANTS

Transplants and newly sprouted seedlings are vulnerable both to unexpected late frosts and to hot, sunny weather. Several easy-to-use devices help protect them.

Glass cloches, available from mail-order seed catalogs, fit over the tops of plants, forming miniature one-plant greenhouses that can save your crops on cold nights. To make your own from a 1-gallon plastic milk jug, cut off the bottom and part of the handle. Place the jug over the plant, and push a stake through the handle to hold it in place. Leave the cap off to allow air ventilation but recap the jug on frosty nights. Or cut out the top of a cardboard box, cut along three edges of the bottom, and turn the box upside down over a young plant. Close the lid at night to protect the plant from cold. Open the lid in the morning.

To protect tender young plants from sudden hot weather and bright sunshine, prop up a piece of plywood or a shingle on the sunny side of each plant to shade it. When the plants are established and growing well, remove the protection. For larger plantings, fasten shade cloth (available from garden supply centers and nurseries) to stakes to form a "ceiling" over crops.

EXTENDING THE SEASON

In cold-winter climates, finding ways to extend the growing season—that is, keeping plants a bit warmer in early spring, in late fall, and even in winter—significantly increases your overall harvest. Even in mild climates, some forms of climate modification are useful, especially for getting warm-season crops started.

plastic sheeting and other products One
way to get a head start in spring is to prewarm the soil. Spreading either black plastic or special infrared-transmitting (IRT) plastic mulch over your planting beds 1 or 2 weeks before you sow seeds or set out transplants warms the soil; it also helps to dry soil that is too wet. This allows you to plant heat-loving crops such as corn, melons, squash, tomatoes, and peppers earlier. For more on plastic mulches, see page 272. Gardeners also use clear plastic to extend the growing season. You can make a low tunnel greenhouse to protect seedlings in spring by stretching clear plastic over a framework of wire hoops or PVC pipe. Some kinds of floating row covers serve similar purposes (see page 276).

Build or buy a cold frame to trap heat.

Mail-order companies offer a heat-capturing product designed especially for tomatoes. It's made up of small, hollow plastic cylinders connected to form a tepee-shaped collar. You place the collar over a tomato plant and fill the cylinders with water. The water absorbs and holds heat, boosting growth and providing frost protection, so you can set out the seedlings a month or more earlier than you would unprotected plants. These devices are tall enough to be left in place until the weather is thoroughly warm.

cold frames Basically a box with a transparent lid, a
cold frame acts as a passive solar energy collector and reservoir. During the day, the sun's rays heat the air and soil in the frame; at night, the heat absorbed by the soil radiates out, keeping the plants warm. Cold frames can be put to many uses in edible gardening. In very early spring, you can sow seeds of cool-season vegetables directly in the frame and grow the plants there until it's time to transplant them to the garden. Later in spring, you can use a cold frame to harden off seedlings of

Protect young plants from frost with glass cloches.

Put up scarecrows to discourage birds.

Shelter crops beneath floating row covers.

warm-season crops started indoors. For fall and winter harvests in cold climates, plant cool-season vegetables in a cold frame base and put on the cover before freezing weather arrives. To make the most of the cold frame's benefits, locate it where a wall or hedge will protect it from harsh wind, and orient it to face south or southwest so that it receives as much sunlight as possible.

Ready-made cold frames are sold by mail-order suppliers and some nurseries, but it is not difficult to make your own. Plan to make the frame about 3 feet wide; it can be as long as you need. Use rot-resistant lumber such as redwood or cedar. Cut the sides so that the frame slopes from about 1^1/$_2$ feet tall at the back to 1 foot tall at the front; an angled surface captures more heat and allows rainwater to run off. For the cover, use a recycled window or staple plastic sheeting to a wooden frame. If the cold frame is longer than about 4 feet, make the cover in sections so it won't be too heavy to lift. Apply weather stripping around the top edges of the box and attach the cover with galvanized steel hinges. Provide ventilation to prevent overheating.

FLOATING ROW COVERS

Made of various lightweight fabrics sold in rolls, floating row covers protect plants from cold temperatures, birds, and many flying insects. The covers are permeable to sunlight, air, and water. Three types are available. A standard floating row cover serves as an insect barrier and protects plants from frost down to 28°F/–2°C. It allows 75 to 85 percent of sunlight to be transmitted to the plant. Remove the cover when temperatures top 80°F/27°C or the plants will overheat. The frost blanket, a second type of floating row cover, offers frost protection down to 24°F/–4°C, with 50 percent light transmission. Since it must be removed during the day when temperatures rise above 32°F/0°C, it does not protect plants from insect pests. The third type, extralight or summer-weight fabric, is used as an insect barrier only. It does not retain heat and allows 85 percent light transmission.

Row covers are designed to be laid directly over seeded beds or plants, though some gardeners support them with stakes. If you plan to leave the covers in place

Drape bird netting over vulnerable crops.

Install fencing where deer or rabbits are present.

for any length of time, allow enough extra fabric so the plants can push up the cover as they grow. Secure the edges by burying them with soil or placing 2-by-4s on them. This seals out insects, though pests already on the plants may proliferate. If your plants require insects to pollinate their flowers (as melons and squash do, for example), remove the covers when blooms appear. At the end of the growing season, row covers help plants survive the first frosts of fall, allowing those last tomatoes to ripen or that fall-seeded lettuce to be harvested over a longer period.

BIRD NETTING

To protect fruit trees and other plants from marauding birds, use netting or screen. Broad-mesh (3/4-inch) nylon or plastic netting is popular for trees, since it readily admits air, water, and sunlight. Enclose trees with netting two to three weeks before fruit ripens, tying it around the trunk beneath the lowest branches or securing it to the ground so birds can't find an opening. For ground-level

crops, you can drape the lightweight netting directly over the plants or make wooden or plastic frames and drape the netting over them.

FENCING

The best boundary for an edibles garden allows free movement of light and air while keeping out pests like rabbits and deer. A post-and-rail fence with wire mesh (or a wood-and-wire fence) is a popular option and relatively inexpensive compared with a solid wood fence. It creates very little shade, and if it is at least 2 feet tall, rabbits can't jump it. Rabbits do burrow, however, so extend the wire mesh 6 inches or more underground. On a gate, make the mesh 12 inches longer than the gate, and fold the mesh into an L shape at the bottom so that it extends away from the garden; when you close the gate, place a stone or two on the extending mesh to secure it. Deer won't be deterred by a fence unless it's taller than 6 feet (see page 291 for more information on controlling deer and other animal pests).

Training and Staking

STAKING VEGETABLES

Training vining edibles such as pole beans, peas, tomatoes, cucumbers, melons, and squash to grow up stakes, trellises, or other supports pays off in several ways. It saves space to grow these plants vertically rather than letting them sprawl across the ground. And you'll harvest more fruits, both because they'll be easier to see and pick and because they won't come into contact with the soil, where they might rot. Put up your stakes and trellises at planting time. If you try to stake plants after they have begun to sprawl, you risk disturbing the roots and breaking the stems. Train or tie the plants as they grow.

Common materials for vegetable supports are wire mesh, wooden stakes and string, and bamboo, but you can also use rustic twigs, decorative metal or wooden structures, copper pipe, or bent reinforcing bar.

1. **A weathered ladder** in the garden makes a fine support. Sink the legs into 6-inch-deep holes so it won't blow over, and wrap string, wire, or wire mesh around it to help plants such as peas, beans, and cucumbers climb.

2. **A sturdy frame** leaning on a sunny wall makes a trellis for cucumber, melon, or squash vines. Support heavy fruits with netting or cloth slings tied to the trellis.

3. **A wire cage** supports a tomato plant; you don't need to tie the stems to it. Buy a 6$^{1}/_{2}$-foot length of 5- or 6-foot-wide concrete-reinforcing wire. Roll it into a cylinder 24 inches in diameter and hold it together with wire. Anchor the cage with stakes.

4. **A wooden obelisk** (purchased or homemade from lumber or tree branches) supports tomatoes and brings height and interest to garden beds. Tie stems to the support as they grow.

5. **Strings stretched** over a wooden A-frame provide support for climbing tendrils of beans and peas.

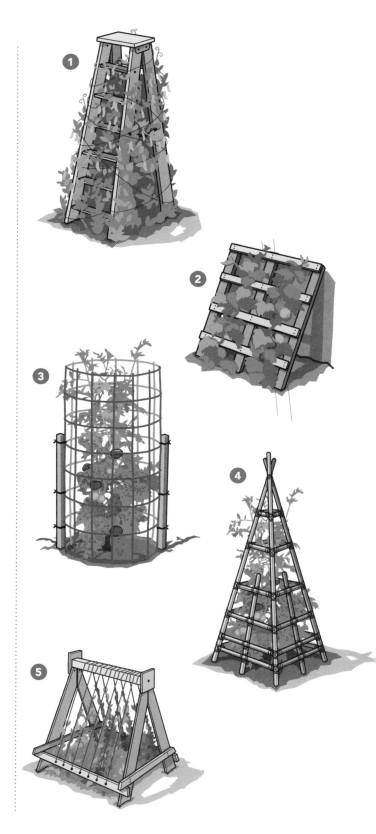

Pruning Fruit Trees

For most edibles, pruning is needed only to direct growth. Fruit trees, however, need special pruning to produce good annual crops.

TRAINING YOUNG FRUIT TREES

While they are young, prune fruit trees only enough to develop the desired framework (too much pruning delays fruiting). There are three primary pruning methods; consult the plant listings for the method recommended for your trees.

central-leader training This type of pruning produces a straight-trunked pyramidal tree, with tiers of branches (called scaffold branches) radiating out from the trunk. Such a tree can become quite tall, so this method is best for dwarf and semi-dwarf trees. Each year, prune to create a new, higher tier of scaffold branches. For good light penetration, maintain open space between tiers and keep the branches toward the top of the tree shorter than those toward the bottom. Don't allow fruit to set on the leader, which could bend it over.

open-center training Trees pruned this way have several main limbs angling outward from the top of a short trunk. Such a tree can be kept shorter than one trained to a central leader. At planting time, cut back the trunk so that it is 2 to 3 feet tall. The next dormant season, prune to create three to five scaffold branches that spiral around the trunk, with at least 6 inches of vertical space between them. Prune back these branches to 2 to 3 feet in length. The following dormant season, choose two strong lateral (side) branches on each scaffold branch, and cut back the scaffolds to the chosen laterals. Prune back the laterals to 2 to 3 feet to force additional lateral branches to grow.

espalier training When space is tight, use this pruning method to make a dwarf tree grow flat. Fasten a trellis or wires to a wall or fence, and set a fruit tree 10 inches away. The tiers of the supports are usually spaced 12 to 18 inches apart. As the tree grows, train branches to grow horizontally along the supports with plastic nursery ties or raffia, and clip off shoots that jut out too far.

DORMANT-SEASON PRUNING

Dormant (winter) pruning of deciduous trees lets you easily see what you're cutting and invigorates the tree. In cold-winter climates, prune late in the dormant season.

Start by removing dead, diseased, crossing, crowded, or broken branches. Then take out suckers growing from the base of the tree or its roots, as well as water sprouts shooting up from horizontal branches or along the trunk. Finally, maximize fruit production by removing old, unproductive growth, thinning out large limbs that shade other fruit-producing branches, and removing small, shaded branches.

Make your cuts about a quarter inch beyond a vigorous side branch. When you remove a whole branch, don't cut flush against the trunk or it opens up the wood to decay. Position your shears or saw just outside the branch collar (the wrinkled area or bulge at the base of the branch); and don't slice into the branch bark ridge (the raised bark in the branch crotch).

SUMMER PRUNING

Summer pruning is done when new growth is slowing down, usually between June and early August. It reduces vigor, helping to keep trees smaller, and improves the color of fruit growing on interior branches by giving them more sunlight. Cut back suckers, water sprouts, and some young branches that grew in the current year. But don't remove too many leaves where sunlight is intense as branches and fruit could sunburn.

Watering

Food crops need a steady supply of water throughout the growing season. If plants are allowed to dry out, they eventually die. Yet too much water, especially in poorly drained soil, deprives plant roots of oxygen, which may also kill them. Figuring out the best ways to water your garden is an ongoing learning process.

HOW OFTEN

Plan to water young vegetable seedlings and transplants frequently—as often as two or three times a day in hot, windy weather—keeping the soil moist but not soggy. As these young plants grow and their roots reach deeper, you can water less frequently. In general, vegetables that are flowering or beginning to set fruit, form heads, or develop edible roots need to be watered more often than older plants. Mature fruit and nut trees and grapes require even less frequent irrigation because they have much deeper roots than annual vegetable crops. See plant entries for more on the water requirements of each crop.

Your soil texture also influences how often you need to water. Clay soils hold lots of water and release it slowly; sandy soils hold less water and release it quickly. Loam soils fall in between, holding less water than clay and more than sand. Subsequently, clay soils need less frequent watering than loam soils, and loam soils can be watered less frequently than sandy soils. (For more on soil texture, see page 262.)

Cool, cloudy weather allows any soil to stay moist longer than hot, dry weather does. Thus cool-season vegetables need less irrigation than those grown in summer. Mulches slow evaporation and are important aids to water conservation. (For more on mulching, see page 272.)

HOW MUCH

Once your plants are established and growing well, water them deeply, applying enough water to moisten the entire root zone. This encourages roots to grow down farther, and deeper roots have access to more moisture, which allows the plants to go longer between waterings. Frequent shallow sprinklings are inefficient because they encourage shallow root growth, which leaves plants subject to stress from heat and drying winds.

How deep a given amount of water will penetrate depends on your soil. On the average, 1 inch of water applied at the surface wets sandy soil 12 inches deep, loam soil 7 inches deep, and clay only 4 to 5 inches deep. To check water penetration in your soil, dig a hole with a trowel after watering.

Water smallest plots by hand.

Use bubblers in shallow furrows to irrigate rows.

WATERING METHODS

hand watering Using a sprinkler nozzle on the end of a hose or a sprinkling can is useful for newly seeded beds, new transplants, and container plants because you can apply the water gently and put it exactly where it's needed. This method rinses away dust and discourages certain pests (especially spider mites). Sprinkling has some disadvantages as well. It wastes water through evaporation, particularly in windy weather. It may also encourage leaf diseases on some crops, especially in humid climates. The best time to hand-water is in the morning (leaves will dry off during the day) when the air is still.

flooding the soil Applying water in basins or furrows is an effective way to irrigate large plants. Basins—used to water trees, shrubby plants, and large vegetables—are doughnut-shaped depressions in the soil surrounding the plants; as the plants grow, you need to expand the basins. Furrows, or shallow ditches, dug near plants in rows work well on level ground. Broad, shallow furrows are generally better than deep, narrow ones: the wider the furrow, the wider the root area you can soak, since water moves primarily downward rather than sideways. Dig basins and furrows before you set out plants or sow seeds, to avoid damaging the roots.

soil soaker hoses These forerunners of drip irrigation systems are useful for slow, steady delivery of water. They are long tubes made of perforated or porous plastic or rubber with hose fittings at one end. When you attach a soaker to a hose and turn on the water supply, water seeps or sprinkles from the soaker along its entire length. Soakers are ideal for watering rows of vegetables; to water beds, snake the soaker back and forth around the plants. Trees can be watered with a soaker coiled around the outer edges of the root zone.

drip irrigation Drip systems deliver water slowly either by drip emitters that you attach to plastic tubing yourself or by emitter lines—tubes with factory-installed emitters spaced at regular intervals. Emitters operate at low pressure and deliver a low volume of water compared with standard sprinklers. They can be adjusted so that the water is applied only to soil directly over plant roots, much reducing the amount of water needed. Drip systems also cut down weed growth, because most of the soil surface is not moistened. By choosing specific kinds of tubing and emitters, you can tailor systems to water individual plants, beds of closely spaced plants, trees, or containers. Drip-irrigation kits and supplies are sold by agricultural supply stores, retail nurseries and garden supply centers, and mail-order suppliers.

Soaker hose (top); installing drip irrigation in a raised bed (middle); a drip system designed for pots (bottom)

Fertilizing

When plants are actively growing, they need a steady supply of nutrients. Though many of these nutrients are already present in soil, water, and air, you generally need to supply others, especially when raising vegetables. Having your soil tested (see page 262) is the best way to determine just which nutrients your garden needs. Your Cooperative Extension Office is another excellent source of information.

PLANT NUTRIENTS

The nutrients that plants need in fairly large quantities, called macronutrients, are nitrogen, phosphorus, and potassium. Be sure to follow package directions carefully, as too much of these nutrients can harm plants or pollute groundwater.

Nitrogen promotes green leafy growth. It is the nutrient most likely to be inadequate in garden soils. Signs of nitrogen deficiency are yellowing and dropping of older leaves and stunted growth. However, if plants get too much nitrogen, they grow so fast that they may become weak and spindly or produce more leaves and stems than flowers, fruits, or edible roots. Excess nitrogen may pollute surface water and groundwater as well.

Phosphorus promotes strong root growth, flowering, and fruiting. Dull green leaves with a purple tint, stunted growth, and reduced yield are signs of deficiency. Too much phosphorus is not likely to hurt your crops, but it is a serious pollutant of water sources.

Potassium regulates the synthesis of proteins and starches that make sturdy plants. It also increases resistance to diseases, heat, and cold. Symptoms of deficiency include reduced flowering and fruiting, spotted or curled older leaves, and weak stems and roots. Excess potassium can cause salt burn on leaf tips, turning them brown.

Plants also need secondary nutrients (calcium, magnesium, and sulfur) and micronutrients (zinc, manganese, iron, and others). Fortunately, most soils are not deficient in these nutrients.

FERTILIZER LABELS

At any nursery, you'll encounter a bewildering array of fertilizers in different forms and formulas. To decide which to buy, start by reading the label. Every fertilizer label states the percentage by weight that the product contains of the three macronutrients: nitrogen (N), phosphorus (P), and potassium (K), listed in that order: N-P-K. For example, a fertilizer labeled 10-3-1 contains

Sprinkle liquid fertilizer onto leaves and soil.

10 percent nitrogen, 3 percent phosphorus, and 1 percent potassium. This example is a complete fertilizer, because it contains all three macronutrients; it is also a high-nitrogen formula, since it contains relatively more nitrogen than phosphorus or potassium. Balanced fertilizers are formulated with equal amounts of each macronutrient, such as a 5-5-5 product; many brands of all-purpose fertilizer are balanced.

In contrast, fertilizers formulated with only one or two of the major nutrients are called incomplete. An incomplete fertilizer containing only nitrogen, for example, is useful when you want to give crops a supplemental feeding after planting.

NATURAL AND CHEMICAL FERTILIZERS

You can buy fertilizers in either natural (organic) or chemical (synthetic) form. Natural fertilizers are derived from the remains of living organisms and include blood meal, bonemeal, fish meal, cottonseed meal, and some animal manures, such as bat guano. Most contain lower levels of nutrients than chemical products do. They release their nutrients more slowly as well. Rather than dissolving in water, the fertilizers are broken down by microorganisms in the soil, providing nutrients gradually as they decay. Natural fertilizers are generally sold and applied in dry form; you scatter the fertilizer over the soil and then dig or scratch it in. A few (fish emulsion, for example) are available as concentrated liquids, which you dilute before applying.

Many natural fertilizers are high in just one of the three major nutrients. For example, blood meal and cottonseed meal are good sources of nitrogen, and bonemeal is high in phosphorus. Some manufacturers combine a variety of organic ingredients in pellet form to make a complete fertilizer.

Chemical fertilizers are manufactured from the chemical sources listed on the label. They may be sold as dry granules or as soluble crystals or concentrated liquids to be diluted in water before use. Because their nutrients are for the most part water-soluble, they act faster than organic fertilizers, but most do not last as long in the soil. Liquid fertilizers provide nutrients especially quickly. Apply the dry kinds as you would natural fertilizers, digging or scratching them into the soil. Some chemical fertilizers come in a controlled-release form, which acts over a relatively long period (three to nine months, depending on the brand) if the soil receives regular moisture.

WHEN AND HOW TO FERTILIZE

Broadcast a complete natural or chemical fertilizer over the soil when preparing a planting bed (see page 263), following package instructions for the amount to use. Work the fertilizer into the soil.

For many vegetables, the fertilizer dug into the soil at planting time will provide sustenance for the entire growing season. Perennial vegetables (such as asparagus), most berries, grapes, and most fruit trees fall in this category. But some long-season crops such as tomatoes and heavy feeders such as corn need supplemental boosts, particularly of nitrogen, during the growing season. (For details, check the individual plant listings on pages 17–238.) Follow-up feedings may also help plants that are growing poorly.

Measure controlled-release fertilizer carefully, then sprinkle evenly around plants.

Use a three-pronged cultivator to scratch fertilizer into the soil.

Organic Methods

Here are some tips to keep your garden healthy, productive, and relatively chemical-free.

pick the right site If you give plants the right amount of sunlight, good soil, and adequate air circulation, insect and disease problems will be few. Trouble most often appears when you try to grow plants in marginal conditions.

consider the soil To grow vegetables or strawberries, first dig about 4 inches of compost into the top foot of soil; compost is equally effective at improving sandy and heavy (clay) soil. To grow shrubs or trees, don't bother amending the soil unless it is very heavy or very light. Just dig a planting hole 12 to 24 inches deep in native soil, set out bare-root stock, water well, and mulch over it with organic matter.

choose disease-resistant plants All categories of plants are susceptible to problems, many of which are listed in this book's individual plant entries. When susceptibility to a specific disease is noted for a plant you want, shop for a resistant variety so you won't have to worry about treatment later.

apply natural fertilizers Fertilizer manufacturers have done a great job of standardizing, labeling, sanitizing, and packaging a wide range of natural fertilizers, from bat guano to cottonseed meal. They've devised fast- and slow-release formulations, liquid and pellet versions, and even included mycorrhizal supplements to enhance the soil food web and improve overall plant growth.

conserve water Mulch saves water by keeping the soil beneath it moister for longer. Drip irrigation cuts water use dramatically, reduces disease problems, and improves plant performance. And rain barrels and cisterns capture rainwater flowing through your house's downspouts for use as needed in the garden.

put beneficial creatures to work Insectaries sell everything from lady beetles and trichogramma wasps to praying mantids, lacewings, predatory mites, and parasitic nematodes. All eat garden pests. But you can also increase the number of natural beneficials in your garden by planting lots of flowers and avoiding the use of broad-spectrum pesticides.

encourage pollinators Hit by major outbreaks of tracheal mites, varroa mites, and colony collapse disorder, North American honeybee populations have plummeted.

Choose the right plants for your site.

You can make your garden more bee-friendly by avoiding the use of broad-spectrum pesticides and by keeping flowers blooming in the garden over as much of the year as possible. To service early-flowering fruit trees and other plants that may need pollination when it is still too cold for honeybees to be active, install mason bee nests in the garden (nurseries and mail-order garden supply companies sell them).

use mechanical pest controls where possible Row covers exclude insects and birds from vulnerable plants. Sticky barriers keep ants out of trees (ants tend and defend aphids), and some sticky traps use pheromones that lure target insects only. Copper barriers can keep slugs and snails at bay. There are even quick-burst sprinklers triggered by motion sensors to frighten deer away.

Invite bees.

Raise chickens.

consider integrated pest management This strategy starts with prevention, using disease-resistant varieties, optimal cultural practices, and pest monitoring. If pests start doing significant damage, integrated pest management (IPM) encourages use of the most targeted, least environmentally destructive control measure available. That might be a mechanical or biological control, but it might also be a hard chemical control. While IPM is environmentally responsible, it isn't strictly organic.

raise chickens Most cities allow you to raise at least a few chickens (but often not roosters). They're great eaters of bugs and vegetable scraps, producers of eggs, and suppliers of high-quality manure. And besides all that, they're fun to raise!

save seed If you raise nonhybrid (open-pollinated) vegetables, you can save seeds from the strongest plants for replanting the following year. Just harvest and dry the seeds and store them in a cool, dark, dry, insect-free place until planting time the next year. Over time, you'll develop varieties perfectly suited to your own garden.

pull or hoe weeds before they set seed Do your hoeing on a clear, dry morning; midday sun will desiccate the remains of tiny weeds by nightfall. Pull bigger weeds the day after a soaking rain; taproots slip easily out of moist soil.

Pests and Diseases

Although few gardens escape pests and diseases entirely, the advice and photos in this section can help you prevent the most common problems and, if troubles do occur, assist you in identifying causes and solutions. Pests and diseases that harm only one or two crops are covered in the individual plant listings.

PREVENTION

Preventing trouble is the most important step in managing pests and diseases: you won't have to solve problems that don't get a chance to start in the first place. Keep your plants healthy and stress-free. Set them out at the recommended planting time in well-prepared soil, and give them the care they need throughout the year. Whenever possible, select plants resistant to specific pests or diseases. A number of insects and diseases overwinter or spend part of their life cycle on plant debris. Pulling up, shredding, and composting spent plants, and tilling the soil, especially in fall, gets rid of winter hiding places. Don't put diseased or insect-infested plants in the compost pile; discard or burn them.

Mix different kinds of plants in your garden. Expanses of just one sort can draw large populations of pests fond of that particular plant. Mixed plantings of several vegetables, other edibles, and flowers not only discourage large numbers of a single pest but also favor beneficial insects.

MANAGEMENT

Check the plants in your garden frequently. A few aphids or chewed leaves are not cause for alarm, and problems often disappear quickly on their own as pests die out naturally, move on, or are controlled by beneficial insects. However, if you are aware that specific problems may be developing, you can keep an eye on the situation and take action if necessary. Following are several methods of pest and disease management.

physical controls The larger pests—such as snails, slugs, grasshoppers, and some beetles and caterpillars—are candidates for removal by hand. Removing infected leaves or even entire branches helps control some pests and diseases. Aim a strong jet of water at plants to dislodge pests such as aphids and mites. Barriers such as floating row covers (see page 276) exclude many insects, while netting can deter hungry birds.

biological controls Living organisms such as beneficial insects (discussed on the opposite page) and certain microorganisms are classified as biological controls. The best-known microorganism is *Bacillus thuringiensis (Bt),* a bacterium that, once ingested by caterpillars or their larvae, causes them to stop feeding and die. Different strains have been identified, each effective against the larvae of specific pests.

natural pesticides These are derived from naturally occurring organisms or other materials and create minimal environmental hazards. A well-known example is insecticidal soap, which combats various pests. Neem oil or extract, derived from a tropical tree, controls many insects, mites, and some diseases. Products containing pyrethrins are lethal to a number of pests; the active ingredient is derived from compounds found in a dried flower. Horticultural oils are highly refined petroleum or vegetable oils that smother pests, pest eggs, and disease spores. Sulfur is used in controlling diseases and mites.

Despite their relatively low toxicity, these natural pesticides can kill beneficial and harmless insects. Use them only on plants that are being attacked and only when pests are present, and follow the label directions exactly. The suggestions for managing pests and diseases listed in the charts that follow do not include recommendations for chemicals that are more toxic, since registration and availability of these products change frequently. If you believe you need stronger controls, consult your Cooperative Extension Office.

crop rotation Because members of the same plant family are often susceptible to the same pests and diseases, planting them in different locations in your garden from one year to the next will help prevent a buildup of pests and disease organisms. Try to plan a rotation that allows at least two years between same or related crops. If serious diseases strike, a longer interval will be necessary. Here are some representative plant families:

cabbage (cole or mustard) family: broccoli, brussels sprouts, cabbage, cauliflower, kale, mustards, radishes, turnips

carrot family: carrots, cilantro, dill, fennel, parsley

gourd family: cucumbers, melons, pumpkins, squash

grass family: corn and some cover crops

lily family: garlic, leeks, onions, shallots

nightshade family: eggplant, peppers, potatoes, tomatoes

pea (legume) family: beans, peas, and some cover crops

Assassin bug

Damsel bug

Lacewing

Beneficial Insects

Hundreds of species of beneficial insects help gardeners keep pests at bay. Those described here and many others are likely to be present naturally in your garden; some (as noted) can be purchased from nurseries or mail-order firms. To encourage flying beneficials, grow flowering plants that provide the nectar and pollen they need at certain times in their life cycles. Good choices include yarrow, feverfew, coreopsis, cosmos, and sweet alyssum, as well as the herbs cilantro and fennel, among others. In addition to these insects, you can buy beneficial parasitic nematodes. These microscopic worms destroy pests such as maggots and cutworms.

Assassin bugs Slim $^1/_2$- to $^3/_4$-inch-long insects; may be red, black, brown, or gray. They feed on a wide variety of pests.

Damsel bugs Dull gray or brown, $^1/_2$-inch-long, very slender insects with long, narrow heads. Nymphs resemble the adults but are smaller and have no wings. Both nymphs and adults feed on aphids, leafhoppers, and small worms.

Ground beetles Shiny black, $^1/_2$- to 1-inch-long insects. The smaller species eat other insects, caterpillars, cutworms, and grubs; some larger species prey on slugs and snails and their eggs.

Lacewings The adults are 1-inch-long flying insects that feed only on nectar, pollen, and honeydew; but the larvae, which resemble $^1/_2$-inch-long alligators, devour aphids, leafhoppers, thrips, and other insects, as well as mites. The larvae are commercially available.

Lady beetles Also known as ladybugs. These beetles and their larvae (which look like $^1/_4$-inch-long alligators) feed on aphids, mealybugs, and the eggs of many insects. You can buy lady beetles, but they often fly away as soon as you release them. Freeing them at night or keeping them in cages for a few days may encourage them to remain in your garden.

Trichogramma wasps These very tiny parasitoid wasps attack the eggs of caterpillar pests. Commercially available species are adapted for gardens or for fruit trees. Because they are short-lived, repeated releases may be needed.

Lady beetle

common pests

Pest	Management
APHIDS	
Soft-bodied, rounded insects that range from pin- to match-head size. May be black, white, pink, or pale green. They cluster on new growth, sucking plant juices. Some kinds transmit viral diseases.	Use floating row covers. Release lacewings and lady beetles. Hose off aphids with a strong blast of water. Spray with insecticidal soap or a product containing pyrethrins.
APPLE MAGGOTS	
Larvae of a type of fruit fly. Flies are smaller than houseflies, with banded or spotted markings on their wings. Flies lay eggs inside apples and crabapples, and larvae destroy crops from within.	Place spherical, red sticky traps baited with fruit-flavored or pheromonic lures in the branches of fruit trees. Remove dropped fruit immediately to prevent larvae from entering the soil to pupate.
CABBAGE LOOPERS	
Greenish caterpillars, also called inch-worms, that feed on cabbages and related crops.	Use floating row covers. Handpick adults and small white egg clusters. Release tricho-gramma wasps, which attack the eggs. Spray with *Bacillus thuringiensis (Bt)* or a product containing pyrethrins.
CABBAGE ROOT MAGGOTS	
Small, white fly larvae with pointed heads. They destroy the root systems of cabbage-family crops; plants are stunted and may wilt. Similar maggots attack onions and corn seedlings.	Cover seedbeds or transplants with floating row covers. Place a tar-paper disc around the base of each plant to prevent flies from laying eggs. Remove and destroy infected plants. Release parasitic nematodes.
CABBAGEWORMS	
Greenish caterpillars, the larval form of white cabbage butterflies. They eat the leaves of cabbage-family plants.	Handpick adults and eggs, which are yellow to orange, on leaves. Use floating row covers. Release trichogramma wasps, which attack the eggs. Spray with *Bacillus thuringiensis (Bt)* or a product containing pyrethrins.
CODLING MOTHS	
Moth larvae under 1 in. long with a pink or whitish body and dark brown head. The usual culprits found inside spoiled apples, crabapples, pears, and quinces; they may also attack plums and walnuts.	Clean up fallen leaves and dropped fruit. In spring, set out sticky traps with pheromone bait. Wrap trunks with sticky barriers. *Bacillus thuringiensis (Bt)* is effective if sprayed directly on larvae before they enter fruit.
COLORADO POTATO BEETLES	
Yellow-and-black-striped beetles and their reddish larvae. Both eat the leaves of potatoes, tomatoes, and eggplant.	Handpick. Discard infested plants. Spray with *Bacillus thuringiensis tenebrionis,* the form of *Bt* that targets this pest, or with neem or a product containing pyrethrins.

	Pest	Management
	CUCUMBER BEETLES	
	Oval-shaped, greenish yellow beetles with black spots or stripes. They eat all parts of cucumbers, squash, and melons. The beetles also transmit bacterial wilt, which attacks cucumbers, and other diseases.	Use floating row covers. Remove infested plants; clean the garden in fall to prevent the beetles from overwintering. Release parasitic nematodes. Spray with a product containing pyrethrins.
	CUTWORMS	
	Dull brownish caterpillars that live in the soil and cut off stems of seedlings at ground level. Some kinds climb into plants and eat leaves.	Clear and till beds to destroy cutworms. Use protective collars around stems of young seedlings. Handpick at night when the cutworms are active. Release parasitic nematodes.
	FLEA BEETLES	
	Very small, shiny, oval beetles that jump like fleas. May be blue-black, brown, or bronze. Adults chew holes in leaves of seedlings, often killing them. Vigorous older plants usually survive.	Remove dead or damaged leaves and plants. Till the soil in fall. Use floating row covers. Spray with neem.
	GRASSHOPPERS	
	Also called locusts. Adults are 1–2 in. long and may be brown, green, or yellow. During their periodic outbreaks, they can cause severe damage, defoliating most plants.	Cultivate the soil in fall, winter, and early spring to destroy egg clusters. Use floating row covers. Try the biological control *Nosema locustae*, which targets only grasshoppers; it works best when used in large areas.
	HARLEQUIN BUGS	
	Black adults with distinctive red markings. They and the wingless immature nymphs suck plant juices from the leaves of cabbage-family plants.	Handpick and destroy the bugs and egg masses, which resemble rows of barrels on leaf surfaces. Use floating row covers. Discard infected plants. Spray with insecticidal soap.
	LEAFHOPPERS	
	Many species of small green, yellow, brown, or mottled insects that run sideways, hop, or fly. They damage the foliage of many plants and the fruits of apples and grapes. Some transmit plant diseases.	Use floating row covers. Release lacewings and lady beetles. Spray with neem.
	LEAF MINERS	
	A catchall term for certain moth, beetle, and fly larvae that tunnel within plant leaves, leaving a nearly transparent trail on the surface. They damage leafy crops such as chard and spinach.	Plant under floating row covers. Spray with neem to discourage adults from laying eggs; once the larvae are inside the leaves, sprays are not effective. Remove infested leaves.

Continued on page 290 ▶

	Pest	Management
	MITES Tiny spider relatives found on leaf undersides. Webbing is often present where they live. Mites suck plant juices; the damaged leaf surface is pale and stippled, and the leaves often turn brown, dry out, and die.	Hose off plants with strong jets of water. Release predatory mites, which feed on the harmful mites; lacewings are also effective. Spray with insecticidal soap, neem, or sulfur.
	NEMATODES Microscopic worms that live in soil and feed chiefly on roots of plants. Some kinds cause plants to form root galls. All cause plants to be weaker and less productive.	Use soil solarization (see page 294) to reduce the population. Plant resistant varieties. Practice crop rotation. Remove and destroy infected plants. Dig in organic matter, which encourages a beneficial fungus.
	SNAILS AND SLUGS Night-feeding mollusks. Snails have shells; slugs do not. Both feast on the seedlings and leaves of many vegetables.	Handpick and destroy. Set out shallow containers filled with beer to drown the pests. Enclose potted plants and raised beds with copper strips. Use bait containing nontoxic iron phosphate.
	SQUASH BUGS Dark brown or black adults and smaller, pale green nymphs. Both suck plant juices on the vines and fruit of squash and pumpkins. The stems wilt and blacken, and the fruits are disfigured.	Handpick adults, nymphs, and reddish brown eggs. Use floating row covers. Spray undersides of leaves with insecticidal soap.
	THRIPS Near-microscopic insects that feed by rasping soft leaf tissue. Look for small black droppings on the undersides of leaves. Leaf surfaces take on a shiny, silvery, or tan cast.	Hose off plants with strong jets of water. Trap thrips with yellow sticky traps. Release lacewings. Spray with insecticidal soap or neem.
	WHITEFLIES Tiny white pests that fly up in a cloud when disturbed. The larvae and adults suck plant juices from leaf undersides. Foliage may show yellow stippling, curl, and turn brown.	Trap with yellow sticky cards or traps. For greenhouse infestations, release *Encarsia formosa*, a predatory wasp. Spray leaves with strong jets of water, insecticidal soap, or neem.
	WIREWORMS Shiny, reddish brown larvae of click beetles. May damage root crops (especially carrots and potatoes). Often found in soil where a lawn or pasture grew.	Till the soil deeply before planting root crops. Rotate crops. Trap pests by placing mature carrots in the soil; pull them up after a few days, destroy the wireworms, and repeat.

Deer

Rabbit

Raccoon

Squirrel

Animal Pests

Some of the worst troublemakers are described here, with suggestions for control. Dogs can be effective guards against deer and rabbits, but not raccoons, which often fight them (and win).

Birds The best way to deal with birds that eat seeds, seedlings, transplants, berries, and fruits is to keep them at bay. Protect plants with floating row covers or bird netting (see pages 276–277).

Deer Hungry deer can eat most of a harvest in just a few hours. An 8-foot-tall fence is optimal, but a 6-foot fence may suffice if the ground slopes downhill outside the fence. Because deer cannot high-jump and broad-jump at the same time, a horizontal "outrigger" extension on the top of a fence makes it harder for deer to clear. Parallel 5-foot-tall fences 4 feet apart have the same effect. Electric fencing also works, as do motion-activated sprinklers and commercial deer repellents (but keep the latter off crops unless the label says otherwise).

Gophers and moles Gophers feed on roots, bulbs, and occasionally foliage. They leave mounds of soil, usually with visible entry holes. To protect individual plants, line the sides and bottom of planting holes with $1/2$-inch mesh hardware cloth, or plant in raised beds whose bottoms are lined with hardware cloth (see page 252). Moles eat earthworms and grubs, not plants, but they often tunnel just below the surface, uprooting or damaging young plants. Their mounds have no visible entry holes. Trap if necessary, or bait with commercial repellent worms.

Rabbits These opportunists sneak into gardens to eat young seedlings and tender shoots, as well as many vegetables. Stop them with a wire-mesh fence (see page 277).

Raccoons These bandits are most active at night and have a special taste for corn, melons, and berries. Wire-mesh fencing or single-strand electrical fences will exclude them.

Squirrels Tree squirrels feed on fruits, nuts, vegetables, tender shoots, and bark. Cover berry vines, ripening fruits, and tomato plants with bird netting. Protect low-growing container crops with wire baskets turned upside down.

common diseases

	Disease	Management
	ANTHRACNOSE	
	A fungal disease that affects many edible plants but seldom kills them. Sunken gray or tan to dark brown spots appear on leaves, stems, or fruit. Leaves wither and drop.	Plant resistant varieties. Clip off and destroy affected plant parts. Avoid overhead watering and provide good air circulation around plants.
	CLUBROOT	
	A fungal disease that causes the roots of many cabbage-family plants to become swollen and twisted. Plant growth is stunted; on hot days, plants wilt. Eventually roots rot. Most common in acid soils.	Add lime to raise the soil pH to at least 7.2. If clubroot is present in the soil, do not plant cabbage-family plants in that spot for 7 years. Dig up and discard infected plants. Clean tools. Solarize soil (see page 294).
	DAMPING OFF	
	Various soil fungi that cause seeds to rot in the soil before they sprout or cause young seedlings to collapse at or near the soil surface. Most common in poorly drained or too-wet soils.	Improve drainage and reduce watering. Do not plant seeds of warm-season crops when the soil is still cold. When starting seeds indoors, disinfect containers and use sterile potting soil. Thin crowded seedlings.
	DOWNY MILDEW	
	A fungal disease that occurs during cool, rainy, or foggy weather. In most plants, a downy substance appears on the undersides of leaves; yellow to brown spots appear on both upper and lower surfaces.	Plant resistant varieties. Water in the morning and allow plants to dry. Discard diseased plants. Rotate crops. Spray with neem to help prevent infection.
	EARLY BLIGHT	
	A fungal disease that causes small dark spots on leaves of eggplant, potatoes, and tomatoes. Eventually leaves turn yellow and die. Tomato fruits develop dark, leathery spots near the stem.	Plant certified disease-free seed potatoes and resistant varieties of other crops. Rotate crops. Avoid overhead watering. Keep plants well fertilized and vigorously growing to resist infection. Destroy debris after harvest.
	FIREBLIGHT	
	This bacterial disease attacks apple, pear, quince, and others. Shoots blacken, appear scorched, and die suddenly. Occurs in moist weather, especially early spring. Spread by insects and splashing water.	Plant resistant varieties. Remove and discard diseased branches, cutting 6–8 in. below blighted tissue. Spray at 3- to 5-day intervals during the bloom season with Serenade or copper compounds.
	FUSARIUM WILT	
	A fungal disease that invades the water-conduction tissues of a number of vegetables, causing plants to wilt and the lower leaves or whole plant to turn yellow and die. Can live in the soil for years.	Plant resistant varieties. Fertilize and water to promote vigorous growth. Rotate crops. Discard infected plants. Try soil solarization (see page 294) to help control the fungus.

	Disease	Management
	LATE BLIGHT	
	A fungal disease that affects potatoes and tomatoes. Small, dark, water-soaked spots on leaves and stems expand rapidly in cool, moist conditions. Tomato fruits are malformed; potatoes rot in storage.	Choose resistant varieties. Avoid overhead irrigation. Rotate crops. Discard infected plants and any plant debris after you harvest.
	OAK ROOT FUNGUS	
	A fungal disease that destroys fruit and nut trees, raspberry, grape, and strawberry. Look for patches of dull or yellowed leaves, white fungal tissue or dark strings under the bark, or tan mushrooms around the plant base.	Plant resistant species. Excavate soil from the plant's base so it can dry. Remove turf grass or other plants growing within 6–8 ft. of the trunk. Water sparingly. Replace infected plants. There are no effective chemical controls.
	POWDERY MILDEW	
	A fungus that causes a powdery white coating on leaves, stems, buds, and fruits. Shade, humidity, and poor air circulation are contributing factors, but unlike downy mildew, it needs dry leaves to become established.	Thin crowded plants to improve air circulation. Plant in a sunny area. Spray with water to wash off fungus. Discard infected plants. Spray with sulfur, copper soap fungicide, or neem.
	RUST	
	Various fungal diseases, many plant-specific, that cause powdery pustules to appear on undersides of leaves. Upper surfaces may be spotted with yellow or orange; eventually the entire leaf may discolor, then drop.	Plant resistant varieties. Remove infected leaves or dig up badly infected plants. Provide good air circulation. In winter, clean up all debris. Avoid overhead watering. Spray with a garlic-based or copper soap fungicide.
	VERTICILLIUM WILT	
	A long-lived soilborne fungus that affects many vegetables, cane berries, and some fruit trees. On trees, scattered branches may die. Vegetable plants wilt; the leaves turn yellow then brown, and eventually die.	Plant resistant varieties. Rotate crops. Prune out and discard infected growth on trees; discard infected plants. Try soil solarization (see next page) to help control the fungus.

Weeds

Weeds are plants growing where gardeners don't want them to grow. Weeds rob your other plants of water, nutrients, and sunlight. Some harbor insects and diseases. Most are unattractive, and a weedy garden is uninviting. Despite their undesirable qualities, weeds do have a few redeeming features. An assemblage of weeds can help prevent erosion. Some kinds of weeds provide nectar and shelter for beneficial insects and butterflies. When they die and decompose, weeds add organic matter to the soil. However, these few positive aspects of weeds do not justify leaving very many of them in the garden. Learning to manage weeds, whether by removing them or preventing their growth in the first place, is an on-going part of successful gardening.

CONTROL METHODS

Identifying the weeds in your garden is the first step in successful management. Weeds are often classified by the length of their life cycle. Annual weeds grow shoots and leaves, flower, set seed, and die within less than a year. They reproduce by seed, and even a few plants can produce lots of seeds. Almost all perennial weeds, which live for several years, also reproduce by seed. Once they mature, however, most produce spreading roots, rhizomes, or tubers as well, making control more difficult. Various control methods are described below.

You can compost annual weeds if they don't have flowers or seeds that might survive the composting process. The top growth of perennial weeds that have not yet seeded can also be composted. But the roots of perennials (dandelions and quack grass, for example) and any weeds that have set seed should be tossed in the trash.

hand pulling or hoeing For established gardens, this is your first line of defense against most weeds. If you're diligent for several consecutive years about pulling or hoeing out annual weeds early in the season, before they set seed, their numbers will decline significantly. These methods also help control perennial weeds, as long as you catch the plants while they're young. Once perennials have matured, you usually have to dig out their roots to clear them. If you just pull off the tops, they'll resprout from bits of roots left in the soil.

herbicides If you're planning to convert a neglected spot into an edible garden, you'll need to clear the area of weeds. Herbicides can be useful, if chosen and used carefully. Most gardeners elect not to apply synthetic herbicides in food gardens; however, a couple of natural products can be used. Herbicidal soap is made from selected fatty acids. It kills the top growth of young, actively growing annual weeds less than 5 inches tall. Undiluted white household vinegar (5 percent acetic acid) also kills weeds if applied during their first two weeks of life. Spray herbicidal soap or vinegar when the air is still, taking care not to spray desirable plants.

rotary tilling When preparing new gardens or working in large gardens with plenty of space between the rows, rotary tilling can also be an effective weed control (at least for a while). Weeds that are totally plowed under will decay, but perennials usually sprout again from roots.

presprouting This is another useful technique for preparing planting areas for vegetables. Add needed soil amendments and till or dig them into the soil. Water the bed, and wait a week or two for weed seeds to germinate. When they're only a few inches high, scrape weeds away with a hoe. Then sow or transplant your vegetables, disturbing the soil as little as possible to avoid bringing more seeds to the surface.

soil solarization Another option is soil solarization, a process that eliminates many kinds of weed seeds and harmful organisms by trapping the sun's heat under clear plastic sheeting. It is done in summer and works best in regions that have hot, sunny weather for four to eight weeks straight; daytime temperatures above 80°F/27°C are ideal. Plan to solarize beds you will use for late summer and fall vegetable crops.

Follow these steps: Cultivate the soil, clearing it of weeds, debris, and large clods of earth. Make a bed at least 2½ feet wide (narrower beds may not build up enough heat to have much effect). Carve a small ditch around the perimeter and rake the bed level. Soak the soil to a depth of 1 foot. Cover the soil with 1- to 4-mil clear plastic; use UV-resistant plastic if it's available, since it won't break down during solarization. Stretch the plastic tightly so that it is in contact with the soil. Bury the edges in the perimeter ditch. An optional second layer of plastic increases the heat and makes solarization more effective; use empty soda cans laid on their sides as spacers between the two sheets. Leave the plastic in place for four to eight weeks (the maximum for really persistent weeds). Leaving it longer than eight weeks may harm the soil structure. Remove the plastic, and plant. After planting, avoid cultivating deeper than 2 inches, as weed seeds at lower levels may still be viable.

common garden weeds

Weed	Management
BERMUDA GRASS (*Cynodon dactylon*)	
A fine-textured, fast-growing perennial frequently planted as a lawn in warm climates. It spreads rapidly by underground stems, aboveground runners, and sometimes seed.	Use 8-in.-deep barriers to keep lawn in bounds. Dig up clumps in garden beds before they form sod, making sure to remove all the underground stems; any left behind can start new shoots.
BINDWEED (*Convolvulus arvensis*)	
Also called wild morning glory or field bindweed. This perennial forms 1- to 4-ft.-long stems that crawl over the ground and twine over and around other plants. The trumpet-shaped flowers are white to pink.	Forms a deep, extensive root system, so hand-pulling seldom controls it—the stems break off, but the weed returns from the root. To kill it, cultivate or hoe every 6 weeks throughout the growing season.
CHICKWEED (*Stellaria media*)	
This annual weed favors cool weather and appears in very early spring. It is a low-growing plant with smooth pointed leaves ¼–1 in. long, bright green on the upper surface and paler on the underside.	Chickweed is easy to pull when the plants are young. A thick layer of mulch will prevent germination of seeds. Solarization kills seeds.
CRABGRASS (*Digitaria* species)	
A shallow-rooted annual weed that grows in spring and summer, thriving in hot, moist areas. As the plant grows, it branches out at the base; stems can root where they touch the soil.	Crabgrass is most likely to be a problem in areas that receive frequent surface watering; infrequent deep watering of established vegetables, berries, and fruit trees can dry out the roots, killing or weakening the weed.
DANDELION (*Taraxacum officinale*)	
Low-growing perennial with dark green, lobed leaves, a deep taproot, and bright yellow flowers. It reproduces both by seed and by any root fragment left in the soil.	Pull young plants before they flower, or take out the entire taproot of older plants to prevent regrowth.
LAMB'S QUARTERS (*Chenopodium album*)	
Also called fat hen. This annual weed grows in spring and summer, producing triangular leaves with wavy edges. A white, mealy powder coats the leaves. The plants grow 1–6 ft. tall. Seeds are extremely long-lived.	Lamb's quarters is fairly easy to pull, especially when young. Remove the plants from the garden before they set seed. A thick layer of mulch around edibles prevents seeds already in the soil from germinating.
MALLOW (*Malva* species)	
An annual in some climates, a biennial in others, sprouting in fall and setting seed the following summer. The plants grow quickly, ranging in height from a few inches to 4 feet tall.	Plants are easiest to pull when young; older plants develop a deep taproot.

Continued on page 296 ▶

	Weed	Management
	OXALIS (*Oxalis corniculata*) An aggressive perennial that spreads quickly by seed. Small yellow flowers develop into long seed capsules that can propel seed as far as 6 ft. Cape oxalis (*O. pes-caprae*) is a larger relative that forms persistent bulbs.	Dig out small plants before—or as soon as—they flower. To manage cape oxalis, dig the whole plant in late winter, sifting through the soil to remove as many of the small bulbs as possible. Soil solarization may also help.
	PURSLANE (*Portulaca oleracea*) A low-growing annual weed with fleshy stems and leaves and small yellow flowers. It thrives in moist conditions but can survive considerable drought. The seeds germinate in late spring.	Though purslane is easy to pull or hoe, pieces of stem reroot readily, so be sure to remove them from the garden.
	QUACK GRASS (*Elytrigia repens*) This perennial weed can reach 3 ft. tall and produces an extensive underground network of long, slender, branching, yellowish white rhizomes that can spread laterally 3 to 5 ft.	Because it reproduces readily from even small pieces of rhizome left in the soil, quack grass is difficult to eliminate. Before planting, thoroughly dig the area and remove all visible pieces of rhizome.
	SOWTHISTLE (*Sonchus* species) An annual weed that grows 1–4 ft. tall in summer. Has a stout taproot and a hollow stem. Milky sap oozes out when a leaf or stem is broken. The yellow flowers look like those of dandelions.	Pull out the plants before they flower and set seed.
	SPOTTED SPURGE (*Chamaesyce maculata*) Also listed as *Euphorbia maculata*. This aggressive annual produces many seeds that may germinate immediately, producing several generations in one summer. Cut or broken stems exude a milky juice.	Hoe or pull out plants early in the season, before they bloom and set seed. Mulch to prevent seeds already in the soil from germinating. Spot-treat with herbicidal soap when plants are young.
	YELLOW NUTSEDGE (*Cyperus esculentus*) This perennial weed resembles a grass, but its stems are solid and triangular in cross section. Spreads by small, roundish tubers (nutlets) at the tips of its roots as well as by seed.	Remove plants when they are still small. Older plants are mature enough to produce tubers that remain in the soil to sprout when you dig or pull the weed.

Enjoy the fruits of your labor.

Glossary

Annual A plant that completes its life cycle (sprouting from seed, maturing, and producing seeds) in one growing season.

Balled-and-burlapped (B-and-B) A term for a nursery plant whose root ball is wrapped in burlap or synthetic fabric.

Bare-root A term for a plant sold with the soil removed from its roots.

Biennial A plant that develops roots and foliage in its first year, then blooms, seeds, and dies during its second year.

Blanching The process of blocking light from a plant to keep it from turning green; it also results in increased tenderness, reduced bitterness, or both.

Bolt To go to seed prematurely.

Bud union (or graft line) The point at which a woody plant's rootstock joins the variety budded or grafted onto it; it is often swollen and usually just inches aboveground.

Bulb A true bulb (an onion, for example) consists of an underground stem base that contains an embryonic plant surrounded by scales (modified leaves that overlap one another).

Cane An elongated fruiting stem (as on a blackberry or grape), usually arising directly from the roots.

Chilling hours The number of cool-season hours when the air temperature is between 32° and 45°F/0° and 7°C.

Compost A rich organic soil amendment made from decayed organic matter—usually vegetation and/or manure.

Crown The point at which a plant's roots join its stem (top structure), at or near the soil line. It can also refer to a tree's entire branch structure, including foliage.

Deciduous A term for any plant that loses all its leaves each year at the end of the growing season.

Espalier A method for training branches to grow flat against a vertical surface.

Evergreen A term for any plant that keeps its leaves longer than one growing season, remaining green year-round.

Family A group of plants whose shared characteristics set them apart from plants in other families. Plants from the same family often have similar growing requirements and pest problems.

Genus (plural: genera) A subdivision of family referring to a group of plant species that have many characteristics in common and probably evolved from the same ancestor. The first word in a plant's botanical name is the genus name.

Grafting The process of splicing the top growth of one plant onto the rootstock of another.

Habit A plant's growth pattern; for example, weeping, columnar, upright, spreading, or trailing.

Hardening off Exposing a plant that has been growing indoors to increasing periods of time outside, easing it through the transition into the garden's chilly nights and direct sunlight.

Hardiness A plant's ability to tolerate cold temperatures. It does not mean tough, pest-resistant, or disease-resistant.

Hybrid A plant whose parents are from two different species, subspecies, varieties, strains, or any combination thereof. Hybrid names are written with the symbol ×, as in *Musa × paradisiaca*.

Leader The central upward-growing stem of a single-trunked tree or shrub.

Loam A desirable soil that consists of sand, silt, clay, and organic matter.

Mulch Plastic, gravel, or organic matter layered over garden soil to minimize weed growth and evaporative water loss.

Perennial A nonwoody plant that lives for more than two years.

pH A measure of soil acidity or alkalinity on a scale from 0 (very acid) to 14 (very alkaline). Pure water has a pH of 7 (neutral). Most plants grow best when soil pH is between 5.5 and 7.5.

Pollenizer A plant whose pollen fertilizes the flowers of another plant.

Pollinator An insect, bird, or animal that transfers pollen from one part of a flower to another or from flowers on one plant to flowers on another.

Rootstock (understock) The part of a budded or grafted plant that furnishes the root system.

Root zone The soil area inhabited by a plant's roots, usually concentrated in the top 18 inches of soil and spreading at least as wide as the plant's canopy.

Row cover A translucent, lightweight fabric placed over plants to protect them from insects, birds, and frost while letting in light, air, and water.

Self-fruitful A term for a plant that successfully pollinates itself.

Species A subdivision of genus referring to groups of closely related plants with only minor differences. The second word in a plant's botanical name is its species name.

Spur A short, spikelike twig on grapevines and fruit trees (particularly apples and cherries) that bears the plant's fruit.

Sucker A vigorous shoot emerging from below the bud union on a grafted or budded plant, or any vertical shoot (water sprout) that grows from the trunk or horizontal branches.

Taproot A thick, deep-growing, central root that is sometimes edible. Carrots are edible taproots.

Tender A term for plants intolerant of cold temperatures.

Tuber A swollen underground stem with multiple growth points. Potatoes are tubers.

Variety A natural or cultivated variant of a species. Names of natural variants are written in italics as the third word in a plant's botanical name. Cultivated varieties (cultivars) may be of hybrid origin or selected varieties of plants that occur in the wild. Cultivar names are enclosed in single quotation marks.

Index

Photography Credits

AGStockUSA/Alamy: 171; courtesy of Ames True Temper: 263-1, 263-2, 263-3, 263-4; Jan Baldwin/Photolibrary: 23; Bill Barksdale/AGStockUSA: 222; Bill Beatty/Visuals Unlimited: 289-1; Anthony Blake/Photolibrary: 37; Marcus Botzek/Corbis: 287-3; Michael Boys/Corbis: 110; Marion Brenner: back cover right, 7 bottom, 209, 248 bottom right, 254 left, 255 bottom, 261 bottom; Rob D. Brodman: 4, 17, 27, 40, 55, 56 right, 59 both, 63 top right, 63 bottom right, 69, 70 top right, 71, 72, 76, 91, 94 top right, 101 top left, 108, 117, 122, 148, 153, 154, 244 bottom right, 253 bottom, 259, 261 top, 265 all, 267 bottom, 273, 280 both, 282, 283 both; Kimberley Burch: 18, 25 top right, 45, 75 top left, 85 top right, 94 top left, 101 bottom left, 107, 123, 155 left, 165, 175, 246 top right, 251, 285 left, 288-1; Burke/Triolo Productions/Getty Images: 127; Rob Cardillo: 43; James Carrier: 98 right; Christi Carter/Photolibrary: 52; Nigel Cattlin/Alamy: 220, 288-4, 292-3, 292-7, 293-2; Nigel Cattlin/Visuals Unlimited: 288-6, 293-5; David Cavagnaro: front cover middle, 61, 83 right, 137, 146, 147, 174, 295-5, 295-6, 295-7, 296-2; Jennifer Cheung: back cover middle, 8 bottom, 129, 250 left, 255 top left, 255 top right; Jack Coyier: 260; Grey Crawford: 80; Rosalind Creasy: 149 top; R. Creation/Getty Images: 215; Robin Bachtler Cushman: 25 bottom right, 68, 70 top left, 70 bottom right, 75 bottom left, 85 bottom right, 88, 145, 197, 211, 217, 281 top; Darcy Daniels: 6, 7 top, 8 top, 9; Francois De Heel/Photolibrary: 109; Frederic Didillon/Mise au Point: 29, 36; Wally Eberhart/Visuals Unlimited: 295-4; Food-Collection/Photolibrary: 106; Fresh Food Images/Photolibrary: 48; David Goldberg: 295-1; David Goldberg/Susan A. Roth & Co.: 296-3; David T. Gomez/©iStockPhoto.com: 49; Thayer Allison Gowdy: 112 top; Alexandra Grablewski/Getty Images: 152; John Granen: 244 top right; Steven A. Gunther: 143, 224, 250 top right; Jerry Harpur: 254 bottom right; Marcus Harpur: 53; Jim Henkens: 25 top left, 26, 73 top, 94 bottom left, 99, 112 bottom, 120, 248 top right, 285 right; Saxon Holt: front cover left, 101 bottom right, 179, 201, 281 middle; D. A. Horchner/Design Workshop: 253 top; ©iStockPhoto.com: 170; Jon Jensen: 134 right; Andrea Jones/Garden Exposures Photo Library: 1, 57, 70 bottom left, 75 top right, 81, 85 bottom left, 86, 125, 149 bottom, 187 bottom, 275, 276 left; Lynn Keddie/Photolibrary: 274; Susanne Kischnick/Alamy: 237; courtesy of S. T. Kolke/The American Phytopathological Society: 293-4; Ernst Kucklich: 111, 121; Holly Lepere: 51, 242 bottom, 248 left, 249; Chris Leschinsky: 62, 188, 189; Janet Loughrey: 187 top, 247 top, 272; Allan Mandell: 139 bottom; Jennifer Martiné: 184; Jim McCausland: 78; Joshua McCullough/PhytoPhoto: 28, 63 top left, 200, 219, 234, 244 left, 288-2; Marcus Mok/Photolibrary: 177; Morales Morales/Photolibrary: 178; Daniel Nadelbach: 97, 139 top; Jerry Pavia: 83 left, 186, 238; courtesy of J. Pawlak/The American Phytopathological Society: 292-1; Pam Peirce: 289-2, 292-6, 295-3; Pam Peirce/Susan A. Roth & Co.: 65, 180, 231, 289-3, 293-1, 296-5, 296-6; David E. Perry: 67 bottom, 213, 225, 287-4, 290-1, 290-3, 296-1, 296-4; Linda Lamb Peters: 105; Norman A. Plate: 25 bottom left, 46 left, 64 both, 73 bottom left, 73 bottom right, 133, 150 left, 151 all, 160, 240 left, 241 both, 243 bottom, 269; Norm Plate: 239, 252 all, 277 right; Andrey Pustovoy/©iStockPhoto.com: 216; Ian Reeves: 263-5; Sue Riseley/©iStockPhoto.com: 221; Valentin Rodriguez/Photolibrary: 226; Lisa Romerein/Getty Images: 218; Susan A. Roth: 47, 75 bottom right, 191, 203, 240 bottom right, 290-6, 290-7, 293-3, 295-2; Science Vu/Visuals Unlimited: 292-2, 292-4; Carol Sharp/Photolibrary: 103; Vladimir Shulevsky/Photolibrary: 235; J S Sira/Photolibrary: 21; Inga Spence/Alamy: 233; Inga Spence/Getty Images: 208 bottom; Inga Spence/Photolibrary: 236; Thomas J. Story: back cover left, front cover right, 2, 5, 19 right, 20, 24, 31, 33, 34 both, 35, 41 top left, 41 top right, 41 bottom right, 44 both, 46 right, 50, 56 left, 58, 60, 66, 79, 85 top left, 87, 89, 90-1, 90-2, 90-3, 90-4, 94 bottom right, 98 left, 101 top right, 114, 115, 116, 118, 119, 126, 134 left, 135, 138, 162, 173, 240 top right, 242 top, 243 top, 245 both, 250 bottom right, 254 top right, 266, 268 all, 281 bottom, 284, 297; Mike Tomlinson/Dave Wilson Nursery: 210; E. Spencer Toy: 54, 262, 267 top; Mark Turner: 30, 32, 41 bottom left, 63 bottom left, 67 top, 82, 96, 102, 104, 113, 130, 131, 132, 150 right, 155 right, 169, 183, 190, 246 left, 246 bottom right, 247 bottom, 276 right, 291-1, 291-4; Juliette Wade/Photolibrary: 22; Jonelle Weaver: 19 left; William J. Weber/Visuals Unlimited: 290-2; Rachel Weill: 77; Ron West: 287-1, 287-2, 288-3, 288-5, 288-7, 289-4, 289-5, 289-6, 289-7, 290-4, 290-5, 292-5; Jo Whitworth/Photolibrary: 38; Bob Wigand: 124, 167, 185, 202, 291-2, 291-3; Mark Winwood/Photolibrary: 277 left; Jack Wolford: 192, 227, 229, 230, 232; Francesca Yorke/Photolibrary: 39; Ed Young/AGStockUSA: 176, 207, 208 top, 223; Ebbe Roe Yovino-Smith: 90 right.

Sunset

©2010 by Sunset Publishing Corporation
80 Willow Road, Menlo Park, CA 94025

ISBN-13: 978-0-376-03918-7
ISBN-10: 0-376-03918-3
Library of Congress Control Number: 2009934635

10 9 8 7 6 5 4 3 2 1
First Printing January 2010
Printed in the United States of America.

OXMOOR HOUSE, INC.
VP, Publishing Director: Jim Childs
Brand Manager: Fonda Hitchcock
Managing Editor: L. Amanda Owens
Editorial Director: Susan Payne Dobbs

SUNSET PUBLISHING
President: Barb Newton
VP, Editor-in-Chief: Katie Tamony
Creative Director: Mia Daminato
Garden Editor: Kathleen Norris Brenzel

Western Garden Book of Edibles
CONTRIBUTORS
Author: Jim McCausland
Managing Editor: Tom Wilhite
Art Director: Catherine Jacobes
Production Specialist: Linda M. Bouchard
Photo Editor: Linda Lamb Peters
Copy Editor: Julie Harris
Illustrator: Damien Scogin
Proofreader: Denise Griffiths
Indexer: Marjorie Joy
Front Cover Photography: Saxon Holt (left), David Cavagnaro (middle), Thomas J. Story (right)

For additional photography credits, see page 303.

To order additional publications, call 1-800-765-6400

For more books to enrich your life, visit oxmoorhouse.com

Visit Sunset online at sunset.com

For the most comprehensive selection of Sunset books, visit sunsetbooks.com

For more exciting home and garden ideas, visit myhomeideas.com

Special Thanks

Sam Benowitz, Raintree Nursery; VJ Billings, Mountain Valley Growers; Paul Bosland, New Mexico State University; Charles Brun, Washington State University; Kimberley Burch; Sharon Cohoon; Curt Daehler, University of Hawaii; Darcy Daniels, Bloomtown Garden Design & Nursery; Michael Dolan, Burnt Ridge Nursery & Orchards; John R. Dunmire; Phil Edinger; Gloria Geller; Kevin Hauser, Kuffel Creek Apple Nursery; Mark Hawkins; Gary Ibsen, TomatoFest.com; Ed Laivo, Dave Wilson Nursery; Dennis Leong; Marianne Lipanovich; Dick Mombell, Fall Creek Farm & Nursery; Gary Moulton, Washington State University; Gary Nabhan, University of Arizona; Rose Marie Nichols McGee; Marie Pence; Ross Penhallegon, Oregon State University; Lon Rombough, Bunchgrapes.com; Janet Sanchez; Renee Shepherd, Renee's Garden; Alex Silber, Papaya Tree Nursery; Bernadine Strik, Oregon State University; Paul Vossen, University of California; Lance Walheim; Hazel White

Resources

Mail-order suppliers such as the following offer a wealth of plant and cultural information in their catalogs and online.

FRUIT TREES, GRAPES, AND BERRIES
Bunchgrapes.com (bunchgrapes.com)
Burnt Ridge Nursery & Orchards (burntridgenursery.com)
Cloud Mountain Farm (cloudmountainfarm.com)
Kuffel Creek Apple Nursery (kuffelcreek.com/applenursery)
One Green World (onegreenworld.com)
Raintree Nursery (raintreenursery.com)

SEEDS AND SEEDLINGS
Johnny's Selected Seeds (johnnyseeds.com)
Kitazawa Seed Company (kitazawaseed.com)
The Natural Gardening Company (naturalgardening.com)
Nichols Garden Nursery (nicholsgardennursery.com)
Renee's Garden Seeds (reneesgarden.com)
Seeds of Change (seedsofchange.com)
Stokes Seeds (stokeseeds.com)
Territorial Seed Company (territorialseed.com)
TomatoFest (tomatofest.com)
West Coast Seeds (westcoastseeds.com)
Wood Prairie Farm (woodprairie.com)

SUPPLIES
Charley's Greenhouse & Garden (charleysgreenhouse.com)
Gardens Alive! (gardensalive.com)
Kinsman Company (kinsmangarden.com)
Peaceful Valley Farm & Garden Supply (groworganic.com)

GENERAL INFORMATION
California Rare Fruit Growers (crfg.org)
Cooperative Extension System Offices (csrees.usda.gov/Extension)
Sunset Publishing (sunset.com)